THE BOOK OF
VISUAL BASIC 2005

D1560757

THE BOOK OF™
VISUAL BASIC
2005

.NET Insight for Classic VB Developers

by Matthew MacDonald

NO STARCH PRESS

San Francisco

Publisher: William Pollock
Managing Editor: Elizabeth Campbell
Associate Production Editor: Christina Samuell
Cover and Interior Design: Octopod Studios
Developmental Editor: Jim Compton
Technical Reviewer: Dan Mabbutt
Copyeditor: Neil Ching
Compositor: Riley Hoffman
Proofreader: Stephanie Provines

For information on book distributors or translations, please contact No Starch Press, Inc. directly:

No Starch Press, Inc.
555 De Haro Street, Suite 250, San Francisco, CA 94107
phone: 415.863.9900; fax: 415.863.9950; info@nostarch.com; www.nostarch.com

Library of Congress Cataloging-in-Publication Data

```
MacDonald, Matthew.
  The Book of Visual Basic 2005 : .NET Insight for Classic VB Developers / Matthew MacDonald.
      p. cm.
  Includes index.
  ISBN 1-59327-074-7
 1.  Microsoft Visual BASIC. 2.  BASIC (Computer program language) 3. Microsoft .NET Framework.
I. Title.
  QA76.73.B3M282 2005
  005.2'768--dc22
                                        2005028823
```

For Faria

ACKNOWLEDGMENTS

The collection of .NET titles on bookstore shelves is embarrassingly large. When writing a book about a language as popular as Visual Basic, the challenge isn't finishing it, but making sure that it's *really* insightful, friendly, and useful beyond the standard Microsoft documentation. To that end, I have to thank countless other developers and .NET aficionados whose words—in books, articles, websites, discussions groups, and emails—have provided the seeds of insight that have enhanced the pages of this book. I hope the readers of this book will also learn from and become a part of the broader .NET community.

Closer to home, I should thank all the pleasant people at No Starch Press who have worked with me throughout this project, for both this edition and the previous one, including Bill Pollock, Karol Jurado, Christina Samuell, Elizabeth Campbell, and Amanda Staab. I also owe a heartfelt thanks to this book's reviewers, Dan Mabbutt of About.com fame and Jim Compton, and its copyeditor, Neil Ching.

Lastly, I need to thank my parents (all four of them) and my loving wife.

BRIEF CONTENTS

CONTENTS IN DETAIL

4
WINDOWS FORMS

5
OBJECT-ORIENTED PROGRAMMING

135

6
MASTERING OBJECTS

173

7
ASSEMBLIES AND COMPONENTS

211

8
BUG PROOFING

9
DEALING WITH DATA: FILES, PRINTING, AND XML

10
DATABASES AND ADO.NET

311

11
THREADING
355

12
WEB FORMS AND ASP.NET
387

14
SETUP AND DEPLOYMENT   451

INDEX   475

INTRODUCTION

Since its creation, Visual Basic (VB) has steadily grown into the world's most popular programming language. But popularity doesn't always mean respect, and for years the development community has been split between those who think Visual Basic is a revolutionary way to solve just about any programming problem and those who think VB should be sent to the bargain bin to make room for a return to "serious" C++ or Java coding. As a result, Visual Basic programmers have a reputation for being a slightly paranoid bunch.

Recently, Visual Basic has been through the greatest change of its life. It's morphed into a modern, object-oriented language that's built on Microsoft's .NET Framework—the same plumbing that powers such heavyweights as C#. Although most VB developers believe that the .NET Framework will eventually replace old-style Visual Basic 6, a surprising number haven't made the jump yet. Some don't trust the new technology (and the never-ending name changes). Others are too busy with real work to think about making a move. And a few are scared off by the radical new model and inevitable migration headaches.

Now Microsoft has introduced Visual Basic 2005, along with the second version of the .NET Framework. Microsoft's developers have expended considerable resources making Visual Basic 2005 easier to understand, use, and embrace, and they're earmarking this release as the version that will finally make die-hard classic VB-ers switch to .NET. So have they succeeded?

As you'll discover in this book, there's still no easy migration path—Visual Basic 2005 is entirely unlike Visual Basic 6, and there's no turning back now. However, if you're ready to step up to a new language—one that cleans out old cobwebs, levels the playing field between VB and other programming languages, and introduces an avalanche of elegant, flexible, and easy-to-use new features—Visual Basic 2005 fits the bill. In fact, it's the Visual Basic makeover many programmers have spent years waiting for.

This book provides a guided tour through the world of Visual Basic 2005. In it, you'll learn how you can use your existing VB skills and master the .NET way of thinking.

Who Should Read This Book

This book is aimed at Visual Basic 6 developers who want to shed some of their current habits and start learning about how the .NET platform works and thinks. We won't spend any time rehashing basic syntax, but we will spend a *lot* of time exploring new .NET concepts.

To get the most out of this book, you should have some experience developing with Visual Basic. You don't need to have tackled advanced subjects, such as Internet applications and object-oriented programming—these are well explained in the book—but you should be familiar with all the "Visual Basic basics," such as variables, controls, loops, conditions, and functions. If you've never programmed with Visual Basic or another programming language like Java, this isn't the best book for you. (You might want to start with Wallace Wang's *Visual Basic 2005 Express: Now Playing*, also from No Starch Press.)

If you're a master programmer with an earlier version of .NET, you already know most of what there is to learn in this book. You may want to check out a book like my own *Visual Basic 2005: A Developer's Notebook*, which concentrates exclusively on new features that have been added to .NET 2.0.

If you're an experienced programmer who's new to .NET, welcome aboard! You'll soon get a handle on Visual Basic 2005's most exciting new innovations and pick up some invaluable tricks on the way.

What You Will Learn

Many of the chapters in this book could be expanded into complete books of their own. It's impossible to cover all the details of .NET, so this book strives to give you the essential facts and insights. The emphasis isn't on becoming a "language nerd" (learning every syntax trick in the book), but on gaining the insights you'll need in order to understand .NET development and to continue learning on your own. We'll go about our journey in a lively, no-nonsense way.

Each chapter begins with a "New in .NET" section that gives experienced developers a quick introduction to what has changed since Visual Basic 6. The rest of the chapter takes a lightning tour through a single aspect of programming with VB 2005. The code examples are tightly focused on specific concepts—you won't find toy applications that are written just for the book. (Those tend to look great while flipping through the book in the bookstore, but end up being much less helpful once you get started.)

A "What Comes Next?" section at the end of every chapter provides some ideas about where you can find more information on the current topic and maybe even become a VB 2005 guru.

NOTE *No single book can teach you the entire .NET platform. The emphasis here is on introducing fundamental techniques and concepts, and giving you the resources you'll need in order to continue exploring the areas that interest you most. To accomplish all this, the text is complemented by code examples, references to additional online material, and helpful tips about planning, design, and architecture. For best results, try to read the chapters in order, because later examples will use some of the features introduced in earlier chapters.*

Code Samples

Practical examples often provide the best way to learn new concepts and see programming ideas in action. Following that principle, this book includes a wealth of code samples to help stimulate your mind and keep you awake. The design philosophy for these samples is straightforward: demonstrate, as concisely as possible, how a .NET developer thinks. This means that all examples are broken down to their simplest elements. The hope is that these code samples represent kernels of coding insight.

The code samples in this book are provided online, grouped by chapter, at www.prosetech.com. These examples aren't exactly the same as the code fragments in the book. For example, they might have a little extra code or user interface, which would just be a distraction in a printed example. These samples provide an excellent starting point for your own .NET experimentation.

Complaints, Adulation, and Everything in Between

While I'm on the subject of online support for the book, I should probably add that you can reach me via email at p2p@prosetech.com. I can't solve your Visual Basic 2005 problems or critique your own code creations, but I would like to hear what this book does right and wrong (and what it may do in an utterly confusing way). You can also send comments about the website and the online samples.

Chapter Overview

Here's a quick guide that describes what each chapter has to offer. Some of the later chapters build on concepts in earlier chapters, so it will probably be easiest to read the book in order, to make sure you learn the basics about Windows forms, object-oriented programming, and Visual Basic 2005 syntax changes before moving on to the more specialized topics such as web applications and database programming.

Chapter 1: The .NET Revolution
What is this thing called .NET, anyway? Learn why Microsoft decided to create a whole new framework for programming and what it threw in.

Chapter 2: The Design Environment
Visual Basic's integrated design environment (IDE), known as Visual Studio, is every programmer's home away from home. In VB 2005, it's been given a slick makeover and new features such as enhanced IntelliSense, macros, and a collapsible code display.

Chapter 3: VB 2005 Basics
I warned you that things had changed. Here you'll get your first real look at the .NET world, with an overview of language changes, an exploration of the class library, and an introduction to namespaces.

Chapter 4: Windows Forms
Windows forms are an example of the good getting better. Visual Basic has always made it easy to drag and drop your way to an attractive user interface, and with the revamped Windows Forms model you'll get some long-awaited extras, such as automatic support for resizable forms, a variety of new controls, and the ability to finally forget all about the Windows API.

Chapter 5: Object-Oriented Programming
At last, Visual Basic 2005 is a full object-oriented programming language. This chapter teaches you the basics of object-oriented development, the most modern and elegant way to solve almost any programming problem. VB 2005 is built almost entirely out of objects, and understanding them is the key to becoming a .NET expert.

Chapter 6: Mastering Objects
In this chapter, we'll continue to explore VB 2005's object-oriented features and advanced class construction techniques including interfaces and inheritance, the most anticipated Visual Basic enhancement ever.

Chapter 7: Assemblies and Components
Modern applications work best when designed as a collection of separate, collaborating components. In this chapter, you'll learn how to make your own components and get the essentials you need to know in order to transfer your applications to other computers.

Chapter 8: Bug Proofing
Visual Basic 2005 retains most of VB's legendary debugging tools, with a few refinements. This chapter describes debugging in the IDE, outlines some tips for making bug-resistant code, and introduces structured exception handling.

Chapter 9: Dealing with Data: Files, Printing, and XML

Traditional Visual Basic data-handling functions have been replaced with objects that let you manage files, serialize objects, print data, and manipulate XML. But the greatest enhancement may be the print preview control.

Chapter 10: Databases and ADO.NET

Visual Basic 2005 includes ADO.NET, a revamped version of ADO that allows you to connect to just about any database and extract the information you need (or make the changes you want) quickly and efficiently. Again, the .NET team has been up late at night tweaking things, and the changes are bound to surprise you.

Chapter 11: Threading

Visual Basic 2005 now goes where only C++ and other heavyweights could venture before: multithreading. But just because you can thread doesn't mean you should. In fact, threading is still the best way to shoot yourself squarely in the foot. Read this chapter for some advice about when to create threads (and when not to) and how to use them safely.

Chapter 12: Web Forms and ASP.NET

This chapter describes the basics of ASP.NET, Microsoft's all-in-one solution for creating web-based applications. Finally, after years of promises, creating scalable web applications with a rich user interface is just as easy as creating a desktop application.

Chapter 13: Web Services

Central to the .NET platform is the vision of software as a service, with worldwide web servers providing features and functions that you can seamlessly integrate into your own products. Read this chapter to start creating web services and, best of all, let .NET take care of all the plumbing.

Chapter 14: Setup and Deployment

Need a quick way to deploy an application or a full-fledged setup program complete with shortcuts, registry tweaking, and an uninstall feature? In this chapter you'll learn two ways to deploy your application: the streamlined web-based ClickOnce model, and the more comprehensive Visual Studio setup project.

What Comes Next?

If you've made it this far, I'll assume you're continuing for the rest of the journey. For best results, you should already have a copy of Visual Basic 2005. The professional edition is best (it includes support for every type of project), but you can also complete many of the examples in this book using a combination of the Visual Basic 2005 Express Edition (for Windows applications) and Visual Web Developer 2005 Express Edition (for web applications). You can get the details on these low-cost versions at http://msdn.microsoft.com/vstudio/express.

But first, before you touch any code, we'll start with Chapter 1—and clear up the cloud of jargon and hype that surrounds .NET. Along the way, you'll discover why so many people find Microsoft's new platform so exciting.

1

THE .NET REVOLUTION

This chapter presents the "big picture" of Visual Basic and the .NET Framework. You'll get an overview of what has changed, why it's different, and just what life will be like in the .NET world. Along the way, we'll sort through Microsoft's newest jargon, demystifying the Common Language Runtime (CLR), "managed" code, and the .NET class library. This chapter is for anyone wondering, "What the heck is .NET?" or, "Why do we need a new programming philosophy?" or, "What has Microsoft promised us this time?"

A Brief History of Visual Basic

Visual Basic has its roots in BASIC, a simple teaching language that programmers once learned before graduating to more serious languages like C. Visual Basic inherited at least part of the BASIC legacy, beginning its life with the goal of being the easiest way for anybody to program . . . anything.

It's probably because of this history that Visual Basic developers have always had their hands full demonstrating that their favorite language is more than just a toy. Time and time again, as programming methodologies and application demands have changed, it has seemed that Visual Basic's time in the spotlight was about to end. Instead, VB has not only kept stride; it has made the world rethink computer programming—first with version 1.0, which introduced the easiest way to create a graphical user interface; then with version 4.0, which provided the easiest way to talk to a database; and then with version 5.0, which gave us the easiest way to go "object-oriented."

Enter .NET

When Visual Basic .NET hit the scene, life changed dramatically. That's because VB .NET 1.0 was the first version of Visual Basic that broke language compatibility. And it didn't do it meekly. Suddenly, commands that VB programmers had been able to use since Visual Basic 1.0 earned a blank stare from the VB .NET compiler. Traditional VB programming tricks and hacks either failed or risked serious side effects. And there was no way to drop projects from earlier versions of Visual Basic into the new VB .NET world.

So how does Visual Basic 2005 fit into this evolution? Visual Basic 2005 *is* VB .NET 2.0. Microsoft marketers decided that the .NET moniker was confusing the heck out of pretty much everyone, so they dropped it. However, they didn't change the language to make it one iota closer to classic VB. In fact, Visual Basic 2005 is almost identical to VB .NET 1.0. The only differences are a few new language frills (many of which are introduced in Chapter 3), a revamped design environment (which is really more about Visual Studio than about the VB language itself; see Chapter 2), and a return of the long-lost (and much-loved) run-edit-and-continue debugging feature (Chapter 8).

But it's important to understand that Visual Basic 2005 is still VB .NET. And well it should be. VB .NET may pose a migration challenge and a whole new learning curve, but it also represents a major redesign and refinement of the Visual Basic language. The features it adds are too good to give up.

One more thing has to be said—don't believe the marketing hype about migration. Microsoft is trying to make Visual Basic 2005 look like a more natural step up from classic VB, and it's claiming it works a lot more like classic VB does. In a few superficial cases, this is true (as with the return of edit-and-continue). But overall, it's no easier to move to Visual Basic 2005 than it was to move to VB .NET 1.0.

The Limitations of "Classic" Visual Basic

Have you heard the argument, "Before you can understand the solution, you have to understand the problem"? In this case it's true, so before we go any further, let's take a look at some of Visual Basic's most infamous shortcomings that VB.NET was designed to address.

Visual Basic's Quirky Mix

Visual Basic's evolution has been so quick that the last version (6.0) was a mixture of cutting-edge features and Paleolithic throwbacks. For example, Visual Basic 6 provided a great framework for creating a graphical user interface, allowing you to configure controls and windows just by setting convenient properties. But if you went one step further into an unsupported area, you quickly felt abandoned. Want to stop a window from resizing to specific minimum dimensions? Want to add your program's icon to the system tray? How about disabling a window's Maximize button without hiding its Minimize button? To perform any of these common tasks, you had to plunge into the Windows API, a library of perplexing C routines. And watch out: If you misused an API function, you could easily crash your program—and even the entire development environment!

I could go on to talk about a number of other hangovers from the past, like Visual Basic's "evil" type-conversion mechanism, which tries to make your life easier by letting you convert data types without following the proper rules—thus allowing you to overlook serious errors. Then there is the archaic practice of referring to open files with numbers. And who can explain why a world-class object-oriented programming language still has the Goto command?

Isolated Languages

If you've dabbled in more than one programming language, you've probably realized that each one does things a bit differently. This was certainly true for Windows programming without .NET, where C++ uses the MFC library, J++ uses WFC, and Visual Basic uses its own framework (with sprinkles of the Windows API thrown in for good measure). Basically, programmers suffered endless headaches trying to understand each other, and they had to consider the quirks and idiosyncrasies of every language before they could choose one to use for development. And even if a problem was solved in C++, Visual Basic developers usually still needed to solve it all over again.

Enterprise Development Headaches

Three-tier design. Distributed objects. Load balancing. It all sounds good on paper. Data objects reading and writing to the database, business objects processing the results, and a Windows application displaying the results, with everyone talking together using the *Component Object Model (COM)*.

But if you've ever tried to create a distributed program, you've probably discovered that setting it up, registering your components, and maintaining version compatibility add a whole new set of agonizing problems that have nothing to do with programming.

DLL Hell

DLL Hell is a particularly ugly example of the problem with component-based programs. Most Visual Basic programs rely heavily on specialized components and controls, sometimes without the programmer even realizing it. These programs work fine when the correct version of every dependent file is present on the system, but if the user installs an application that mistakenly overwrites one of these files with an older version, or updates some but not all of a set of dependent files, then strange problems start to come out of the woodwork. Such problems are a nightmare to try and identify, and the worst part is, they usually appear long after a fully functional application has been installed. The end result? Fragile programs that can easily be disrupted when other applications are updated or uninstalled.

Incomplete Support for Object-Oriented Programming

Before I even knew what polymorphism and inheritance were, I knew that classic Visual Basic didn't have them. Never mind that VB had all the other tools needed to write elegant programs based on objects; there was no escaping the talk about its OOP limitations. No other limitation did more to crush the personal self-esteem of the dedicated VB programmer.

The .NET Vision

Most people were expecting Microsoft to deal with some of these complaints by bolting on a few new features, as it did for the previous few versions of Visual Basic. As advanced developers started to expand the types of programs that Visual Basic was used to develop, cracks in the VB picture started to appear—everywhere. Applications became more complicated, and language enhancements only brought more inconsistencies and deficiencies to light. At some point, the people at Microsoft decided to start over and build a new set of languages from the ground up. The .NET Framework is the result of that effort.

The Ingredients of .NET

Like COM and ActiveX, the .NET Framework means a lot of different things, depending on whom you talk to in Microsoft's marketing department. On the programming side, .NET is made up of the *Common Language Runtime (CLR)* and a set of *unified classes*. The .NET Framework sits on top of the Windows platform, which provides its own set of services (for example, the IIS server built into Windows lets your computer be a web server). Figure 1-1 shows the relationship.

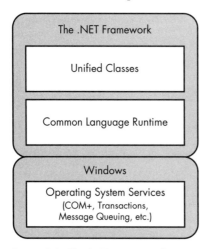

Figure 1-1: The .NET Framework

The Common Language Runtime (CLR)

The CLR (see Figure 1-2) is a runtime environment that processes, executes, and manages Visual Basic code. It's a little like the traditional Visual Basic runtimes (for example, VBRUN300.dll or MSVBVM60.dll), but with increased responsibility.

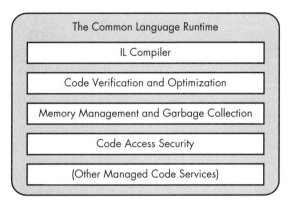

The Common Language Runtime

- IL Compiler
- Code Verification and Optimization
- Memory Management and Garbage Collection
- Code Access Security
- (Other Managed Code Services)

Figure 1-2: The Common Language Runtime (CLR) environment

What does the CLR code offer to your applications? Here are some examples:

- It prevents operations that could corrupt memory and cause the system to become unstable.
- It automatically cleans up objects you don't need.
- It catches common mistakes and halts your program with an error, rather than letting it run on with scrambled data.
- It compiles your code on the fly into native machine code, ensuring optimum performance.

Many of these features have been available in the Visual Basic world for years, albeit in a somewhat less ambitious form. In fact, much of the excitement about C# (another .NET language released about the same time as VB.NET 1.0) came from C++ programmers who had never experienced some of the advantages that VB programmers take for granted, like automatic memory management.

Code that executes inside the CLR is called *managed code*. Visual Basic 2005 code is always managed code, which means that it works with CLR services and operates under the CLR's careful supervision.

The .NET Classes

The .NET classes contain the tools that let you perform all kinds of tasks, from writing to a database to reading from a web page (see Figure 1-3). In the past, these capabilities either were hard-coded into the language with special functions, or provided through separate components. Think of the integrated class library as a supremely well-organized programming toolbox.

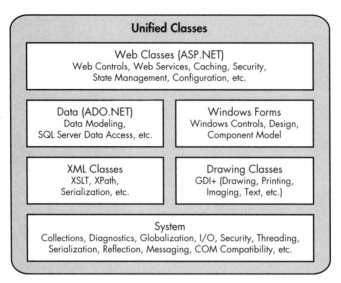

Figure 1-3: The unified classes in .NET

Speaking the Same Language

Within .NET, each programming language still has its own syntax. For example, every line in a C# program ends with a semicolon (;), unlike Visual Basic. But these differences are really just superficial.

- Every .NET language is built on the CLR.
- All .NET languages share a common set of class libraries, which they use to do everything from displaying a Windows message box to retrieving a file from the Internet.

For example, look at the similarity of these two .NET-based programs, which accomplish the same thing—first in Visual Basic, and then in C#:
Here is the VB 2005 version:

```
Private Sub CreateTextBox()
    ' This function makes a new text box,
    ' and puts some text in it.
    Dim MyText As New Textbox()
    MyText.Location = New Point(25,25)
    MyText.Size = New Size(25,125)
    MyText.Text = "This was made in VB!"
    Me.Controls.Add(MyText)
End Sub
```

And here is the C# 2005 version:

```
private void CreateTextBox()
{
    // This function makes a new text box,
    // and puts some text in it.
    Textbox MyText = new Textbox();
    MyText.Size = new Size(25,125);
    MyText.Location = new Point(25,25);
    MyText.Text = "I come from C#...";
    this.Controls.Add(MyText);
}
```

There are some obvious superficial differences here; for instance, you're probably wondering what's going on with all the curly brackets, slashes, and semicolons in C#. However, if you study the two programs carefully, you'll realize that their differences are simply matters of syntax. Every line in the VB program has a direct "translation" into a line in the C# program. The code is written a little differently, but it uses the same concepts. Or to be more picturesque, the two languages use different words, but have the same grammar.

The full effects of these changes are amazing. At last, Visual Basic programmers can interact with the full Windows developer community! If someone has solved your problem in C#, you can now benefit from their experience and translate their solution into VB 2005 without a lot of trouble.

Deep Language Integration

The power of CLR integration extends beyond the way you code. Behind the scenes, the same engine is processing code from different .NET languages. This deep integration means, for instance, that code written in Visual Basic can inherit procedures and properties from classes written in C#, and that errors thrown from code written in C# can be caught by code written in Visual Basic.

In fact, every CLR language compiles into the same CPU-independent bytecode when you create a .exe or .dll file: the *Microsoft Intermediate Language* (*MSIL*, or *IL* for short). This means that ultimately, different .NET languages have essentially the same performance—so programming in VB 2005 instead of C# 2005 is nothing more than a lifestyle choice.

Prebuilt Infrastructure

If you're an experienced developer, it has probably dawned on you that developers are paid to solve the same problems over and over again. Most internal business applications boil down to databases, web development always involves tackling site-management issues, and every first-person game requires the traditional 3D-rendering engine. In the past, Microsoft has been tremendously successful designing some of the basic infrastructure that we all need, creating such tools as ADO for universal database access and COM+ for managing transactions. Microsoft's philosophy has been that they should supply the infrastructure, while the programmer writes the specific "business logic" that distinguishes one project from the next. And it's likely that you heartily agree (unless you want to spend your time wrestling with low-level details such as state management, database-specific APIs, and messaging).

The .NET Framework extends this philosophy with its common class library. Here you can find cutting-edge tools for creating everything from a Windows service to an ASP.NET web application ready to serve thousands of eager e-shoppers.

Web Services and the Next-Generation Internet

Microsoft is also using .NET to expound its vision of "software as a service." The story goes a little bit like this: Many years ago, Windows applications were isolated. Integrating parts of different applications was difficult unless they resided together in a rigorously thought-out .dll. Code sharing really only occurred inside the walls of individual companies. Then, along came COM and ActiveX technology. All of a sudden, programmers had exciting new ways to communicate. Dozens of vendors offered custom controls that you could easily and painlessly drop into your applications. Other developers discovered how easy it was to use automation features to drive COM programs by "remote control." For example, you could create a spreadsheet in Excel from within VB, or even perform a search operation in Word from within C++, using an easy-to-understand object model.

Where am I going with this? The idea is that the Internet is now at roughly the same stage in its evolution. We finally have interactive web applications for tracking stock portfolios and ordering books, and yet we don't have an easy way to integrate parts of web applications without resorting to awkward tricks such as "screen scraping," where information is read from a predefined line in a web page. These techniques are difficult to maintain and to extend. What happens if a website changes its content or goes out of business? In short, a better solution is needed.

That's where web services come in. A *web service* is an application that exposes its functionality over the Internet using standard Internet protocols, such as HTTP and XML. A developer can use a web service just as easily as a local component, without worrying about the technology involved.

Open Standards: XML, SOAP, WSDL, and Other Letters from the Alphabet

Open standards? *Microsoft?* That's what flashed through my mind when I heard that the .NET Framework was going to have key technologies based on open standards such as XML. Finally, Microsoft has recognized that the world of the Internet is a diverse one, and that in order for developers to adopt Microsoft tools, they need innovations based on a solid foundation of platform-independent, widely accepted open standards. This means that

.NET can transfer a database table using XML markup, and provide web services that can be used by applications on Unix or Macintosh computers.

But how open are their "open standards?" Or, to put it another way, is the Microsoft implementation of these open standards really able to interact with other operating systems and programming languages? Suprisingly, yes. Today, .NET applications can communicate with services written in competing languages like Java, and Java clients can communicate with .NET services. At first, minor implementation differences caused the odd hiccup. Remarkably, Microsoft and other technology vendors have worked to remove these complications, rather than defending them in a desperate bid to lock in their customers. The .NET Framework just might be Microsoft's first truly open platform.

NOTE *However open .NET is, it definitely isn't an open source or cross-platform product. (*Open source *means the source code is available for other developers to improve, or at least peruse.* Cross-platform *means you can use it to build applications that run on different operating systems.) Even though .NET plays nicely with others, your code still needs to run on a Windows computer. However, if you want to create applications that everyone can enjoy, why not build a web application (Chapter 12)? Even though your code runs on a Windows-powered web server, any type of computer can surf it happily.*

Metadata: The End of DLL Hell?

Programs in .NET are *self-describing*. In other words, when you create a .NET .exe file, it doesn't just contain your compiled program; it also has information that describes the other components it needs in order to work, and which version of each component is supported. Previously, this information was buried in the Windows registry, which meant that every application had to go through a registration process, and that its registry information had to be rigorously updated to keep from becoming out-of-date and conflicting with the application itself.

So is DLL Hell really over? The answer is yes. And no. Well, as you'll find out in Chapter 7, there *is* a Global Assembly Cache (GAC) where applications can share components, just as they always have. No one wants to distribute a separate version of the .NET Framework with every application they make. However, you don't need to use it just to use a simple component in a few applications. Even better, the amazing version control and management features provided by the Global Assembly Cache should guarantee that DLL Hell will never appear again. Probably.

Is VB 2005 Still VB?

Microsoft has played it a little risky and completely tossed out some of the old Visual Basic nightmares. As a result, VB 2005 looks quite a bit different from classic Visual Basic. In fact, many time-honored commands are no longer available in .NET. Following are some of the advances that you should cheer about . . . and some other changes that you won't be celebrating.

Ten Enhancements You Can't Live Without

1. Visual Basic is truly object-oriented—at last.

2. The new Windows Forms model for programming a user interface is more powerful than ever, and bundles convenient controls for everything from system tray icons to print previewing to web browser windows.

3. There's no automatic type conversion: `Option Strict` lets you turn off this dangerous "convenience."

4. Structured error handling makes it as easy to trap an error in Visual Basic as in any other modern programming language.

5. ASP.NET provides the easiest and most powerful system to date for programming web applications.

6. Method overloading now allows you to create different versions of methods with the same name, but with different arguments. Visual Basic 2005 will use the correct one automatically.

7. Even critics can't deny that the new development environment is heart-stoppingly beautiful. Does any other language offer collapsible code, intelligent dynamic help, and an entire programming language for creating macros?

8. A new event model lets you connect multiple event handlers to a single control and store function references in special variables, called *delegates*.

9. Initializers let you set the value of a variable on the same line where it is declared.

10. Metadata means that DLL Hell may finally be a thing of the past. You can now set up a program just by copying its directory—a capability that hasn't existed in the Windows world for years.

Ten Changes That May Frustrate You

1. Arrays must always have a lower boundary of 0.

2. Existing Internet projects using Web Classes or DHTML aren't supported, so you will need to rewrite them from scratch as ASP.NET applications.

3. There are no more default properties, so you can't abbreviate `Text1.Text` as just `Text1`.

4. The techniques you used in the past to print documents, draw graphics, read text files, and provide context-sensitive help have changed—get ready to learn these basics all over again.

5. There is no deterministic finalization. That fancy jargon means that when you're finished with an object, it may still hang around in memory for some time until it's cleaned out. As a result, you can't rely on events that take place when an object is unloaded, because they won't occur at a predictable time.

6. Older database access methods, such as RDO and DAO, are not fully supported. (For example, they can't be used for data binding.)

7. Even if you use the upgrade wizard, a great deal of code may need to be rewritten, including routines for reading from and writing to files, and for creating printouts. In fact, for complex applications, you may have to abandon the whole idea of migration.

8. There is no way of accessing pointers. In classic Visual Basic, pointer access was dangerous and unsupported, but could still be done by those who knew the "secret" functions, such as `StrPtr()` and `ObjPtr()`.

9. `Goto`, `Gosub`, and line numbers are no longer supported.

10. The model for drawing on a form has changed. If you did custom drawing in the past, you'll need to rewrite it from scratch.

The Dark Side of .NET

Not every Visual Basic programmer is happy with the radical changes Microsoft made. To some critics, .NET's drive to modernize programming has left Visual Basic 2005 looking more like Java than .NET.

They argue that years of Visual Basic legacy are being left behind, and that compatibility with old code is being rudely broken. There's more than a grain of truth to these complaints.

So is .NET worth it? Yes. Visual Basic 2005 has changed enough to make life a little painful for developers, but once you understand the new changes, your coding days will be easier and more productive. In a sense, Microsoft is gambling that developers will be so eager to program with an elegant, revitalized version of Visual Basic that they'll sacrifice backward compatibility. Sometimes change hurts.

What About COM?

COM is the *Component Object Model*, the fundamental technology that allows programs to communicate together, and allows parts of programs (their *components*) to interact as well. Until now, COM was supposedly the basis of Windows programming—so where has it gone?

This is a question that's bound to be asked again and again. As Microsoft points out, there are hundreds of millions of COM applications, including such heavyweights as Microsoft Office. COM will be around as long as Windows is around; in fact, Windows won't boot without COM.

That said, .NET is not built on top of COM. Programs written in .NET communicate natively; because their languages are all based on the CLR, they don't need to work through obscure COM interfaces. In fact, .NET is really a next-generation version of COM. (At one early stage, parts of it were even called COM+ 2.0.) But don't panic. Microsoft has worked long and hard to make sure that COM applications can communicate seamlessly with .NET. One day you may wake up to a world without COM . . . but it won't be any time soon.

What Comes Next?

Throughout the rest of the book, the .NET Framework will never be far from our discussion. Even though this is a book about writing software using the VB 2005 programming language, our time will be evenly divided between VB syntax and the common classes that are part of .NET. You just can't master VB 2005 development without spending a good amount of time becoming familiar with the class library. Conversely, many VB concepts like objects, exceptions, and threading are built into the CLR and shared by all .NET languages.

There is an advantage to this organization: once you've mastered VB 2005, you aren't all that far from becoming an accomplished C# coder—if it interests you. Perhaps the most exciting fact about life in the .NET world is that language wars are (mostly) dead, and the broad community of .NET developers can share tips, tricks, and insights across language boundaries.

2

THE DESIGN ENVIRONMENT

The changes in the Visual Studio 2005 *integrated design environment (IDE)* haven't generated the same amount of attention as other new features such as language enhancements and web services. That's because the IDE doesn't determine what you can and can't do with a well-written program. In fact, you can create a Visual Basic project using nothing more than Notepad and compile it at the command line using the vbc.exe utility included with the .NET Framework, even if you don't have the complete Visual Studio package installed. The IDE is really nothing more than a helpful work area for designing programs.

On the other hand, there are several good reasons to explore the IDE in detail, as you'll see in this chapter. For one thing, it's changed so much since Visual Basic 6 that even experienced programmers may find themselves somewhat lost. Most importantly, though, if you master the IDE, you'll become a more productive developer, with tools such as integrated help, flexible macros, and a customizable code display ready at your fingertips. Look at the new IDE features in Visual Studio 2005 as your reward for upgrading to the .NET platform. Stepping up to Visual Basic 2005 requires some relearning and a little hard work, but in the end you'll get to spend your programming hours in a state-of-the-art environment equipped with conveniences that no other programming tool can boast.

This chapter describes each part of the Visual Studio interface, along with additional tips for configuring the IDE and working with macros and other time-savers. You'll round up with a look at the simplest possible .NET application that you can create—a command-line program called a *Console application*.

New in .NET

The IDE in Visual Studio has evolved from a mix of different ancestors. It combines the best of Visual InterDev, Visual Basic, and Visual C++. It also throws in some of the attractive new interface elements turning up in such products as Office and Windows XP. Some of the most important changes are summarized in the following paragraphs.

True integration

It's always been called the "integrated" design environment, but up until .NET it's been anything but. While different Visual Studio products, such as Visual Basic, Visual C++, and Visual InterDev, have had similar interfaces, they've also had a whole host of subtle differences. As you discovered in the first chapter, one of the core goals of the .NET Framework is to integrate different languages, and this strategy extends to the development environment. With Visual Studio, programmers of all stripes share the same IDE, and they can use identical components such as debugging tools and menu designers.

The new "look"

Could Microsoft release a groundbreaking new product without revamping the interface? Probably not. As we've seen with Windows 95, 98, 2000, and XP, Microsoft tries to combine technological advances that are buried under the hood with painstaking design enhancements. Visual Studio follows this trend. Depending on your outlook, it's a welcome improvement, an inconsequential change, or a distracting nuisance. In any case, get ready to look at a new set of hand-detailed icons and learn to use windows that dock, tab, collapse, and hide automatically.

Enhanced IntelliSense

Visual Basic programmers have always been able to count on catching typos and minor mistakes, thanks to the built-in syntax checker. IntelliSense remains in Visual Basic 2005, with a few refinements. Now errors are underlined (as they are in Microsoft Word, for example), and a tooltip explains the problem when you hover your mouse over the offending code. When you start a conditional or loop structure, Visual Basic 2005 automatically adds the last `End If`, `End Case`, or `Loop` line. And, if you let it, the editor will automatically format your code with the appropriate indenting.

Macros

Visual Basic 2005 allows you to record simple macros or create more complex ones using a built-in macro editor. It's the first indication of Visual Studio's *Automation model*, which allows developers to interact with the development environment to create enhanced add-ins and customized programming tools.

Code snippets

Need the code for a common task, but can't quite remember what functions to use? Visual Basic 2005 adds a new Code Snippets feature that lets you quickly insert ready-made code and tweak it to suit your needs. Although you're initially limited to what Visual Studio includes, you'll be able to download more great examples from Microsoft or third-party developers in the future and add them to your snippets collection.

A little more like classic VB

Visual Studio 2005 adds a few refinements that are designed to make it behave like the Visual Basic 6 environment developers remember and love. Two key features include edit-and-continue debugging (which you'll study in Chapter 8) and the ability to create a new project without saving it right away. Of course, there's a whole pile of annoying VB 6 quirks that will never return (like the in-your-face VB 6 error checker, which stopped you in your tracks every time you made a minor mistake).

Starting Out in the IDE

You know the drill. It's time to load up the design environment by browsing to the Visual Studio shortcut in your Start menu.

Although it's well organized, the Visual Studio interface is somewhat complicated, with a wealth of features packed into every corner of the IDE. In the following sections, we'll look at different aspects of the interface one by one and explore the concepts you need to know to become completely comfortable in your new programming home.

NOTE   *To be technically correct, Visual Basic 2005 is the programming language that you use, while Visual Studio 2005 is the IDE that provides all the conveniences from automatic syntax checking to a built-in form designer. For familiarity, though, this book sometimes refers to the editor as though it were a part of Visual Basic 2005.*

The Start Page

When you first open Visual Studio, a detailed Start Page appears (as shown in Figure 2-1). The Start Page gathers several types of information together, along with links that let you open recent projects.

Recent MSDN articles (from the Web)

Single-click access to applications you worked on recently

Jump to the MSDN Help or a useful section of the MSDN website

Breaking news (from the Web)

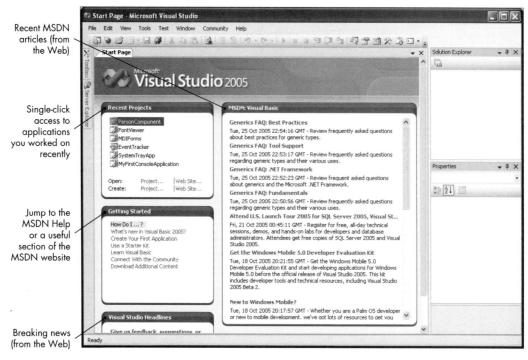

Figure 2-1: The Start Page

The most useful part of the Start Page is the Recent Projects section, which shows a list of applications you worked on recently (and allows you to open one of them with a single click). However, the other portions of the Start Page offer some interesting frills. They consist of information that's drawn from Microsoft's own MSDN (Microsoft Developer Network) website (http://msdn.microsoft.com). You could browse to this information on your own using a web browser (and many developers do), but Visual Studio incorporates it into the interface to spare you the trouble of having to search around on the Web. It's a simple idea, but it can help you stay up to date with the latest developments, trends, and bug fixes. Of course, all these web-based features rely on you having a live Internet connection ready to go. If you're not currently connected to the Internet, the links won't be updated and they obviously won't work when you click them.

NOTE *Microsoft is following its own advice with Visual Studio's seamless Internet integration. As you'll find out in Chapter 13 on web services, Microsoft (like many other leading technology companies) sees the computer industry evolving into a model in which numerous discrete components provide services to other applications over the Internet.*

Features like the Start Page resemble web services in that they seamlessly incorporate a piece of Internet functionality (like late-breaking articles) into a Windows application (in this case, Visual Studio).

The Start Page includes three panels with MSDN content, which are described in the following sections.

MSDN: Visual Basic

This large section provides a list of recent articles from the MSDN website. Check here frequently, and you can keep an eye out for developments that interest you, say, a new optional add-in or a tutorial that describes a thorny problem you're grappling with. To read one of these articles, just click the link. The related web page will open inside the Visual Studio interface.

Getting Started

This section includes links that lead to the Visual Studio Help (on your computer) and valuable sections of the MSDN website. For example, you can click "How Do I?" for task-specific help, "What's New in Visual Basic 2005" if you're a longtime user getting up to speed with the latest version, or "Learn Visual Basic" for a comprehensive (if a bit dry) tutorial on the VB language. All of these sections are great for browsing, but the other links lead to even more treasures. Try "Download Additional Content" to hunt for useful sample code, and "Connect With the Community" to head to the Microsoft newsgroup forums, where you can pose your most head-scratching VB questions to the VB community.

Visual Studio Headlines

This section is used for important announcement from the MSDN website. (Oddly enough, this section of supposedly vital information is buried at the bottom of the Start Page, where most developers are likely to overlook it.)

Changing the Startup Behavior

Visual Studio gives you a very limited ability to configure what it should do on startup. To see your options, select Tools ▶ Options from the menu. The Options dialog box will appear, with a tree of settings. Make sure the Show All Settings check box is selected, so that you see every section of settings. Then drill down to the Environment ▶ Startup section shown in Figure 2-2.

The "At startup" list allows you to choose what action Visual Studio should take when you first fire it up. The default is to show the Start Page described in the previous section. If you just can't warm up to the Start Page, however, or if you don't have an Internet connection to make the most of all those web-enhanced features, you might want to choose something different. Your options include loading the project you used most recently, showing the New Project or Open Project dialog boxes, or doing nothing at all, which starts you off with a blank, uncluttered window.

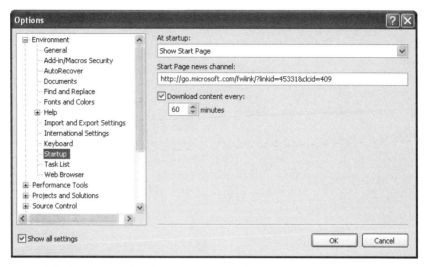

Figure 2-2: Configuring Visual Studio's startup behavior

If you decide to keep the Start Page, there's a little more you can control. You can choose the web URL from which Visual Studio reads all its content. (Unfortunately, you can't use just any URL—it needs to be in the format Visual Studio expects, which makes this setting relatively useless.) You can also choose how often the Start Page is refreshed with newly downloaded web data. The default is once an hour.

TIP   *You can also configure the number of projects in the recent project list. Head to the Environment ▶ General section, and set the Items Shown In Recently Used Lists setting. It's 6 by default.*

Creating a Project

Before you go any further, you may want to create a project so that you can see the interface components this chapter describes. You won't actually do much with this first program—not even make it display a "Hello, World!" message—but you will get your first look at the full design-time environment.

To create a new project, click the Create Project . . . link in the Recent Projects section of the Start page, or just choose File ▶ New Project from the menu. A window will appear (see Figure 2-3) listing the different project types you can create.

For now, keep the default (Windows Application), and click OK to continue. A new project will created with a single form.

When you create a new project in Visual Studio 2005, you aren't forced to save it right away. Instead, your project files are tucked away in a user-specific temporary folder, which allows you to tweak your application, compile it, and debug it, all without saving it to a specific location on your hard drive. When you're ready to keep your work around for the long term, just choose File ▶ Save *[ProjectName]* from the menu.

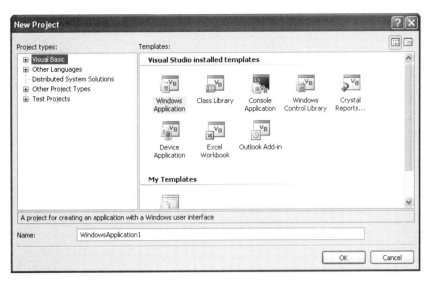

Figure 2-3: Creating a project

If you're curious and you want to track down the real code files, search for a temporary directory like C:\Documents and Settings*[UserName]*\Local Settings\Application Data\Temporary Projects*[ProjectName]*. Visual Studio creates these directories automatically to store new, unsaved projects. Once you save a project, it's moved to the location you choose.

NOTE *If you want to ensure that projects are always saved when they're created, you can change Visual Studio's behavior. Select Tools ▸ Options, browse to the Projects and Solutions ▸ General section, and turn on the Save New Projects When Created check box. If you install Visual Studio as a multilanguage or C# developer (rather than choosing the VB profile in the setup program), this check box is selected initially.*

Tabbed Documents

You might notice that you didn't really leave the Start Page behind when you created your application. Instead, you've just opened a new window (which displays the one default form that's added to all new Windows applications). You can find out which windows are open (and move back and forth from one to another) using the row of tabs just under the Visual Studio menu (see Figure 2-4). The IDE uses tabbed windows to organize a great deal of information without creating excessive clutter.

As with Visual Basic 6, there are two ways to edit any form. You can use the design view to arrange and configure the controls on a window, and use the code view to add the event handlers that run when specific actions take place. You can switch back and forth between code and design views with the buttons at the top of the Solution Explorer window, described later in this chapter (or you can use the less convenient View ▸ Code and View ▸ Designer menu commands). Once you show these additional views, you can switch between them quickly by clicking the appropriate tab.

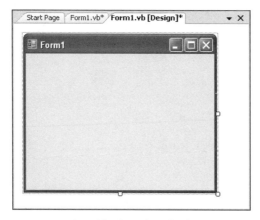

Figure 2-4: The tabbed window display

In the tabbed window list, the name of the tab indicates the file and the view. If it's a code display window, you'll just see the filename (for example, Form1.vb contains the event-handling code for Form1). Form design windows add the word "design" (for example, Form1.vb [Design] provides a graphical look at Form1). Thus, Figure 2-4 includes three tabs—one for the Start Page, one for the code view of Form1, and one for the design view of the same form.

Docked and Grouped Windows

Most of the windows in Visual Studio support docking, which allows them to latch onto a side of the main IDE window rather than floating together in a jumbled mess. In addition, some windows are docked together, which means that when they appear, you'll need to switch from one to another by clicking the appropriate tab. For example, the Breakpoints, Locals, and Immediate windows (which are used for debugging) are shown in a tabbed group (see Figure 2-5). Similarly, the Toolbox and Server Explorer are also grouped (on the left of the IDE). Windows that are grouped together in this way aren't necessarily related. It's just Visual Studio's way of saving screen real estate.

Window tabs

Figure 2-5: Grouped windows

If you just won't feel comfortable until you've customized every avenue of Visual Studio, you can drag windows to different areas of the screen to change the way they are docked and grouped. Rearranging windows on your own is a little tricky. After a prolonged bout of experimentation, you're likely to wind up with windows in the wrong places or grouped with the wrong windows. Correcting these problems can be awkward, and you may find it easiest to reset the display to its default layout. To do this, select Window ▸ Reset Window Layout from the menu. Everything will be restored to its original layout.

Touring Visual Studio

One of the most remarkable features of the IDE is that just about everything you need is only a few clicks away . . . once you understand how to get there.

NOTE *You can't realistically use the IDE with a small monitor (or with a large monitor using a low resolution). If your current screen resolution is less than 1024 × 768, be ready to endure some clutter and suffer a severe reduction in quality of life while using the IDE. With Visual Studio, the greater your resolution is, the more convenient the IDE will be. Generally, a monitor that's 19″ or larger is best.*

Just as with Visual Basic 6, the IDE is built out of a collection of different windows. Some windows are used for writing code, some for designing interfaces, and others for getting a general overview of files or classes in your application. Now that you understand how windows work in Visual Studio, it's time to take a look around the design environment, and find out the role each window plays.

The Solution Explorer

The Solution Explorer window shows all the files that are part of the current project. The Solution Explorer replaces the Project Explorer in Visual Basic 6, and it works similarly, with a couple of important differences. The Solution Explorer can contain multiple projects (as shown in Figure 2-6), much like a project group in Visual Basic 6. The Solution Explorer can also contain other files that are used in your project but contain data rather than code. For example, you can include pictures, XML documents, and other files. Having the Solution Explorer track these dependencies for you is a substantial improvement. In the past, an obscure part of a program might fill controls using external bitmap files. If you didn't know about this requirement, you might not have remembered to make sure the bitmap files were in the application directory, which would be sure to cause a problem when you ran the program.

NOTE *Technically speaking, a solution is a group of one or more projects. Every new project is automatically placed inside a new solution. In Chapter 7 you'll learn how to get fancier and place multiple projects in a solution.*

One nice feature about the Solution Explorer is that it provides significant file management capabilities, enabling you to create folders to organize dependent files. You can easily rearrange and rename files without breaking other portions of your code.

Figure 2-6: The Solution Explorer with
two projects

By default, the Solution Explorer ignores files that happen to be in your
project directory but weren't created in Visual Studio (and haven't been
explicitly added to the project). However, if you want to take a look at *everything* in the project directory, just click the Show All Files button at the top
of the Solution Explorer (or choose Project ▶ Show All Files). This trick
uncovers some hidden resource files, such as the automatically generated
code for forms that you'll explore in Chapter 4.

The Toolbox

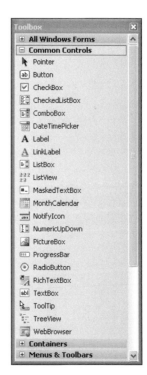

The Toolbox window (see Figure 2-7) is similar to
the toolbox in Visual Basic 6, but it's more carefully
organized. It provides controls you can use when
designing a graphical interface.

By default, the Toolbox uses automatic hiding
to slide out of the way when it's not being used.
An icon is displayed at the left edge of the screen,
and if you hover over it, the Toolbox slides out.
(You've probably encountered the same feature
with the Windows taskbar.)

Although the automatic hiding feature
conserves screen space, this behavior is frustrating
when you are designing a form's interface, both
because the window constantly slides in and out
of view and because when it appears, it obscures
part of the form you're editing. When you need
to work with the toolbox, click the pushpin in
the top right corner of the window when it slides
into view. This disables the automatic hiding
feature (until you click the pushpin to "unpin"
the window).

Figure 2-7: Some of the
controls in the Toolbox

Similarly, you can free up real estate by unpinning other Visual Studio windows. In practice, you'll probably prefer to have everything you need on the screen waiting for you, rather than interactively bouncing on and off it, but the auto-hide feature does give you some ability to free up space when needed.

When you have a design view of a form open, the Toolbox displays all the controls you can drop on the form, subdivided into several groups. You can see all the possible controls using the first group, which is named All Windows Forms.

By default, these controls are displayed in a list view that displays the name of each item, but you can also change it to the more compact icon display used in Visual Basic 6 by right-clicking and clearing the check box next to the List View option.

NOTE   *If your toolbox is empty, it's probably because you aren't currently designing a Windows form. If you haven't started a project, or if you are in code view, no controls will be shown.*

Customizing the Toolbox

If a third-party developer releases a custom control that you're eager to use, you can add it straight to the Toolbox. Just right-click the Toolbox, and select Choose Items. Select the .NET Framework Components tab, click Browse, and find the appropriate .dll file. You can then choose exactly which controls to display by adding a check mark next to the appropriate items (see Figure 2-8).

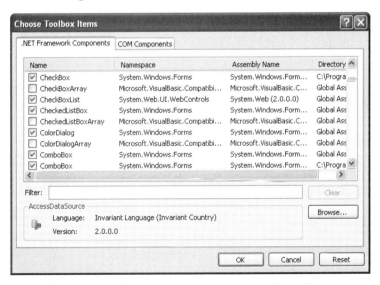

Figure 2-8: Choosing which items to display in the Toolbox

You can also use the .NET Framework Components tab to hide items that are currently shown. But what's the point of having a component if you can't use it?

You'll find that the list of Toolbox components is longer than you expect, because it includes certain items (such as web controls) that only appear in specific project types. It also includes some items that were originally included in .NET 1.0 for backward compatibility—such as controls for control arrays—but that are no longer recommended and are therefore never included in the Toolbox.

NOTE *You can also use this window to add an ActiveX control—just use the COM Components tab instead of the .NET Framework Components tab. Most ActiveX controls can be wedged into .NET applications without a problem, and Visual Studio will automatically generate interoperability code that makes it work almost seamlessly. However, it's a better idea to stick with .NET controls where possible. They provide more features, fewer headaches, and better performance.*

The Properties Window

The Properties window is the IDE window that has changed the least from classic versions of Visual Basic. It still occupies the same place in the IDE, and it is used for the same purpose: setting the properties for the controls in your application.

One enhancement is the collapsible interface, which allows you to show or hide categories by clicking the plus (+) or minus (−) boxes next to the category heading (see Figure 2-9). Category headings are indicated with a gray background. The collapsible interface also applies to some properties that use complex data types. For example, forms have a Font property that references a Font object. You can set the information for this font object by clicking the ellipsis (. . .) next to the word *Font*, or you can expand the Font property to show all the subproperties. These are the properties of the related font object, such as Name, Size, and Unit.

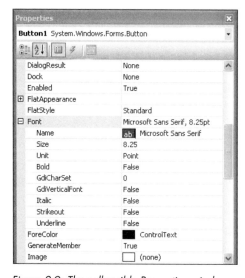

Figure 2-9: The collapsible Properties window

The Code Display

The code display window in Visual Studio has some impressive refinements. One of these is the auto-formatter, which automatically applies the correct indenting to block structures. However, one of the most innovative features is the collapsible display, which allows you to choose portions of the code to view while hiding those that don't interest you. This allows you to control screen clutter and navigate through your code files more easily.

There are two ways to collapse a section of code. One way is to place code in a #Region block. These blocks have no effect on the function of your code and are ignored when the code is compiled. The hash (#) indicates that this is a special instruction for the IDE.

For example, suppose you want to create a region named *Secret Algorithm*. Here's how you define that region:

```
#Region "Secret Algorithm"
#End Region
```

Inside the Region block, you can place any ordinary code. For example, here's a region that wraps two procedures:

```
#Region "Secret Algorithm"

    Public Function CalculateCodes() As String
        ' (Code goes here).
    End Function

    Public Function ValidateCodes(code As String) As Boolean
        ' (Code goes here).
    End Function
#End Region
```

Figure 2-10 shows how this code can be tucked neatly out of sight.

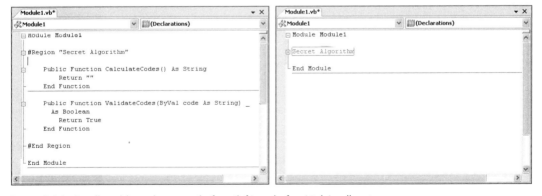

Figure 2-10: A collapsible code region before (left) and after (right) collapsing

Additionally, any code in a class, module, subroutine, or function is automatically made collapsible. Figure 2-11 shows both an expanded and a collapsed procedure.

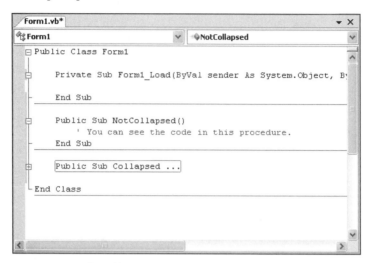

Figure 2-11: Collapsible code without a region

Splitting Windows

In a large project you may sometimes need to work with more than one document at a time, and the IDE makes it easy to do that. Here's how it works. First, right-click the tabbed list of documents, and choose either New Horizontal Group or New Vertical Group. New Horizontal Group creates two rows of tabs, one above the other (as shown in Figure 2-12). New Vertical Group creates two rows of tabs: one on the left and one on the right. You can repeat this process to create even more tab groupings.

To move a document tab from one window to another, you can drag the tab (the easiest approach), or you can right-click it and choose Move to Next Tab. This trick allows you to organize your environment when editing a large project. If you empty out a tab group, it disappears, and life reverts back to normal.

You can also split each individual code editing window so that you can see two parts of the same *document* at once. To do this, select Window ▶ Split from the menu while you're editing the appropriate code file (and use Window ▶ Remove Split to take it away). This technique allows you to see more than one portion of the code in a single file (as shown in Figure 2-13).

Even though you have a split in your window, there's still just one document. All views are updated automatically when you make a change in either section.

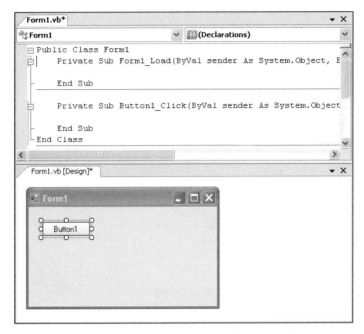

Figure 2-12: Organizing windows with multiple (horizontal) tab groups

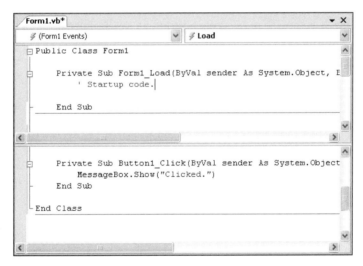

Figure 2-13: Using split windows

The Task List

The Task List (see Figure 2-14) is another convenience that helps you manage programming tasks while working on a project. The Task List acts like a developer's to-do list. To show the Task List, select View ▶ Other Windows ▶ Task List.

To add an item to the Task List, click the clipboard icon, and type a description. You can also give each task a priority (Low, Medium, or High) by choosing an option in the ! column. When you're finished with the task, you can mark it completed by adding a check mark, or you can right-click and choose Delete to remove it altogether.

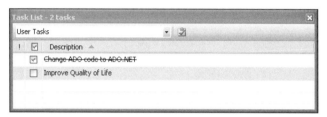

Figure 2-14: User tasks

So far, you've seen how to add *user task* items to the Task List. However, the most interesting part of the Task List is the way you can link it to your code using predefined *comment* items. For example, any time you add a comment that starts with 'TODO, it will be automatically added to the list. You can then double-click the item to jump directly to the relevant place in code. This allows you to keep track of locations in code where further work or revision is required.

Figure 2-15 shows how comment items work. The 'TODO comment in the upper pane (the code view) is linked to the task item in the bottom pane (the Task List). Notice that comment items appear only when you select Comment in the drop-down list at the top of the Task List, instead of User Tasks.

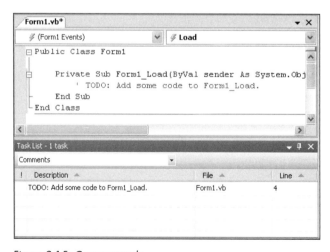

Figure 2-15: Comment tasks

You don't need to add `'TODO` in front of all the comments you want to track. Instead, you can set the predetermined comment types that will be automatically added to the Task List. To do so, select Tools ▶ Options, and then choose the Environment ▶ Task List section. You can add a new type of comment (called a "comment token") by typing the prefix the comment must start with (leave out the apostrophe), setting the default priority, and clicking Add (Figure 2-16).

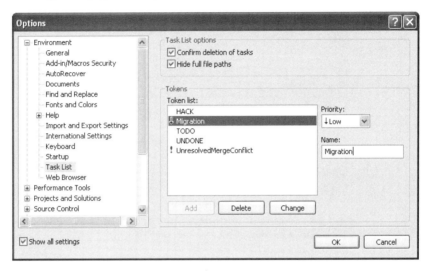

Figure 2-16: Adding custom comment tokens

Code Snippets

Every day, developers write similar code to solve similar problems. The creators of VB wanted to take some of the pain out of hunting for code examples and to put the syntax for basic tasks right at your fingertips. Visual Basic 2005 addresses this challenge with a new feature called *code snippets*.

The idea behind the code snippets feature is that you can quickly dig up a few elusive lines of code for a common task and then customize them to suit your exact needs. Visual Studio helps you out by organizing snippets into groups and using some innovative highlighting.

Inserting a Snippet

To try this out, move to the appropriate location in your code, right-click the mouse, and select Insert Snippet. A pop-up menu will appear with a list of snippet categories, such as Common Code Patterns, Data, Security, and Windows Forms Applications. Once you select a category, you'll see a full list of all the snippets that are available. You can then select one to insert it at the current position.

For example, Figure 2-17 shows the result of inserting the code snippet named *Get a Random Number using the Random class* from the Math category.

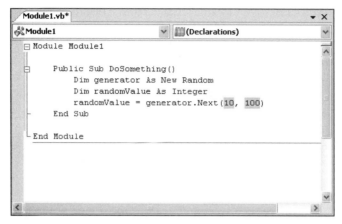

Figure 2-17: Inserting a snippet

The best feature snippets provide is that they highlight any hard-coded values in green. For example, the snippet shown in Figure 2-17 includes two hard-coded values (the numbers 10 and 100, which represent the lowest and highest random numbers you're willing to consider). When you hover over either of these values, a tooltip pops up with an explanation about what value you should type in to replace the hard-coded number (Figure 2-18). And for a real shortcut, you can jump from one highlighted region to the next, just by pressing TAB.

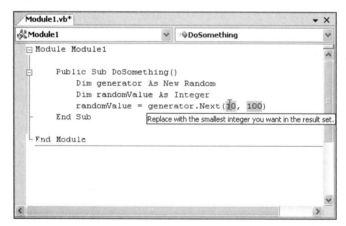

Figure 2-18: Replacing the hard-coded values in a snippet

Managing Snippets

Snippets are only as useful as the code they contain, and Visual Basic 2005 ships with a relatively small collection of snippets that range from genuinely useful (like "Compare Two Files") to absurdly trivial (like "Define a Function"). Many useful topics aren't dealt with at all. However, there's still hope, because the snippets system is extensible. That means you can hunt down .vbsnippet files on the Internet and add them to your collection.

To get an overview of all the snippets that are currently on your computer or to add new ones, you need to use the Snippet Manager. Select Tools ▶ Code Snippets Manager (Figure 2-19). Select a snippet, and you'll get a brief description that indicates who created it.

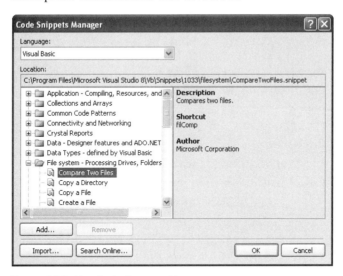

Figure 2-19: The Code Snippets Manager

The hidden gem in the Code Snippets Manager window is the Search Online button. Click this to launch a search that goes beyond your local computer and into the CodeZone community. (You may find that this search isn't quite as refined as should be. If you're digging up irrelevant links, try adding the word "snippet" to the search to home in on the code.)

TIP   *Want to take your snippets to the next level? Microsoft offers a surprisingly powerful free tool for managing and customizing code snippets—you can download it at http:// msdn.microsoft.com/vbasic/downloads/tools/snippeteditor. Using this tool you can edit and test existing snippets, set author, title, and keyword information for your own snippets, and even convert your snippet into a .vsi (Visual Studio Content Installer) file for easy sharing with other programmers.*

Macros

Macros are a new and welcome feature for Visual Basic 2005 users. At their simplest, macros are little pieces of functionality that help you automate repetitive coding tasks. For example, consider the following code example. (I've abbreviated it considerably to save space, but you get the idea.)

```
' Assigning to oddly named controls.
FirstNamelbl.Text = FirstName
LastNamelbl.Text = LastName
Streettxt.Text = Street
Countrycbo.Text = Country
```

The programmer who wrote these lines made a common naming mistake and put the control identifier (for example, txt for text box) at the end of the name instead of the beginning. In this case, using Visual Studio's Find and Replace feature isn't much help, because even though the mistake is repeated, many different variables are incorrectly named. If you're a seasoned problem-solver, you may already realize that this mistake can be fixed by repeating a set of steps like this:

1. Start at the beginning of the line.
2. Press CTRL and the right arrow to jump to the position right before the period.
3. Highlight the last three letters (hold down SHIFT and press the left arrow three times).
4. Use CTRL+X to cut the text.
5. Press HOME to return to the front of the line.
6. Press CTRL+V to paste the variable prefix in the right position.
7. Move one line down by pressing the down arrow.

Easy, right? Just repeat these steps for each of the next dozen lines, and the problem is solved. Of course, now that we've realized that the process of editing a line is just a sequence of clearly defined steps, we can automate the whole process with a macro.

To do this, select Tools ▶ Macros ▶ Record TemporaryMacro (or press CTRL+SHIFT+R). Follow the steps, enter the appropriate keystrokes, and then click the Stop button on the macro toolbar. Now you can play the temporary macro (CTRL+SHIFT+P) to fix up the remaining lines.

The Macro IDE

When you record a macro, Visual Studio stores a series of instructions that correspond to your actions. If you've created macros in other Microsoft applications such as Microsoft Word or Microsoft Access, you'll already be familiar with this system. The interesting thing in Visual Studio is that the macro language used to record your actions is exactly the same as ordinary Visual Basic 2005 code. The only difference is that it has built-in objects that allow you to interact with the IDE to do things like insert text, open windows, and manage projects. In fact, an entire book could be written about the object model used in Visual Studio's macro facility.

To view the code you created with your temporary macro, select Tools ▶ Macros ▶ Macro Explorer. In the Macro Explorer window (which is paired with the Solution Explorer by default), find the TemporaryMacro routine in the RecordingModule, as shown in Figure 2-20.

Right-click the TemporaryMacro routine, and select Edit to view the code, which looks like this:

```
Sub TemporaryMacro()
    DTE.ActiveDocument.Selection.StartOfLine(VsStartOfLineOptionsFirstText)
```

```
      DTE.ActiveDocument.Selection.WordRight()
      DTE.ActiveDocument.Selection.CharLeft(True, 3)
      DTE.ActiveDocument.Selection.Cut()
      DTE.ActiveDocument.Selection.StartOfLine(VsStartOfLineOptionsFirstText)
      DTE.ActiveDocument.Selection.Paste()
      DTE.ActiveDocument.Selection.LineDown()
End Sub
```

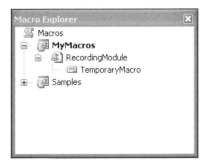

Figure 2-20: The Macro Explorer window

This code is bound to look a little unfamiliar, as it uses the DTE object model, which allows you to interact with the IDE. The important thing to understand is that every macro corresponds to a subroutine, and all recorded actions are defined in code. To interact with the IDE, you use DTE commands.

TIP *When you open a macro project, you'll end up with what looks like two design environments. The easiest way to switch from your regular project to your macro project is using the taskbar, which shows both.*

The Temporary Macro

Macros help you while you are writing a program. In fact, most macros have a limited usefulness: They are created to solve a specific problem and are not used once that problem is solved. For that reason, a Visual Studio macro is recorded as a "temporary" macro. There can only be one temporary macro at a time, and when you create a new temporary macro, the old one is replaced.

If you want to create a permanent macro, you'll have to open the macro editor and move the code in the TemporaryMacro subroutine into a new subroutine that you've just created for that purpose. To run this new macro, double-click its name in the Macro Explorer window.

Macros with Intelligence

In practice, macros often take over where more mundane find-and-replace or cut-and-paste operations leave off. For example, you might want to make a macro that could intelligently examine the currently selected text and decide what correction or insertion to make based on some test. You could even build an entire wizard, complete with Windows forms and file access. Some examples of advanced macros are included in the sample code for this chapter.

Following is a straightforward example that swaps the code on either side of an equal (=) sign in the selected range. For example, it could convert the line of code StringA = StringB to StringB = StringA.

```
Public Sub InvertAssignmentLine()

    ' Retrieve the text.
    Dim str As String
    Dim i As Integer
    DTE.ActiveDocument.Selection.SelectLine()
    str = DTE.ActiveDocument.Selection.Text

    ' Trim the final hard return.
    str = Left(str, Len(str) - 2)

    ' Find the equal sign.
    i = InStr(str, "=")

    ' Reverse the text if it had an equal sign.
    If i > 0 Then
        str = Mid(str, i + 1) & "=" & Left(str, i - 1)
        DTE.ActiveDocument.Selection.Text = str & vbNewLine
    End If

    ' "De-select" the current line.
    DTE.ActiveDocument.Selection.Collapse()

End Sub
```

The structure of this code should be clear, but the DTE commands will be new. A good way to start learning about DTE commands is to record a task in the IDE, and then look at the automatically generated code. For comprehensive information about the DTE, check out the Visual Studio Help.

Incidentally, this code also uses traditional Visual Basic 6 string manipulation functions such as Len() and Left(), which are still supported but whose use is discouraged in favor of VB 2005's new object-oriented equivalents. The online samples for this chapter include a rewritten version of this macro that uses .NET-style string manipulation. After you've read the next chapter and learned the basics of .NET, you might want to take a look at that sample.

Macros and Events

Visual Studio also provides a special EnvironmentEvents macro module, which contains macros that react to IDE events for windows, documents, and build and debugging operations. Once again, you need to know some non-VB features to perfect this type of macro—namely, the object model for the IDE.

The next macro example uses the WindowActivated event. Whenever you change focus to a new window, this macro closes all the other windows that are part of your project (the dockable Visual Studio windows and the Start Page won't be closed) in an attempt to reduce screen clutter. It may seem a little foreign because we haven't yet explained how .NET handles events, but it gives you an interesting idea of what is possible with the IDE. For example, you could create a macro that executes every time a user starts a new project and preconfigures the toolbox or initial code files.

```
Public Sub WindowEvents_WindowActivated(GotFocus As EnvDTE.Window, _
  LostFocus As EnvDTE.Window) Handles WindowEvents.WindowActivated

    ' Exit if the current window doesn't correspond to a document.
    If GotFocus.Document Is Nothing Then Exit Sub

    Dim Doc As Document
    Dim Win As EnvDTE.Window

    ' Scan through all the windows.
    For Each Win In DTE.Windows
        ' Ignore the window if it doesn't correspond to a document
        ' or is the currently active window.
        If Not Win.Document Is Nothing And Not Win Is GotFocus Then
            Win.Close()
        End If
    Next

End Sub
```

Remember, this macro will work only if it's placed in the EnvironmentEvents module. Only that module has the automatically generated code that makes all the Visual Studio events available.

NOTE   *These macro examples are by no means comprehensive. Visual Studio allows you to write and integrate all sorts of advanced add-ins, control designers, and macros. Macros can even use the .NET class library, display a Windows interface, and examine your code. For a rich set of macro samples, check out the macro project named Samples, which is installed automatically with Visual Studio and will appear in the Macro Explorer.*

The Simplest Possible .NET Program

Now that you've made your way around the Visual Studio environment, it's time to take a closer look at the project and solution system by generating your first real program.

The simplest possible .NET program doesn't use any Windows forms. Instead, it is a *Console* or *command-line* application. This type of application takes place in something that looks like an old-fashioned DOS window, but it is really just a text-based Windows program. Console applications are sometimes used for batch scripts and other extremely simple utilities. Mainly, though, Console applications are used to create every computer writer's traditional favorite: the "Hello, World!" program.

To create a Console application, just start a new project and select Visual Basic Projects ▶ Console Application (Figure 2-21).

Figure 2-21: Creating a Console application

The following sample program, called MyFirstConsoleApplication, uses the Console object (found in the System namespace) to display some basic information on the screen. The project is configured to run the Main subroutine at startup.

```
Module Module1

    Sub Main()
        Console.WriteLine("What is your name?")
        Dim Name As String = Console.ReadLine()
        Console.WriteLine()
        Console.WriteLine("Hi " & Name & ". I feel like I know you already.")

        ' This stops the application from ending (and the debug window
        ' from closing) until the user presses Enter.
        ' If you were interested, you could examine the return value
        ' of ReadLine() to find out what the user typed in.
        Console.ReadLine()
    End Sub

End Module
```

To launch this program, choose Debug ▶ Start Debugging (or just press the F5 key). The result is shown in Figure 2-22.

This book won't feature anything more on Console applications, because Windows and web applications provide much richer interface options. The only significance of MyFirstConsoleApplication (and the only reason it's included in this book) is the fact that it shows you a complete Visual Basic 2005 application in its simplest form. That application is a module (although a class could be substituted) and a single subroutine that contains all of the program's operations. Nothing is hidden in this example. You could write this program in a text file, give it the .vb extension, and compile it the old-fashioned way using the vbc.exe command-line compiler.

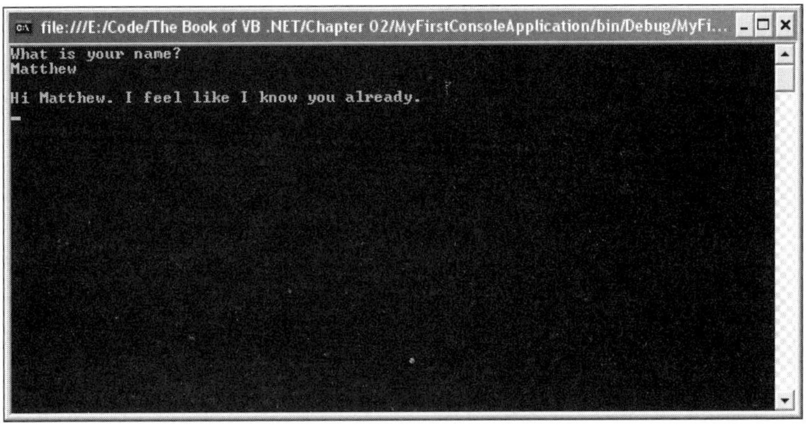

Figure 2-22: An unimpressive .NET application

MyFirstConsoleApplication Files

The essential logic for this application is contained in a single .vb file, named Module1.vb. However, Visual Studio uses a few extra files to keep track of additional information about your solution.

- MyFirstConsoleApplication.sln contains information about the projects in the solution and their build settings (which determine whether the project is compiled or ignored when you click the Start button).
- The MyFirstConsoleApplication.suo file contains binary data that preserves your view settings for the solution, making sure that Task List items, breakpoints, and window settings are retained between sessions. This is a major improvement over Visual Basic 6.
- The MyFirstConsoleApplication.vbproj file is the most interesting. It uses an XML format to store information about your application, including the assemblies it needs, the configuration settings it uses, and the files it contains. This information is required only when programming and testing your application—as you'll see in Chapter 7, all the necessary details are embedded into the final executable when you compile it.

MyFirstConsoleApplication Directories

There are also three extra subdirectories created inside every VB project:

- The My Project directory includes some resource files that support various Visual Basic features that you may or may not use, such as the My object, application settings, and embedded resources. You'll learn about all of these details later in this book. But for now, don't worry about this directory. It doesn't include any nondefault content for the MyFirstConsoleApplication project.

- The obj directory contains some temporary files that are created while building the application (every time you press the Start button to run it in Visual Studio). These files can be safely ignored.

- The bin directory contains the actual application once it's compiled. There are two ways to compile your application—in debug mode (for testing) and in release mode (once you've perfected it). When you launch your application for debugging (by pressing F5, clicking the Start button in the toolbar, or selecting Debug ▶ Start Debugging), your application is compiled in debug mode and placed in the bin\Debug folder. On the other hand, when you choose Build ▶ Build *[ProjectName]* from the menu, your application is compiled in release mode (which gives it that extra performance edge) and placed in the bin\Release folder.

The compiled MyFirstConsoleApplication consists of one executable file, which is named MyFirstConsoleApplication.exe. However, you'll find that some extra support files turn up in the bin\Debug directory, such as the .pdb file that Visual Studio uses for debugging. When you distribute your application to other computers, you won't need these extra files. For more information about .NET compilation and deployment, refer to Chapter 14.

NOTE *Unlike in Visual Basic 6, all programs are fully compiled before you can run them. When debugging, Visual Studio will create a .pdb file along with the executable. This file contains the debug symbols that allow you to pause, resume, and debug your application.*

Project Properties

Visual Studio introduces a new control panel for configuring projects. To take a look, double-click My Project in the Solution Explorer, or choose Project ▶ *[ProjectName]* Properties. Either way, you'll see a new page appear, with a list of tabs on the left (see Figure 2-23).

You'll consider the options in this window at various points throughout this book, whenever they relate to a specific feature. But if you want to start exploring by tweaking the options in MyFirstConsoleApplication, here's a quick guide that explains each tab:

Application
This tab lets you choose the filename for your final .exe file, the icon, and how it starts. You'll learn how to use it to set a startup form and respond to application events in Chapter 4.

Compile
This tab lets you supply settings for the VB compiler. For example, you can turn off certain warnings, and require cleaner coding by turning on Option Explicit and Option Strict. Chapter 8 has more about these two options.

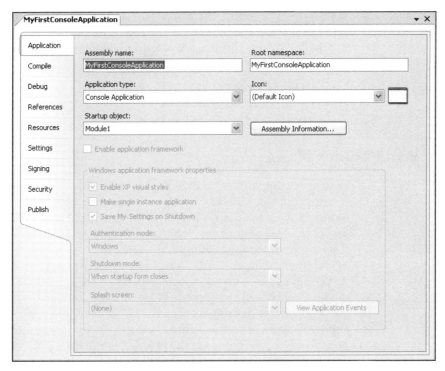

Figure 2-23: Managing project properties

Debug

This tab lets you supply command-line arguments, set the startup directory, and set a few more settings that affect debugging sessions. Chapter 8 explores debugging in detail.

References

This tab shows you your project *references*, which are other components that your application is using. You'll learn more in Chapter 3.

Resources

This tab lets you add *resources*, text or binary information that's embedded right inside your compiled application file. You'll learn more in Chapter 7.

Settings

This tab lets you set application settings, which are automatically stored in a configuration files. You'll use settings to keep track of database connection strings in Chapter 10, but you can use them for almost any type of simple data.

Signing

This tab lets you give your compiled project a *strong name*, so that it can be placed in the computer-specific component repository called the *Global Assembly Cache (GAC)*. You'll try this out in Chapter 7.

Security

> This tab lets you fine-tune security settings for ClickOnce, a specialized deployment technology described in Chapter 14.

Publish

> This tab lets you publish your application as a ClickOnce publication, so it can be easily installed from the Web or a network (and updated seamlessly). You'll learn how in Chapter 14.

What Comes Next?

In this chapter you learned about Visual Studio, the integrated environment where you will perform all your programming. Visual Studio is an indispensable tool, correcting simple mistakes, making code easily readable and navigable, organizing resources, and providing designers for HTML pages, XML documents, graphics, and icons.

Though the focus of the remainder of this book is on the Visual Basic 2005 language, an entire book could easily be written on the features in Visual Studio (and several have been). The customization and macro features alone are probably the most sophisticated ever bundled into a Windows application, and it will take some time before developers have explored all the benefits and possibilities they can provide. If these features have captured your interest, go ahead and start experimenting! One great starting point is the Visual Studio Extensibility website provided by Microsoft at http://msdn.microsoft.com/vstudio/extend.

3

VB 2005 BASICS

So far you've read about the fundamental goals of the .NET platform, and you've learned how to work in the remodeled Visual Studio programming environment. But before you can start creating *real* VB 2005 programs, you need a basic understanding of a few .NET concepts. These concepts—the basics of Visual Basic 2005—range over every aspect of the language. They include everything from small details, such as changes to assignment syntax and variable scoping, to the namespace feature, which is the basis of .NET's overall organization. Understanding how namespaces work is your key to accessing the common class library—the all-in-one repository of functionality used for everything from downloading a file from the Internet to printing a document.

We'll begin this chapter with an introduction to namespaces, the common class library, and Visual Basic 2005's file format. These are the aspects of Visual Basic programming that have changed the most in the .NET world. Next, you'll learn about how the basic data types have evolved and their hidden object structure. Finally, you'll explore the changes that have been made to assignment syntax and functions, and you'll learn about delegates, another .NET newcomer. By the end of the chapter you'll be familiar with .NET's most fundamental innovations, and you'll be ready to get to work with the Visual Basic 2005 language.

NOTE *Although a handful of language refinements are new in Visual Basic 2005, almost all of the changes you'll learn about in this chapter apply to all .NET versions of Visual Basic. The most notable exception is the My object, which makes its debut in Visual Basic 2005.*

New in .NET

You might wonder what a chapter on basics is doing in a book designed for developers who already understand details such as functions, variables, and events. The answer? VB 2005 and its predecessor, VB.NET, represent a complete overhaul of the Visual Basic language. The changes from classic Visual Basic range from minor tweaks all the way to a radical new programming model based on the class library. Some of the features you'll read about in this chapter include:

The common class library

Java has one. Windows programmers have had dozens, ranging from C++ tools such as MFC and ATL to the built-in Ruby engine in Visual Basic 6. Unfortunately, none of these class libraries has offered a truly complete and integrated solution, so developers have been forced to work with a mix of different components and even resort to the Windows API. With .NET, developers finally have a complete, modern class library providing all the programming capabilities that were previously available only in countless different bits and pieces.

The My object

In a bid to demystify the sprawling class library, the designers of VB added a new My object that provides shortcuts to some of the most useful features. Sadly, My isn't all it's cracked up to be (for example, it lacks access to some of .NET's most powerful features), but it does have a few genuinely useful tricks in store.

Redefined arrays

Arrays are the most obviously changed basic elements from classic VB. Gone are the days when arrays could take any shape and size. In order to work with the Common Language Runtime and be consistent, VB 2005 arrays always begin at element 0. And that's only the start. Be sure to review the data type descriptions in this chapter to learn why arrays now act like objects, not like structures.

Shortcuts and cosmetic changes

Facing the need to implement sweeping changes to support the Common Language Runtime, the VB design team decided to revise the whole language for .NET, introducing minor refinements like new assignment shortcuts, mandatory function parentheses, better support for optional parameters, and keywords that allow you to exit a function quickly or skip to the next iteration of a loop. Many of these hit the scene with .NET 1.0, but VB 2005 continues to evolve.

Method overloading

You can use the Overloads keyword to create multiple procedures that have the same name, but different parameters. Visual Basic 2005 will decide which procedure to use depending on the variables you supply.

Delegates

A *delegate* is a variable that can store a reference to a function or subroutine. You can then use this variable to execute the procedure at any time, without needing to call it directly. Delegates help you write flexible code that can be reused in many different situations.

TIP   *If you want a detailed look at the entire VB 2005 language, from the ground up, why not take a look at the Visual Basic Language Specification 8.0. (VB 2005 is also known by the version number 8.) You can search for this document at www.microsoft.com/ downloads, or just use http://tinyurl.com/8rne5 to get there.*

Introducing the Class Library

The cornerstone of .NET is the common class library, which provides several thousand useful *types* (programming objects) that you can drop directly into a Visual Basic 2005 program. Essentially, the class library is filled with prebuilt pieces of functionality. For example, you'll find that it contains all the ingredients you need to build graphical Windows applications, web pages, and modest command-line applications (like the one shown in Chapter 2).

The class library is enormous. Even after you have finished this book and learned VB 2005 programming style and syntax, you'll continue to return to new parts of the class library as you add new features to your applications. But before you start considering any of the types in the class library, it helps to understand two of its basic organizing principles: namespaces and assemblies.

Namespaces

Every piece of code in a .NET program exists inside a conceptual construct known as a *namespace*. Namespaces prevent .NET from confusing one program with another. For example, suppose the Acme Insurance Company uses a namespace called AcmeInsurance for all of its programs. The code for a program that provides insurance policy information might then exist in a namespace called `AcmeInsurance.PolicyMaker` (which is really a `PolicyMaker` namespace inside the `AcmeInsurance` namespace).

Namespaces are hierarchical, like directories on a hard drive. `AcmeInsurance` is a company-specific namespace that can contain other namespaces representing programs; those namespaces can themselves include still more namespaces. This is useful, because Acme's PolicyMaker program might use a class named `Policy`. Somewhere in the world, another program probably uses a `Policy` class. However, there's no chance of confusion, even if you install both of these programs at once, because Acme's `Policy` class really has the full name `AcmeInsurance.PolicyMaker.Policy`, which is almost certainly unique.

NOTE *A dramatic comparison can be made between namespaces and the Windows API. Essentially, all the capabilities of the Windows API exist in a single namespace that is stuffed full of hundreds of functions. Without a very thorough, cross-referenced guide, there is no way to tell which functions belong together. The problem is compounded by the fact that procedures in the Windows API must have less-than-ideal names just to avoid colliding with existing function names. This is one of the main reasons that using the Windows API is the secret nightmare of many VB programmers.*

Namespaces aren't just used in your own applications. They're also an important organizing principle for the class library. The thousands of types that are included with .NET are organized into more than 100 namespaces. For example, if you want to build a Windows application, you'll use the types from the `System.Windows.Forms` namespace.

To take a look at the class library namespaces and start exploring them, you can refer to the indispensable *class library reference*. To find it, fire up the Microsoft Visual Studio 2005 Documentation (you'll find the link in the Start menu), and then dig through the table of contents to this location: .NET Development ▶ .NET Framework SDK ▶ Class Library Reference. Figure 3-1 shows this all-important location.

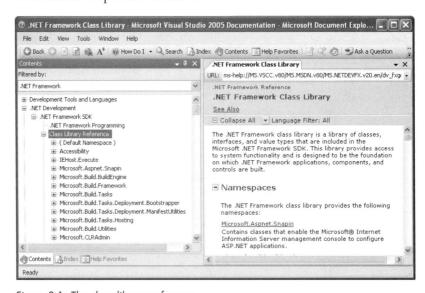

Figure 3-1: The class library reference

The class library is arranged like a giant tree structure, and each branch (namespace) contains a few dozen or a few hundred types. The core namespaces of the .NET Framework begin with System (for example, System.Data or System.Windows.Forms).

To find out what's inside a namespace, just expand the node in the tree. For example, Figure 3-2 shows a partial list of the types in the System namespace, which is the most fundamental .NET namespace. It includes basic data types and core ingredients such as the Console class demonstrated in Chapter 2. To get more information about one of these types, select it.

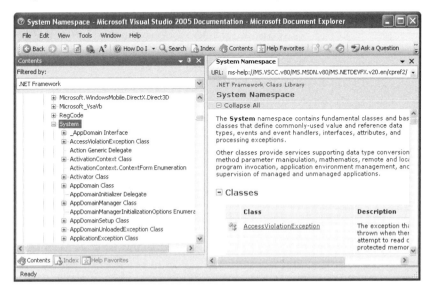

Figure 3-2: Documentation for the System namespace

The class library is intimidating at first glance. However, as you become more familiar with VB 2005, and after you study its object-oriented underpinnings in Chapters 5 and 6, you'll start to feel more at home.

TIP   *To jump straight to the documentation that details a specific class, just look up the class name in the index of the Visual Studio Help.*

Assemblies

Although namespaces are used to organize types logically into separate groups, that's not the whole story. In order to use any namespace in your application, you need to have access to the right *assembly*, which is the physical file (a .dll or .exe) that contains the corresponding compiled code. For example, if you want to use the controls in the System.Windows.Forms namespace, you need to have access to the System.Windows.Forms.dll file, where the code is stored. (In this case, the namespace name and the assembly name match, but this isn't a requirement. An assembly can contain code in many different namespaces, and different assemblies can use the same namespace.)

In other words, there are two ways to think about the class library. You can picture it as a collection of types that are organized into namespaces, all of which you can use in your programs. Or, you can think of it as compiled code in a set of .dll files, stored in a system-specific location on your computer.

TIP　*In Chapter 7 you'll explore assemblies in much more detail. You'll learn what these files look like on the inside and how you can divide your own applications into multiple components.*

Types

At this point, you might be wondering exactly what the class library contains. The answer is *types*—a .NET concept that includes classes, events, structures, and more exotic creations such as enumerations and delegates. In Chapters 5 and 6 you'll get to the technical details of this arrangement, but for now you can think of the class library as a collection of objects you can use in your programs.

This model is dramatically different from pre-.NET versions of VB. Visual Basic 6 provided a few built-in objects that you could use (such as `Printer`, `Screen`, `App`, and `Err`) and allowed you to add more objects by adding references to COM libraries (for example, those used for databases or XML support). Visual Basic 2005, on the other hand, provides hundreds of objects that are sorted into namespaces according to function and at your fingertips through the .NET class library.

If you aren't quite clear on what an object is, keep reading. The next sections explain the bare minimum you need to know to start using objects.

NOTE　*Objects are programming constructs that contain properties, methods, and events (all of which are called* members*).*

Properties

Properties store information about objects. For example, a `TextBox` control in a Windows application has a property called `Text`, which stores the text that appears in the text box. (A *control* is really just a special type of object.) If you had a `TextBox` control named `Text1`, you could use `str = Text1.Text` to copy the text out of the text box and into a variable named `str`.

Methods

Methods are commands that cause an object to do something. For example, `MessageBox.Show()` uses the `Show()` method of the `MessageBox` object to display a message, and `MyDoc.Print()` uses the `Print` method of the `MyDoc` object to send some data to the printer. In this book, you'll recognize method names because they are always followed by empty parentheses.

Events

Events are notifications that an object sends you, which you can then either listen to or ignore. For example, a button object sends a `Click` event, which gives you the chance to respond and perform an operation in your code.

Instance members and shared members

One of the most confusing aspects of object-oriented programming, at least for the newcomer, is that some objects need to be created, while others don't. The reason for this difference is that objects can have both *shared* members, which are available even if you haven't created an object, and normal *instance* members, which are available only once you've created an object. For example, `Console.WriteLine()`, used to display a line of text in a command-line application, and `MessageBox.Show()`, used to display a message box in a Windows application, are two examples of shared methods. You don't need to create objects of the `Console` or `MessageBox` types in order to use the `WriteLine()` or `Show()` methods. On the other hand, `TextBox.Text` is an instance member. Instance members don't have any meaning without an object—for example, you can't talk about the `Text` property of a `TextBox` unless you're talking about a specific `TextBox` object in a window.

In VB 2005, any class can have a combination of shared members and instance members. For example, you'll consider the `DateTime` type a little later in this chapter. It provides a shared `Now` property that you can use to retrieve the current date and time without creating an object first. `DateTime` also contains ordinary instance properties, including `Day`, `Month`, `Year`, and `Time`, which get individual components of a date stored in a particular `DateTime` object.

Using the Class Library

Now that you've learned about the nifty class library, you're no doubt eager to put it to use in your applications.

In order to use the types in the class library, you need to make sure they're accessible to your code. This feat requires two steps. First you need to make sure your project has a reference to the correct assembly where the code is stored. Next, you need to consider *importing* the namespace that contains the types you're interested in so that they're easier to code with. The following sections have the full details.

Adding a Reference to an Assembly

Before you can use the objects provided in a namespace, you must make a *reference* to the appropriate assembly. A reference is simply your application's way of letting Visual Basic know which components it's using. Often, you won't need to worry about this issue at all, because when you create a new application in Visual Studio, you start out with references to a small set of assemblies you're likely to use. For example, Windows applications always have a reference to System.Windows.Forms.dll.

You can use the Solution Explorer to see a list of all the references used by your project. However, Visual Studio hides this information from you by default (assuming that it's more information than you really want to know). To take a look, select Project ▸ Show All Files. The Solution Explorer will now include several new ingredients: files that are in the project directory but aren't a part of your project, the compiled version of your application in the bin directory, and a group of references. Figure 3-3 shows the references that are added, by default, to all new Windows applications.

Usually, these references will be all you need. Of course, sometimes you will decide to use a component of the class library that exists in a different assembly. The process works like this:

1. You find an exciting component in the class library that does exactly what you need.

2. You look at the top of the class information page to find out which assembly you need. For example, the System.Xml.XmlNode class lives in the assembly named System.Xml.dll (as indicated in Figure 3-4). If your application already has a reference to this assembly, you don't need to take any additional steps.

Figure 3-3: Basic references in a Windows application

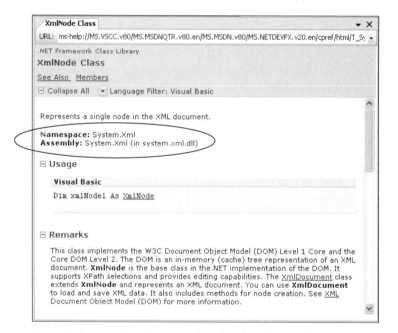

Figure 3-4: Assembly information from the class library reference

3. Then you right-click the References item in the Solution Explorer and select Add Reference.

4. Last, you find the appropriate file (System.Xml.dll in this example) in the list under the .NET tab, and select it (see Figure 3-5).

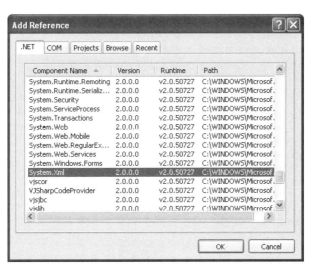

Figure 3-5: Adding a reference

5. Click OK. Visual Studio will add the reference (and you'll see it in the References group in the Solution Explorer). Now the components in that part of the class library are available for you to use.

NOTE *Don't become confused between assemblies and namespaces. Logically speaking, the objects in the class library are grouped in namespaces. Physically speaking, the code that defines these types is stored in assemblies. Once you have the correct assemblies referenced for your project, you can forget about them entirely, assume the point of view of your code, and start thinking in terms of namespaces.*

Importing a Namespace

As long as you have a reference to the appropriate assembly, you can access an object in a namespace by writing its fully qualified name (as in *[Namespace].[Class]*). This can be cumbersome, though, because many objects are stored several levels deep, in namespaces with long names. For example, the .NET version of the VB 6 App object is called Application and is found in the System.Windows.Forms namespace. This means, for example, that in order to retrieve the product version of your application, you have to write code like this:

```
VersionString = System.Windows.Forms.Application.ProductVersion
```

Admittedly, the line looks far more complicated than it needs to be. To improve on this, you can make things simpler by using the Imports statement.

Essentially, the Imports statement tells the VB compiler what namespaces you're using. It's strictly a time-saver to help reduce the number of long, fully qualified names you have to type. The Imports statement must occupy the first line in your code window, before any classes or modules are defined, and the Imports statement doesn't use a block structure.

Here's an example of code without the `Imports` statement. This snippet of code simply uses the `MessageBox` class (from the `System.Windows.Forms` namespace) to show a message box.

```
' This code has no Imports statement.
' A reference to the System.Windows.Forms assembly exists in the project.
' (VB 2005 added it automatically because we chose to create a Windows
' application.)

Public Module MyModule
    Public Sub Main
        System.Windows.Forms.MessageBox.Show("You must enter a name.", _
          "Name Entry Error", System.Windows.Forms.MessageBoxButtons.OK)
    End Sub
End Module
```

The following example rewrites the code with the benefit of the `Imports` statement. The Imports statement saves us some typing in two places:

```
Imports System.Windows.Forms

Public Module MyModule
    Public Sub Main
        MessageBox.Show("You must enter a name.", _
          "Name Entry Error", MessageBoxButtons.OK)
    End Sub
End Module
```

You can import as many namespaces as you want by adding additional Imports statements at the top of your code file. The `Imports` statement won't slow your code down in any way—in fact, the compiled code won't change at all. It's simply a coding convenience.

NOTE   *If you try this example for yourself, you'll find that you can use the nonqualified names (in the second example) without adding the `Imports` statement. That's because the `System.Windows.Forms` namespace is already imported by default in a new Visual Studio project—read the next section to find out more.*

Project-wide Imports

An `Imports` statement only applies to the file that it's used in. You can also create project-wide imports that apply to all the files in your project. In fact, if you create a new Windows project, you'll find that `System.Windows.Forms` is already imported at the project level, so you can write code like the preceding `MessageBox.Show()` example *without* typing the `Imports` statement or using a fully qualified name.

To see all the project-wide imports, right-click your project in the Solution Explorer and select Properties. Then click the References tab (as shown in Figure 3-6). The top portion of this page shows the assemblies that are referenced; the bottom portion shows namespaces that are imported automatically.

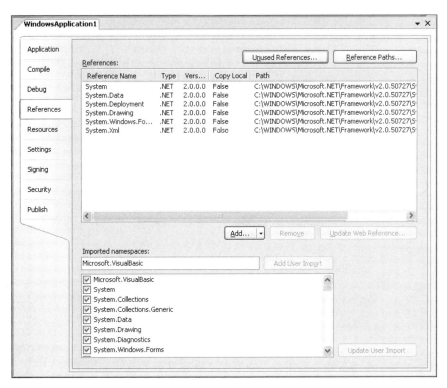

Figure 3-6: Project imports

Using this window, you can easily add, edit, and remove any of the project-wide imports.

Aliases

You can also use the Imports statement to create an *alias*, which is typically a short form that you can use to refer to a namespace. For example:

```
Imports Wn = System.Windows.Forms
' Now we can use statements like Wn.MessageBox.Show
```

An alias is useful if you want to import namespaces that have classes with the same names. Using an alias, you can still make it much easier to work with these types (and ensure that the resulting code is much more readable), but you won't have to worry about conflicts between identically named types.

Exploring the Class Library Namespaces

Throughout this book you will discover various parts of the class library and learn how to use them in your programs. But just to get yourself oriented and help you understand the structure of the class library, the following sections provide a quick overview of some of the more important namespaces.

System

This is the core namespace that you'll begin learning about in this chapter. The System namespace includes the definitions of basic data types such as strings, arrays, and events. It also introduces exceptions, which you'll study in Chapter 8.

System.Collections and System.Collections.Generic

These namespaces provide *collection classes*—objects that can contain groups of objects. You'll explore these in Chapter 6, which focuses on object-oriented programming.

System.Data

This namespace includes the types needed for ADO.NET, which is discussed in Chapter 10. Other namespaces that start with System.Data are used for specific parts of ADO.NET, such as SQL Server and Oracle support.

System.Drawing

This namespace provides types that allow you to work with colors and fonts and draw directly on a form. Many of these features go under the collective name GDI+ and are quite different from the drawing features provided in Visual Basic 6. These features aren't described in this book, because manually drawing a form's interface in code is an unsatisfying experience for most all programmers. It's difficult to produce content that looks attractive, and it's nearly impossible to generate anything like an animation program that works with respectable speed. However, GDI+ does make a brief appearance in Chapter 9 with printing.

System.Drawing.Printing

This is a namespace used to support print and print preview features, which you'll explore in Chapter 9.

System.IO

This namespace is used for file access, including file management and reading and writing your own files. It's also covered in Chapter 9.

System.Net

This namespace contains low-level network communication classes, as well as some useful objects you can use to retrieve information from the web without delving into ASP. Chapter 9 provides a taste of these features.

System.Reflection

This namespace provides support for *reflection*, a technique that allows you to do various interesting and slightly unusual things, such as examining a class you don't have information about and finding out what it is ("reflecting" on it). Reflection is further discussed in Chapter 7.

System.Runtime.Serialization

This branch of the class library contains several namespaces that allow you to serialize objects (convert them to a block of bytes for long-term storage) and then restore them effortlessly. This impressive feature makes an appearance in Chapter 9.

System.Threading

This namespace provides the tools you'll need for creating multithreaded programs. Chapter 11 will give you a solid grounding in threading.

System.Web

This is the namespace to use for ASP.NET applications. The root System.Web namespace provides the basic built-in ASP.NET objects. Other namespaces that start with System.Web include additional important types, such as those used to create Web Forms interfaces. You'll learn about ASP.NET in Chapters 12 and 13.

System.Windows.Forms

This namespace includes all the types you need for building the user interface in a Windows program, including classes that support forms, text boxes, buttons, and countless other controls. You'll learn all about Windows programming in Chapter 4.

System.Xml

This namespace contains objects that allow you to interact with XML data and create your own XML documents. You'll be introduced to XML in Chapter 9.

Microsoft.VisualBasic

This tiny namespace provides the classic built-in VB functions (the string manipulation functions Left() and Mid(), along with other blasts from the past). You won't use this namespace directly.

Microsoft.Win32

This is a small namespace that lets you access the registry and respond to certain global system events. You'll use the registry in Chapter 9.

Other namespaces

Of course, the class library provides many more capabilities than this book has space to cover, including advanced string manipulation, regular expressions, sockets and other tools for FTP-type programs, and low-level classes for managing the sticky details of security and COM. There are even whole namespaces of classes that do little more than support features in the Visual Studio IDE and that provide design-time support for controls and the Properties window.

The class library integrates features that previously required a combination of dozens of separately developed components and the Windows API. Throughout this book, I'll introduce you to the most exciting parts of the class library, the Visual Basic 2005 programming language, and the Visual Studio interface where you'll do your work, all at once.

The My Object

After releasing VB .NET 1.0, Microsoft discovered that developers often had trouble finding the specific classes they needed in the sprawling .NET class library. In a bid to improve this situation, Visual Basic 2005 introduces quick access through a built-in object that's always available. Oddly enough, this one-stop shop is called the My object.

Obviously, the My object can provide hooks into only a very small subset of the total .NET Framework. (After all, the more features it provides, the more complex it will become, until it's much more confusing than the class library it's trying to replace!) However, Microsoft has made a reasonable attempt to centralize some of the most commonly used features in My.

For example, imagine you want to grab a few commonly used pieces of information, such as the current time, the name of the computer where your code is running, the name of the user running the code, and the current directory where the application is stored. All of these details are available in the class library, but they're easier to find using the My object. To get a sense of the information you can find, try out this code:

```
MessageBox.Show(My.Computer.Clock.LocalTime)
MessageBox.Show(My.Computer.Name)
MessageBox.Show(My.Computer.FileSystem.CurrentDirectory)
MessageBox.Show(My.User.Name)
```

My Core Objects

Without a doubt, the best feature of My is that its features are *discoverable*—in other words, you have a good chance of finding them using Visual Studio IntelliSense. To help you out, the My object divides all its features into seven key branches (see Figure 3-7).

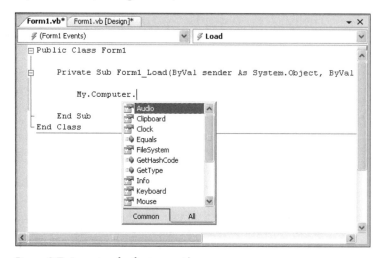

Figure 3-7: Browsing for features with My

Five of these branches have core objects that centralize functionality from the .NET Framework and provide computer information.

`My.Computer`

This object provides information about the current on which your code is running. For example, you can access the clipboard (`My.Computer.Clipboard`), play sounds (`My.Computer.Audio`), retrieve information from the Windows registry or a file (`My.Computer.Registry` and `My.Computer.FileSystem`), and even check the network status (`My.Computer.Network`).

`My.Application`

This object provides information about the current application, including the assembly and its version number, the folder where the application is running, and the command-line arguments that were used to start the application. You can also use this object for quick-and-easy logging.

`My.User`

This object provides information about the current user. You can use this object to write security code that checks the user's account or group membership.

`My.Settings`

This object allows you to retrieve custom settings from your application's configuration file. You'll use configuration settings in Chapter 10.

`My.Resources`

This object allows you to retrieve *resources*—blocks of binary or text data that are embedded in your application when you compile it. Resources are a great way to store items such as pictures that your application needs to use, and you'll learn more about them in Chapter 7.

Default Instances

There are also two `My` objects that provide *default instances*. Default instances are objects that .NET creates automatically for certain types of classes defined in your application.

`My.Forms`

This object provides a default instance for each form. This allows you to communicate between forms, as you'll see in the next chapter.

`My.WebServices`

This object provides a default proxy object for every web service your application uses. You'll learn about web services in Chapter 13.

The Dark Side of My

At first glance, the `My` objects seem like a great idea. However, they aren't without their critics. One problem is that even though the `My` objects simply provide access to features that are already in the .NET class library, they do so in a slightly different way—and having to learn two ways to solve the same problem can get confusing. A more significant problem is that the `My` objects usually don't give you all the power that you get by using the corresponding classes directly from the .NET class library. In many cases, you'll need to use the real .NET classes anyway, so many developers question why they should spend time learning a scaled-down model. Finally, the My objects are unabashedly VB-centric. Even though C# developers (and programmers working in other .NET languages) can, technically, use the My objects, most won't go to the extra work. As a result, VB code that relies heavily on the My objects isn't as easy to convert into pure C# code, which is a drawback if you like to exchange ideas and insights with programmers of other stripes.

Throughout this book, you'll occasionally dip into the My objects. You'll learn when they provide the quickest, neatest solution. However, we won't shy away from getting more power by delving into the .NET Framework on our own either.

Code Files

In Visual Basic 6 (and older versions), there were several specialized types of files that went into a project. Form files (.frm) contained the graphical layout and event-handling code for a form. Class files (.cls) contained individual classes that you created on your own. Module files (.mod) contained variables and functions that could be made globally accessible. The whole collection of files was grouped into a project, which was described by the familiar Visual Basic project file (.vbp) and could be further bundled into project group files (.vbg). Keeping all these different file types straight could be a bit of a challenge.

Visual Basic 2005 takes a different approach.

- When you start a new application, you create a *solution* file (.sln), as shown in Figure 3-8.

- Each solution can hold one or more project files (.vbproj).

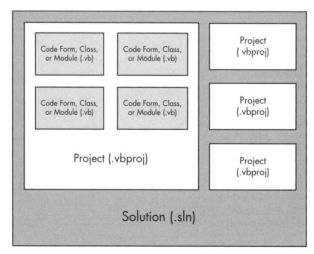

Figure 3-8: A solution file

- All the other files are code files (.vb). These code files can contain multiple classes, modules, and forms (which are really just a special type of class). In other words, the logical grouping of your program into classes, modules, and forms doesn't necessarily determine the physical division of your code into files on the hard drive.

NOTE   *As you'll discover in Chapters 12 and 13, Internet applications are a little different from other programs and contain a variety of distinct file types.*

Class and Module Blocks

In order to make this model possible, Visual Basic 2005 use various block structures to hold classes, modules, and forms. For example, here's a code file that contains a class and a module:

```
Public Class MySampleClass
    ' Code here.
End Class

' No man's land...code can't exist here.

Public Module MySampleModule
    ' Code here.
End MyModule
```

Inside a class or module definition, you can add procedures and write your code as normal. However, you can't place any type of variable or procedure declaration *outside* of these definitions. The following example illustrates the difference.

```
Public i As Integer              ' This is not allowed!

Public Class MySampleClass
    Public j As Integer          ' This is OK.
    Public Sub MySub()           ' This is also fine.
    End Sub
End Class
Public Sub MySub2()              ' This has no meaning!
End Sub

Public Module MySampleModule
    Public Sub MySub3()          ' This is OK.
    End Sub
End Module
```

All classes and modules are contained in a root element that you don't see: your project's namespace. For example, if you place the code shown above into a .NET component (something you'll try in Chapter 7), another application can access MySub3() using the fully qualified name MyProject.MyModule.MySub3().

Bear in mind that Visual Basic 2005's multipart file format should not be seen as a good reason to combine dozens of classes and modules into a single file. Organization at the file level still makes sense. The only difference is that now you have the ability to group together small, interconnected classes in one file.

Namespace Blocks

All the code you enter in your project is contained in a *root namespace*. By default, Visual Basic 2005 will assign it the name of your application. To rename your project's root namespace, right-click your project in the Solution Explorer, and choose Properties. Then edit the text in the Root Namespace text box. You can also change the *assembly name* of your program at the same time (the name the final .exe file will have when you build it).

It's all well and good to learn how to change your root namespace, but a logical question is why bother? Technically, you care about your project's namespace only if you want it to be used by other applications. For example, if you're creating a database component for a Fortune 100 company, it makes more sense to use the namespace DatabaseLibrary rather than MyProject0043. Of course, even if you aren't building a component, it's a good rule of thumb to choose respectable namespace names just in case you want to reuse your code in the future.

You can also create additional namespaces to help you organize your code in a large application. To do this, use the Namespace/End Namespace block. Namespaces have to be defined outside all other constructs. This means that you can't create a namespace inside a class or a module; it has to be the other way around. Here's an example of how you might create a new namespace (named Configuration) to hold a module named ConfigTools:

```
Namespace Configuration

    Module ConfigTools
        Public Sub UpdateSettings
            ' Some code goes here.
        End Sub
    End Module

End Namespace
```

In this example you can access the UpdateSettings() procedure from another namespace in your project as Configuration.ConfigTools.UpdateSettings() or from another application as [ProjectName].Configuration.ConfigTools.UpdateSettings().

Adding Code Files

You can easily add modules, forms, and ordinary code files to a Visual Basic 2005 project using the Project menu. Choose Project ▶ Add New Item to get a full list of choices, as shown in Figure 3-9.

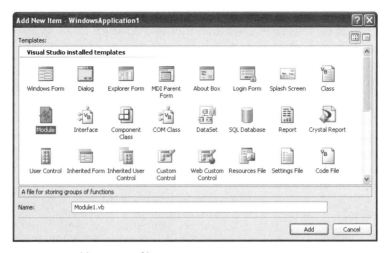

Figure 3-9: Adding a new file

Visual Basic 2005 projects aren't limited to code files. You'll also see some templates for quickly creating About boxes and other common windows. You can even add other resources such as bitmap files, HTML pages, and icons. The ability to add these files directly into your project ensures that you can keep track of important resources.

Data Types

Most Visual Basic 6 data types remain the same in VB 2005, at least on the surface. For example, all of the following statements are still valid:

```
Dim MyInteger As Integer
Dim MyString As String
Dim MyDate As Date
```

These may look the same as the built-in data types in Visual Basic 6, but in fact they are not. Each one of these variable types is mapped to a corresponding type in the System namespace. For example, the Date keyword really corresponds to System.DateTime, and the String keyword represents System.String.

The System Types

The types in the System namespace are shared by every .NET language, and they form part of the infrastructure that lets you integrate code components written in different languages without running into any trouble. Of course, in order for this integration to work, the built-in variable types in Visual Basic 6 had to be harmonized with those from other programs to create the best possible common type system. This is the reason for most of the data type changes that you'll find in VB 2005. For example, Integer now maps to

System.Int32—a 32-bit integer that can store a number as great as
2,147,483,647—rather than to Visual Basic's traditional 16-bit integer,
which could accommodate numbers only up to 32,767.

```
Dim MyInteger1 As Integer          ' This is a 32-bit integer.
Dim MyInteger2 As System.Int32     ' This is also a 32-bit integer.
```

This is quite a convenience for new VB developers, who often use integers
as loop counters without realizing the size limitations. One manifestation of
this problem is a VB 6 report-generating program that fails with an overflow
error if it finds more than 32,767 records in a database.

If you're moving from VB 6, you'll find a slew of minor changes to many
of your favorite data types. Strings work more or less the same way that they
did in VB 6, although you can't create a fixed-length string anymore. User-
defined types (those created with Type/End Type statements) are another
casualty, but they can be replaced by structures and classes, as you'll see in
Chapters 5 and 6. Another change is that the Currency data type is no longer
available. You'll have to use Decimal instead, which is optimized for financial
calculations that require exact fractions.

Multiple Variable Declaration

Visual Basic has always allowed you to create more than one variable on a
single line. In the past, however, the results weren't always what you might
have expected. Consider the following example:

```
Dim intA, intB, intC As Integer
```

In Visual Basic 6 this line of code would create one integer (intC) and
two Variants. (A Variant was the default variable type in VB 6.) In Visual
Basic 2005, however, all the variables in this line will become integers. In fact,
Visual Basic 2005 no longer supports Variants. If you want to create a variable
that can accommodate different data types, you will need to use the generic
System.Object type.

Initializers

Initializers are a convenient VB 2005 feature that lets you assign a value to a
variable on the same line where you define it. Here's an example:

```
Dim i As Integer = 1
```

This technique even works with arrays (in which case you need to
enclose all the values in a set of curly braces) and objects:

```
' Define an array and fill it (with four numbers) in one step.
Dim NumberArray() As Integer = {1, 2, 3, 4}
```

```
' Define and initialize an object in one step, using its constructor.
Dim MyFile1 As System.IO.FileInfo = New System.IO.FileInfo("c:\readme.txt")

' or...
Dim MyFile2 As New System.IO.FileInfo("c:\readme.txt")
```

You can also create new variables inside other code statements, such as function calls, by using the New keyword:

```
ProcessFile(New System.IO.FileInfo("c:\readme.txt"))
```

Don't overuse this convenience, though, because it can make your code difficult to read.

Data Types as Objects

Visual Basic 2005 is object-oriented to the core. If you haven't had any experience with object-oriented programming and design, you may have to wait until Chapters 5 and 6 before the .NET picture really becomes clear. However, I can't wait that long to divulge one more unusual secret: *Every type in Visual Basic 2005 is really a full-fledged object.*

The most important consequence of this shift is the fact that all data types have built-in methods for handling associated tasks. For example, you may remember that Visual Basic 6 included a whole host of functions for calculating such values as the length of a string or the upper boundary of an array. One of the goals of .NET was to remove this collection of disorganized, language-specific functions and provide equivalent or better capabilities through the elegant class library.

Accordingly, you might expect to find classes in the System namespace that contain similar helper methods, organized according to function. But there's a weakness to this design—in order to use this approach, you'd need to know which class to use. For example, in order to manipulate a string, you'd need to find a (hypothetical) StringManager class. Learning about all these helper classes would be a significant bit of extra work.

A better option is to organize these features so that they're actually a part of related data type. For example, the length of a string should be a characteristic of the String object. That way, you can get the length information without resorting to another class or a miscellaneous function that's built into the VB language. The following section demonstrates this principle and gets under the hood with the System.String type.

Strings

In .NET, every string is an object based on the System.String type. That means a string contains all the basic methods that it needs, bundled right with it.

The following example shows how string manipulation works in the
.NET world. This code compares two ways to find the length of a string—
using the Len() function, which is a part of the VB language, and using the
Length property, which is a part of every String object.

```
Dim MyString As String = "This is some sample text."
Dim StringLength As Integer

' The old fashioned way, which is still supported in VB 2005
StringLength = Len(MyString)

' The .NET way, which treats the string as a System.String object.
StringLength = MyString.Length
```

In order to use the first approach, you need to know that the built-in
Len() function exists. In any language, there could be hundreds of built-in
functions. The worst part is that they aren't organized in any way. The only
way to know what functions work with what data types is through hard-won
experience.

The second approach is much nicer. The Length property is built into
your String object. To find out about it, you simply need to type your variable
name (MyString), hit the period key, and look through the IntelliSense list of
string-related functionality (see Figure 3-10).

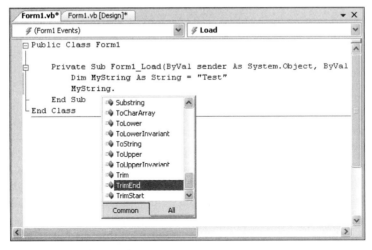

Figure 3-10: IntelliSense for a string

These techniques work for both string variables and string literals
(text enclosed in quotation marks). Here are a few more examples of string
manipulation code:

```
Dim MyString As String

' Capitalize a string and trim spaces, all in one line.
MyString = "lower case   ".ToUpper().Trim()          ' = "LOWER CASE"
```

```
' Get the portion of the string that starts at the second character
' and is four characters long. Note that strings start numbering at 0,
' which represents the first character.
MyString = MyString.Substring(1, 4)                    ' = "OWER"

' Replace all occurrences of the characters "W" with "LD".
MyString = MyString.Replace("W", "LD")                 ' = "OLDER"

' Get a string from an integer.
Dim MyInteger As Integer = 42
MyString = MyInteger.ToString()                        ' = "42"
```

These examples only scratch the surface. Table 3-1 provides a more comprehensive look at what a String object can do. For even more details, check out the class library reference in the Visual Studio Help. In the following sections you'll learn about some of the object smarts that are built into other common data types.

Table 3-1: Members of the String Class

Member	Description
Length	Returns the number of characters in the string.
ToUpper() and ToLower()	Return a copy of the string with all the characters changed to be uppercase or lowercase.
Insert()	Puts another string inside a string at a specified (zero-based) index position. For example, Insert(1, "pre") adds the string "pre" after the first character of the current string.
Remove()	Removes a specified number of strings from a specified position. For example, Remove(0, 1) removes the first character.
Replace()	Replaces a specified substring with another string. For example, Replace("Hi", "Bye") changes all occurrences of "Hi" in a string to "Bye".
Substring()	Extracts a portion of a string of the specified length at the specified location (as a new string). For example, Substring(0, 5) retrieves 5 characters starting at position 0 (the start of the string).
StartsWith() and EndsWith()	Determine whether a string ends or starts with a specified substring. For example, StartsWith("The") will return either True or False, depending on whether the string begins with the word "The".
IndexOf() and LastIndexOf()	Find the position of a substring in a string. This returns the first match. IndexOf() starts searching at the beginning, while LastIndex() starts at the end and works backward. There are also versions of these methods that accept an integer indicating the position where you want to start the search.
Split()	Divides a string into an array of substrings. It splits the string by looking for a delimiter you indicate. For example, use Split(" ") to split a sentence into individual words, by dividing it wherever a space occurs.
Join()	Fuses an array of strings into a new string. You can specify a separator that will be inserted between each element.

(continued)

Table 3-1: Members of the String Class (continued)

Member	Description
Trim(), TrimEnd(), and TrimStart()	Remove spaces (or some other character) from the sides of a string. You can use Trim() to remove this character from both sides, or TrimStart() or TrimEnd() to remove them from just the beginning or end.
PadLeft() and PadRight()	Add the specified character to either side of a string, the number of times you indicate. For example, PadLeft(3, MyString) returns a string with three additional spaces on the left side.

TIP *Remember, many traditional Visual Basic functions are still supported for backward compatibility. However, the object-oriented way of doing things is often more elegant and more organized. You'll learn far more about objects and how to use them in Chapters 5 and 6 of this book.*

More Efficient Strings

The .NET string is easy to work with, but it doesn't always perform well. For example, it's not very efficient when you need to paste together a new string out of several smaller strings. Because of the way the String data type is designed, this type of operation actually generates a new String object for each new addition, and creating a new object takes a short amount of time. Multiply that by several thousand (for an intensive string-processing algorithm), and you may wind up with a sluggish application.

To see the problem in action, try out the following code, which stitches together a new string out of 10,000 snippets:

```
Dim BigString As String = ""
For i As Integer = 1 To 10000
    ' Enlarge BigString.
    BigString &= " This is string part " & i.ToString()
Next
```

This code is slow because it requires creating (and abandoning) 1,000 string objects. Fortunately, .NET doesn't expect you to give up string parsing. In situations where you need fast processing (for example, when combining a large number of strings), you can use a more specialized System.Text.StringBuilder class. When you create a StringBuilder, it latches on to a buffer of memory where it can store its string. As you enlarge the string (by calling the StringBuilder.Append() method), it simply grabs more memory as needed, rather than generating a whole new object. When you're finished your string operations, you can convert your StringBuilder back into a conventional string by calling the ToString() method.

Here's an example that rewrites the earlier code snippet to use a StringBuilder:

```
Dim BigStringBuilder As New System.Text.StringBuilder()
For i As Integer = 1 To 10000
```

```
' Enlarge BigStringBuilder.
    BigStringBuilder.Append(" This is string part ")
    BigStringBuilder.Append(i.ToString())
Next
Dim BigString As String = BigStringBuilder.ToString()
```

If you run both of these code sections, you'll discover that the StringBuilder works almost instantaneously, while the ordinary string code is sluggish. Try the StringProcessing test project (available with the samples for this chapter) to see the difference in action.

Dates and Times

Date variables also have some interesting built-in features. For example, you'll find members that make it easy to retrieve portions of a date and perform date calculations. You can also use the TimeSpan class to store a measured interval of time, instead of a specific date. Here's an example:

```
Dim MyDate As Date
Dim MySpan As TimeSpan

' Set the date to today and the timespan to one day.
MyDate = Date.Now
MySpan = TimeSpan.FromDays(1)

' This displays the current hour.
MessageBox.Show(MyDate.Hour)

' This moves the date to tomorrow.
MyDate = MyDate.Add(MySpan)

' Here's another way to modify dates, which moves us back to today.
MyDate = MyDate.AddDays(-1)
```

Arrays

Arrays in Visual Basic 2005 always start counting at element 0. The types in the class library also follow this convention. (This is a change from VB 6, where some collections were 0-based and others 1-based, with little real consistency.)

When declaring an array, you specify only the upper boundary, as shown in our next example. The total number of elements in the array is always one greater than the number you specify.

```
Dim MyArray(10) As String   ' This creates an array with 11 elements,
                            ' numbered from 0 to 10.

Dim MyArray(1 To 10) As String ' This doesn't work!
                              ' The To keyword is allowed,
                              ' but the lower bound must be 0.
```

Opinions vary about this change. Many programmers resent the fact that arrays have been limited, while other developers have accepted it as a cost of integration with the Common Language Runtime. It also adds a level of commonality that helps programmers share code and know what to expect.

If you don't want to specify your array bounds at all, you can create and fill an array in one step using the new initializer syntax. Here's an example:

```
' This creates a three-element array with the numbers 1, 2, and 3.
' Notice that you don't need to explicitly indicate the array size,
' because it's based on the number of values you supply.
Dim NumberArray() As Integer = {1, 2, 3}

' Here's the much longer way of doing this:
Dim NumberArray(2) As Integer
NumberArray(0) = 1
NumberArray(1) = 2
NumberArray(3) = 3
```

NOTE   *It is technically possible to create a .NET array with a lower bound other than zero by resorting to some very strange commands. I certainly don't recommend this ugly work-around. Instead, if you need a more flexible type of array, consider a more object-oriented solution and create a custom collection class.*

Arrays and IEnumerable

One useful addition to arrays is the IEnumerable interface, which lets you move through an array with a For Each command instead of looking up the appropriate upper and lower boundaries and then specifying the coordinates. The following example shows how you can examine every string in an array with a few lines that are very light on manual code. The only drawback is that you receive a read-only element from the array, which is suitable for a display or print operation but not for a modification.

```
Dim Foods() As String = {"cheese", "meat", "sugar", "soy milk"}

' Define a variable that has the same type as your array.
Dim Food As String

' Loop through the array, getting each string.
For Each Food In Foods
    ' Display the string in a list box.
    lstStrings.Items.Add(Food)
Next
```

Built-in Array Features

Just like strings and dates, arrays are also objects. They're based on the System.Array class.

It's interesting to look at some of the built-in features of an array. For example, you can find the bounds of an array using methods `GetLowerBound()` and `GetUpperBound()`. That means you can iterate over an array with a loop like this:

```
For i = MyArray.GetLowerBound(0) To MyArray.GetUpperBound(0)
    ' Some code here.
Next
```

The methods shown here replace the old `UBound()` and `LBound()` functions, although those functions are still supported if you want to code in the traditional (and slightly outdated) way. The 0 in this example specifies the first element. Remember, VB 2005 starts counting array elements at 0, so 0 means "first." Note that we don't really need to check the lower boundary, because we know that all arrays start numbering at 0. (So you could hard-code the number 0 in your loop.)

The `Array` class also includes shared methods. The methods and properties shown so far use instance methods, which means you need to create an array in order to use them. Shared methods, however, can be used independently. To use a shared method, you use the name of the class, which in this case is `Array`.

For example, you can reverse an entire array in one blow with the following code:

```
Dim NumberArray() As Integer = {1, 2, 3}
Array.Reverse(NumberArray)

' NumberArray now contains the sequence of elements 3, 2, 1.
```

You can use similar shared methods for even more value-added features:

```
Dim NumberArray() As Integer = {143, 242, 7}
Array.Sort(NumberArray)

' NumberArray now contains the sequence of elements 7, 143, 242.
```

This code works as long as the array contains elements that can be sorted and has only one dimension. Examples include numbers or strings.

Even array searching is automated:

```
Dim Foods() As String = {"cheese", "meat", "sugar", "soy milk"}

Dim MeatPosition As Integer
MeatPosition = Array.IndexOf(Foods, "meat")

' MeatPosition is set to 1, representing the second element.
' If you receive -1, the item could not be found.
```

For more information, refer to the `System.Array` class in the class library reference.

Arrays as Reference Types

Another interesting detail about arrays is that they are actually *reference types*, not value types like the other simple variables. That means that, behind the scenes, an array variable holds a *reference* to an array object that's floating around in memory. (Essentially, a reference is a memory pointer, but you'll never get a chance to actually take a look at that memory pointer, because it's managed by .NET.) By comparison, a value-type variable contains its information directly. Both reference and value types are objects. However, reference types are more common when dealing with complex objects, because they provide a more efficient way to manage large amounts of memory. Numeric data types and dates are simple value types.

In most situations, the technical different between reference types and value types won't affect your code. You'll be happy enough to manipulate both using variables. However, there are two cases where reference types may produce slightly unexpected behavior because of their differences. This quirkiness appears when you write code that attempts to copy an array or test whether two arrays are equal.

Here's an example of this weirdness in action. Setting two arrays equal to each other doesn't copy the contents of an array—only the reference. You end up with two array variables that access the same array. If you modify one of these variables, the other will be updated as well.

```
' Integers are value types.
Dim Integer1 As Integer = 100
Dim Integer2 As Integer
Integer2 = Integer1        ' Copies the value 100 into Integer2.
                           ' We end up with two copies of the
                           ' same information.


' Arrays are reference types.
Dim NumberArray1() As Integer = {1, 2, 3}
Dim NumberArray2() As Integer
NumberArray2 = NumberArray1   ' Copies the reference into NumberArray2.
                              ' We end up with two variables accessing
                              ' the same array!

' This change affects the first element of both
' NumberArray2 and NumberArray1.
NumberArray2(0) = 52
```

To create a real copy of an array, you just need to use its built-in Clone() method, as shown here:

```
NumberArray2 = NumberArray1.Clone()  ' A duplicate copy is created.
                                     ' We have two copies of the array.
```

Once again, the Clone() method is one of the many features provided to all array objects.

You'll learn more about reference types and how they differ from value types when you dig into object-oriented programming in Chapter 5. All reference types behave like the array when you attempt to create a copy (although not all provide a Clone() method to get around the problem).

Changes to Operations

Operations look the same in Visual Basic 2005 as they did in previous releases, so you won't have any trouble combining strings and adding numbers. However, you can make use of a few elegant shortcuts. The following sections explain what's new.

Assignment Shorthand

Visual Basic 2005 provides timesaving ways to perform simple arithmetic operations. They look a little strange at first, but they let you save a few extra keystrokes and condense overly verbose code. If you have used C#, Java, Perl, or a similar language, you will be familiar with these already.

```
intA += 1          ' Equivalent to intA = intA + 1
intA += intB       ' Equivalent to intA = intA + intB
intA -= 10         ' Equivalent to intA = intA - 10
strName &= "End"   ' Equivalent to strName = strName & "End"
```

You can use this trick with all the basic numeric operators, including addition (+), subtraction (-), multiplication (*), division (/), and exponents (^).

Converting Variables

Most professional applications use the Option Strict statement to prevent automatic variable conversions. These automatic conversions (famously called "evil type coercion" in classic versions of Visual Basic) are dangerous because they may work under some circumstance and fail under others. The problem is explored in much more depth in Chapter 8, which deals with bug proofing your code. For now, it is enough to know that conversions that might fail, such as converting a string to a number or a 32-bit integer to a 16-bit integer, can't occur automatically if you have Option Strict enabled. You have to do the work manually, using either the shared functions of the System.Convert class or the CType() function that is built into Visual Basic 2005.

CType() works by taking two parameters: the variable you want to convert and the type that you want to convert it to. Consider this example:

```
' This converts a string to a number.
MyInteger = CType(MyString, Integer)
```

Here is another example that uses conversion with basic objects, VB 2005's replacement for the Variant:

```
Dim objA As Object, objB As Object
objA = 3
objB = "3"

' Will not work if Option Strict is on!
' VB 2005 doesn't know how to add mysterious objects.
objA = objA + objB
' This works, provided the objects can be converted to integers.
objA = CType(objA, Integer) + CType(objB, Integer)
```

Math

The Math class contains a number of shared properties and methods that support mathematical operations. For example, you can get the value of the constant pi by using the Math.Pi property. A few other examples are shown here:

```
MyValue = Math.Sqrt(81)        ' MyValue is 9.
MyValue = Math.Abs(-42)        ' MyValue is 42.
MyValue = Math.Round(4.779, 2) ' MyValue is 4.78.
MyValue = Math.Log(4.22)       ' I'll let you calculate this one.
```

Random Numbers

It's easy to generate random numbers in Visual Basic 2005. This is another programming capability that Microsoft has moved out of the dark alcoves of specific languages and into the common class library. This example uses the System.Random class to automatically generate an integer between 0 and 5:

```
Dim MyNumber As Integer
Dim RandomGenerator As New Random()

' Retrieve a random number from 0 to 5.
' (You can add one to get a random number from 1 to 6.)
MyNumber = RandomGenerator.Next(5)

' Retrieve another random number, but this time make it an integer
' from 1 to 6. (VB 2005 interprets this as a value of 1 or larger,
' but always less than 7.)
MyNumber = RandomGenerator.Next(1, 7)
```

Some New Rules for Scope

Scope is the measure of a variable's life and of the ability of other parts of your code to access it. You are probably familiar with the fact that a Private variable in a module or class can't be accessed by any code outside of that module or class. Similarly, a variable created inside a procedure exists only as long as the procedure does and can't be accessed in any other routine.

Visual Basic 2005 tightens scoping another notch. Variables defined inside block structures (such as loops and conditional blocks) can't be reached from outside the block. This probably won't affect you, but it is still good to know.

```
If MyCondition = True Then
    ' Create a variable with If-block scope.
    ' (This scoping behavior is automatic and unchangeable.)
    Dim NewInteger As Integer = 12
End If
' NewInteger cannot be accessed here.
```

Short-Circuit Logic

In previous versions of VB, you could use two logical operators to make comparisons: And and Or. VB 2005 adds two new operators to the mix: AndAlso and OrElse.

AndAlso and OrElse work in a similar way to And and Or. The difference is that they use short-circuit logic, which allows you to evaluate just one part of a long conditional statement.

Here's how it works. Imagine you want to perform a certain task only if two conditions are true. This is a situation that's tailor made for an And.

```
If MyString <> "" And MyInteger > 0 Then
    ' Code here runs if MyString isn't empty and MyInteger is more than 0.
End If
```

In this situation, VB always evaluates both conditions. In other words, it tests whether MyString is blank, and then it checks MyInteger. But if you use AndAlso, VB decides to use a bit of a shortcut:

```
If MyString <> "" AndAlso MyInteger > 0 Then
    ' Code here runs if MyString isn't empty and MyInteger is more than 0.
End If
```

Now VB begins by checking whether MyString is blank. If MyString is blank, it doesn't bother to check MyInteger at all. That's because it's clear that the condition can't be met, because one of the criteria has already failed. This process of skipping the second check when it's not required is called *short-circuit evaluation*.

In this example, it doesn't matter much whether you use And or AndAlso. The end result is the same, and the performance is roughly equal. However, there are some cases where it could make a difference. For example, your condition might call a function that runs some code. Here's an example:

```
If MyString <> "" AndAlso TestIfValid(MyInteger) Then
    ' Code here runs if MyString isn't empty and the TestIfValid()
    ' function returns true.
End If
```

If `MyString` is blank, the `TestIfValid()` function isn't called. If `MyString` isn't blank, the `TestIfValid()` function is called, and its return value is checked. This is important, because the code in `TestIfValid()` could conceivably take some time or affect other details in your program.

The same principle holds with `OrElse`.

```
If MyString <> "" OrElse TestIfValid(MyInteger) Then
    ' Code here runs provided one of the following is true:
    ' MyString isn't blank or TestIfValid() returns true.
End If
```

In this case, if `MyString` isn't blank, there's no need to run `TestIfValid()`. That's because the condition is already satisfied by the first part of the expression. On the other hand, if `MyString` is blank, VB will call `TestIfValid()` and run the conditional code if it returns true.

`AndAlso` and `OrElse` are handy when dealing with objects that might contain null references. Consider this example:

```
If MyObject Is Nothing Or MyObject.Value > 10 Then
    ' (Do something.)
End If
```

Technically, an object with a null reference hasn't been created yet, so it's not safe to do anything with it. That means this code will generate an error if `MyObject` is `Nothing` (a null reference). That's because the second condition will still be evaluated, even though it isn't valid.

The solution is to use short-circuit evaluation:

```
If MyObject Is Nothing OrElse MyObject.Value > 10 Then
    ' (Do something.)
End If
```

Now the object won't be examined if it doesn't really exist.

Quickly Skipping Through a Loop

VB 2005 adds a `Continue` statement that you can use inside any loop. The `Continue` statement exists in three versions: `Continue For`, `Continue Do`, and `Continue While`. You use the version that corresponds to the type of loop (`For...Next`, `Do...Loop`, or `While...End While`). When the `Continue` statement is executed, it automatically skips any remaining code in the loop and starts the next iteration.

To see the `Continue` statement in action, consider this code:

```
For i = 1 to 1000
    ' (Code goes here.)

    If i > 10 Then
        Continue For
```

```
    End If

    ' (More code goes here.)
Next
```

This code loops 1,000 times, incrementing a counter i. The first ten times, both blocks of code execute. But once i is greater than 10, the behavior changes. For example, when i is 11, the first block of code runs, and then the condition is evaluated. Because 11 is greater than 10, the Continue For statement springs into action. Execution skips over the remaining code in the loop, and the next iteration starts, with i set to 12.

In this example, the Continue For statement isn't really required. You could solve the problem by making the second block of code conditional. However, if you have deeply nested code in which you evaluate multiple conditions, the Continue statement can be a handy way to jump out of the mess.

Enhanced Procedures

Just as in previous versions of Visual Basic, VB 2005 incorporates two types of procedures: the function, which returns a value, and the subroutine, which does not. In the following sections, you'll learn about the changes .NET has in store.

NOTE   *In object-oriented speak, procedures are also known as* methods. *The term* methods *includes both functions and subroutines. It's the .NET standard, and you'll see it used throughout this book—starting now.*

Calling a Method

One minor change with method calls is that they now require parentheses. In the past, parentheses were used only when a return value was needed:

```
' Visual Basic 6 code

' No parentheses allowed.
MsgBox "Hi there!", vbOKOnly

' Parentheses required.
Response = MsgBox("Delete file?", vbYesOrNo, "Confirm")
```

Visual Basic 2005 always uses parentheses. It's only a cosmetic change, but it makes code a little more consistent, and it aids readability because you can distinguish a method call from another type of statement at a glance:

```
' Visual Basic 2005 code

' Parentheses are always required.
```

```
MessageBox.Show("Hi there!" , MessageBoxButtons.OK)

Response = MessageBox.Show("Delete file?", "Confirm", _
  MessageBoxButtons.YesNo)
```

(Notice here also that the MsgBox function has also been replaced with the MessageBox class.)

Parentheses are even used when a function or subroutine doesn't require parameters, as in this line, which shows a window:

```
Form1.Show()
```

ByVal and ByRef

ByVal is the new default for method parameters, and Visual Studio inserts that keyword automatically and incessantly to emphasize the point. ByVal parameters are passed as copies. Any changes to a ByVal parameter affect the copy, not the original. The following method, for example, is free to change the Number parameter without affecting the variable that was supplied in the calling code.

```
Public Function CheckForPrimeNumber(ByVal Number As Integer) As Boolean
    ' What happens to Number here, stays here.
End Function
```

That said, there are some subtleties that you need to be aware of when passing certain data types by value. With reference types (like the array), a copy of the *reference* is passed for a ByVal parameter, not a copy of the actual data. This copy still refers to the same in-memory object. As a result, if you access the object and change it in some way, the change will still affect the one and only original object, contrary to what you might expect!

In other words, changes you make to simple data types won't return to your calling code. However, any reference type will be modifiable whether passed by reference or by value.

```
Public Function CheckForPrimeNumber(ByVal Number() As Integer) As Boolean
    ' If we change a value in the Number() array, it will affect
    ' the original array in the calling code, even though it was
    ' passed ByVal.
End Function
```

You could take extra, potentially painful, steps to change this behavior. For example, you could use the array's built-in Clone() method. However, it's better just to rely on your code to behave properly and refrain from tampering with values it shouldn't touch. Incidentally, this design makes a fair bit of sense—after all, if .NET created a copy of a huge array every time you called a method like CheckForPrimeNumber(), it could end up slowing down your application.

The Return Keyword

One nice addition to methods is the Return keyword, which allows you to write this kind of code:

```
Public Function Add(intA As Integer, intB As Integer)
    Return intA + intB      ' Instead of Add = intA + intB

    ' Any code here will not be executed.
End Function
```

The Return command combines two actions together: setting the function's result to the specified value and exiting the function immediately (as though an Exit Function statement had been used). The nicest thing about using Return is that you don't need to specify the function's name to provide the return value. This allows you to sidestep some minor but annoying problems, such as mistyping the method name or having to update your method code if you change the name of the method.

Optional Parameters

A method can still use optional values by incorporating a parameter array. A *parameter array* is an array provided to your function that contains "everything extra" that was added in the function call. For example, this function:

```
Public Function GetRecordCount(EndDate As Date, _
  ParamArray OtherOptions() As String) As Integer

    ' (Function code goes here.)
End Function
```

could be called with this statement:

```
NumberOfRecords = GetRecordCount(Date.Now, "John", "California")
```

The OtherOptions array would contain the string "John" at index 0 and the string "California" at index 1.

Parameter arrays allow you to collect any extra information, and that makes them very flexible, especially when the method being called doesn't need to know a lot about the extra information and can just write it to disk, pass it to another method, or use it in a predefined way. However, a method with a parameter array can be difficult to use, particularly for other developers, because it doesn't define what information is required or provide any type checking. Consequently, the method might easily end up with a lot of mysterious information that it can't interpret.

Generally, parameter arrays are an awkward means of using optional values. Visual Basic 2005 provides two other options: *default values* and *overloaded methods*, both of which are more convenient and aesthetically pleasing.

Default Values

With default values, you explicitly mark parameters that are optional. These can be included, or just left blank by the calling code. If they are left blank, the default value that you have specified will be used automatically.

For example, this method,

```
Public Function GetRecordCount(ByVal EndDate As Date, _
  Optional ByVal Person As String = "", _
  Optional ByVal State As String = "Kentucky") As Integer

  ' (Some code here.)
End Sub
```

can be called like this:

```
NumberOfRecords = GetRecordCount(Date.Now)
```

or like this:

```
NumberOfRecords = GetRecordCount(Date.Now, , "California")
```

or like this:

```
NumberOfRecords = GetRecordCount(Date.Now, "John", "California")
```

Default values may seem just about perfect. They allow you to create methods that accept a variety of different information, but they also define all the possible pieces of information. In practice, however, optional values aren't always ideal. One problem is that they sometimes allow too *much* flexibility. The method might end up making assumptions about what information will be supplied, or you might end up using default values that are inappropriate for certain situations. There is also no way to find out whether a value hasn't been supplied or the user has supplied a value that is identical to the default value.

NOTE   *Once you declare an optional parameter, any parameters to the method that are declared after the optional parameter must also be optional.*

Method Overloading

If you want to create more flexible functions and subroutines—ones that can accept different combinations of parameters—it's recommended that you use *method overloading* instead of default parameters. Method overloading allows you to provide different versions of the same function or subroutine. These methods have the same name, but they have different parameter lists (and are preceded with the Overloads keyword).

For example, consider the following `Combine()` functions:

```
Public Overloads Function Combine(intA As Integer, intB As Integer) _
  As Integer
    Return(intA + intB)
End Function

Public Overloads Function Combine(strA As String, strB As String) As String
    Return(strA & strB)
End Function
```

In this scenario, if you call the `Combine()` function in your code, Visual Basic 2005 will look at the parameter list you provide and match it with the appropriate version of `Combine()`.

```
IntegerValue = Combine(1, 2)      ' Uses the first version to return 3.
StringValue = Combine("1", "2")   ' Uses the second version to return "12".
```

In this case, we overload the `Combine()` function because "combine" means two different things, depending on the data type that's used. Combining numbers involves adding them, whereas combing strings involves joining them together. This type of differentiation already existed in the Visual Basic language with the addition operator (+), which adds numbers but concatenates strings, just like the `Combine()` function. This is an example of operator overloading, which is built into the VB 2005 language.

Another common use of method overloading is to provide database access routines that work with different criteria. For example, if you have ever created a database program, you've probably used such functions as `GetRecordByID()`, `GetRecordByName()`, and `GetRecordsByDate()`. There is nothing wrong with this system, but it can get awkward when you have several different databases and need to create long function names, such as `GetClientSalesByClientName()`.

You can provide a cleaner solution with overloaded methods:

```
Public Overloads Function GetUser(ID As Integer) As UserObject
    ' Code here.
End Function

Public Overloads Function GetUser(Name As String) As UserObject
    ' Code here.
End Function

' And so on...
```

However, you will need to make sure that the methods take different numbers of parameters or require parameters with different data types. A common technique is to start by creating a very basic method and then add overloaded versions that introduce new parameters, one by one. It's not enough to give the parameters different names, because you don't use these names when you call the method.

TIP   *There's another good reason to learn about method overloading. The .NET library uses this technique extensively in its own classes (and never uses optional parameters). This allows you to concentrate on the information you need from a function rather than worry about what kinds of information you can supply as parameters.*

Delegates

Visual Basic 2005 includes an interesting feature called delegates, which gives you another way to work with functions and subroutines. A *delegate* is a special type of variable that can store the location of a method. Before you can create a delegate, you have to define its type, in a statement like this:

```
Public Delegate Function ProcessFunction(StringIn As String) As String
```

This statement doesn't create a variable. Instead, it defines a type of delegate. Based on this definition, the ProcessFunction delegate type can be used to store the location of a function that accepts a single string argument and has a string return value. (The names you give the parameters in the declaration really don't matter.)

Once you have this definition in place, you can use it to create a delegate variable as you would any other variable:

```
Dim MyDelegate As ProcessFunction
```

A delegate can store references only to methods that have exactly the same *signature* as the delegate definition. In other words, they need to have the same number of parameters, the same parameter data types, and the same return value data type. This is how delegates enforce type safety and also prevent you from referring to the wrong function or subroutine by accident.

```
Public Function CapitalizeName(Name As String) As String
   ' A reference to this function can be stored in MyDelegate.
End Sub

Public Function MyFunction(Name As String, Optional ID As Integer = 0) _
   As String
   ' This function is different. It cannot be stored in MyDelegate.
End Sub

Public Sub Process(Name As String)
   ' This won't work either. It's a subroutine, not a function.
End Sub
```

Once you create a variable based on a delegate, you can assign a method to it by using the `AddressOf` operator. The `AddressOf` operator lets Visual Basic 2005 know that you are using a reference to a method, not trying to run it directly.

```
Dim MyDelegate As ProcessFunction
MyDelegate = AddressOf CapitalizeName
```

Once you set a delegate, you can run the method later, just by using the delegate:

```
' Calls the CapitalizeName() function and assigns its return value
' to UCaseName.
Dim UCaseName As String
UCaseName = MyDelegate("samantha jones")
```

This is a useful technique, because it allows what programmers call an extra *layer of indirection*. This means that the code you create is more generic and has a better chance of being reused.

Here's a function that accepts a delegate as an argument and uses the function specified by the delegate to perform a task:

```
Public Sub ProcessArray(MyArray As String(), _
  FunctionToUse As ProcessFunction)

    Dim i As Integer
    For i = 0 to MyArray.GetUpperBound(0)
        MyArray(i) = FunctionToUse(MyArray(i))
    Next i

End Sub
```

You call the subroutine like this:

```
Dim CustomerNames() As String = {"bob evans", "chan park", "jill svetlova"}
ProcessArray(CustomerNames, AddressOf CapitalizeName)
```

The result of this sleight of hand is that each element of `CustomerNames` will be modified according to the `CapitalizeName()` method.

By using a delegate, you can create a single `ProcessArray()` subroutine that can process array elements in a variety of different ways, depending on the `FunctionToUse` reference that you supply. You only need to write the code in `ProcessArray()` once, but you still get ultimate flexibility (and the envy of your colleagues).

NOTE   *It can become a little confusing to keep all of these ingredients in mind at once. To perform this delegate test successfully, you need to define the delegate, create a delegate variable, point the delegate variable at the right method, and then run the method through the delegate. You can see these steps in action by using the sample code available online—check out the DelegateTest1 and DelegateTest2 projects.*

Delegates won't receive much more attention in this book, for two reasons. First, delegates can often be replaced by objects and methods. For example, we could rewrite the preceding ProcessArray() example to use a collection of special Customer objects that support a Process() method. (If the following example is a little perplexing, don't worry; all will be explained in Chapters 5 and 6.)

```
Public Sub ProcessArray(MyArray As Customer())
    Dim MyCustomer As Customer
    For Each MyCustomer In MyArray
        MyCustomer.Process()
    Next
End Sub
```

A second use of delegates is to allow communication between different objects, by having one object store a delegate that contains a method in another object. However, there is also a better alternative for this type of communication—events, which are really just delegates with some added conveniences. You'll learn how to work with events in detail in Chapter 5.

What Comes Next?

This chapter has provided a whirlwind tour through dozens of different language changes introduced when VB.NET replaced Visual Basic 6. The most fundamental concept presented here was the common class library, which is a complete programmer's toolkit stocked with most of the features you could ever need in any language.

This chapter also explained how and why many of the features that VB programmers have relied upon for years are now changing from stand-alone functions into class methods and are being grouped with the objects that they relate to. The key to understanding the new .NET world is realizing that *everything* is an object. The next step is to dive into object-oriented programming with the next few chapters. Additionally, you might want to start making forays into the class library reference to find out what methods and properties are exposed by the common data types.

4

WINDOWS FORMS

Windows forms are the building blocks of the traditional graphical programs designed for the Windows operating system. Most of the applications you use, from office productivity software such as Microsoft Word to interactive games and multimedia products, can be considered Windows Forms applications. The hallmark of a Windows Forms program is that every part of its user interface is built out of windows.

Windows Forms applications are all-purpose solutions to many programming problems. And .NET 2.0 makes it easier than ever to design a rich interface with support for resizing forms, splitting windows, and anchoring and docking controls. VB 2005 also takes the confusion out of Multiple Document Interface (MDI) applications, adds enhanced designers that let you build trees and lists by hand, and introduces the most powerful toolbars and menus yet.

Perhaps the most remarkable shift from classic VB is the fact that each form, along with all the controls on it, is now completely defined in Visual Basic code. This means that as you use the designer to rearrange your user interface and set control properties, the IDE actually quietly stores the information in a .vb code file. This allows you to tweak these settings by hand, or even to dynamically create a portion of the user interface while the application is running. All in all, it gives you greater control over your application.

New in .NET

.NET introduces a whole new model for working with forms—one that could easily occupy an entire book. It saves C++ developers the effort of wrestling with the MFC framework and gives Visual Basic programmers a level of control they've never had before.

A unified model for Windows applications

All .NET languages share the same Windows Forms (or WinForms) technology, which means that Microsoft won't introduce new controls that are available only to developers using a certain language. Just as all .NET languages share a common runtime, they also all use exactly the same user interface toolkit.

The component tray

In earlier versions of Visual Basic, controls were such a popular and easy way to add functionality to a program that they were used even when the "control" (for instance, a timer) didn't require a visual interface. In VB 2005, these invisible components are no longer placed on a form's drawing area. Now they are organized in a dedicated component tray.

Anchoring and docking

These are the kind of little frills that win the hearts of developers. Anchoring and docking let you make controls move and change size automatically, so that you never need to write resizing code again. And if you have a more sophisticated layout in mind, you'll get a great start with .NET's intelligent panel controls.

Forms are classes

Visual Basic 6 forms had a dual identity, acting both as objects and as classes at the same time. In Visual Basic 2005, a form is just another class that inherits from System.Windows.Forms.Form. Even better, all of its characteristics—including such details as its position and the properties of the contained controls—are included automatically in the class code.

MDI enhancements

.NET removes many traditional restrictions on your ability to work with windows, and nowhere is that more apparent than with MDI windows. Not only can you turn any form into an MDI parent by setting a simple property, but you can also turn any other Windows form into a child at runtime with a single command.

Extender providers

In a bid for even greater organization, Visual Basic 2005 introduces the concept of *providers*, which are controls that enhance other controls on the same form with additional properties. For example, if you want your controls to have tooltips, you can add a `ToolTip` control to the component tray, and voilà!—every control has a new `ToolTip` property.

Getting Started

Windows Forms applications get their name from the fact that they are built out of a number of windows, or *forms*. Different applications use windows differently. For example, multiple document (MDI) applications, such as Visual Studio, can designate that several windows be manipulated inside a larger "container" window. Other applications—Windows Explorer, for example—use a single window that divides itself into several resizable panes. Each of these types of interfaces is easy to create with Visual Basic 2005.

At this point, it's a good idea to start a Windows Forms project and try adding some controls to it. Much as in earlier VB versions, you add a control by selecting the icon and drawing it on the design surface. You can also add more forms by right-clicking your project in the Solution Explorer and choosing Add ▸ Add Windows Form.

NOTE *In this section, we explore how you can design the interface for a project with a single form. As you start adding more forms and writing code to handle events and to communicate information from one form to another, the VB 2005 world takes a couple of twists. We'll explore the implications of multiple forms, and their underlying architecture, later in the chapter.*

The new Windows Forms engine works like the traditional Visual Basic 6 Form Designer when it comes to creating and designing forms. Properties are still configured in a Properties window. Controls can be moved, copied, and aligned with the grid, exactly as they could be in classic VB. But you'll notice that the Toolbox packs in a great deal more—it's now divided into several subgroups, each with its own collection of related controls. You'll find the familiar Windows standards in the Common Controls group.

The Component Tray

In classic VB, some features would be implemented through "invisible" controls, the most common example being the Timer control. This was a convenient way to add functionality, but it was a little messy—after all, controls were designed to provide user interface, not to replace .dll files and other code components. Visual Basic 2005 provides a cleaner implementation through a tool called the *component tray*.

You'll notice this new addition as soon as you try to draw an "invisible" control on the design surface. (For example, try one of the items in the Components section of the Toolbox.) Instead of appearing on the form, where they might be obscured by other, legitimate controls, the invisible components will now appear in a special area of the window, as shown in Figure 4-1.

This lets you easily add support for menus, timers, and standard Windows dialog boxes (such as Open, Save, and Print, and selection windows for Font, Color, and Print Settings). You could create these controls directly using a couple of lines of code that access classes in the System.Windows.Forms namespace, but the component tray makes the process effortless.

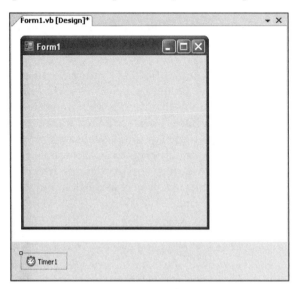

Figure 4-1: A timer in the component tray

Custom Designers

Some controls have complex properties that can't be specified by simply entering strings in the Properties window. A typical example is the TreeView control, which contains a hierarchy of different elements (called *nodes*). In the past, the content for complex controls like the TreeView couldn't be created at design time—instead, you needed to generate it programmatically. However, .NET outfits many of its most impressive controls with *custom designers* that solve this problem.

For example, a ListBox control can be filled at design time using the handy ListBox designer. Just find the Items property in the Properties window, and click the ellipsis (. . .) next to the word *Collection*. A designer window will appear where you can enter your list items (see Figure 4-2). A similar tool is available for the Items property in the ListView control and for the Nodes property in the TreeView control. These custom designers are lightweight and straightforward.

Figure 4-2: Configuring list items with the designer

The best way to get used to this new system is to try it out. The basic principle is that you start by adding items (for example, individual nodes and buttons) to the list on the left.

Then, to configure the properties for an individual item, you select the item from the list and modify the property list that appears on the right. And remember, if you want to add an image to an item, you'll need an associated ImageList control, which will provide a collection of pictures to choose from. Thankfully, the ImageList control also has its own designer, so inserting and rearranging graphics files is a breeze.

Locking Your Controls

It used to be that getting controls to line up perfectly in a complex interface could be a slow and tricky process. It sometimes involved turning off the Snap to Grid feature in order to position some of the controls exactly, and then re-enabling it so that other controls could easily be placed in positions that lined up consistently. And once you finally had your controls perfectly arranged, you risked scattering them with an accidental mouse click.

Locking is a convenient design-time feature that can help you prevent this type of accident. It existed in Visual Basic 6, but only in a crude "all or nothing" form. As soon as you locked a VB 6 form, you couldn't change anything until you unlocked it, which often didn't allow enough flexibility. The locking feature still exists in Visual Basic 2005—just right-click your form and select Lock Controls (and do it again to unlock them).

However, VB 2005 also provides a more useful version of this feature that allows you to lock individual controls. To use it, select the control and change its Locked property to True. You can then add new controls and rearrange existing ones, without having to worry that you'll accidentally move the locked control that you've positioned perfectly.

Control Layout

As any Windows developer knows, it's easy to add controls to a form, but it's much harder to arrange those controls in a perfectly pleasing layout. The task becomes even trickier when you need to take into account different window sizes and screen resolutions. Fortunately, .NET offers a set of features that allow you to build flexible layouts that adapt easily to different conditions. In the following sections, you'll tour the highlights.

Anchoring

Anchoring is a simple idea that saves a lot of trouble. The best way to understand anchoring is to see it in action. Examine the window shown in Figure 4-3.

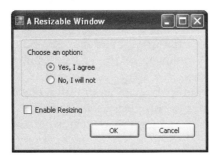

Figure 4-3: An ordinary window

By default, Windows controls are "anchored" to the upper-left corner of a form. This used to mean that as a form was resized, the controls stayed put, because the position of the upper-left corner does not change. As a result, unless you wrote explicit resizing code, the embarrassing blank borders at the bottom and right edges of your form would grow wider, as shown in Figure 4-4.

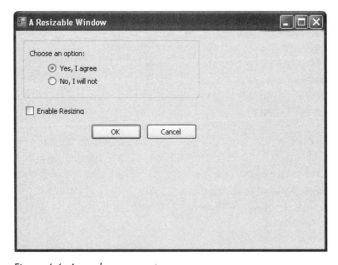

Figure 4-4: An embarrassment

If, on the other hand, a control could be anchored to the bottom of the form, its position would drop as you lengthened the form, guaranteeing that the distance between the control and the bottom edge of your form always remained constant. This anchoring to any side of a form is exactly the ability that .NET forms provide.

To change a control's anchoring, find its Anchor property in the Properties window, and then change it using the special drop-down control (see Figure 4-5). Click to select the edge or edges that your control should bind to. For example, you might want to anchor a control to the lower-right corner, thus ensuring that the control will always be a fixed distance away from the bottom and right edges of your form.

Figure 4-5: Anchoring options

You can even anchor a control to more than one side. In this case, the control has to grow automatically to maintain a consistent distance away from the form edges as the form is resized. In our sample resizable form shown in Figure 4-6, the command buttons are anchored to the bottom right, the group box is anchored to the left, right, and top (so it will grow to fit the form width), and the radio buttons are anchored to the top left (the default). A check box allows you to test anchoring by turning it on and off. (You can try this example with the Anchoring project that's included with the sample code for this chapter.)

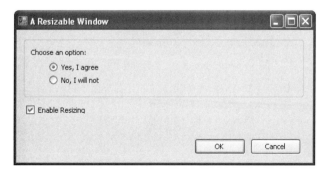

Figure 4-6: A basic resizable form

There are some controls that you'll never want to be resized. For example, buttons should always be a standard, consistent size—they look bizarre if they start to grow as a form changes size. This is one of the main problems with many of the commercial add-ins for automatic resizing that were in vogue before .NET hit the scene.

A sophisticated program will resize the areas of its interface that can benefit from more screen real estate. For example, if you are creating a window with a group of check-box settings, you should probably give it a fixed border, because the window will not need to change size. On the other hand, if you have a window that contains a control with a lot of scrollable information (a RichTextBox, a ListView, or a DataGridView, for example), you should allow it to grow when resized, by docking it to opposite sides.

NOTE *Anchoring is always relative to the container that holds the control. For example, if you put a button inside a panel, you can use anchoring in two ways. You can anchor the panel so it moves or changes size when the form is enlarged, and you can anchor the button so it moves or changes size as the panel is resized.*

Docking

Docking allows a control to latch onto an edge of a window and resize itself automatically. To add docking to a control, find the Docking property in the Properties window, and choose an edge on which to dock (Figure 4-7). You can only dock against a single edge (or choose to fill the entire form), and you can't dock *and* anchor a single control.

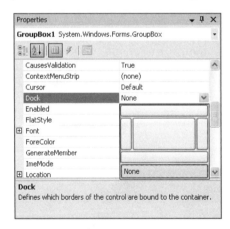

Figure 4-7: Docking options

The first time you use docking, you're likely to become slightly frustrated. While docking does what it claims, it also forces the control to sit flush against the docked edge and take its full width. This often means that your control is squeezed up against the side of the form, without enough of a border, as shown in Figure 4-8.

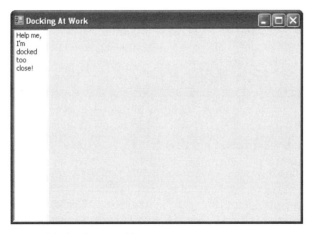

Figure 4-8: Docking problems

Thankfully, there is a way to fine-tune control docking and create a perfectly resizable form. The secret to successful docking is *padding*. Padding allows you to insert a buffer between the docked control and the form to which it's docked. To set some extra padding for your form, find the `Padding` property in the Properties window, expand it, and set `All` to 15. Now the docked control will still bind to the side and be resized, but it will have some much needed spacing around it.

Of course, form padding doesn't help if you are trying to dock multiple controls next to each other and you want to increase the spacing between them. To have more fine-grained control over spacing and docking, place your controls inside separate `Panel` controls. The `Panel` control provides its own `Padding` property. The process works like this: You dock the panel to the side of the form, and then you configure the panel's padding to make sure the control it contains is placed perfectly. The online sample code includes a simple application named Docking that allows you to play with different docking settings (see Figure 4-9).

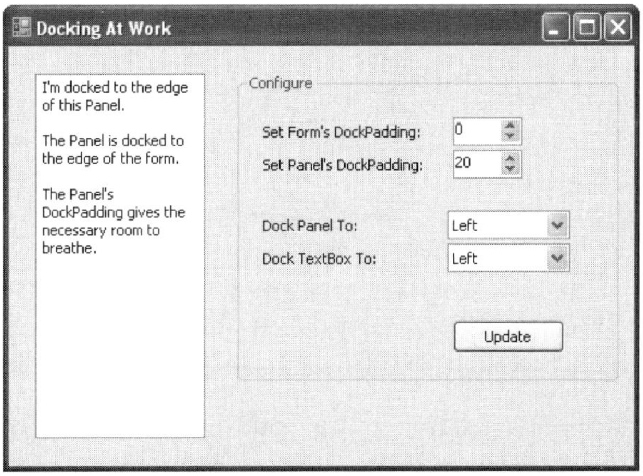

Figure 4-9: Adding space with docking

It will take some experimentation before you master this system well enough to create the interfaces you want. Many articles about Visual Basic 2005 just gloss quickly over the whole affair and don't admit that fine-tuning an interface is still a labor of love, even with Visual Studio's enhanced anchoring and docking features. To get started, you might want to start experimenting with the sample code included for this chapter, which shows some examples of how you can use panels to help organize groups of controls.

Maximum and Minimum Window Sizes

In VB 2005, all forms provide `MinimumSize` and `MaximumSize` properties that allow you to set limits on how a form is resized. When these properties are set, they stop users cold when they try to resize a form beyond its pre-established dimensions. For example, you could cap a window at a height of 200 pixels and a width of 400 pixels by setting the `MaximumSize.Height` and `MaximumSize.Width` accordingly. (The default values of both are 0, which means that no limit is enforced.)

`MinimumSize` and `MaximumSize` offer a great improvement over the manual techniques to which Visual Basic programmers have traditionally resorted, which involved reacting to a form's `Resize` event, determining whether the form had been made too small or too large, and then manually resizing it if necessary. There were two significant problems with that approach: the Form Designer had to be careful not to trigger an extra `Resize` event and get trapped in an endless loop, and code in the `Resize` event handler reacted only *after* the form had been changed to an invalid size. The latter meant that, depending on the user's display settings, the window would sometimes flicker noticeably as it fought between the user's attempted change and the programmer's stubbornly resistant code.

Automatic Scrolling

Have you ever wound up with too much content to fit on a single form? You might need a more compact design, or you might be trying to cram too much information into one place. Or, you may want to try out .NET's automatic scrolling feature, which gives any form instant scrollbars.

Here's how it works. If you set the `AutoScroll` property of a form to `True`, and you resize the form so that some controls "fall off the edge," scrollbars will be provided automatically so that the user can scroll through the form and access the hidden controls. `AutoScroll` is a fairly crude option for large windows, and you can usually achieve more professional results by using anchoring and docking. However, if you use your imagination, you might find some interesting uses for `AutoScroll` forms.

One useful technique is to use automatic scrolling within another container control, like the `Panel` control. For example, you could create a list of scrollable options by adding several controls inside a panel and then setting its `AutoScroll` property to `True`. Figure 4-10 shows the difference between a scrollable form and a scrollable panel.

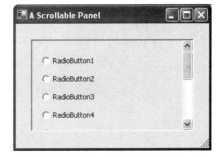

Figure 4-10: Two ways to scroll

Split Windows

The split-window interface is one of the hottest design features these days, and the applications that use it are replacing traditional MDI programs. For example, the system utilities component introduced with Windows 2000, which is used for everything from configuring your hardware to adding user accounts, has a Windows Explorer–like interface that divides a single window into multiple, sizable components. Even applications (such as Visual Studio) that still use the MDI paradigm usually combine it with dockable windows and other split-window displays.

Split-window designs were somewhat of a rarity in classic Visual Basic programs, however. That's because before .NET they were a chore to program, sometimes requiring reams of extra resizing code. One of Visual Basic 2005's best-kept secrets is that it can not only dock and anchor controls, but can also create resizable split-window programs that require no extra code.

To create a split window, you start by adding the SplitContainer control from the Containers section of the Toolbox. Technically, the SplitContainer is a container control that uses two panels and includes a user-resizable splitter bar in between them. The user can drag the bar to one side or another to change the amount of space given to each panel. Although the split container always consists of two panels, you can change the orientation of these panels. If you set the Orientation property to Orientation.Vertical (the default), the splitter runs from top to bottom, creating left and right panels. The other option is Orientation.Horizontal, which stacks a top and a bottom panel with a splitter bar running between them.

Once you've added the SplitContainer (and anchored or docked it to fill the appropriate portion of your form), you can add content inside the SplitContainer. For example, Figure 4-11 shows a split window with a TreeView in one panel (the left) and a PictureBox in the other (the right).

Of course, in this example, you want to make sure that the TreeView and PictureBox change size when the splitter bar is moved. To do this, you need to make sure the controls inside the SplitContainer use anchoring or docking. For example, you could anchor the TreeView to all sides or set the Dock property to Fill so that the TreeView automatically resizes itself to occupy the entire panel. That way, the user can move the splitter bar at runtime to change the size of the PictureBox and the TreeView controls. Figure 4-12 shows the result of resizing the panel. (You can try this example out in the SplitWindow project.)

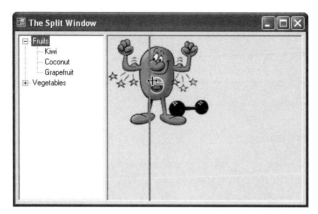

Figure 4-11: Adjusting a split window

You can also set the Panel1MinSize and Panel2MinSize properties of the SplitContainer to configure the smallest size (in pixels) to which the two panels can be resized. When these properties are specified, users won't be able to make one panel too small (the splitter bar can then only be dragged down as far as the minimum-size position). You can also stop resizing altogether by setting the IsSplitterFixed property to False. With that setting, the only way to change the size of the two panels is to set the SplitterDistance property programmatically, which positions the splitter bar. You can even hide a panel on a whim by setting the Panel1Collapsed or Panel2Collapsed property to True.

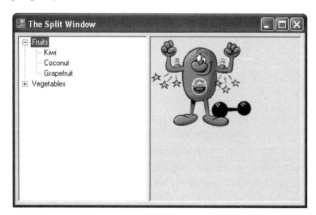

Figure 4-12: A resized panel in a split window

Once again, you'll have to experiment with these techniques in order to master them, but you now understand the fundamental concepts.

NOTE *Here's a mind-bending puzzle. You create a form with a* SplitContainer, *and you anchor that container to all sides of the form. The user enlarges the form, and so the* SplitContainer *also expands to fit. But inside the* SplitContainer, *which panel gets the new space? By default, both panels grow or shrink proportionately. However, you can change this behavior with the* FixedPanel *property. A fixed panel doesn't change when the* SplitContainer *is resized. So if you designate* Panel1 *as the fixed panel, the second panel will grow as the window is resized. (In Windows Explorer the directory tree is in a fixed panel. It doesn't change size when you expand or shrink the window.)*

Container Controls

Although the SplitContainer is one of the most useful containers, you'll find several other choices in the Containers section of the Toolbox.

The GroupBox and the Panel are the most straightforward of the containers. The GroupBox is a long-standing Windows staple, which simply adds a curved border and a title around a group of controls. The Panel is a little more versatile—it supports scrolling and a configurable border. Unlike the GroupBox, it can't show a caption. The Containers section also includes the TabControl, which works as a group of tabbed containers, only one of which can be shown at a time.

The Panel is the basis for several other container controls. You've already seen the SplitContainer, which wraps two Panel controls, but you haven't explored the more exotic FlowLayoutPanel and TableLayoutPanel controls. These layout panels implement a more weblike way of arranging content. When you place controls in either of these panels, the location information is ignored. Instead, controls in the FlowLayoutPanel are arranged from top to bottom (or side to side), one after the other in such a way that if one control grows in size, the others are bumped out of the way. Controls in the TableLayoutPanel are arranged similarly in a resizable (yet invisible) grid, with one control in each cell.

Figure 4-13 shows an example of a left-to-right FlowLayoutPanel with several controls. The WrapContents property is set to True, so that the controls are arranged in multiple rows to fit the bounds of the panel, and the BorderStyle property is set to show a sunken border around the edge. To add more space around individual controls, you could tweak the Margin property of the appropriate control, which works like the Padding property discussed earlier.

This flexibility requires a different style of user interface design, but it's more flexible in situations where you have dynamically generated content (if, for example, you're reading large quantities of text from a file or database and then displaying it in different controls). It's also a good choice if you need to localize your application for different languages, because your controls can resize and rearrange themselves to fit changing text sizes.

Figure 4-13: Miscellaneous controls in a
FlowLayoutPanel

NOTE *If you aren't sure whether all the content will fit inside a FlowLayoutPanel or
TableLayoutPanel, you can use the same automatic scrolling property described
earlier. Just set AutoScroll to True.*

Controls and Events

For a good part of its lifetime, the average Windows applications sits idle,
waiting for something to happen. For example, it's not until a user clicks a
button or types into a text box that your code springs into action.

For that reason, you'll spend a good amount of time thinking about the
event handlers for your controls. Event handlers, as their name suggests, are
dedicated subroutines that spring into action when the corresponding event
takes place. Generally speaking, an event handler allows your application to
respond to notifications from a control that something has happened.

To create an event handler, switch to code view (choose View ▶ Code
from the menu). Then select the desired control from the control list at the
top left of the code window (see Figure 4-14).

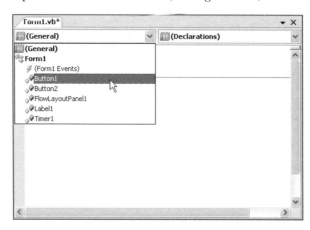

Figure 4-14: Choosing a control

Next, choose the desired event from the list on the right side (see Figure 4-15).

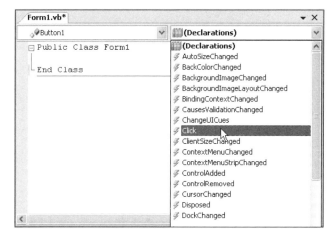

Figure 4-15: Choosing an event

NOTE *Of course, dedicated VB developers know there's a shortcut for most controls. Double-click the control on the design surface, and Visual Studio will create an event handler for the default event (the event that's most commonly used). For example, the default event of a* Button *is* Click, *the default event of a* Form *is* Load, *and the default event of a* TextBox *is* TextChanged.

Here is a sample event handler for a button's Click event:

```
Private Sub Button1_Click(ByVal sender As System.Object, _
   ByVal e As System.EventArgs) Handles Button1.Click
      ' Show a message box.
      MessageBox.Show("You clicked me.")
End Sub
```

All Visual Basic 2005 event handlers look pretty much the same—another valuable break from Visual Basic tradition, in which every event handler had its own idiosyncratic collection of parameters. This new uniformity allows you to write event handlers that can deal with more than one type of event, and it makes it easier to figure out the correct method signature for your event handlers.

The .NET convention for events states that they must have two parameters. One, called sender, provides a reference to the object that sends the event. Thus, you can always examine the sender parameter to find out where the event originated. The other parameter, called e, is an object that bundles together any additional information that you need from the event. Different events will use different objects for e, depending on their needs. The default event style, which is used for a button's Click event, doesn't require any additional information, and so it sends an empty e object.

On the other hand, the MouseMove event does include important extra information: the current coordinates of the mouse pointer. In the following example (see Figure 4-16), the event handler retrieves and displays this information.

Figure 4-16: Tracking the mouse

Here's the code that makes it work:

```
Private Sub MouseTracker_MouseMove(ByVal sender As Object, _
  ByVal e As System.Windows.Forms.MouseEventArgs) Handles MyBase.MouseMove
    lblPosition.Text = "The mouse is at X: " & e.X & " Y:" & e.Y
End Sub
```

You can try this example in the MouseMoveHandler project.

Handling More Than One Event

Another profound change in Visual Basic 2005 is that an event handler can work with multiple controls. This allows you to reuse code. For example, imagine a form with a dozen labels. When the mouse moves over a label, you want the label to change color. You could write a separate MouseEnter and MouseLeave event handler for each label, but this would force you to write and maintain reams of code, which is a certain nightmare (unless you're paid by the hour). A better choice is to write a single set of event handlers that can respond to mouse movements for any label.

NOTE   *In Visual Basic 6, the solution to this problem was control arrays. Control arrays aren't available in VB 2005, and for good reason—they're just too awkward to program with. As you'll see, the VB 2005 solution is much neater.*

In VB 2005, an event handler is connected to an event through the Handles keyword, which appears at the end of the definition of the event handler. By default, functions use VB 6 naming conventions, so a Click event for Button1 is named Button1_Click. However, you can change the name of the event handler without causing any problem because the actual link between an event and a control is specified explicitly with the Handles keyword.

One advantage of this system is that it's easy to create event handlers that work with more than one control. All you have to do is add the names of the additional controls to the Handles clause. Consider our next example (see Figure 4-17), which receives Click events from three different buttons, and examines the sender object to find out where the event occurred:

```
Private Sub ClickHandler (ByVal sender As System.Object, _
  ByVal e As System.EventArgs) Handles cmdA.Click, cmdB.Click, cmdC.Click

    ' Convert the unidentified sender object to a more useful form.
    Dim ctrl As Control = CType(sender, Control)

    MessageBox.Show "You clicked the button called " & ctrl.Name
End Subinsert
```

Figure 4-17: A generic event handler

Notice that before this code can use the sender object, it has to convert it into a recognized type. In this case, we cast convert the sender object to the Button class, but instead we use the more generic Control class, which supports some basic properties that are shared by all controls. This includes the Name property. If the code didn't make the conversion, and tried to use the sender object directly, it would cause an error, because the System.Object class only supports a few basic operations.

Accept and Cancel Buttons

All controls are not created equal. Forms have two properties that let you designate special buttons: AcceptButton and CancelButton. These properties single out the button that will be "clicked" automatically when the user presses the ENTER key (to "accept" the window) or the ESC key (to "cancel" it). Thus, if you add a button named cmdOK, and set the Form.AcceptButton to cmdOK, the cmdOK.Click event handler will run automatically when the user presses the ENTER key.

The feature existed in Visual Basic 6, but it was implemented by adding the Default and Cancel properties for button controls. This state of affairs was a little confusing, as it didn't clearly indicate that a form could have only one Default and one Cancel button.

Exploring .NET Forms

So far, you've learned how to combine controls to build a snazzy form and how to write the code that drives them. The next step is to assemble a suitable group of forms into a complete multiwindow application.

As in Visual Basic 6, every .NET form comes with some built-in capabilities. Technically, every form you create inherits all the features of the prebuilt Form class that can be found in the System.Windows.Forms namespace. *Inheritance* allows an object to access the features of another class. This means that System.Windows.Forms.Form provides your form with the basic functions that it needs in order to look and act like a form. In addition, your form possesses other features all its own (depending on the controls you've added). The hierarchy is shown in Figure 4-18.

I've actually simplified the relationships a bit here. In fact, the System.Windows.Forms.Form class itself inherits qualities from other, more basic classes in the .NET class library. (You'll learn more about inheritance in Chapter 6.)

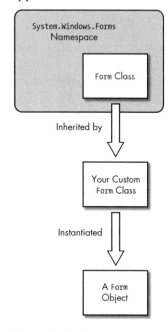

Figure 4-18: Form inheritance

Two Ways to Show a Form

Forms have existed in Visual Basic since its first release, and along the way, they've evolved from static templates to full-featured objects. Unfortunately, this evolution has led to a few inconsistencies. A form in Visual Basic 6 can act like both a class definition and a special kind of ready-made object.

NOTE *If you haven't used classes before, you may wonder what the difference is between a class and an object. Essentially, a class is a definition from which an object can be created. For example, there is one text box class (System.Windows.Forms.TextBox) that provides all the features that let a text box work the way it does, including properties such as Text that your program can interact with. There may be many text box objects in your program that are built with this class. For all the explicit details about classes and objects, be sure to read Chapters 5 and 6.*

The fact that a form plays a strange dual role as both a class and an object means that there are two ways to show a form:

Explicit creation

In this case, you're in control, and it's up to you to create the form object you need. This is the .NET standard.

Implicit creation

With this shortcut, the form object is created on the fly as soon as it's needed. This is a VB 6 tradition, but it can lead to headaches down the road.

For example, imagine you've added a form named MyForm to your project. Here's the correct object-oriented approach to showing it, using explicit creation:

```
Dim MyDynamicallyCreatedForm As New MyForm()
MyDynamicallyCreatedForm.Show()
```

In this example, the first line creates the form object. The second line uses that form object, displaying it on the screen. This two-step approach gives you a lot of flexibility when creating multiple-document applications. For example, you could use this technique in a word processing application to create a new window whenever the user opens a document. Code like this can handle as many simultaneous windows as you want, with no extra programming required.

You can also use the traditional implicit creation approach that harkens back to VB 6. Here's how that works:

```
MyForm.Show()
```

This shortcut uses the *default instance* of MyForm. Essentially, Visual Basic is willing to create one MyForm object automatically, as needed. It creates this object as soon as you attempt to interact with it. Assuming you haven't used any of the methods or properties of MyForm yet, Visual Basic creates the default instance when you call MyForm.Show(). If you call MyForm.Show() again sometime later, the default instance already exists, so you end up showing the same form object (if it's not already visible).

This automatic-form-creation shortcut seems convenient at first, but it actually hides a few dangerous thorns. For example, it's all too easy to make the mistake shown here:

```
Dim MyDynamicallyCreatedForm As New MyForm()
MyForm.Show()
```

In this case a new (non-default) form object is created, but the default instance is displayed. The newly created `MyDynamicallyCreatedForm` object drifts off into memory, abandoned.

Conceptually, the default instance approach is a little ugly. Because it doesn't require you to explicitly create the form object, you never know for sure where the form object is created (and when its initialization code runs). The default instance approach also breaks down if you want to show more than one copy of the same window at the same time, in which case you need to head back to the explicit creation approach. In fact, implicit creation acquired such a bad reputation that it was removed entirely from VB .NET 1.0—and rightly so. But in VB 2005, Microsoft caved in to the pressure to make VB respect its roots and added implicit creation back.

Using implicit creation is a bit of a minefield. But you can improve on it a bit by using another approach—the `My` object. The `My` object gives you the same implicit creation behavior, but it makes your code clearer. That's because when you see a line of code that shows a form with the `My` object, you know that implicit creation is at work.

Forms and the My Object

.NET 1.0 introduced the new object-based form system, and it made a lot of a sense. However, irate VB programmers were quick to complain that their much-loved environment had changed. To try to keep them happy, Microsoft added a shortcut to VB 2005 that allows you to access the default instance of a form without bringing back all the confusion. This shortcut is based on the `My` object.

Here's how it works. The `My.Forms` object provides one default instance of every form in your application. You access this form object by name. So, if you have a form named `SuperCoolWindow`, you can access the default instance as `My.Forms.SuperCoolWindow`. You can show the form with this single line of code:

```
My.Forms.SuperCoolWindow.Show()
```

This is equivalent to this:

```
SuperCoolWindow.Show()
```

But the `My` approach is nicer, because it makes it easier to see what's taking place.

Remember, the default instance isn't actually created until the first time you refer to it in code. This behavior can get a bit tricky, because you don't have any way to know when your form will be created and therefore when its initialization code will run.

However, there's a definite benefit to the `My` syntax. Namely, you can always get a reference to your form, no matter where you are in code. This is important if one form needs to interact with another. For example, one form might want to call a subroutine that's coded inside another. Using the `My` object, it's easy to get there.

The My object also has a dark side (see Chapter 3 for more details). First of all, it's clearly not going to work if you need to show more than one copy of a form (for example, most professional word processing applications let the user edit several files at once). In this case, it's up to you to create your forms and track them. The second problem is that the default instance isn't necessarily the one you want to use. For example, suppose your application creates a form with the following code:

```
Dim MyFormObject As New SuperCoolWindow()
MyFormObject.Show()
```

This won't be the same form object as My.Forms.SuperCoolWindow. Even worse, imagine what happens if another window tries to interact with your form object using code like this:

```
My.Forms.SuperCoolWindow.RefreshData()
```

This code compels Visual Studio to create a new SuperCoolWindow object (assuming it doesn't already exist), and call its RefreshData() method. This can be a tricky problem. It might lead to a situation where one form tries to interact with SuperCoolWindow, but actually ends up talking to the invisible default instance. You'll never be alerted with an error, but the task you want to perform won't take place on the form where it should.

So what's the best option—creating form objects explicitly or using the default instances through the My object? The best advice is to use the My object in simple applications. If you have an application that shows more than one instance of the same form, or needs complex interactions between forms, you should take control of form creation and tracking on your own. You'll learn how later in this chapter, in "Interaction Between Forms" on page 120. And to avoid problems, stick to one approach (the My object or explicit creation). Don't mix and match.

Modal Forms

The preceding example uses the Show() method, which displays a modeless form. A *modeless* form is one that doesn't disable other forms in your application. This means that a user can access several different modeless windows at once and enter information into any one of them. Sometimes, modeless forms have to be built with custom communication and refresh routines, which allow them to update themselves in response to changes in other currently open forms. Interaction between different forms is examined later in this chapter.

Some parts of an application's interface are *modal*. For example, About windows, Open/Save windows, and Preferences windows are, by convention, almost always modal. Once a modal window appears, the user cannot access any other part of the application until the window has been dealt with and closed. Usually, the user does this by entering or selecting any necessary information and then clicking OK or Cancel, at which point you can call Form.Close().

To show a modal form in Visual Basic 2005, you use the `ShowDialog()` method instead of `Show()`:

```
Dim MyFormObject As New MyForm()
MyFormObject.ShowDialog()
' Any code here is executed only after MyFormObject is closed.
```

The `ShowDialog()` method stops your code. For example, any code that falls after the `ShowDialog()` statement in the example above won't be executed until the new form is closed.

The Startup Form and Shutdown Mode

In a Windows application, you'll typically end up with many forms. One of these forms plays a special role—it's the startup form, and it's shown automatically when the application starts.

To choose your startup form, double-click the My Project node in the Solution Explorer, select the Application tab, and set the Startup Form. You'll be given a list of all the forms in your project to choose from.

The startup form is shown automatically when your application first launches. From that point on, you're free to create as many modal or modeless forms as you want. By default, your application ends as soon as the startup form is closed. However, you can change this behavior by setting the Shutdown Mode option to When Last Form Closes, which keeps your application alive until every form is explicitly closed. If you want even more control, you can explicitly end the application at any point by calling `Application.Exit()`.

Application Events

In some applications, you might want to show more than one form when your application first starts up. So how do you do it? In previous versions of VB, the best choice was to choose to start your application with a `Sub Main` method—a code routine where you can explicitly show whatever forms you want. This option is still available in VB 2005, but in order to use it you need to clear the Enable Application Framework check box in the project properties, which disables several useful features. A better option is to respond to special application events to show the extra forms you need.

To create event handlers for application events, you need to click the View Application Events button in the project properties window. The first time you do this, it creates a new code file named ApplicationEvents.vb.

Here are the events you can react to:

Startup

Fires when the application starts but before the startup form is created. If you want to show a form before the main form, you could show it here. This is also a great place to put initialization code that should run before the first form appears.

Shutdown

Fires after all the forms in application are closed, just before your program ends. This is a good place to save user preferences and last-minute settings. This event isn't raised if the application fails with an error.

UnhandledException

Fires if the application ends with an unhandled error. If you perform application-wide cleanup in response to the Shutdown and UnhandledException events, you've covered your bases. (Exceptions and error handling are covered in Chapter 8.)

StartupNextInstance

Fires when the application is launched for a second time (in other words, one copy is already running). Usually you won't use this event. Instead, you can select the Make Single Instance Application setting in the project properties to allow only one copy of your application to run at once. If the user tries to launch a second copy, the first instance is brought to the foreground.

NetworkAvailabilityChanged

Fires when a network connection is connected or disconnected. This is useful if you have some features that depend on Internet connectivity (such as when you use a web service, as discussed in Chapter 13).

For example, if you want to perform some initialization code and show a splash screen when your application first starts, you could handle the Startup event like this:

```
Partial Friend Class MyApplication
    Private Sub MyApplication_Startup(ByVal sender As Object, _
      ByVal e As StartupEventArgs) Handles Me.Startup
        ' Show this form modelessly, so your code keeps running.
        ' Note that this form doesn't show a close box or title bar
        ' (Form.ControlBox is false) so the user can't close it.
        Dim Splash As New SplashForm()
        Splash.Show()

        ' (Put time-consuming initialization code here.)

        ' Hide the splash screen.
        Splash.Close()

        ' On to the main form...
    End Sub
End Class
```

You can also add a splash screen using the Splash Screen option in the project properties, but the approach shown here gives you much more control. You could use a similar approach is you wanted to show a Login window to collect user credentials before starting an application or show a window with a license message.

Several of the application events also provide extra information through an event argument object. For example, in the Startup event, you can retrieve the command-line parameters used to start the application (e.CommandLine), which is useful if you want to open a user-specified file automatically. You can also use set the e.Cancel property to true to cancel a startup (for example, if the user doesn't supply required login credentials).

Form Oddities

Forms have a few unusual extra properties, two of which we'll briefly examine here. You probably won't need to use them, but they can provide a few hours of design-time fun. Both of these strange behaviors are on display in the FormOddities project included with the sample code.

Opacity

One of these interesting features is *opacity*, which allows you to make a form partially transparent (see Figure 4-19). For example, if you change a form's Opacity property to 10% (actually 0.10), the form and all its controls will be almost completely invisible, and the background window will clearly show through. If you set the background window's Opacity property to 90% (0.90), the background will show through only slightly.

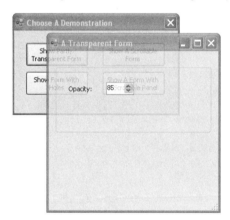

Figure 4-19: A transparent window

This feature is supported only in Windows 2000 and later operating systems (and has sketchy support with some color and graphics card settings). For this reason, the opacity feature should never be used indiscriminately in business applications. A master user-interface designer might be able to use it to create floating controls or menus that don't mask underlying content—or to enable some nifty effect in a logo animation or graphic display. In general, however, such enhancements won't be supported by older computers and will do little more than complicate an application.

TransparencyKey

You can use the TransparencyKey property to make portions of a window invisible. The color that you specify with this feature will become transparent when your program is running (much as a form does when you alter its opacity). For example, if you choose light red, any occurrence of light red in your form—whether it is in the form's background, in another control, or even in a picture contained in a control—will become invisible, and the application behind your program will show through. However, unlike sections altered with the Opacity property, transparent areas act like "holes" in your application's window (see Figure 4-20). A user can even click to activate another window if it's visible through a transparent region.

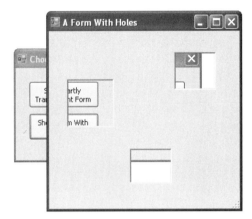

Figure 4-20: Cutting out bits of a form

The FormOddities sample code uses a form with three red PictureBox controls, which disappear at runtime. Once again, this feature is only supported in Windows 2000 or later. Can it be useful? It all depends. If you're trying to create a next-generation user interface, you might decide to create an irregularly shaped form by hiding parts of a background image. It's eye candy when it works, but difficult to perfect.

The Inner Workings of Forms

There's a lot more to forms than you might suspect. In fact, forms are complex classes that contain detailed initialization code, all of which is generated automatically (thanks to Visual Studio). In this section, you'll take a closer look and see how forms really work, and why they are a dramatic change from pre-.NET versions of Visual Basic.

Visual Basic 6 Forms "Under the Hood"

In Visual Basic 6, every form is stored in a file with the extension .frm, and any binary information (pictures, for example) is stored in a corresponding file with a .frx extension. If you open a VB6 .frm file in a text editor, you'll see information like this:

```
Begin VB.Form frmHello
   Caption        =    "Hello World Program"
   ClientHeight   =    3195
   ClientLeft     =    60
   ClientTop      =    345
   ClientWidth    =    4680
   LinkTopic      =    "frmHello"
   ScaleHeight    =    3195
   ScaleWidth     =    4680
   StartUpPosition =   3  'Windows Default
   Begin VB.CommandButton cmdQuit
      Caption        =    "Quit"
      Height         =    495
      Left           =    1440
      TabIndex       =    1
      Top            =    2520
      Width          =    1815
   End
   Begin VB.Label lblHello
      Caption        =    "Hello World (of Visual Basic 6)!"
      Height         =    495
      Left           =    1080
      TabIndex       =    0
      Top            =    960
      Width          =    2535
   End
End
Attribute VB_Name = "Form1"
Attribute VB_GlobalNameSpace = False
Attribute VB_Creatable - False
Attribute VB_PredeclaredId = True
Attribute VB_Exposed = False
Option Explicit

Private Sub cmdQuit_Click()
   Unload Me
End Sub
```

This code was generated when I created the simple "Hello, World!" form shown here in Figure 4-21, with a label control and a Quit button.

If you've never looked at VB 6 code before, this might come as a bit of a surprise. At the end of this file is all of the Visual Basic event handler code that you created (in the preceding example, it's just the Click event handler for the cmdQuit button). But before that is a great deal of information that sets the properties and position of all the interface elements in your program.

This code resembles Visual Basic code somewhat, but closer examination shows that it's actually sort of a strange hybrid. For example, controls are defined with a statement like `Begin VB.Label lblHello`, which follows the C style of syntax by indicating the type of element to be created (`VB.Label`), followed by the name of the item (`lblHello`). Though this code is clearly present and accessible, it wasn't shown anywhere inside the Visual Basic 6 IDE.

Figure 4-21: A basic VB 6 form

The "code" in a VB 6 .frm file is untouchable, because there is no guarantee that your changes won't break it. If you want to modify your user interface, you have to do it manually, using the built-in Form Designer. Usually, this is the most convenient option; however, every once in a while a problem appears that could easily be solved by tweaking a few values if you could only have direct access to the form file. Instead, these changes always require time-consuming manual repositioning or resizing.

Visual Basic 2005 handles this kind of situation quite a bit differently.

Visual Basic 2005 Forms "Under the Hood"

Every Visual Basic 2005 file has the extension .vb, whether it is a form, a class, or a module. However, when you create a form VB 2005 actually creates *two* files. These two files are definitions for the same form class, but there's a clear division. The file you see in the Solution Explorer contains the event handling code you've written. The other file is made up of the automatically generated code that initializes your form and configures its controls—what I'll call *infrastructure* code. Ordinarily, this file is hidden from view—but it's not too hard to peel back the curtain and see what's going on inside.

Take a close look at Figure 4-22. It shows an ordinary form named Form1.vb. (An initial, blank form named Form1.vb is added to all new Windows application projects.) If you look at the code for this form (choose View ▸ Code from the menu), you'll see an empty class definition that's just waiting to receive your code:

```
Public Class Form1
End Class
```

Figure 4-22: A basic VB 2005 form

However, there's more here that meets the eye. To see the other side of the story, choose Project ▶ Show All Files from the menu. Now you'll find that every form is paired with a designer file. For example, Form1.vb has Form1.Designer.vb. (Visual Studio generates this name automatically by adding .Designer on the end of your form name.) Figure 4-23 shows the designer file for Form1.

Figure 4-23: The designer code file

If you look into this code, you'll find quite a bit more content. The key section is a subroutine named InitializeComponent(). Essentially, every time you do something in Visual Studio that affects your form (like add a new control, or configure an existing control), Visual Studio adds the corresponding code in the InitializeComponent() method. In other words, InitializeComponent() has every code statement that's needed to construct your form from scratch.

This code frees Visual Basic from its dependence on the IDE. A Visual Basic application now consists of nothing but pure VB code and could be created with nothing more than a text editor. Most times, you'll want to stay away from this infrastructure code, because it's long, tedious, and sometimes convoluted. Generally, it's easiest to configure your forms through the designer in Visual Studio.

However, you may find that going behind the scenes to see how Visual Basic creates your interface not only provides some interesting information, but also allows you to perform some otherwise time-consuming rearrangements just by modifying a few automatically generated values. For example, if you've been forced to change your naming convention, you can quickly change all the names of your interface elements with a simple Find and Replace operation in your code display. In other words, you *won't* need to click each control in the Form Designer and manually make the change to the Name property through the Properties window. Or, you might find that this code allows you to understand how a specific control really works—sort of like a condensed tutorial.

Stepping Through the "Muck and Goo"

Some developers refer to this portion of the Visual Basic code as "muck and goo" (and others have likely invented less flattering euphemisms). Once you understand it, however, you'll gain a unique programming edge and a better understanding of the .NET Framework.

In the sample .frm file shown earlier, I showed the code that would be needed for a simple "Hello, World!" form. In Visual Basic 2005, the same window would create code like this in the designer file:

```
Friend WithEvents lblHello As System.Windows.Forms.Label
Friend WithEvents cmdQuit As System.Windows.Forms.Button

'Required by the Windows Form Designer
Private components As System.ComponentModel.Container

'NOTE: The following procedure is required by the Windows Form Designer
'It can be modified using the Windows Form Designer.
'Do not modify it using the code editor.
<System.Diagnostics.DebuggerStepThrough()> _
Private Sub InitializeComponent()
    Me.lblHello = New System.Windows.Forms.Label()
    Me.cmdQuit = New System.Windows.Forms.Button()
    Me.SuspendLayout()
    '
    'lblHello
    '
    Me.lblHello.Location = New System.Drawing.Point(80, 40)
    Me.lblHello.Name = "lblHello"
    Me.lblHello.Size = New System.Drawing.Size(208, 40)
    Me.lblHello.TabIndex = 1
    Me.lblHello.Text = "Hello World"
    '
    'cmdQuit
    '
    Me.cmdQuit.Location = New System.Drawing.Point(128, 264)
    Me.cmdQuit.Name = "cmdQuit"
    Me.cmdQuit.Size = New System.Drawing.Size(80, 40)
    Me.cmdQuit.TabIndex = 0
    Me.cmdQuit.Text = "Exit"
    '
    'HelloForm
    '
    Me.AutoScaleBaseSize = New System.Drawing.Size(5, 13)
    Me.ClientSize = New System.Drawing.Size(440, 373)
    Me.Controls.AddRange(New Control() {Me.lblHello, Me.cmdQuit})
    Me.Name = "HelloForm"
```

```
Me.Text = "Hello World Program"
Me.ResumeLayout(False)

End Sub
```

Looking at this code, you can make the following observations:

- Every control is defined as a variable in a form. The Friend accessibility keyword is used, which means that other forms in your program can access these controls.

- All these controls are initialized in the InitializeComponent() subroutine that is called automatically when the form is loaded. This subroutine has a special DebuggerStepThrough attribute (see the text enclosed in the < > angle brackets) that tells Visual Studio to ignore the code during debugging.

- The properties of each control are set in separate blocks, each identified with a comment indicating the control name.

- The Me.Controls.AddRange() statement ads all the controls to the form at once. The Me keyword represents the current form, which has a Controls property that represents all the controls it contains.

- At the end of the InitializeComponent() subroutine, some additional properties are set for the current form.

- The SuspendLayout() method is invoked at the beginning of this process, and the ResumeLayout() method is called at the end. This stops the form from rearranging and refreshing its controls while the initialization is underway, which optimizes performance.

Perhaps the most useful thing you can do once you understand the infrastructure code is to copy and paste parts of a user interface from one form to another. With the Form Designer, you have to manually select the correct controls—and positioning them on another form can be tricky. If you understand the muck and goo, however, it's just a matter of copying text.

What About Binary Information?

Not all information can be represented in code. For example, you might load a picture into a picture box, a form, or an image list at design time. When you do this, Visual Basic 2005 stores the appropriate information in a resource file and then writes the code needed to read the information from that file. As with Visual Basic 6, each form can have a resource file, but instead of having the extension .frx, every VB 2005 resource file ends with .resx. As with the designer file, the .resx files are hidden until you choose Project ▶ Show All Files. (You'll learn more about resources in Chapter 7.)

Adding Controls Dynamically

A common question from Visual Basic programmers is how to add controls to a form *dynamically*—in other words, while the program is running. For example, you might want to create a diagramming program that allows users to drag and drop various symbols onto a form. Rather than manually painting the individual graphics, a better way to handle this problem is to use button or picture controls. With this technique, you can easily move pictures using their properties, and let the Windows operating system worry about painting the form in such a way that the existing controls aren't overwritten. This approach also allows you to easily capture mouse clicks and allows the user to drag and move your icons after they have been placed.

In Visual Basic 2005, the distinction between controls added at runtime and those added at design time has been blurred. As you've already learned, all the controls that you add using the Windows Form Designer are really created by the code in the InitializeComponent() routine when your form is first loaded. This code looks almost exactly the same as the code you would use to add a control later in a program's execution. The only difference is its location in your program.

Thus, one easy way to add a control dynamically is to add it at design time and configure its properties. Then, find the corresponding automatically generated code, and cut and paste it into another method. Be aware that this code may exist at several different places in the Windows Designer code region.

Examine the following infrastructure code, which is used to create a new label:

```
' The declaration in the class:
Friend WithEvents Label1 As System.Windows.Forms.Label

' From the InitializeComponent() subroutine:
Private Sub InitializeComponent()
    Me.Label1 = New System.Windows.Forms.Label
    Me.Label1.Location = New System.Drawing.Point(96, 100)
    Me.Label1.Name = "Label1"
    Me.Label1.Size - New System.Drawing.Size(112, 48)
    Me.Label1.Text = "Permanent label"
    ' (Code for other controls has been left out.)
    Me.Controls.AddRange(New Control(){Me.Button1}, Me.Label1)
End Sub
```

This code, with some minor modifications, could be inserted into a button's Click event to create the label dynamically, as shown in our next example. There are two significant changes. First, the Controls.AddRange() method, which adds a whole group of controls from an array, has been replaced with the `Controls.Add()` method, which adds only a single control. Second, the declaration for the label has been changed to a `Dim` statement, because the `Friend` and `WithEvents` keywords are not valid when you create an object inside a method.

```
Private Sub Button1_Click(ByVal sender As System.Object, _
  ByVal e As System.EventArgs) Handles Button1.Click

    Dim LabelNew As New System.Windows.Forms.Label()
    LabelNew.Location = New System.Drawing.Point(96, 200)
    LabelNew.Name = "LabelNew"
    LabelNew.Size = New System.Drawing.Size(112, 48)
    LabelNew.Text = "Dynamically created label"
    Controls.Add(LabelNew)

End Sub
```

This code does have a couple of drawbacks, however. For one thing, the control variable is created inside the button's `Click` event, so it is destroyed as soon as the `Click` event is over. Does this mean that the control itself disappears? In fact, the control remains, but it's a little bit more difficult to access. The only way you can reach it is through the `Controls` property of your form (with `MyForm.Controls("LabelNew")`, for instance), which contains a collection of *all* the controls on the form. A better solution is to use your own collection for groups of dynamically added controls. To use your own collection, add this line to your form at the class level:

```
Private DynamicControls As Collection
```

Then, when you create the label, use the following line of code to store it in the collection:

```
DynamicControls.Add(LabelNew)
```

Of course, if you are creating a control that you won't need to access again, these lines aren't necessary.

Dynamic Event Hookup

Alternatively, you might be adding a control whose prime purpose is receiving events (such as a button control). In this case, you may not need to explicitly keep track of the control, but you do need a way to receive its events. Unfortunately, controls that are created at runtime can't be defined with the `WithEvents` keyword. Even if they could, it wouldn't help you; all that `WithEvents` really does is to make it easier for you to wire up an event handler with the `Handles` keyword. But if you haven't created a control yet (and you don't know when or if you'll create it), it's impossible to connect the event handler ahead of time.

You can solve this problem by dynamically wiring up a new control at runtime with the `AddHandler` statement. Consider the following example, which adds a new button at a random location, and sets it to use the same event handler as the first button. Every time you click this button, you add a new button that, when clicked, adds yet another new button.

```
Private Sub Button1_Click(ByVal sender As System.Object, _
  ByVal e As System.EventArgs) Handles Button1.Click

    ' Create a random number generator for choosing the
    ' new button's position.
    Dim Rand As New Random()

    ' Generate and configure the new button.
    Dim NewButton As New System.Windows.Forms.Button()
    NewButton.Left = Rand.Next(Me.Width)
    NewButton.Top = Rand.Next(Me.Height)
    NewButton.Size = New System.Drawing.Size(88, 28)
    NewButton.Text = "New Button"

    ' Add the button to the form.
    Me.Controls.Add(NewButton)

    ' Wire up the new button's Click event.
    AddHandler NewButton.Click, AddressOf Button1_Click

End Sub
```

To see this random button reproduction in action, try out the DynamicRandomButtons sample program (Figure 4-24).

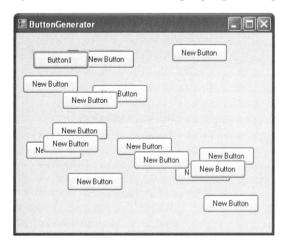

Figure 4-24: Buttons that spawn other buttons

NOTE *Assigning dynamic event handlers is another technique that you can use to replace the control arrays that were used in classic VB.*

Interaction Between Forms

You're about to learn several ways that forms can interact with one another in more sophisticated applications. In particular, you'll look at dialog windows (the easiest case), at owned forms, and at MDI applications. But first, we'll set the stage by considering one of the challenges that can arise with form interaction.

A Sample Form Interaction Problem

As you learned earlier in this chapter, forms can come into existence in two different ways:

- You can create the form object explicitly in your code.
- You can use the default instance using the My.Forms object, in which case the form object is created automatically when needed.

It's important to decide which approach you're using in an application, because it determines how forms will interact.

Imagine you've created a form named RecordList with a list of product records drawn from a database. The user can choose a product record and start editing it by clicking a button. At this point, you fire up a second form, called EditRecord.

Once the user completes the change in EditRecord, the user clicks an update button. At this point, the record is updated, but the edit form isn't closed. (Let's assume that the user might want to make more changes.) However, there's now a problem—the list that's shown in the RecordList window now has out-of-date information.

Depending on the exact behavior you want, there are several ways you can solve this problem. One option is for the EditRecord form to call a custom subroutine in the RecordList form. (Let's call this the RefreshRecords() method of the RecordList form.) The challenge here is that in order for EditRecord to access RecordList, it needs a way to access the form.

If you've embraced the My object, this code does the trick:

```
' This may work (if you showed the form through My).
' Be careful.
My.Forms.RecordList.RefreshRecords()
```

But there's a potential problem with this approach. If you didn't use My to show the RecordList form in the first place, the current RecordList window won't be the default instance. In that case, when the EditRecord form accesses the default instance, it will actually be interacting with a different form object from the one you intend. This form will be generated on demand. And unless you've already called the Show() method on this form, it won't even be visible.

So what's the solution if the My object isn't your cup of tea? You need to explicitly keep track of the form yourself. That means you need to keep the form variable stored somewhere. One option is a module. For example, you could create this module for the sole purpose of tracking forms:

```
Public Module FormTracker
    Public RecordListForm As RecordList
End Module
```

Now you simply need to remember to set this form variable. You could do it at the same time you create the form:

```
Dim NewRecordList As New RecordList()
FormTracker.RecordListForm = NewRecordList
FormTracker.RecordListForm.Show()
```

Or you could use an event handler in the form so it always happens automatically whenever the form is created. (This assumes you'll only have one copy of the form in existence at a time.)

```
Public Class RecordList

    Public Sub Form_Load(ByVal sender As System.Object, _
     ByVal e As System.EventArgs) Handles RecordList.Load
        ' Set the reference so others can access this form.
        FormTracker.RecordListForm = Me
    End Sub

End Class
```

Either way, you can access the form later through the form variable you've created.

Dialog Windows

Dialog windows offer another way to communicate information. The MessageBox object is a special kind of built-in dialog window. You choose the options you need, display them in the window, and then examine the user's choices through the return value:

```
Dim Result As DialogResult
Result = MessageBox.Show("Is this a yes or no question?", _
  "Question", MessageBoxButtons.YesNo)

If Result = DialogResult.Yes Then
    ' The user clicked Yes.
Else
    ' The user clicked No.
End If
```

NOTE *You may receive a Visual Studio warning when you check the* DialogResult. *That's because there's a name conflict between the* DialogResult *property of the current form, and the* DialogResult *enumeration, which provides the list of constants that correspond to different actions (such as Yes, No, OK, Cancel, and so on). This warning is harmless, but you can remove it by replacing every reference to* DialogResult *with the fully qualified name* System.Windows.Forms.DialogResult, *which makes it clear you aren't using the property of the current form. To learn more about enumerations and get a deeper understanding of how* DialogResult *works, refer to Chapter 5.*

A custom Windows form isn't this convenient. You can display the window, but your window won't return a value. That means you need to rely on global variables, or check the state of other variables in the form to find out what choices the user had made.

.NET provides a new model for dialog windows that lets you get simple results from a custom form without needing to maintain extra variables. It also gives you the ability to put code where it belongs rather than scattering it among various event handlers. This method won't help you if you must have complex or detailed information returned from a window, but if all you need is a simple yes or no, your code will be cleaner and more standardized than it would have been in the past.

A good example of a dialog window is a custom confirmation window. For example, you may have an email feature in your application that allows the user to send you a purchase order. Before sending the order, a confirmation window might display additional information and ask whether or not the user wants to proceed. This window requires very little code. Essentially, it displays some information and then closes when the user clicks OK or Cancel. However, you also need a special control or format to display the required information, so you can't use the typical MessageBox object.

To solve this problem, select the OK button, and set the DialogResult property to OK. This is the value that will be returned from your window automatically if the user clicks this button. Now select the Cancel button, and set the DialogResult property to Cancel. There's no need to write any extra code or even to add an event handler. Once the user clicks one of these buttons, Visual Basic 2005 will automatically close the form and return the result to you.

The code for displaying your custom confirmation window will look something like this:

```
Dim Result As DialogResult
Dim Confirm As New ConfirmationForm()
Result = Confirm.ShowDialog()

If Result = DialogResult.OK Then
    ' The user clicked your OK button.
Else
    ' The user clicked your Cancel button.
End If
```

If necessary, you can add additional code to the button event handlers to store extra information on the form, and you can check those variables from within your calling code. Keep in mind that even after the window is closed, the form object remains in memory, along with all its information, until the form variable goes out of scope.

The dialog model is extremely convenient. However, it may not work for more complicated scenarios—for example, when a user has a variety of different options that aren't covered by the preset DialogResult variables. And remember, it's only valid when you're showing a modal window with the ShowDialog() method. If you use Show() instead to pop up multiple windows at once, there's no return value, and you'll need to devise other ways to communicate between your forms.

Owned Forms

.NET introduces the concept of *owned forms*. An owned form belongs to another form. When the owner window is minimized, all of its owned forms are also minimized automatically. When an owned form overlaps its owner, it is always displayed on top. Owned forms are usually used for floating toolbox and command windows. One example of an owned form is the Find and Replace window in Microsoft Word.

Any form can own another form, and you don't need to set up the relationship at design time. Instead, you just set the Owner property, as shown here:

```
' Show the main window.
Dim Main As New MainForm()
Main.Show()

' Create and display an owned form.
Dim Search As New SearchForm()
Search.Owner = Main
Search.Show()
```

MDI Interfaces

A Multiple Document Interface (MDI) program is generally based on a single parent window that can contain numerous child windows (see Figure 4-25). Usually this model is used to allow a user to work with more than one document at a time. (A "document" might be a report, a data grid, a log, a text listing, or something entirely different.)

Any window can become an MDI parent (container) if you set the IsMdiContainer property to True. Many of the restrictions that were placed on MDI parents in pre-.NET versions of Visual Basic have now been lifted. For example, parent windows can now contain regular controls, such as buttons, along with the standard menus and command bars. This makes it possible to create a wide variety of bizarre forms that look nothing like a conventional window should. For respectable interfaces, an MDI parent should contain only dockable controls, such as status bars and menu bars, which latch onto an edge of the window and provide a clear working area for any child windows.

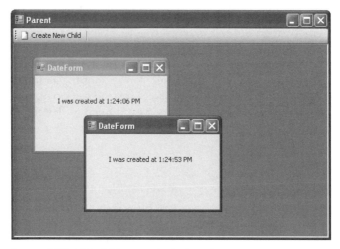

Figure 4-25: MDI children are locked inside MDI parents

Turning a window into an MDI child is similar to making it an owned form.

```
Private Sub NewChild(ByVal sender As System.Object, _
  ByVal e As System.EventArgs) Handles cmdNewChild.Click
    Dim Child As New DateForm()
    Child.MdiParent = Me
    Child.Show()
End Sub
```

Of course, at the end of this subroutine, the Child variable will be lost, and you won't be able to use it to access the MDI child. However, MDI forms include some extra conveniences that make them easy to work with, and free you from manually keeping track of forms. Every MDI parent provides a collection named MdiChildren that contains all of the currently opened MDI forms. Every MDI parent also has an ActiveMdiChild property, which tells you which child window currently has focus. This allows the following kind of information exchange:

```
' This code is in the MDI child class.
Public Sub RefreshData()
    ' Some code here to update the window display.
End Sub

Private Sub InfoChanged(ByVal sender As System.Object, _
  ByVal e As System.EventArgs) Handles cmdRefresh.Click
    ' Calls a function in the parent.
    CType(Me.MdiParentForm, ParentForm).RefreshAllChildren()
End Sub
```

NOTE *This example assumes the child form class is named* ParentForm, *and it contains a custom method named* RefreshAllChildren() *that performs the refresh. To see the complete code, refer to the MDIForms project included with the samples for this chapter.*

Note that in order to call the RefreshAllChildren() subroutine, the code needs to convert the reference to the MDI parent form into the appropriate form class. Otherwise, you'll only be able to access the standard form properties and methods through the reference, not the custom ones you may have added to the class.

The RefreshAllChildren() subroutine is found in the parent:

```
' This code is in the MDI parent class.
Public Sub RefreshAllChildren()
    Dim Child As DateForm
    For Each Child in Me.MdiChildren
        If Not Me.MdiChildren Is Me.ActiveMdiChild
            Child.RefreshData()
        End If
    Next
End Sub
```

This form has an extra feature that determines whether an MDI child is the one that called it, and if so it doesn't bother to call the refresh procedure. The reasoning here is that the active MDI child will already be up to date, as it was the form that originated the refresh request. Of course, the real reason I've included this code is to demonstrate the ActiveMdiChild property. Notice that the code uses the Is statement, instead of an equal sign, to compare the forms. This is because both forms are objects (reference types), which cannot be compared with an equal sign.

To see this logic in action, try out the MDIForms project, which automatically refreshes all windows when you click a button in any one of the child forms (see Figure 4-26).

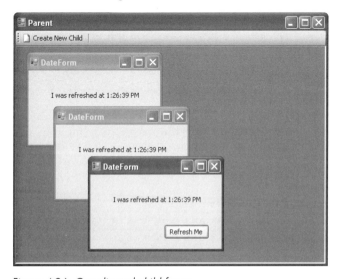

Figure 4-26: Coordinated child forms

More .NET Controls

So far this chapter hasn't described the individual controls that you can work with. For essentials like the Button, TextBox, CheckBox, PictureBox, RadioButton, and Label controls, there's no need—most of these controls are similar to those provided in earlier versions of Visual Basic, and are fairly straightforward, with similar sets of properties, events, and methods. (One obvious difference is that controls that display text now always have a Text property. For some controls, Visual Basic 6 used a Caption property instead.)

However, along with these standbys are a dizzying array of genuinely new controls that do everything from displaying web pages to validating text boxes. You've already seen a few of these—namely, advanced container controls like the Panel, SplitContainer, and FlowLayoutPanel—and you'll see some more useful widgets throughout this book. (For example, the printing controls are featured in Chapter 9, the DataGridView control makes an appearance in Chapter 10, and the Timer shows up in Chapter 11.)

NOTE *There's no way to walk you through all the available controls in a single chapter. In the following sections, you'll consider three nifty additions: the ToolStrip, the NotifyIcon, and the ToolTipProvider. However, there's lots more out there for those who want to experiment!*

Strips and Menus

.NET 2.0 includes the most powerful model for menus and toolbars that VB developers have ever laid their hands on. Without any programming effort, you get frills like automatic overflow menus, drag-and-drop rearrangement, support for Windows XP visual styles, and a slick modern look. More ambitious users can dig into the menu and toolbar internals to change nearly every drawing detail.

Collectively, the menus and toolbars in .NET 2.0 are known as the "strip" controls, because they all share some core functionality that's built into the System.Windows.Forms.ToolStrip class. You'll find all of these controls in the Menus and Toolbars section of the Toolbox. Here are the highlights:

ToolStrip

Use this for toolbars that you can latch to the top or sides of your windows.

MenuStrip

Use this for the familiar Windows menu, complete with optional thumbnail icons next to any command.

ContextMenuStrip

Use this for a pop-up menu that you can show when the user right-clicks something. Use ContextMenuStrip.Show() to pop the menu into view at the right time. (You'll see an example in the following section, which demonstrates a system tray application.)

StatusStrip

Use this for a status bar. Status bars are similar to toolbars, although they tend to have a slightly different visual appearance and they usually rely on static text more than clickable commands. (However, you can technically put all the same ToolStrip ingredients into a StatusStrip.)

ToolStripContainer

This oddball container control allows the user to drag and rearrange ordinary ToolStrip controls. It's composed of five panels: one panel for each side, and one panel that fills the remaining content in the middle (where you put other content). When you place a ToolStrip in a ToolStripContainer, it's automatically made mobile.

Learning everything there is to know about these controls would require at least one lengthy chapter, but, fortunately, you don't need much expertise to get started. The basic concept is that all strips are really collections of one or more ToolStripItem objects. (This collection is provided through the Items property of the strip control.) Each ToolStripItem represents a separate element on a strip or menu. This item could be a clickable button or menu command, an ordinary label, a separator, a text box, and so on.

Technically, the ToolStripItem objects aren't genuine controls. However, they provide nearly as much functionality, including properties for the font (Font), colors (BackColor and ForeColor), the display style (DisplayStyle), the displayed content (Image and Text), the state of the item (Visible and Enabled), and so on. They also provide events, like Click (the most useful one), which fires when the user clicks the item.

To create any strip, whether it's a status bar or menu, you follow more or less the same process. First, you drag the appropriate control onto your form from the Menus & Toolbars section of the Toolbox. Then, you use the Visual Studio design support to start adding ToolStripItem objects. For a menu, you can start typing the text of each command directly on the form design surface. For a ToolStrip, you create each ToolStripItem by selecting it from a drop-down list (see Figure 4-27); then you can select the ToolStripItem and customize it in the Properties window.

The ToolStrip in Figure 4-27 is a simple one, composed entirely of the most useful ToolStripItem types: the ToolStripButton and ToolStripSeparator. Once you've created the ToolStrip you want, it's time to handle the button clicks. Here's an example event handler that responds when the user clicks the New button on the ToolStrip by showing the name of the ToolStripItem. As usual, you can generate this event handler quickly by double-clicking the New button in the design environment.

```
Private Sub NewToolStripButton_Click(ByVal sender As System.Object, _
  ByVal e As System.EventArgs) Handles NewToolStripButton.Click
    Dim item As ToolStripItem = CType(sender, ToolStripItem)
    MessageBox.Show("You clicked " & item.Name)
End Sub
```

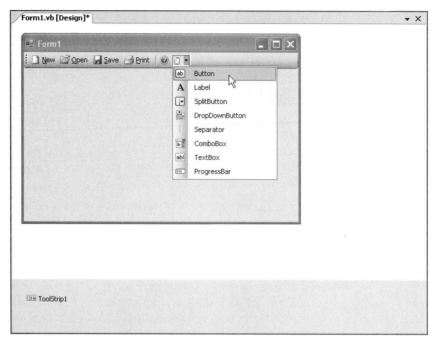

Figure 4-27: Choosing a ToolStripItem to add to a ToolStrip

As you use the ToolStrip, you'll find yourself getting quickly acquainted with it. In the meantime, keep these useful facts in mind:

- By default, the ToolStripButton shows a picture only (as set in the Image property). To change this so that it also shows content set in the Text property, set the DisplayStyle property to ImageAndText. You can even configure where the image goes relative to the text using the TextImageRelation property.

- A ToolStrip can be vertical or horizontal. To change its orientation, change the Dock property. (By default, when you create a new ToolStrip it's dockcd to the top of the form as a horizontal toolbar.)

- A ToolStrip can't float, but it can be moved into different positions using the ToolStripContainer. To try this trick out, start by adding a ToolStripContainer, and docking it to fill your form. Then, add your ToolStrip controls inside the ToolStripContainer, along one of the four sides. At runtime, the user will be able to rearrange ToolStrip objects that are next to each other, or move a ToolStrip from one side to another. (To disable some sides so that they aren't dockable use ToolStripContainer properties like LeftToolStripPanelVisible, TopToolStripPanelVisible, and so on.)

- By default, when a ToolStrip can't fit all its items at once, the ones at the end drop off into an overflow menu (see Figure 4-28). If this isn't the behavior you want, set the ToolStrip.CanOverflow property to False. Or for even more control, set the Overflow property of individual items to determine whether they will be made a part of the overflow menu. This allows you to ensure that the most items will remain visible even as the less important ones are shuffled into the overflow menu.

Figure 4-28: The ToolStrip
overflow menu

• As shown in Figure 4-27, you can add several ToolStripItem types to a ToolStrip. However, you aren't limited to just these options; you can add a ToolStripControlHost to a ToolStrip programmatically. The ToolStripControlHost can wrap any other type of control, allowing you to quickly put check boxes, date controls, and just about anything else into the ToolStrip. For example:

```
' Create a DateTimePicker control.
Dim Dt As New DateTimePicker()
Dt.Value = DateTime.Now
Dt.Format = DateTimePickerFormat.Short

' Wrap it in a ToolStripControlHost.
Dim Host As New ToolStripControlHost(Dt)

' Place it in the ToolStrip.
MyToolStrip.Items.Add(Host)
```

Use the ToolStrips project to begin playing with the MenuStrip and ToolStrip controls.

System Tray Icons

At last, Visual Basic provides an easy way to add and use a system tray icon. All you need to do is place the NotifyIcon control on your component tray, and supply an appropriate icon using the Icon property (and pop-up text using the Text property). The icon will appear immediately when the form is displayed (Figure 4-29) and will disappear when the form is unloaded.

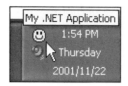

Figure 4-29: A system tray icon

The only problem with this approach is that the NotifyIcon won't appear *until* the form is loaded, which prevents you from creating system tray applications that quietly load themselves in the background without showing anything. Unfortunately, this sort of background application is quite useful. It can linger in the background performing periodic tasks automatically, or it could wait for the user to click the icon and choose a menu command before performing any operations.

To create a background application that works this way, you need to switch off the VB application framework. It's a little counterintuitive, but not terribly difficult. Here's how to get started:

1. Double-click the My Project node in the Solution Explorer.
2. Clear the check mark next to the Enable Application Framework setting.
3. Choose Sub Main for the startup object.
4. Select File ▶ Add Component, and create a new component with any file-name. (In the following example, we use the name *ApplicationStartup*.) This component will contain the Main() method that launches your application.

You must use a component to start your application (rather than an ordinary class or module) because only a component gives you a design surface where you can create controls and other components. In other words, although the ApplicationStartup component isn't a form, you can still use Visual Studio to design it. That means you can add objects like the NotifyIcon by dragging them from the Toolbox and dropping them onto your component, without having to write all the code by hand.

In this example, you need both a NotifyIcon and ContextMenuStrip. Drop both of these ingredients onto the design surface of your component, which looks like the component tray of a form (see Figure 4-30). You can select items here and configure them further in the Properties window.

Before going any further, set the text and icon for the NotifyIcon (using the Text and Icon properties), and add two menu comments to the ContextMenuStrip: Show Clock and Exit. To add these items, right-click the ContextMenuStrip and select Edit Items.

Now, set the NotifyIcon.ContextMenuStrip property to refer to the ContextMenuStrip that you've created so that the the NotifyIcon will automatically show the menu when a user right-clicks the system tray icon.

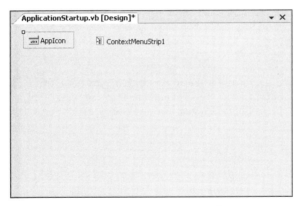

Figure 4-30: Adding a system tray icon and context menu to a component

Next, it's time to add event handlers for the two context menus. Here's the code you need:

```
Public Class ApplicationStartup
    Private Sub cmdExit_Click(ByVal sender As Object, _
      ByVal e As System.EventArgs) Handles cmdExit.Click
        AppIcon.Visible = False
        Application.Exit()
    End Sub

    Private Sub cmdShowClock_Click(ByVal sender As Object, _
      ByVal e As System.EventArgs) Handles cmdShowClock.Click
        ' You could show another form here, but we
        ' simply show a message box.
        MessageBox.Show(Date.Now.ToString, "Date", _
          MessageBoxButtons.OK)
    End Sub

    Public Shared Sub Main()
        ' (Code omitted.)
    End Sub
End Class
```

The real trick is the Main() method, which starts your program. The Main() method must be declared with the Shared keyword so that it's always available, even before your component has been created. (You'll learn more about shared methods in Chapter 5.) Your task in the Main() method is to create the form, perform any other initialization you need, and get things started. Here's the code that does the trick:

```
Public Shared Sub Main()
    ' Make sure we get the Windows XP look, if available.
    Application.EnableVisualStyles()
```

```
' Create this component.
' At this point, the NotifyIcon appears automatically
' (assuming its Visible property is True).
Dim App As New ApplicationStartup

' Because no forms are being displayed, you need this
' statement to stop the application from automatically ending.
' The application will just wait for menu clicks from this point on.
Application.Run()
End Sub
```

NOTE
If you choose to switch off the application framework in this way, make sure you include the command Application.EnableVisualStyles() *before you show any forms to ensure that your application will support Windows XP visual styles when running under Windows XP. (On earlier operating systems, this command has no effect.) Without this step, you'll always get the old-fashioned buttons, for a decidedly dated look.*

This completes a background application that uses the system tray. When you first load it, the icon appears but no forms show up. Right-click to see the menu and start interacting with your application. If the user clicks Exit, the program ends; if the user clicks Show Clock, the current time is displayed. (This application is provided with the examples for this chapter in the SystemTrayApplication project.)

The possible uses for an application like this are countless. For example, you could create a task-logging program that records the amount of time spent on each project by simply "punching in" and "punching out" on the system tray icon menu. The program would then write the appropriate information to a file or database.

Providers

Providers are an innovative type of component. Providers extend the properties of other controls on the current form. For example, to add a tooltip to a control, all you need to do is drag a ToolTipProvider onto the component tray. Once you do so, every control on the current form automatically acquires a new property (courtesy of the ToolTipProvider) named ToolTip. You can set this with the tooltip text that you want to appear when the user hovers the mouse over the corresponding control.

You can also tweak various ToolTipProvider properties to configure global tooltip settings, such as how many milliseconds your program will wait before showing the tooltip, or how long the tooltip will remain displayed if the user doesn't move the mouse. Usually, however, the default settings are best.

NOTE *Remember that a tooltip should be reserved for graphical controls such as toolbar buttons, not used with label controls or ordinary buttons.*

You'll find two other providers with .NET:

HelpProvider

This provider lets you show help messages or launch a help topic in another window. Best of all, you can create context-sensitive help that shows different help for different windows and controls. The HelpProvider springs into action when a user presses F1 while positioned over another control.

ErrorProvider

This provider lets you show a flashing error icon (with a Tooltip error message) when invalid data is entered. You can use it with your own validation routines to alert a user when a mistake is made in an input control like a TextBox.

What Comes Next?

The future is bright for user interface programming with Windows forms. Because all .NET languages share the same WinForms technology, Microsoft won't be introducing new controls that are only available to developers using a certain language.

To learn more, your best bet is to master the full-featured suite of controls bundled with Visual Basic 2005. Complete reference information for every control can be found in the class reference portion of the Visual Studio Help, in the System.Windows.Forms namespace. Or, for a detailed look at each and every Windows Forms control, you can try a book like my own *Pro .NET 2.0 Windows Forms and Custom Controls in VB* (Apress, forthcoming).

5

OBJECT-ORIENTED
PROGRAMMING

Visual Basic first introduced support for object-oriented programming in version 4.0, and the response was varied. Some cutting-edge VB developers began to push forward with object-oriented concepts, using them to build sophisticated component-based programs that could scale to serve thousands of simultaneous users, while the rest of the VB developer community continued as it always had. As time went on, the group of object-oriented programmers grew larger, and most books about Visual Basic programming began to include at least some reference to its OOP features. With Visual Basic 2005 these features are greatly expanded—in fact, they've swallowed the entire language!

If you want to do anything in .NET, you'll need to use objects. For example, you create and manage files by using `File` and `Directory` objects, print out reports using `PrinterDocument` objects, and interact with databases using `DataSet` and `DataReader` objects (as you'll discover in Chapter 9). In fact, in Visual Basic 2005 *everything* is an object, whether you realize it at first or not. You had a glimpse of this in Chapter 3, which examined how fundamental

Visual Basic 2005 data types, such as arrays, strings, and even integers, are actually full-featured objects. In Chapter 4 the plot thickened with forms, which were also exposed as a special type of object. As this book continues, you'll learn how to create your own custom objects and use them for a variety of programming tasks. But before you can get there, you need a crash course in object-oriented programming. That's where this chapter comes in.

To make the best use of .NET objects, and to enhance your own applications, you should develop a good understanding of object-oriented concepts. You may have already learned how to use classes and objects with a previous version of Visual Basic or another programming language. Even so, you'll probably still want to read through the majority of this chapter and the next to explore the object-oriented features of VB 2005 and to get the big picture of the world of classes, interfaces, and object relationships.

New in .NET

Visual Basic 2005's enhanced OOP features first appeared in .NET 1.0, when they were among the most hotly anticipated language changes. Visual Basic 2005 keeps all of these features (and adds a few more, which you'll learn about in Chapter 6). At last, Visual Basic includes all the hallmarks of a true object-oriented language.

In this chapter, you'll see some of the following changes:

The `Class` keyword

In Visual Basic 6, each class required a separate file. Now you can group your classes any way you want, as long as you place all classes inside declarations (for example, start with `Public Class MyClassName` and end with `End Class`).

The `Is` keyword

In VB 2005, you test whether two objects are the same by using the `Is` keyword (for example, `If objOne Is objTwo Then`), not the equal sign.

Constructors

You can now use constructors to preload information into an object in a single line. Initializing objects can't get any easier.

Garbage collection

Garbage collection replaces deterministic finalization. When you set an object to `Nothing`, it doesn't disappear until the next time the garbage collector runs, which means that you can't use an event handler to do the cleanup.

Enumerations

Need to use constants, but tired of using hard-coded numbers and strings? Enumerations give you the ability to define groups of related values and give each value a descriptive name, which makes for cleaner coding.

Shared members

The Shared keyword allows you to create properties, variables, and methods that are always available, even when no instance object exists. Visual Basic 6 allowed you to create modules that were entirely made up of shared methods, but it didn't provide anything close to the features and fine-grained control afforded by the Shared keyword.

Introducing OOP

Visual Basic is often accused of being a loosely structured language, and many VB developers lapse into an event-driven style of programming that scatters code fragments everywhere. If you want to write a program that has any chance of being extensible, reliable, and even fun to program, it's up to you to adopt a more systematic programming methodology—and none is nearly as powerful, or as natural to the way Windows works, as object-oriented programming.

It's hard to imagine anything in the past ten years that has so completely caught the imagination of developers as object-oriented programming. What started off as an obscure philosophy for "language nerds" has grown into a whole assortment of nifty, easy-to-use techniques that can transform a complex, bloated application into a happy collection of intercommunicating objects. Quite simply, object-oriented programming makes it easier to debug, enhance, and reuse parts of an application. What's more, object-oriented principles are the basis of core pieces of the Windows operating system—first with COM, and now with the .NET Framework.

What Is Object-Oriented Programming?

One of the more intimidating aspects of object-oriented programming is the way its advocates tout it as a philosophy (or even a religion). To keep things straight, it's best to remind yourself that object-oriented programming really boils down to the best way to organize code. If you follow good object-oriented practices, you'll end up with a program that's easier to manage, enhance, and troubleshoot. But all these benefits are really the result of good organization.

The Problems with Traditional Structured Programming

Traditional structured programming divides a problem into two kinds of things: data and ways to process data. The problem with structured programming is that unless you've put a lot of forethought into your application design, you'll quickly end up with a program that has its functionality scattered in many different places.

Consider a simple database program for sales tracking that includes a basic search feature. Quite probably, at some point, you'll need to add the ability to search using slightly different criteria than you originally defined. If you're lucky, you've built your search routine out of a few general functions. Maybe you're really lucky, and your changes are limited to one function. Hopefully, you can make your changes without reworking the structure of your existing code.

Now consider a more drastic upgrade. Maybe you need to add a logging feature that works whenever you access the database, or perhaps your organization has expanded from Access to SQL Server and you now have to connect to an entirely new and unfamiliar type of database. Maybe you need to have your program provide different levels of access, to change the user interface radically, or to create a dozen different search variants that are largely similar but slightly different. As you start to add these enhancements, you'll find yourself making changes that range over your entire program. If you've been extremely disciplined in the first place, the job will be easier. By the end of the day, however, you'll probably end up with a collection of loosely related functions, blocks of code that are tightly linked to specific controls in specific windows, and pieces of database code scattered everywhere.

In other words, the more changes you make in a traditionally structured program, the more it tends toward chaos. When bugs start to appear, you'll probably have no idea which part of the code they live in. And guess what happens when another programmer starts work on a similar program for inventory management? Don't even dream of trying to share your code. You both know that it will be more difficult to translate a routine into a usable form for another program than it will be to rewrite the code from scratch.

In Chapter 6 you'll see some examples that explain how object-oriented programming overcomes these disasters. But for now, it will help if you get a handle on how you can create an object in Visual Basic 2005.

First There Were Structures . . .

The precursor to classes was a programming time-saver called *structures*. A structure is a way of grouping data together, so that several variables become part of one conceptual whole.

NOTE *In earlier versions of Visual Basic, structures were called types. As you learned in Chapter 3, the word type has a completely different meaning in .NET—it encompasses all the different ingredients you'll find in the class library. This is a potential point of confusion for classic VB developers migrating to .NET.*

For example, suppose you need to store several pieces of information about a person. You could create separate variables in your code to represent the person's birth date, height, name, and taste in music. If you leave these variables separate, you've got a potential problem. Your code becomes more complicated, and it's not obvious that these separate variables have anything to do with each other. And if you have to work with information for more than one person at a time, you have to create a frightening pile of variables to keep track of all the information. It's likely that you'll soon make the mistake of changing the wrong person's age, forgetting to give someone a birth date, or misplacing their favorite CD collection. Here's where structures come into the picture.

A Very Simple Person Structure

To group this information together, you can create the following structure:

```
Public Structure Person
    Dim FirstName As String
    Dim LastName As String
    Dim BirthDate As Date
End Structure
```

Where can you place this code? In VB 2005 you can put public structures anywhere at the file or module level. The only limitation is that they can't be inside a function or a subroutine. If you define a private structure, you can put it inside the class or module where you want to use it.

Now you can use this structure to create a Person object in some other place in your code, and you can set that Person's information like so:

```
Dim Lucy As Person
Lucy.FirstName = "Lucy"
Lucy.LastName = "Smith"
Lucy.BirthDate = DateTime.Now
```

In this case, we set the birthday to the current time to indicate that Lucy has just been brought to life.

The preceding code is easy to read. When you change a variable, you know which person it relates to. If you want to create more than one Person object, it's easy, and there will be a lot less code. Best of all, you can pass an entire Person through just one parameter to a function or subroutine that uses it, as follows:

```
Public Sub GoShopping(ByVal Shopper As Person)
    ' Some code here to manage the mall process.
End Sub
```

NOTE   *The word* object *is often used in a fairly loose fashion to mean all sorts of things. But technically speaking, an object is a live instance of a structure or a class that's floating around in memory. In other words, you use a structure to define a person at design time, and you use that structure to create as many* Person *objects as you need at runtime, each of which stores its own personal data.*

Structures are really "super variables." You're probably familiar with this concept if you've worked with databases, even if you've never actually created a structure or a class. In a database, each person is represented by a *record* (also known as a *row*), and each record has the same series of *fields* to describe it.

Basically, there is one important similarity between structures and classes: Both are defined only once, but can be created as many times as you want, just about anywhere in your code. This means you only need to define one Person structure, but you can build families, convention centers, and bowling clubs without introducing any new code.

Making a Structure That Has Brains

What about a structure with built-in intelligence? For example, what if we could make a Person structure that wouldn't let you set a birth date that was earlier than 1800, could output a basic line of conversation, and would notify you when its birthday arrives?

This is what you get with a *class*: a structure that can include data and code. (Actually, Visual Basic 2005 structures can contain code, though there are subtle differences between structures and classes, which we'll explore a little later in this chapter. In practice, classes are usually the way to go because structures have subtle limitations. Most programmers see structures simply as examples of backward compatibility—like little pieces of living history accessible from the modern Visual Basic programming language.)

Consider our Person as a full-fledged class:

```
Public Class Person

    ' Data for the Person
    Public FirstName As String
    Public LastName As String
    Public BirthDate As Date

    ' Built-in feature to get the Person object to introduce itself.
    Public Function GetIntroduction() As String
        Dim Intro As String
        Intro = "My name is " & FirstName & " " & LastName & ". "
        Intro &= "I was born on " & BirthDate.ToString()
        Return Intro
    End Function

End Class
```

Notice that this Person class looks similar to the Person structure you saw earlier. It has the same three variables, except that now you must be careful to mark them with the Public keyword. (By default, variables inside a class are private, which means that only the code inside the class can see or change them. In this case, this behavior isn't what you want, because it would prevent your code from changing or retrieving this information.) The Person class also adds a *method* (here, a function) called GetIntroduction(), which is placed right in the class. This means that every Person object is going to have a built-in feature for introducing itself.

To create a file quickly for a new class in Visual Studio, load up a project and choose Project ▸ Add Class from the menu.

Similarly, if you were to make a class modeling a microwave oven, you might have data such as the microwave's manufacturer and the current power level, along with a CookFood() method. Now you can see how classes help organize code. Methods that are specific to a particular class are embedded right in the class.

Instantiating an Object

Returning to our Person class, you'll find that it's quite easy to use it to create a live object (a process called *instantiation*):

```
Dim Lucy As New Person()
Lucy.FirstName = "Lucy"
Lucy.LastName = "Smith"
Lucy.BirthDate = DateTime.Now
MessageBox.Show(Lucy.GetIntroduction(), "Introduction")
```

This code produces the output shown in Figure 5-1.

Figure 5-1: An introductory class

NOTE *To see this code in action and create a Lucy object, you can use the ObjectTester project included with the samples for this chapter.*

Notice that to create an object based on a class, you use a Dim statement with the New keyword. The New keyword is required to actually create the object. Alternatively, you could use the following code:

```
Dim Lucy As Person    ' Define the Lucy object variable.
Lucy = New Person()   ' Create the Lucy object.
```

This code is almost exactly the same. The only difference is that it gives you the ability to separate the two lines. This approach could be useful if you want to define the Lucy *variable* in one spot and then create the Lucy *object* in another spot, such as a separate method. Notice that there is no Set statement used. (The Set statement was a hallmark of objects in Visual Basic 6.)

TIP *In classic Visual Basic, using the* New *keyword in a* Dim *statement could get you into trouble by defining a dynamically creatable object that could spring to life at any moment and just wouldn't stay dead. Now the syntax* Dim VarName As New ClassName *defines a variable and instructs Visual Basic to instantiate the object immediately, just as you would expect.*

To release an object, set it equal to Nothing, as shown here:

```
Lucy = Nothing
```

This tells Visual Basic that the object is no longer needed. Strictly speaking, you won't often need to use this statement, because the variable will be automatically cleared as soon as it goes out of scope. For example, if you define a variable in a subroutine, the variable will be set to nothing as soon as the subroutine ends. If you want to clear an object variable before this, use the Nothing keyword.

Objects Behind the Scenes

When you create an object based on a class, you'll find that it behaves differently from other variables. This unusual behavior was introduced in connection with arrays in Chapter 3, although it is significant enough to examine in more detail here. The issue is that classes are *reference types*, which means that, behind the scenes, .NET tracks them using a reference that points to some location in memory. All reference types exhibit some quirky behavior when you copy or compare instances.

Copying Objects

Consider the following code:

```
' Create two people objects.
Dim Lucy As New Person()
Dim John As New Person()

' Enter information in the Lucy object.
Lucy.FirstName = "Lucy"

' Copy the reference, not the value. The original John object is abandoned.
John = Lucy
```

The last line is the most significant. If you were expecting objects to behave like variables of the Integer or String data type, you might expect that this line copies Lucy's information into John. Instead, the existing John object is abandoned, and the reference to it in the John variable is replaced by a reference to the Lucy object. At the end of the last line, there is really only one object (Lucy) remaining, with two different variables that you can use to access it.

Let's continue with the following code:

```
John.FirstName = "John"
' Now Lucy.FirstName is also John!
```

This is an example of *reference equality*. In most cases it is more useful than value equality for working with objects. It's definitely faster, because all .NET needs to do is copy a memory pointer from one variable to another (rather than copy the entire block of memory that represents the object, which could be quite large).

NOTE   *This is the key difference between VB 2005 structures and classes: Structures are value types, while classes are reference types. As with all value types, assignment and comparison operations work on the contents of the object, not the memory reference. This can make large structures much slower and less efficient to work with than classes.*

Many classes support *cloning*, which allows you to copy the contents of an object when needed by calling a `Clone()` method. The familiar `Array` class is an example. To create an object that supports cloning, you need to go to a little extra work and implement a special interface. The next chapter explains interfaces and demonstrates this technique.

Comparing Objects

Reference types also have their own rules for comparison. Notably, you can't use the equal sign (=). This is to eliminate confusion regarding the true meaning of an "equals" comparison. With two variables, a comparison determines whether the values of both variables are the same. With two objects, a comparison doesn't determine whether the contents are the same, but rather whether both object *references* are pointing to the same object. In other words, if `objOne Is objTwo`, there really is only one object, which you can access with two different variable names. If `intOne = intTwo`, however, it means that two separate variables are storing identical information.

Here's an example that demonstrates this oddity:

```
If Lucy Is John Then
    ' Contrary to what you might expect, the Lucy and John
    ' variables are pointing to the same object.
End If

' The following won't work, because you can't compare object contents
directly.
' If Lucy = John Then
    ' This comparison can't be made automatically.
    ' Instead, the object would need to provide a method that
    ' compares every property (or just the important
    ' ones that are necessary to define equality).
End If
```

The difference between reference equality and value equality takes a little getting used to. Sometimes it helps to understand why the creators of VB (and most other modern languages, such as Java and C#) choose to implement this sort of behavior. The reality is that objects are often large blobs of memory with plenty of information and functionality packed in. Although it's possible for an environment like the Common Language Runtime to provide a standard way to compare two blobs of memory to see whether they contain the same data, it would be unacceptably slow. Simple value types tend to be much smaller scraps of information that are readily available and can be compared with lightning speed.

There's also the issue of *identity*, which reference types have and value types don't. Essentially, if two value types have the same data, they are the same. However, if two reference types have the same data, they are equivalent but separate. In other words, it's possible to have two identical but separate Person objects. (Maybe it's just a freakish coincidence.)

The Null Value Error

The most common error you will receive while working with reference types is the common NullReferenceException, which warns you that "Value null was found where an instance of an object was required." What this means is that you've tried to work with an object that you have defined but have not instantiated. Typically, this is caused when you forget to use the New keyword. Here's the mistake in action:

```
Dim Lucy As Person      ' No New keyword is used; this is a definition only.
Lucy.FirstName = "Lucy" ' Won't work because Lucy doesn't exist yet!
```

It's a small mistake that you will soon learn to avoid, but being able to recognize it ensures that it will never frustrate you for long.

Classes in Pieces

As you've already learned, Visual Basic 2005 is flexible enough to let you define as many classes as you want in the same file. This feature has been around since .NET 1.0 first hit the scene. However, VB 2005 adds a new wrinkle. Now, not only can you place multiple classes in one file; you can also *split* a single class across different files. (This might be worthwhile if you're working with extremely large classes.)

In order to pull off this trick, you need to add the Partial keyword to your class declaration. Otherwise, the VB compiler assumes you've made a mistake. For example, you could split the Person class into two pieces in several ways. First, put this part of the declaration in a file named Person1.vb:

```
Partial Public Class Person
    Public FirstName As String
    Public LastName As String
    Public BirthDate As Date
End Class
```

Then put this part into a file named Person2.vb:

```
Partial Public Class Person
    Public Function GetIntroduction() As String
        Dim Intro As String
        Intro = "My name is " & FirstName & " " & LastName & ". "
        Intro &= "I was born on " & BirthDate.ToString()
        Return Intro
    End Function
End Class
```

This doesn't change how your program works one bit. When you compile your application, these two pieces are fused together into one class, exactly as though you had coded them in the same file.

NOTE   *Technically, you only need to add the* Partial *keyword to one of the class declarations. In other words, if you split a class into ten pieces, you need to use* Partial *on at least one of those pieces. However, it's good style to use it on every declaration, so you don't forget that you only have a piece of the picture when you're editing one of the files.*

You probably won't use partial classes too often. Although they can help you break down large classes into more manageable bits, the presence of large classes in the first place probably indicates that you need a better design (one that splits your code into smaller classes). However, Visual Studio uses partial classes to hide details that you don't need to see, like the automatically generated form code that you saw in Chapter 4. The idea is that the class is split into two pieces—the one you fill with your application code and the other that has the low-level plumbing you can safely ignore.

Enhancing a Class with Properties

A class provides another important ingredient, called *properties*. Right now, the Person class uses three variables, and all of these variables are exposed to the outside world. This exposure makes life convenient but dangerous. Suppose a microwave oven did not have a control panel; instead, the user was supposed to control it directly through the circuitry in the back. In such a situation, numerous problems could occur, ranging from unsatisfactory results (for example, burning dinner by forgetting to turn the power off at the right time) to safety hazards (for example, burning people by running the microwave with the door open).

In order to make sure that a class does only the legitimate things it is intended to do, its developer has to make it a well-encapsulated black box, hiding as much of the internal details as possible and providing it with a control panel. This means that every class should perform its own basic error checking. It also means that a class should use only private variables, which are hidden from the outside world. To let the calling code change a private variable in a class in a controlled manner, you use properties.

Properties are really special procedures that allow a private variable to be changed or retrieved in a more controlled way. For example, to use a property instead of a public variable for a Person's first name, you can remove the FirstName variable and add this code instead:

```
Private _FirstName As String

Public Property FirstName() As String
    Get
        Return _FirstName
    End Get

    Set(ByVal Value As String)
        _FirstName = Value
    End Set
End Property
```

The code breaks the public FirstName variable into two parts: a private _FirstName variable that stores the actual information behind the scenes, and a public FirstName property that the class user sees. The internal _FirstName variable uses an underscore in its name to distinguish its name from the property name. This is a common technique, but is definitely not your only possible choice. (Some developers prefer to add a prefix; for example, m_ to indicate "member variable.")

The code for setting and retrieving FirstName is still exactly the same. In fact, the property procedure hasn't introduced any new code, so we haven't gained anything. You can also use the same approach to change the LastName variable to a property. But let's look at what we can do with the BirthDate variable:

```
Private _BirthDate as Date

Public Property BirthDate() As Date
    Get
        Return _BirthDate
    End Get

    Set(ByVal Value As Date)
        If BirthDate > Now Then
            MessageBox.Show("You can't create an unborn person")
        Else
            _BirthDate = Value
        End If
    End Set
End Property
```

Now, if you attempt to set a birthdate that occurs in the future, the property procedure will refuse to comply and will scold you with a message box. Be aware that for a class to display message boxes in response to invalid input is bad design. A Person class has nothing to do with your program's user interface; it should limit its functions to setting and retrieving data about persons. To handle invalid input correctly, you should throw an *exception*, which would be received by the code setting the property and would be interpreted as an error. The code where the class properties are being set could then decide how to handle the problem. (Throwing and catching of exceptions are discussed in Chapter 8.)

You may have also noticed that the limitations imposed by this code don't necessarily make a lot of sense. For example, assigning the Person a birth date in the future might make a lot of sense for performing certain types of calculations. The restrictions in the preceding code example are really just designed to give you an idea of how a class can review data and refuse to accept information that is not appropriate.

Properties also provide another layer of abstraction. For example, when you set a microwave to defrost, several different internal properties are set, including settings for a maximum and a minimum power level, and a frequency between which the two are alternated. These details are hidden from the user. If the user had to set all this information directly, not only would a typical microwave operation take a lot more effort, but different microwave models would require different steps to operate.

Read-Only Properties

Sometimes you might want a property to be visible but not directly changeable. For example, in our microwave analogy, there could be a LastServiceDate property that indicates when the microwave was most recently repaired or examined. You wouldn't want the microwave user to change this date, although the microwave class itself might update it in response to its ServiceMicrowave() method.

To make a property read-only, you leave out the Set procedure and add the keyword ReadOnly to the definition. In the case of the Person object, you might want to make the BirthDate property read-only, because this value can't be changed at will:

```
Public ReadOnly Property BirthDate() As Date
    Get
        Return _BirthDate
    End Get
End Property
```

You can also use the WriteOnly keyword to include a property with only a Set procedure and no Get procedure. This rarely makes sense, however, and is not usually what an ordinary programmer expects from an object. Typically, it's a trick that's used only in unusual scenarios, such as if you're creating a password property that can be set at will but (for security reasons) can't be retrieved.

The preceding code example raises an interesting question. The program has been restricted so that the value of BirthDate can't be changed, which is a reasonable restriction. However, it also prevents you from assigning a BirthDate value in the first place. In order to solve this problem, you need a way to load basic information when the Person object is first created, and *then* prevent any future changes to those values (such as `BirthDate`) that can't ordinarily be modified. The way to accomplish this is to use a `ReadOnly` property procedure, as shown in the preceding example, in combination with a custom *constructor*.

Enhancing a Class with a Constructor

In Chapter 3 you learned that with initializers you can preload variables with information using the same line that you use to create them. Initializers allow you to convert this:

```
Dim MyValue As Integer
MyValue = 10
```

into this:

```
Dim MyValue As Integer = 10
```

Constructors work the same kind of magic with classes that initializers do with variables. The difference is that classes, being much more complex than simple variables, can require significantly more advanced initialization. For example, you will typically have to set several properties, and in the case of a business object, you might want to open a database connection or read values from a file. Constructors allow you to do all this and more.

A constructor is a special subroutine that is invoked automatically in your class. This subroutine *must* have the name `New`—that's how Visual Basic 2005 identifies it as a constructor.

Consider the following `Person` class:

```
Public Class Person
    ' (Variable definitions omitted.)
    ' (Property procedures omitted.)

    Public Sub New()
        _BirthDate = DateTime.Now
    End Sub

End Class
```

Notice that we've included a constructor that assigns a value for the internal `_BirthDate` variable. Now, every time you create a `Person` object, a default birth date will be automatically assigned. This technique can allow for some shortcuts in your code if you frequently rely on certain default values.

Constructors That Accept Parameters

The previous example only scratches the surface of what a well-written constructor can do for you. For one thing, constructors can require parameters. This allows for a much more flexible approach, as shown here:

```
Public Class Person
    ' (Variable definitions omitted.)
    ' (Property procedures omitted.)

    Public Sub New(ByVal FirstName As String, ByVal LastName As String, _
    ByVal BirthDate As Date)
        _FirstName = FirstName
        _LastName = LastName
        _BirthDate = BirthDate
    End Sub

End Class
```

NOTE *You might notice that the parameter names in the previous example conflict with the property names of the class. However, the parameter names have precedence, so the code will work the way it is written. To refer directly to one of the properties with the same name in the* New *subroutine, you would need to use the* Me *keyword (as in* Me.FirstName*).*

The constructor in this example allows you to preload information into a Person object in one line. Best of all, it's done in a completely generic way that lets you specify each required piece of information.

```
Dim Lucy As New Person("Lucy", "Smith", DateTime.Now)

' This can also be written with the following equivalent syntax:
' Dim Lucy As Person = New Person("Lucy", "Smith", DateTime.Now)
```

Bear in mind that it makes no difference in what order you place your methods, properties, variables, and constructors within a class. To make it easy to read your code, however, you should standardize on a set order. One possible standard is to include all your private variables first, followed by property procedures, then constructors, and then other methods. Visual Basic 2005 gives you as much freedom to arrange the internal details of a class as it gives you to arrange different classes and modules in a file.

To try out the Person class and see how a simple client interacts with it, you can use the ObjectTester project included with the sample code for this chapter (see Figure 5-2).

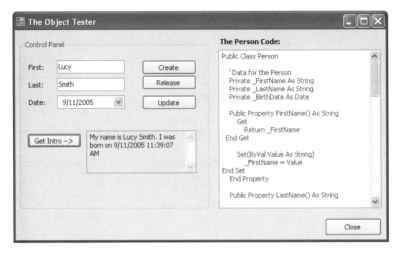

Figure 5-2: Testing the Person object

Multiple Constructors

Another exciting feature of VB 2005 is the ability to define multiple constructors for a class. Once you've done this, then when you create an instance of that class, you can decide which constructor you want to use. Each constructor must have its own distinct parameter list. (In other words, multiple constructors can't share the same signature.)

How does it work? Conceptually, it's the same process as for overloading procedures, which was demonstrated in Chapter 3. The only difference is that you don't use the Overloads keyword.

Here's a Person class with more than one constructor:

```
Public Class Person
    ' (Variable definitions omitted.)
    ' (Property procedures omitted.)

    Public Sub New(ByVal FirstName As String, ByVal LastName As String, _
    ByVal BirthDate As Date)
        _FirstName = FirstName
        _LastName = LastName
        _BirthDate = BirthDate
    End Sub

    Public Sub New(ByVal FirstName As String, ByVal LastName As String)
        _FirstName = FirstName
        _LastName = LastName
        _BirthDate = DateTime.Now
    End Sub

    Public Sub New(ByVal FirstName As String, ByVal LastName As String, _
    ByVal Age As Integer)
```

```
        _FirstName = FirstName
        _LastName = LastName
        _BirthDate = DateTime.Now.AddYears(-Age)
    End Sub
End Class
```

These overloaded constructors allow you to create a `Person` by specifying all three pieces of information or by specifying only the name, in which case a default date will be used. You can also use a variant of the constructor that calculates the `BirthDate` using a supplied `Age` parameter.

The technique of multiple constructors is used extensively in the .NET class library. Many classes have a range of different constructors that allow you to set various options or load information from different data sources. Overloaded constructors are also much more flexible than optional parameters, which are never used in the .NET class library.

When you create an object that has more than one constructor, Visual Studio shows you the parameter list for the first constructor in a special IntelliSense tooltip (see Figure 5-3). This tooltip also includes a special arrow icon that you can click to move from constructor to constructor (you can also use the up and down arrow keys).

Multiple constructors are a way of life in .NET. The concept is fairly straightforward, but as you learn about the .NET class library, you'll realize that creating classes with the perfect set of constructors is as much an art as a skill.

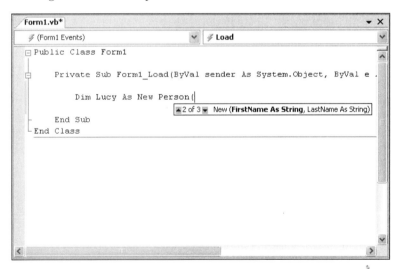

Figure 5-3: Visual Studio.NET's IntelliSense tooltip for a constructor

TIP   *You can create multiple versions of any method in a class. You just need to use the* Overloads *keyword, along with the techniques that were introduced in Chapter 3. Overloading methods is another trick that makes a frequent appearance in the .NET class library and provides your objects with increased flexibility.*

The Default Constructor

One other detail about constructors is worth noting. If you don't create a constructor, your class has one. In the case of a class without a specified constructor in code, your object will use a default constructor that doesn't require any arguments and doesn't do anything special.

However, as soon as you add a custom constructor to your class, Visual Basic 2005 will stop generating the default constructor for you. This means that if you add a constructor that requires parameters, that becomes your only constructor. When you create an object based on that class, you will then be forced to use that constructor and provide the required parameters. This restriction can come in very handy, ensuring that you create your objects successfully with valid data.

If you want to be able to create objects without any special parameters, just include the default constructor manually in your class. The default constructor looks like this:

```
Public Sub New()
    ' Initialize variables here if required.
End Sub
```

Destructors

With all this talk about constructors, it might have occurred to you that it would be useful to have a complementary *destructor* method that is automatically invoked when your object is destroyed. A destructor method might allow a lazy programmer to create a class that automatically saves itself just before it is deallocated, or—more usefully—one that cleans up after itself, closing database connections or open files. However, Visual Basic 2005 has no direct support for destructors. That's because .NET uses garbage collection, which is not well suited to destructors. Quite simply, garbage collection means that you can't be sure when your object will really be cleared.

Garbage Collection

It's worth a quick digression to explain garbage collection. Garbage collection is a service used for all languages in the .NET Framework, and it's radically different from the way things used to work in Visual Basic 6.

Object Death in Visual Basic 6

Visual Basic 6 uses a technique called *reference counting* to manage object lifetime. Behind the scenes, it keeps track of how many variables are pointing at an object. (As you've already seen in this chapter, more than one object variable can refer to the same object.) When the last object variable is set to Nothing, the number of references pointing to an object drops to zero, and the object will be swiftly removed from memory. At the same time, the

`Class.Terminate` event occurs, giving your code a chance to perform any related cleanup. This process is called *deterministic finalization* because you always know when an object will be removed.

As with many characteristics of Visual Basic 6, this system had some problems. For example, if two objects refer to each other, they could never be removed, even though they might be floating in memory, totally detached from the rest of your program. This problem is called a *circular reference*.

Object Death in Visual Basic 2005

In .NET, objects always remain in memory until the garbage collector finds them. The *garbage collector* is a .NET runtime service that works automatically, tracking down classes that aren't referenced anymore. If the garbage collector finds two or more objects that refer to one another (a circular reference), and it recognizes that the rest of the program doesn't use either of them, it will remove them from memory.

This system differs from Visual Basic 6. For example, imagine a `Person` object that has a `Relative` property that can point to another `Person` object. A very simple program might hold a couple of variables that point to `Person` objects, and these `Person` objects may or may not point to still more `Person` objects through their `Relative` property. All these objects are referenced, so they will be safely preserved.

On the other hand, consider a `Person` object that you use temporarily, and then release—let's call this object `PersonA`. The twist is that the `PersonA` object itself points to another object (`PersonB`), which points back to `PersonA`. In Visual Basic 6, this circular reference would force the abandoned `Person` objects to remain floating in memory, because neither one has been fully released. With VB 2005 garbage collection, the garbage collector will notice that these objects are cut off from the rest of your program, and it will free the memory.

For example, Figure 5-4 shows the in-memory objects in a sample application. When the garbage collector checks this application, it will start at the application root and discover that three `Person` objects are still in use. However, there are two `Person` objects that aren't in play, so they'll be removed.

A side effect of garbage collection is *nondeterministic finalization*. In other words, in Visual Basic 2005, you *don't* know exactly when an object will be removed. This is because the garbage collection service, handy as is, does not run continuously. Instead, it waits for your computer to be idle, or for memory to become scarce, before it begins scanning. This often allows your program to have better all-around performance. However, it also means that any code that responds to a `Finalize` event (the VB 2005 equivalent of `Class.Terminate`) may not be executed for quite some time. This can be a problem. If you are relying on using the `Finalize` event to release a limited resource, such as a network database connection, the resource remains active for a longer time, thus increasing the resource cost of your application—and potentially slowing life down dramatically.

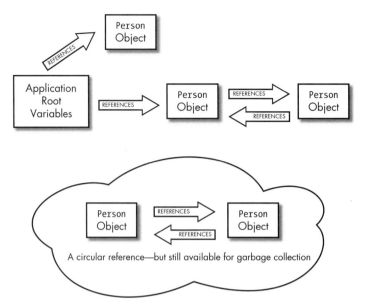

Figure 5-4: Garbage collection and .NET objects

Object Cleanup

You can manually trigger the garbage collection process by using the following code:

```
System.GC.Collect()
```

However, this technique is strongly discouraged. For one thing, it will cause an immediate performance slowdown as .NET scans the entire allocated memory in your application. A much better approach is to create your own "destructor" type of method for classes that use limited resources. This method will have to be called manually by your code. By convention, this method should be named `Dispose()`.

Generally, most classes won't need a `Dispose()` method. However, a few classes might—for example, any object that holds on to a database connection or a file handle needs to ensure that it releases its resources as quickly as possible. In the next chapter, you'll see how to use the `IDisposable` interface to implement a `Dispose()` method in a class in the most standardized way possible.

Before adding a `Dispose()` method, ask yourself whether it is really required. A class that reads information from a database should probably open and close the database connection within the bounds of a single method. That ensures that no matter how you use the class, there's no possibility of accidentally holding a database connection open for too long. Careful programming design can prevent limited resources from being wasted.

Enhancing a Class with Events

Events are notifications that an object sends to other objects. These notifications are often ignored. (Consider, for example, the many different events that are fired from a typical form.) However, the client can choose to pay attention to important events and write an event handler to respond to them.

You can define an event with the Event keyword. An example is shown below in the Person class:

```
Public Class Person
    ' (Other class code omitted.)
    Public Event DataChanged()
End Class
```

Once you have defined an event, you can fire it at a later time from inside any code in your Person class. For example, you can use the DataChanged event in any part of your Person class to notify the rest of your code that a piece of information has changed.

The following code demonstrates how you could modify the FirstName property procedure to fire the DataChanged event:

```
Public Property FirstName() As String
    Get
        Return _FirstName
    End Get
    Set(ByVal Value As String)
        _FirstName = Value
        RaiseEvent DataChanged()
    End Set
End Property
```

An Event in Action

These are the ingredients: an event definition and a RaiseEvent command to fire the event when needed. So how do you link it all together? Events used in classes work the same way as the control events that you are already familiar with. As with control events, you can create an object using the WithEvents keyword and then attach event handlers to its events using the Handles keyword for a subroutine. You can also hook up event handlers dynamically using the AddHandler command, as you saw in Chapter 4.

Our example uses a simple program that creates a Person object and displays the object's information in a window. The fields that show this information are read-only and can't be modified. However, the user can change the first name through another avenue: an additional text box and an update button in a group box with the caption Apply For a Name Change, as shown in Figure 5-5. (This example is also included with the sample code for this chapter, in the EventTester project.)

Figure 5-5: The event tester

The form class looks like this:

```
Public Class EventTester

    ' Create the Person as a form-level variable.
    Private WithEvents CurrentPerson As New Person("Lucy", "Smith", _
      DateTime.Now)

    ' This event handler updates the window when the form is loaded.
    Private Sub frmClassTester_Load(ByVal sender As System.Object, _
     ByVal e As System.EventArgs) Handles MyBase.Load
        RefreshData()
    End Sub

    ' This event handler allows the user to update the class.
    Private Sub cmdUpdate_Click(ByVal sender As System.Object, _
      ByVal e As System.EventArgs) Handles cmdUpdate.Click
        CurrentPerson.FirstName = txtNewFirst.Text
    End Sub

    ' This procedure must be called manually.
    Private Sub RefreshData()
        txtFirstName.Text = CurrentPerson.FirstName
        txtLastName.Text = CurrentPerson.LastName
        dtBirth.Value = CurrentPerson.BirthDate
    End Sub

End Class
```

Here's a quick summary:

- A Person object is created as a form-level variable named CurrentPerson when the form is created. This variable is declared WithEvents, which means that its events are automatically available.

- An event handler for the form's Load event calls the RefreshData() sub-routine when the form is first loaded.

- The RefreshData() subroutine updates the on-screen controls with the information from the CurrentPerson object.

We are now just a step away from putting the DataChanged event to good use, so that our EventTester form can get immediate notification when a name change occurs.

First, we can modify the RefreshData() method so that it is invoked automatically in response to our DataChanged event:

```
Private Sub RefreshData() Handles CurrentPerson.DataChanged
```

Now, when you click the cmdUpdate button, the CurrentPerson object is modified, the event is fired, and the data is refreshed automatically.

Clearly, the preceding example doesn't *need* an event. You could accomplish the same thing by calling the RefreshData() procedure manually after you make your changes. To make life a little more confusing, there's no single rule to determine when you should use events and when you should do the work by explicitly calling methods in your client code. In fact, a lot of thought needs to go into the process of modeling your program as a collection of happily interacting objects. There are many different design patterns for communication, and they are the focus of frequent debate and discussion. A good way to get started is to start thinking of your objects as physical, tangible items. In the case of events, ask the question, "Which object has the responsibility of reporting the change?"

Events are very flexible because they allow multiple recipients. For example, you could add a Handles clause for the CurrentPerson.DataChanged event to several different subroutines. These methods will be triggered one after another, although the order can vary. Events can also be fired across projects and even from event definition code in one language to event handler code in another.

Events with Different Signatures

You can also create an event that supplies information through additional parameters. Remember, the recommended format for a .NET event is a parameter for the sender, combined with a parameter for the additional information. The additional information is provided through a class that derives from System.EventArgs. For example, our DataChanged event might require a special object that looks like this:

```
Public Class PersonDataChangedEventArgs
  Inherits EventArgs

    Private _ChangedProperty As String
    Public Property ChangedProperty As String
        Get
            Return _ChangedProperty
```

```
      End Get
      Set(ByVal Value As String)
         _ChangedProperty = Value
      End Set
   End Property

End Class
```

With this example, we're getting slightly ahead of ourselves. It introduces the concept of inheritance, which Chapter 6 delves into in more detail. The important concept here is that PersonDataChangedEventArgs is a special class used to pass information to our DataChanged event handler. It is based on the standard EventArgs class, but it adds a new property that can hold additional information.

The event definition will now need to be adjusted to accept an argument of the new class. It makes sense to use the typical two-parameter format that's found in all .NET events:

```
Public Event DataChanged(ByVal sender As Object, _
  ByVal e As PersonDataChangedEventArgs)
```

NOTE   *The standard names—sender and e—are used for the parameters.*

The event can be raised like this:

```
' This code would appear in the FirstName property Set procedure.
Dim e As New PersonDataChangedEventArgs
e.ChangedProperty = "FirstName"
RaiseEvent DataChanged(Me, e)
```

This system introduces a few problems. First, the RefreshData() method can no longer receive the event, because it has the wrong signature. We must rectify this before we can use RefreshData(). Second, the process of creating the PersonDataChangedEventArgs object and filling it with information adds a few more lines to our code. In short, we may have added more functionality than is required and needlessly complicated our code.

In a sophisticated scenario, however, multiple parameters can be invaluable. For example, as soon as you create an event handler that can receive events from several different objects, you'll need to make sure it can distinguish which object is sending it the notification and take the appropriate action. In this case, the end result will be shorter and clearer code. The preceding example might be useful if the refresh operation required is particularly time-consuming. Depending on which information has changed, the event handler might refresh only part of the display:

```
Private Sub RefreshData(ByVal sender As System.Object, _
  ByVal e As PersonDataChangedEventArgs) Handles CurrentPerson.DataChanged
```

```
    Select Case e.ChangedProperty
        Case "FirstName"
            txtFirstName.Text = CurrentPerson.FirstName
        Case "LastName"
            txtLastName.Text = CurrentPerson.LastName
        Case "BirthDate"
            dtpBirth.Value = CurrentPerson.BirthDate
    End Select

End Sub
```

This type of design could bring about a significant improvement in performance. Of course, the approach of including the property values as strings isn't very efficient, because it leaves the door wide open to logic errors caused by mistyped variable names. A better way of passing information to a method is to use enumerations, which make their appearance in the next section.

Enumerations

The previous example uses a DataChanged event that fires every time a change was made. The DataChanged event provides extra information, namely the name of the variable that has changed. However, to keep the example as simple as possible, we made a decision that might have had unfortunate consequences in a real application: We used a string to identify the variable name. This makes it all too easy to cause an error by using the wrong capitalization or misspelling a word. Even worse, an error like this has no chance of being caught by the compiler. Instead, it will probably become a hard-to-detect logic error, propagating deep within your application and causing all sorts of mysterious problems.

The problem exposed by the Person.DataChanged event is not at all unusual. A similar error can occur if you are creating any method that can perform one of a set number of different tasks. For example, consider a Person object with a more advanced GetIntroduction() method that allows you to specify the type of environment:

```
Public Function GetIntroduction(EnvironmentType As String) As String
    Dim Intro As String
    If EnvironmentType = "Business"
        ' Set Intro accordingly.
    ElseIf EnvironmentType = "Home"
        ' Set Intro accordingly.
    ElseIf EnvironmentType = "Formal Occasion"
        ' Set Intro accordingly.
    End If
    Return Intro
End Function
```

In this example, the GetIntroduction() method uses a string value that is supposed to be set equal to a specific predetermined value to designate the type of introduction required. The same type of logic could be used with an integer variable that stores a predetermined number. However, there are several drawbacks to this approach:

- A mistake is easy to make, because no checking is performed to make sure that the parameter has a supported value (unless you add such logic yourself).

- The client code has no idea what logic your method uses. If you use an integer, it may be easier to code accurately but harder to guess what each value really represents to your method.

- The code is difficult to read and understand. It may make sense when you write it, but it might become much less obvious a few months later.

- The approach is not standardized. A hundred different programmers may solve similar problems a hundred different ways, with hundreds of different predetermined values; as a result, integration and code sharing can become very difficult.

A somewhat better approach is to define fixed constants. Then you can pass the appropriate constant to the method. This approach prevents casual mistakes from being made, because the compiler will catch your mistake if you type the constant name incorrectly. However, it doesn't really solve the consistency problem. It also introduces a new problem: Where should the constants be stored? If a program is not carefully designed, the constants can be lost in a separate file, or the names of constants used in one method might even conflict with those used for different methods! And what's to stop a careless programmer from bypassing this safety net and (incorrectly) using ordinary numbers instead?

Creating an Enumeration

Enumerations are designed to solve such problems. An *enumeration* is a type that groups a set of constants together. For example, the following enumeration could help with the GetIntroduction() example:

```
Public Enum EnvironmentType
    Business
    Home
    FormalOccasion
End Enum
```

In your code, you would use this enumeration with the name you have created. For example, here's the new GetIntroduction() method:

```
Public Function GetIntroduction(Environment As EnvironmentType) As String
    Dim Intro As String
```

```
    If Environment = EnvironmentType.Business
        Intro = "Hi guys. It's me."
    ElseIf Environment = EnvironmentType.Home
        Intro = "Honey, I'm home!"
    ElseIf Environment = EnvironmentType.FormalOccasion
        Intro = "Pleased to meet you, sir or madam."
        Intro &= "My name is " & FirstName & " " & LastName
    End If
    Return Intro
End Function
```

And here's how you could call the method:

```
ReturnedMessage = GetIntroduction(EnvironmentType.Business)
```

Notice that you don't have to create an instance of an enumeration object to use its values. Those values are automatically available. However, you can create a variable just for storing a value for an enumeration, if you want. Here's an example:

```
Dim EnvironmentValue As EnvironmentType
EnvironmentValue = EnvironmentType.Business
ReturnedMessage = GetIntroduction(EnvironmentValue)
```

One other nice feature is the way that Visual Studio's IntelliSense automatically prompts you with possible values from your enumeration, as shown in Figure 5-6.

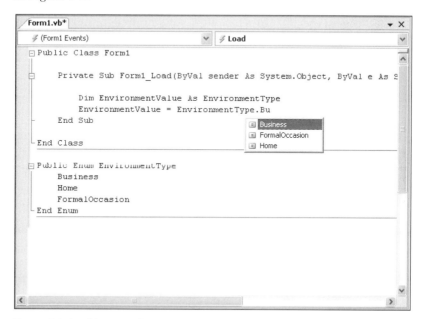

Figure 5-6: IntelliSense with enumerations

Enumerations "Under the Hood"

Behind the scenes, each entry in the enumeration is given its own integer value. In our previous example, Business is given the value 0, Home is 1, and FormalOccasion is 2. This means that the comparison in the GetIntroduction() method is really just examining a number value and comparing it to the values defined in the EnvironmentType definition.

In fact, if you were to look directly at the Environment value you received (for example, by displaying it in a message box without using the ToString() method), you would see that it is really an ordinary number. The use of the enumeration in your code just makes the logic more clear and understandable. It also makes it much more difficult to make a mistake, because you have only a small group of enumerated values, whereas there is no practical limit to the number of different integer values you could use.

```
Dim Environment As EnvironmentType = EnvironmentType.Home
Dim EnvironmentString As String
EnvironmentString = Str(Environment)          ' EnvironmentString = "1"
EnvironmentString = Environment.ToString()    ' EnvironmentString = "Home"
```

In some cases, you might want to define specific number values for your enumerations. This might be required if you are migrating a segment of code from a system of hard-coded integer values or constants to a more modern approach with enumerations. In this case, you might have procedures in your code that still expect certain specific values and that check for these values instead of comparing a value to your enumeration definition.

To create a backward-compatible enumeration for this situation, you could specify values in your enumeration definition, like this:

```
Public Enum EnvironmentType
    Business = 50
    Home = 51
    FormalOccasion = 52
End Enum
```

You could also use this approach if you need an enumeration to correspond to some other value. For example, you might want to create an enumeration that allows you to examine error codes. You would create the enumeration using the error codes with the appropriate values and use it to make your code more clear.

In other words, this:

```
ReturnValue = OpenDB("mydb")
If ReturnValue = 34 Then
    ' Database already open error.
End If
```

would become this:

```
ReturnValue = OpenDB("mydb")
If ReturnValue = DBErrors.AlreadyOpen Then
    ' Database already open error.
End If
```

with the help of this enumeration:

```
Public Enum DBErrors
    AlreadyOpen = 34
End Enum
```

NOTE   *You could also still use the old code and check that* ReturnValue = 34. *Essentially,* AlreadyOpen *is a named numeric constant.*

Using Enumerations with an Event

Enumerations can be placed just about anywhere in your code, but they generally belong in the class that uses them. That prevents them from conflicting with other enumerations and makes sure they will always be available if you copy a class into another project. For example, the Person class could use the following enumeration to support the PersonChanged event:

```
Public Class Person
    ' (Code omitted.)
    Public Enum ChangedProperty
        FirstName
        LastName
        BirthDate
    End Enum
End Class
```

Even if you don't place an enumeration inside a class, it's a good idea to keep it in the same file—just place it before or after your class. This makes sense if you want to use one enumeration in several classes.

Using the ChangedProperty enumeration, you can improve the event handling example you saw earlier. Once you've added the enumeration, the next step is to create a standard EventArgs class that stores the changed property. This PersonChangedEventArgs class will be used to pass the required information with the PersonChanged event.

```
Public Class PersonChangedEventArgs
  Inherits EventArgs

    Private _ChangedProperty As Person.ChangedProperty
    Public Property ChangedProperty() As Person.ChangedProperty
```

```
        Get
            Return _ChangedProperty
        End Get
        Set(ByVal Value As Person.ChangedProperty)
            _ChangedProperty = Value
        End Set
    End Property

    Public Sub New(ByVal ChangedProperty As Person.ChangedProperty)
        _ChangedProperty = ChangedProperty
    End Sub
End Class
```

You would also need to update the PersonChanged event definition:

```
Public Event PersonChanged(ByVal sender As Object, _
  ByVal e As PersonChangedEventArgs)
```

and the code that raises the event:

```
' Raise the PersonChanged event to indicate that the LastName was modified.
' This also involves creating a new PersonChangedEventArgs object to send.
RaiseEvent PersonChanged(Me, _
  New PersonChangedEventArgs(ChangedProperty.LastName))
```

The fully revised code is available as with the code for this chapter (look for the EnumerationTester project).

Keep in mind that to use an enumeration in a class, you will have to specify its full name. Enumerations are always available, even if you don't have a live object. For example, you could use the following code to examine the enumeration in the PersonChanged event handler:

```
Private Sub RefreshData(ByVal sender As System.Object, _
  ByVal e As PersonChangedEventArgs) Handles CurrentPerson.PersonChanged
    Select Case e.ChangedProperty
    Case Person.ChangedProperty.FirstName
        txtFirstName.Text = Lucy.FirstName
    Case Person.ChangedProperty.LastName
        txtLastName.Text = Lucy.LastName
    Case Person.ChangedProperty.BirthDate
        dtBirth.Value = Lucy.BirthDate
    End Select
End Sub
```

This example takes the ChangedProperty value returned in the PersonChangedEventArgs object and compares it to the different possible values in the enumeration. The interesting detail about this code is that the enumeration is accessed directly through the class (Person) instead of through a live object. This is possible because all public enumerations are shared members that are always available, even if you haven't created an object.

Visual Basic 2005 provides this ability because enumerations are part of the basic set of information that you need in order to interact with an object. Because enumerations are essentially unchangeable constants, they don't need to be linked to a specific object instance. Also, because enumerations are shared, you can easily use them in constructors and other shared methods, when you might not have an object instance available. The next section delves into shared members in more detail.

Shared Members

When you first considered objects in Chapter 3, you briefly learned how classes can be potentially confusing because they can have both shared and instance members. So far, all the properties, methods, and events you have seen in the Person class have been instance members. These members have no meaning until you create an instance of the class.

```
Person.FirstName = "Lucy"    ' Has no meaning and will cause an error!

Dim Lucy As New Person()     ' FirstName is an instance member,
Lucy.FirstName = "Lucy"      ' so this will work.
```

We examined a similar distinction with Windows forms in Chapter 4. Windows forms also need to be instantiated from the class description before you can access any members.

Shared members allow you to circumvent these rules. A shared member can be used directly, without requiring a live object.

Shared Methods

Shared methods allow you to provide useful functionality related to a class. Many classes in the .NET class library use shared methods. For example, the System.Math class is composed entirely of useful methods for performing advanced mathematical operations. You never need to specifically create a Math object.

```
' Works even though Math is the class name, not an instance object!
MyVal = Math.Sin(AngleInRadians)
```

Other commonly used classes with shared members are the MessageBox class (use MessageBox.Show() to show a message) and the Console class (use Console.WriteLine() to write text in a command-line application).

Shared methods have a wide variety of possible uses. Sometimes they provide basic conversions and utility methods that support your class. For example, you might have a special class that reads information from a file and provides it through properties. This class might benefit from a shared IsFileValid() method that takes the name of the file you plan to open, determines whether it is in the correct format, and returns True or False.

You could then make a decision about whether to use the file by creating an instance of the class.

The following example uses a shared method named CalculateBirthDate() to enhance the Person class:

```
Public Class Person
    ' (Other code omitted.)

    Public Shared Function CalculateBirthDate(AgeInYears As Integer) As Date
        ' The following line takes the current date (using a shared method
        ' of the DateTime class), subtracts the number of specified years
        ' (using a built-in method), and returns the result.
        Return DateTime.Now.AddYears(-AgeInYears)
    End Function
End Class
```

The Shared keyword indicates that this method is "shared" among all instances of this class and will always be available.

This method is useful if you want to create a new Person object but you don't know the appropriate BirthDate to use. Using this shared method, you could supply the age in years and receive a date value that you could use to create a new Person. (In this example, this method wouldn't actually be needed because the Person class provides an additional constructor that accepts an Age parameter instead of a BirthDate.)

```
Dim BirthDate As Date
' Calculate the appropriate birth date for a 25-year-old
' using the shared method.
BirthDate = Person.CalculateBirthDate(25)

' Now create the person.
Dim CurrentPerson As New Person("Lucy", "Smith", BirthDate)
```

A shared method can't access an instance member, such as a non-shared property or variable. In order to access a non-shared member, it would need an actual instance of your object—in which case it would also have to be an instance method.

```
Public Shared Function GetAgeInYears() As Integer
    ' This will not work because there is no current object!
    ' It would work perfectly well for a non-shared
    ' method.
    Dim Age As TimeSpan
    Age = DateTime.Now.Subtract(BirthDate)
    Return (Age.TotalDays \ 365)
End Function
```

The problem that occurs here is when you attempt to access the BirthDate property. BirthDate is an instance member, so it's not available in the shared method.

Even so, you can still call up a shared method through an instance object. In practice, though, it's best to use the class name instead of a live object when invoking a shared method. That way, it's obvious to anyone looking at your code that the particular procedure you are using is a shared method.

Shared Properties

Just as you can create shared methods, you can create shared variables and properties by adding the Shared keyword. Once again, the possibilities are profound. Here is a simple example:

```
Public Class Person
    ' (Other code omitted.)

    Private Shared _Count As Integer
    Public ReadOnly Property Count() As Integer
        Get
            Return _Count
        End Get
    End Property

    Public Sub New()
        _Count += 1
    End Sub
End Class
```

This example leaves out the basic Person code you've already considered and illustrates a new concept: A class can count how many objects have been created. It works like this:

- A shared variable, _Count, is used to keep track of the number of objects in use.

- Every time an object is created, the _Count variable is incremented in the constructor. The variable exists as long as the program is running, whether or not there are currently any Person objects in use.

- Remember that Count is read-only, so it doesn't have a corresponding Set procedure.

Here's a simple code snippet that tests this counting feature:

```
Dim FirstPerson As New Person("Lucy", "Smith")
Dim AnotherPerson As New Person("Joe", "Xamian")

' This line displays a count of 2.
MessageBox.Show(Person.Count & " people have been created.")
```

Keep in mind that there is no code to subtract from _Count when an object is destroyed. This means that the counter won't be accurate in the long run unless you add additional features, such as a Dispose() method that subtracts one from _Count.

Modules "Under the Hood"

You probably remember that classes aren't the only place to put code in Visual Basic—you can also use modules, which provide procedures and variables that can be accessed at any time.

Modules are usually used for *helper methods*—routines that perform basic conversion or utility methods that may be required in numerous different places in your application. For many Visual Basic programmers, modules were the first tool they had to reuse code throughout an application.

If all this sounds oddly familiar, it's because modules perform the same role as shared methods. You might think that modules are a simpler way to share functionality, but in fact, there is really no difference at all. If you were to peer into the innards of your code, you would see that modules are really special classes that are made up entirely of shared members.

That's right—modules are classes! Because every member is shared, you don't need to create an instance of a module before you use it. This also means that you can work with only a single copy of your module, and any information stored in its variables is available to any code using that module.

Here's an example of a module:

```
Public Module FileAccessTools
    Public FileName As String

    Public Sub OpenFile(ByVal File As String)
        ' Open the file here and set the FileName variable.
    End Sub

    Public Sub CloseFile
        ' Close the current file (indicated by FileName).
    End Sub
End Module
```

This module is identical to the class shown next. There isn't a single difference, other than syntax:

```
Public Class FileAccessTools
    Public Shared FileName As String

    Public Shared Sub OpenFile(File As String)
        ' Open the file here and set the FileName variable.
    End Sub

    Public Shared Sub CloseFile
        ' Close the current file (indicated by FileName).
    End Sub
End Class
```

The more you understand about Visual Basic 2005, the more you'll realize that the language is completely built around objects and the principles of object-oriented programming. Some of the conventions of traditional Visual Basic remain, but really just as a thin veneer over the OO reality.

Assessing Classes

Let's take a step back and answer our original question: Just what is a class? A class is a template we use to create objects. A class consists of three things: properties that allow you to access information about it, methods that you use to make it take actions, and events that it uses to notify your program about certain changes. Some classes might have only properties. In that case they resemble our `Person` structure. Other classes might consist almost entirely of methods that allow us to process information or to perform such tasks as writing to a file. An example of a class like this is the `Math` class featured in Chapter 3. It is made up entirely of shared methods that perform mathematical operations.

The amazing thing about our `Person` class is the way that we, or other programmers, can reuse and expand upon it. Other programmers don't have to understand how the `Person` class works in order to use it. To them, it's just a black box. Can you imagine the excitement you'll feel when a colleague tells you he's taken your `Person` class and incorporated it in a collection within a `NuclearFamily` object that has additional properties such as `Address` and additional methods such as `FindYoungestMember()`?

Types: The Big Picture

As you now know, the .NET class library consists of *types*, a catch-all term that includes several types of ingredients. To help you get your bearings, you might want to review the following sections, which show the full list of .NET types:

Structures

Structures are composite data types. They wrap related variables into a convenient package. One of the main differences between structures and classes is that structures are value types, so they act differently than reference types for comparison and assignment operations. For example, assigning one structure variable to another copies the entire structure, not the object reference.

Classes

Classes are more advanced structures that often add code, constructors, and events into the mix. Classes are the most common type in the class library and the one that you spend most of your time examining in this chapter. The word *classes* is sometimes used interchangeably with *objects* or *types* in casual speech, because classes underlie the most important features of any object-oriented framework (such as .NET). Classes are the basic ingredient for creating a wide array of flexible objects.

Delegates

A delegate defines the signature of a method. Using a delegate definition, you can create variables that point to other methods, as you saw in Chapter 3. In this chapter, you considered events, which build on the delegate feature to allow one object to notify another when something important occurs.

Enumerations

An enumeration is a list of constants, each of which has a descriptive name. Enumerations make it easy for a programmer to choose one of several different options. Enumerations were described in this chapter.

Interfaces

An *interface* is a contract that defines methods or properties a class must provide. Interfaces allow for more sophisticated class design, and they are particularly useful when a class needs to be deployed and enhanced or substituted without breaking existing clients. Interfaces are discussed in the next chapter.

Surveying the Objects in Your Application

You can get started looking at the object structure of your application with the Class View window. To show this window, select View ▶ Other Windows ▶ Class View. Figure 5-7 shows the Class View window as it surveys the ObjectTester application.

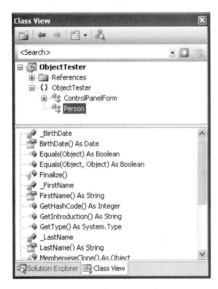

Figure 5-7: An application's class structure

This top portion of the Class View window provides a tree showing all the classes you use, organized by namespace. Figure 5-7 makes it clear that there are exactly two classes in the ObjectTester application—the familiar Person class and a ControlPanelForm class that represents the main window.

When you select a class, the bottom portion display all the information about the properties, methods, events, and private variables contained in that class. Together, these details make up the *members* of the class.

You can see a similar view of namespaces and the .NET class library using the Object Browser. To display the Object Browser, choose View ▸ Other Windows ▸ Object Browser. Each member has a brief associated description. However, you'll probably find that it's easiest to learn about .NET classes by consulting the class library reference in the Visual Studio Help.

What Comes Next?

Objects are central to the philosophy of .NET. You'll continue to explore them in Chapter 6, where you'll learn more about object-oriented philosophy and guiding principles. You'll also tackle some of the most advanced object-oriented concepts, including inheritance and interfaces.

6

MASTERING OBJECTS

This chapter continues our exploration into the world of objects. In Chapter 5 we covered the basics of defining a class, of enhancing it with properties, methods, events, and constructors, and of using it to create live objects. This chapter begins by explaining some more of the philosophy behind *why* you should go to all this trouble, and outlining the principles that can guide you to good object-oriented design. Next, you'll tackle three key topics for classy programming: inheritance (the ability of a class to acquire and extend the functionality of another class), interfaces (contracts that allow you to "lock down" class design), and collections (objects that group other objects together).

As you read this chapter, you'll realize that these features aren't just new frills for OO gurus—instead, they are organizing principles that shape the entire .NET Framework and the Visual Basic 2005 language. The more you learn about objects, the more you'll understand about the .NET class library, and the easier you'll find it to learn about new classes and to integrate them into your programs to provide additional features. In short, if you have time to learn about only one VB 2005 concept, I heartily recommend the theory and practice of using objects. No other topic is as integral to the workings of the Visual Basic 2005 language.

New in .NET

If you're coming from a classic version of VB, you'll find that Visual Basic 2005 has a whole new perspective on objects. Classes and interfaces are no longer just two more features pasted onto the language—they now represent the underlying philosophy of the whole .NET Framework. Here are some of the minor changes, along with some of the more seismic ones:

Inheritance

Inheritance, perhaps the most anticipated feature to ever enter into the Visual Basic language, allows you to create sophisticated objects that share features and functions. In fact, if you've worked through the examples in the preceding chapters of this book, you've already been using inheritance in Visual Basic 2005, most notably to create your own Windows forms.

Interfaces

Interfaces are now directly supported as a separate code construct, instead of a special type of class. This makes using them more straightforward and convenient than ever.

Collections and generics

Visual Basic 2005 goes one step further than Visual Basic .NET 1.*x* with *generics*—a new feature that lets you create more flexible classes. You'll see generics at work with some miraculously adaptable collections. These collections are flexible enough to work with any type of object but can be "locked in" to a type of your choice to prevent errors.

The Philosophy of OOP

Making the shift from traditional programming to an object-oriented approach is a significant adjustment. Before you plunge back into the technical details of Visual Basic 2005's support for object-oriented design and development, it may help to review some of the reasons why object-oriented design and programming are held in such high esteem.

Object-oriented programming encompasses several principles that contribute to reusable, efficient design. Taken together, these principles allow you to create programs and components built out of tightly organized, extremely reusable components.

You already know how to use objects. The following sections will help guide you to using them well.

The "Black Box" Idea

Classes in your program should behave as much as possible like *black boxes*—"black" meaning that you can't see inside them to puzzle out what's going on, and you don't have to. Imagine the difficulty you would have if using your microwave to defrost chicken required you to peer into the microwave object's circuitry and make alterations. Clearly, you would have quite a problem on your hands. If you look at the appliance as a black box (which conceptually it is), you are only concerned with the input and output: Frozen chicken goes in; defrosted chicken comes out. The process of defrosting is "abstracted away," which is a fancy way of saying that the microwave manufacturer worries about it so you won't have to. And I'm sure you'll agree that as a result, your kitchen experience is much more productive.

Similarly, if an entirely new microwave were to come onto the market tomorrow, you wouldn't need to change your cooking habits to accommodate it. You could still rely on the new microwave having the same *interface*. The microwave would plug into the same outlet, accept food through a similar door, and require the same information (cooking time and power level) in order to perform its tasks. Interface design is another important object-oriented concept.

TIP   *Don't confuse the concept of user interface with programming interface. The user interface is how an end user (your customer) interacts with your code. The programming interface is how one part of your code interacts with another part or a separate component from a different developer.*

Any component of a program that can be updated without "breaking" the existing client code that it services is the programming analog of our standardized, functionally encapsulated microwave oven.

TIP   *This chapter frequently refers to "the client code" as though the programmer writing an object and the programmer using it were not the same. In fact, this is not a strange example of multiple personalities, but a healthy way to approach object-oriented design. In order to make sure your applications are built out of complete, well-encapsulated objects that can be reused in different scenarios and even in different programs, you should start thinking of each object as its own individual program. Every object should receive all the information it needs through clear, standardized methods and properties, and it should provide capabilities that can be used directly, without requiring additional processing or the use of specific conversions and undefined rules.*

Loose Coupling

In the preceding example, we hinted at another principle of good object-oriented design: *loose coupling*. In a loosely-coupled system, the various components in your application are as independent as possible. Consider the microwave object again as part of your kitchen system. As the microwave defrosts the chicken, it doesn't need to know whether you're baking a potato in the conventional oven or cooking mashed potatoes or rice on the stovetop. Nor does it matter if you plan to prep ingredients in the microwave and transfer them to the stovetop. To you, all these steps are part of a one conceptual `PrepareDinner()` method. But the appliances you use are loosely coupled, which means you can use them in any combination you see fit.

When you're designing classes, it will help to think about yourself as a component designer and to imagine that other programmers will use your classes in their own highly customized programs. The more interdependencies and requirements you incorporate in a component, the harder it will be to move that component into another program. In the worst-case scenario, another programmer would have to bring along a whole class of unrelated objects, global variables, and helper functions before your object would work properly.

TIP *It's worth noting that although loose coupling is credited as an object-oriented design principle, it isn't really anything new. The best traditional structured programs also incorporate this principle, and their creators design functions that are highly generic. The more generic the code is, the easier it is to reuse, whether it's inside your own program or inside someone else's.*

Cohesion

A related idea is *cohesion*. In a well-designed, highly cohesive program, every portion of code is responsible for one—and only one—task. In traditional structured programming, this means that you carefully separate functions so as to isolate small, reusable units of logic. In object-oriented programs you should apply this principle as rigorously as possible, dividing objects and their methods into the smallest useful components and clearly distinguishing between the types of tasks that each method performs. For example, you would never include presentation-layer code in an object. An object should return information to the calling code, which you can then format and present to the user. If you were to include user interface code in an object, it would be tied to a specific display environment and hard to reuse in different windows or in other programs.

You've probably come across nightmarish situations where user interface, data access, and business logic code were all intermingled in a single procedure. Part of the reason classic version of Visual Basic sometimes have a bad reputation is that it's just too easy to put data access and processing code in an event handler (such as the `Click` event for a button) where it's hard to find, debug, and reuse. You can still make this mistake in a .NET application, but VB 2005 gives you all the object-oriented tools you need to design better code.

TIP *It may help to remind yourself of the black box principle: The object consumer (that is, the program) shouldn't need to know anything about how an object works.*

What Do Classes Represent?

When introducing classes, most programming books use examples with classes that represent concrete, physical *things* in the real world. For example, in Chapter 5 our Person class is clearly designed to model a real-world person. Similar concrete classes might have names like Invoice, Product, TextBox, and Calculator.

However, you should remember that programming classes don't need to correspond to something real. Classes might just represent a programming abstraction. For example, classes like Rectangle, FontUnit, Buffer, and Version may just represent useful ways to combine together related bits of information. Similarly, classes might just group together useful related functionality—Console and Math are two .NET classes that do exactly that.

Inheritance

Inheritance, consistently the most requested addition to Visual Basic, made its debut in Visual Basic .NET 1.0 and is still going strong in Visual Basic 2005. Inheritance allows you to take a class, called a *base class*, that has a basic set of features and procedures and then create from it new classes, called *derived classes*, that inherit this functionality and extend it with their own members. There are three main uses for inheritance:

Inheritance allows code to be reused.
For example, you might create an application with several data objects that read information from various files. Each data object would have its own methods and properties, depending on the types of information it manipulates, but the file access code would probably be almost identical for all of them. In this case, you could create a base class with basic file access code and then create derived classes that would inherit from the base class and extend it in various ways. The individual data objects would then be instantiated from the appropriate derived class. In this way the data object gets all the common file access code and any new functionality you need to include.

Inheritance is required to use key components of the .NET class library.
For example, you create a form by defining a class that inherits from the System.Windows.Forms.Form class and adding your own code elements, such as control variables and event-handling procedures. If you didn't use inheritance, you would have to use the default form that the class library provides to you, unchanged.

Inheritance allows related classes to be standardized.
For example, in .NET every control class (including labels, text boxes, buttons, and so on) inherits from the Control class, which includes basic details such as font, color, and text support. As a result, you could write a piece of code to perform basic formatting with any control class, even one that hasn't been invented yet.

In the preceding chapters, you were introduced to a few important examples of inheritance at work, and more will be explored throughout the book. Some examples where inheritance is used with the .NET class library include:

- Forms, which inherit all their basic functions from `System.Windows.Forms.Form`

- Web services, which inherit from `System.Web.Services.WebService`

- Custom exceptions (which inherit from `System.Exception`), event arguments (`System.EventArgs`), collections, and many more

Inheritance Basics

Here's an example of inheritance at its simplest:

```
Public Class Politician
  Inherits Person
    Private _Elected As Boolean
    Private _Party As Party

    ' Include some sample political parties.
    Public Enum Party
        Independent
        Communist
        National
    End Enum

    Public Property PoliticalParty() As Party
        Get
            Return _Party
        End Get
        Set(ByVal Value As Party)
            _Party = Value
        End Set
    End Property

    Public Property IsInOffice() As Boolean
        Get
            Return _Elected
        End Get
        Set(ByVal Value As Boolean)
            _Elected = Value
        End Set
    End Property

End Class
```

This `Politician` class inherits from (or *derives from*) the original `Person` class, which is `Politician`'s base class or *parent* class. This design is used because a `Politician` has all the basic properties of a `Person`, including a first and last name and a birth date. In addition, there is some information that applies only to politicians, such as the `PoliticalParty` and `IsInOffice` properties.

If you create a Politician, you'll see that it has all the events, subroutines, and properties defined for a person, as shown in Figure 6-1.

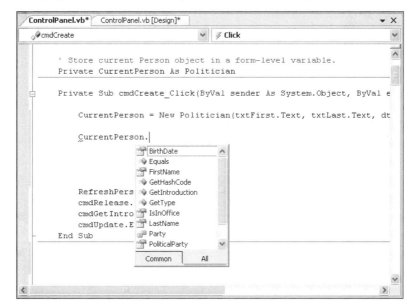

Figure 6-1: IntelliSense display of the events, subroutines, and properties of a Politician

This means that you can easily work with the full set of properties in your code:

```
Dim President As New Politician()
President.PoliticalParty = Politician.Party.National
President.FirstName = "Lucy"
President.LastName = "Smith"
```

Inheritance in Action

The online sample code for this chapter includes an InheritedObjectTester project that shows the Politician class in action (see Figure 6-2).

One interesting feature of this program is how it works with enumerations. The main window displays a list box that allows the user to set the political party for a Politician object. However, the list of political parties is not constructed by hand—to do so would violate encapsulation by mingling Politician details with the user interface code.

Instead, the code uses a special shared method that is built into the System.Enum class: the GetNames() method. This method provides an array of strings that represents all the constant names in the enumeration. Here's how it works:

```
Private Sub ControlPanelForm_Load(ByVal sender As System.Object, _
    ByVal e As System.EventArgs) Handles MyBase.Load
```

```
' AddRange adds a whole array of string items at once.
    lstParty.Items.AddRange(System.Enum.GetNames(GetType(Politician.Party)))
End Sub
```

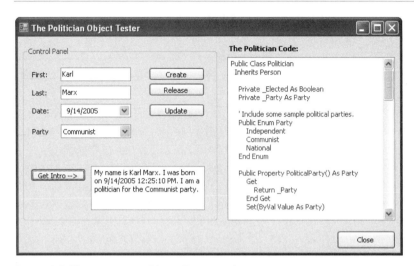

Figure 6-2: The Politician Object Tester window

NOTE   *In order the use the* GetNames() *method, you need to retrieve a special* Type *object that represents the* Party *enumeration type. This* Type *object is obtained with the* GetType() *function, which is hard-wired into the Visual Basic language. (This is an example of reflection, a feature you'll study more closely in Chapter 7.)*

Once a user has chosen a value from the list box, the string has to be reconverted to the appropriate enumerated value (which, as you'll remember from Chapter 5, is really just an integer). To perform this magic, you can turn to another piece of functionality that's built into every enumeration. In this case, it's the Parse() method, which converts a string name to the appropriate enumeration number.

```
Dim PartyChoice As Politician.Party
PartyChoice = System.Enum.Parse(GetType(Politician.Party), _
    lstParty.SelectedItem)
```

Constructors in Inherited Classes

There are a couple of interesting quirks associated with derived classes. First of all, constructors are not directly inherited. Instead, as with any other class, Visual Basic 2005 automatically provides a default constructor for your derived class that takes no arguments. This constructor automatically calls the constructor of your base class (Person, in our example). But our Person class has several different constructors. How does the Politician constructor know which one to call?

By default, the `Politician` constructor calls the parent (`Person`) constructor that has no arguments. If the `Person` class doesn't have a constructor with no arguments, Visual Basic 2005 will generate an error when you try to run the program and compile the `Politician`.

You could get around this problem by adding a constructor with no arguments to the `Person` class, but this is a bit messy—after all, what if you really need to make sure that a `Person` object can't be created without supplying a bare minimum of information? A better way to solve this problem is to create at least one custom constructor for the `Politician` class. This new constructor must explicitly call a constructor in the base `Person` class. You accomplish this with the `MyBase` keyword.

`MyBase` represents the portion of the object that's been inherited. In other words, you can use `MyBase` to access any member (method, property, event, and so on) that's been inherited from another class. In most cases, you don't need to use `MyBase` because you can access inherited members directly. (Consider, for example, the `FirstName` property of a `Politician` object.) However, there are two situations where you do need `MyBase`: if a member is defined in both the current class *and* the inherited class (so there's a name conflict), or if you need to trigger a constructor in the parent class (which you ordinarily can't call directly).

Here's an example of a custom constructor in the `Politician` class that uses a constructor from the `Person` class:

```
Public Sub New(ByVal FirstName As String, ByVal LastName As String, _
  ByVal Age As Integer)
    MyBase.New(FirstName, LastName, Age)
End Sub
```

The parameter list for this constructor is exactly the same as that for the constructor in our `Person` class. Once the constructor receives the information, it passes it along to the `Person` class to set up the basic `Person` values.

This approach to the initialization of derived object is extremely powerful for the following reasons:

- You control exactly which constructors are available in the derived class. For example, a constructor from the `Person` class that does not apply to the `Politician` class doesn't need to be available.

- You can use all appropriate constructor logic from the parent class without having to repeat the code in the derived class.

- You have the chance to perform any additional setup or error checking that is required for the derived object. For example, you can ensure that a `Politician` can't be created with an age less than 18.

- You can use a constructor from the parent class and perform additional logic to extend the initialization process. The following example demonstrates with a `Politician`-specific constructor that initializes the name, age, and party affiliation:

```
Public Sub New(ByVal FirstName As String, ByVal LastName As String, _
  ByVal Age As Integer, ByVal PoliticalParty As Party)
```

```
        MyBase.New(FirstName, LastName, Age)
        _Party = PoliticalParty
    End Sub
```

It's always good practice to begin a constructor in a derived class by calling one of the parent constructors. If you don't, you are at risk of creating redundant code or making it more difficult to update your base class later on. As a rule, if instantiating a derived object is difficult or requires a great amount of special code to alter or override the base behavior, you are not making proper use of class inheritance.

Protected Members

When you inherit from a class, all its public members are available, and all the private members—such as the variables used to store internal details—are hidden. This is generally good encapsulation. It all boils down to proper division of labor. The base class needs to be assured that no other code, including that of its child classes, can reach in and modify its internal variables except through the methods and properties it presents to clients. Thus the base class is responsible for managing its own internal workings, and the derived class is responsible for managing all the additional information it supplies. If your derived class needs to modify one of the base variables, it should go through the appropriate method in the base class—for example, by calling a property procedure.

Sometimes, however, you might want to make a variable available to all derived classes, but not to any other code. This could allow some optimizations among a tightly linked group of related classes. To make a class variable available in subclasses, use the keyword Protected, instead of Private or Public.

The name Protected is a bit of a misnomer. Like a private variable, a protected variable is protected from careless client code, but *it is not* protected from careless code in the derived class. Here is an example that defines a protected variable for the Person class:

```
Protected _BirthDate As Date
```

This variable will be accessible only to code in the Person class and its derived class, such as Politician. However, there is nothing to guarantee that the derived Politician class will use the value properly.

```
Public Class Politician
    ' (Code omitted.)

    Public Sub ChangeBirthDate(ByVal NewDate As String)
        ' Note that the MyBase keyword isn't required, but it makes it clear
        ' that you are modifying a value from the parent class.
        MyBase._BirthDate = NewDate
        ' No error checking!
    End Sub
End Class
```

The same principle can be applied to methods, which can also be protected. This is generally a more useful technique. For example, you might have a utility method that modifies certain variables in your Person class. This utility method shouldn't be made directly available to the client code—instead, it should only be available for use by other class methods or constructors when needed. However, the utility method might also be useful for a derived class, and you can probably trust a derived class, such as Politician, to use it for the right reasons. By declaring the method Protected you can provide access to it from subclasses and still perform any required error checking to create a basic level safety to ensure that no invalid data is supplied.

Overriding Methods

Sometimes, the behavior of a parent class may not suit a derived class. For example, consider the GetIntroduction() method in the Person class. While this is a nice starting point for a conversation, it may not be the most suitable choice for a politician's introduction. You could create a new method (like GetPoliticianIntroduction) in the derived class, but this would mean that the client code would have to treat Politician objects and Person objects differently in order to get the appropriate introduction. One of the goals of object-oriented design is to allow related types of objects to have the same interface so they can be manipulated with the same code. If this is done correctly, a programmer needs to modify only one definition in order to allow a program to use Politician objects just as easily as it can use Person objects, with no coding changes required.

To help facilitate this vision, you can use overridable methods. *Method overriding* allows you to replace a method defined in the base class with a more suitable method in the derived classes. For example, you could make the GetIntroduction() function of the Person class overridable in a derived class by adding the Overridable keyword like this:

```
Public Class Person
    ' (Code omitted.)

    Public Overridable Function GetIntroduction() As String
        Dim Intro As String
        Intro = "My name is " & FirstName & " " & LastName & ". "
        Intro = Intro & "I was born on " & BirthDate.ToString()
        Return Intro
    End Function
End Class
```

Then you could create a specialized version for a Politician using the Overrides keyword:

```
Public Class Politician
    Inherits Person
    ' (Code omitted.)
```

```
Public Overrides Function GetIntroduction() As String
    ' Make use of the original GetIntroduction() method.
    Dim Intro As String = MyBase.GetIntroduction()

    ' Add some additional politician-specific content.
    Intro &= " I am a politician for the " & _
      _Party.ToString() & " party."
    Return Intro
  End Function
End Class
```

This example uses the MyBase keyword to get the original introduction and then extends it. Alternatively, you could have skipped this step and substituted a totally new custom introduction.

Overridden Methods in Action

The technical details of overridden methods are fairly straightforward, but you may not realize the real benefit they provide until you see them in action. The advantage of overridden methods is that they allow a derived class to continue to interact with client code in the same way that the original parent class does, but with customized results.

For example, you might have made a simple program using a Person class:

```
Dim CurrentPerson As New Person("Lucy", "Smith", 44)
' Call a custom procedure to print out the introduction to a printer.
PrintIntro(CurrentPerson)
```

This program uses a custom PrintIntro() method, which accepts a Person object as a parameter:

```
Public Sub PrintIntro(ByVal P As Person)
    Dim StringToPrint = P.GetIntroduction()
    ' (Remainder of code omitted.)
End Sub
```

Now, perhaps you want to update the program to use the new Politician class. The following change is made:

```
Dim CurrentPerson As New Politician("Lucy", "Smith", 44)
```

No other changes are required—the program is now complete and fully functional. The PrintIntro() procedure does *not* need to be changed, even though it expects a Person object. Because the Politician object is really a special kind of Person, the PrintIntro() method automatically supports both.

The PrintIntro() method doesn't explicitly use any Politician-specific features, because it is treating the Politician object as a simple Person. However, when it calls the GetIntroduction() method, it is the Politician object's version of the method that will be invoked. This is because in .NET, the bottommost version of a method is always used in a class, regardless of how the variable is defined (whether as a Politician or a Person, in our example). This ensures that when you call an overridden method, the correct version is executed. The technical term for this behavior is *polymorphism,* and it ensures that you can look at an object in different ways depending on the context (for example, you the CurrentPerson object in the previous example can behave like a Politician or a Person, depending on how you want to interact with it).

Technically, no type conversion actually takes place when the Politician object is passed to PrintIntro() function. Instead, a process called *casting* occurs.

Casting

No information is lost when an object is cast to another type. Instead, Visual Basic just looks at it in a different way. For example, you might receive an object of type Object from some sort of generic function (like a search or sort routine). Essentially, an object is a reference to a blob of memory. When you receive an Object type, there's not much that you can do with it. If, on the other hand, you know what the object is really supposed to be, you can use the CType() function to cast it to the correct type, and start using the associated properties and methods of that type. You can't use these properties and methods without casting it, because the Common Language Runtime can't otherwise verify whether the object will really support them, and that violates type safety.

The key to understanding this process is realizing that casting is *not* a conversion. No matter how you cast an object, it is still the identical blob of data. The only change is which methods and properties are available. Of course, an object can only be cast to a supported type. The only supported types of casting are from a derived class to a parent class (for example, from a Politician to a Person), or from a class to one of its supported interfaces (which is discussed later in this chapter).

Here's a direct example of casting in action, using the Politician class:

```
Dim CurrentPerson As New Politician("Lucy", "Smith", 44)
lblIntro.Text = CurrentPerson.GetIntroduction()

' Now convert the reference to a Person object.
CurrentPerson = CType(CurrentPerson, Person)

' GetIntroduction() still works the same as it did before,
' returning the political introduction, because CurrentPerson
' is still a Politician object.
lblIntro.Text = CurrentPerson.GetIntroduction()

' However, this doesn't work, because though CurrentPerson
' is still a Politician, the code is treating it as a
' simple Person, and so the Party property is not available.
Lucy.Party = Politician.Party.Communist
```

Of course, you can attempt to perform certain casting operations that won't work. For example, if you create a Person object and then try to cast it to a Politician, you're doomed to fail. (Or to put it another way, although all politicians are people, all people aren't necessarily politicians.) If you're in doubt about whether a particular cast will work, you need to remember the exact type of object you created when you used the New keyword.

TIP   *Instead of using CType(), you can use a related function that's new in VB 2005. It's called TryCast(), and it allows you to shave a few milliseconds off type casting code. It works like CType(), with one exception—if the object can't be converted to the requested type, a null reference is returned. You can test for a null reference by checking if your object is Nothing. If you make the same mistake with CType(), an InvalidCastException occurs, which you need to catch with exception-handling code, as described in Chapter 8.*

MustInherit (Abstract Classes)

There are a couple of additional tools you can use when modeling objects. One is *abstract classes*. You cannot create an instance of an abstract class; you can only derive new classes based on it.

Abstract classes are defined using the MustInherit keyword. Here's an example:

```
Public MustInherit Class DBRecord

End Class
```

Inside a MustInherit class, you can add ordinary methods and properties, just like you would in any other class. Of course, these properties won't ever be used on their own—instead, they'll be inherited by other classes. For example, the DBRecord class shown above could be used to group together some functionality that's commonly used in classes that represent database records. Along those lines, the DBRecord class might define a Connect() method like this:

```
Public MustInherit Class DBRecord
    Public Sub Connect(ByVal ConnectionString As String)
        ' Code goes here.
    End Sub
End Class
```

Keep in mind that the DBRecord class has no meaning on its own. In order to actually get something accomplished, you need to know exactly what type of record is being used. For example, if it's employee records, you might want this EmployeeRecord class:

```
Public Class EmployeeRecord
    Inherits DBRecord
    ' Employee-specific members go here.
End Class
```

This design ensures that you can reuse common pieces of functionality (like the code for the Connect() method) without allowing a programmer to inadvertently create a meaningless object (like an instance of the base DBRecord class).

MustOverride

In the previous section, you saw how an abstract class can allow you to share code with different derived classes, while remaining safely inactive. Abstract classes also play another role as *class templates*.

To understand how this works, you need to realize that there are some members that you might want to declare in a MustInherit class even though you can realistically supply the code. For example, when you're designing the DBRecord class, you might decide that all the classes that derive from DBRecord should have basic SaveData() and LoadData() methods, which gives them the ability to update or retrieve a single record. However, you can't actually write the code to perform this task, because it depends on the type of record.

Here's where the MustOverride keyword fits in. The MustOverride keyword indicates a method whose implementation must be provided by the derived class. In other words, a MustOverride method has no code! For that reason, a MustOverride method can only be placed inside a MustInherit class. Here's an example:

```
Public MustInherit Class DBRecord

    Public Sub Connect(ByVal ConnectionString As String)
        ' Code goes here.
    End Sub

    Public MustOverride Sub LoadData()
    Public MustOverride Sub SaveData()

End Class
```

In this example, we assume that the Connect() method, which is used to open a database connection, is standard enough that it can be coded directly into the DBRecord class. However, the other declared methods, which retrieve and save data from the database, have no default implementation that can be given because they depend upon the contents of the database in question and their types. Therefore we leave them to be overriden (actually, implemented) by methods in derived classes.

When you define a method in an abstract class with MustOverride, you do not specify any code other than the method declaration. You don't even include a final End Sub statement. The derived class *must* implement all MustOverride methods declared in its parent. It can't ignore any of them (unless it too is a MustInherit class).

The approach illustrated in this example is a powerful one. It ensures consistency, and it allows you to use classes with different code (for example, an EmployeeRecord and an OrderRecord) in the same way, using common methods like `Connect()`, `SaveData()`, and `LoadData()`. However, in .NET it's more common to create reusable class templates in a different way—using interfaces, which are presented later in this chapter.

Multiple-Level Inheritance

Visual Basic 2005 allows you to use unlimited layers of inheritance. For example, we could create a new class called `DemocratPolitician`, or even `President`, that inherits from the `Politician` class, which in turn inherits from the `Person` class. Some classes pass through many levels of inheritance to build up all their features. For example, every .NET type originates from the ultimate base type `System.Object` which is enhanced by a number of subsequent derived classes. Figure 6-3 shows the inheritance diagram for a common Windows form.

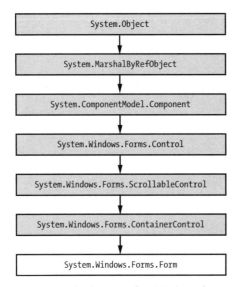

Figure 6-3: The lineage of a Windows form

Of course, the architects of the .NET class library are experienced OO developers, and multiple-level inheritance is used to great effect in the class library. In general, however, levels of inheritance should be viewed with cautious skepticism. As a rule of thumb, you should try to keep the levels of inheritance to as few as possible (perhaps just a single level), particularly if the intermediate levels are not used. For example, if your application will only ever use `Politicians`, it's best to create only a `Politician` class, rather than a base `Person` class and a derived `Politician` class.

Visual Basic 2005 does *not* allow you to inherit from more than one class at the same time. (This is a limitation of all .NET languages.) If you have multiple classes whose features you want to include in a new class, it's often best to create a compound class that brings together different subobjects through its properties. These objects can "plug in" to instances of the new type to provide more features. For example, you could create a `Person` class that can contain an instance of an `Occupation` class to specify job-related information and a `Car` object that describes the primary vehicle used by that person.

Is Inheritance a Good Idea?

Inheritance can be a bit tricky to use properly, and with overuse it can lead to more problems than it's worth. A common problem arising with inheritance is *fragile classes*. These can emerge when you have a complex hierarchy of objects and multiple layers of inheritance. In such a situation, it's often extremely difficult to change any characteristics of your base classes, because the changes would affect countless derived classes. In other words, your program reaches an evolutionary dead end, because any enhancement would break existing classes and require a cascade of changes that would be difficult to track down and deal with.

When using inheritance, you should ask yourself if there are other available solutions to your problem. In some cases, you can share code by creating a utility class with appropriate functions. For example, you might redesign the `DBRecord` data object described earlier by placing file access routines into a common class or code module. Another way to avoid inheritance is to design objects that can contain other objects, which in turn provide the desired functionality. This technique is called *containment*, and it's usually used in combination with a technique called *delegation*.

For example, suppose you want to create an `OrderRecord` object with a `Connect()` method that opens a database connection. You could use containment and delegation to implement this functionality, without inheriting it from a parent class, as follows. First, a `DBAccess` class is designed whose instances can be used to manage communication with the database. The definition of the `OrderRecord` class then includes an internal variable of this type. When the `OrderRecord.Connect()` method is called, it uses the contained `DBAccess` object in the appropriate way to make the connection. In other words, `OrderRecord` *delegates* the responsibility of connecting to `DBAccess`. Here's a rough outline of the code:

```
Public Class OrderRecord
    Private objDB As New DBAccess()

    Public Sub Connect(ByVal ConnectionString As String)
        objDB.Connect(ConnectionString)
    End Sub
End Class
```

Using Inheritance to Extend .NET Classes

This chapter has concentrated on using inheritance with business objects. Business objects tend to model entities in the real world, and they usually consist of data (properties and variables) and useful methods that allow you to process and manipulate that data.

Inheritance also allows you to acquire features and procedures from the .NET class library for free. You've already seen how to do this with Windows forms, but we haven't yet discussed the full range of possibilities. This section provides two quick examples designed to illustrate the power of inheritance.

Visual Inheritance

Every form inherits from System.Windows.Forms.Form. However, you can also make a form that inherits from another form. Here's how to do it:

1. Start a new Windows project. Rename the form you start off with to BaseForm. This is the form you'll use as the standard for other forms.

2. Before going any further, add a couple of buttons to BaseForm. Then, right-click your project in the Solution Explorer, and choose Build.

3. Now, choose Project ▸ Add Windows Form to add a second form. But instead of starting with the standard blank template, choose the Inherited Form option shown in Figure 6-4.

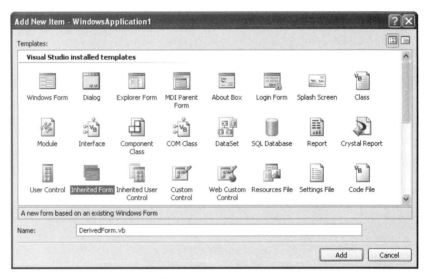

Figure 6-4: Adding an inherited form

4. Name your new form DerivedForm, and click OK.

5. The Inheritance Picker dialog box will show you all the forms in your project (and any other components you're using). You need to choose the form you want to inherit from. In this case, it's BaseForm, as shown in Figure 6-5.

6. Click OK.

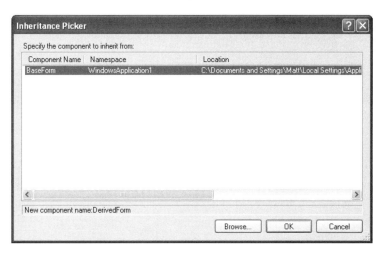

Figure 6-5: Choosing the base form

Your new form, DerivedForm, will contain all the controls you created on BaseForm. In fact, DerivedForm will look exactly the same as BaseForm, because it will have inherited all of BaseForm's controls and their properties. In the designer, you'll see a tiny arrow icon next to each inherited control (see Figure 6-6).

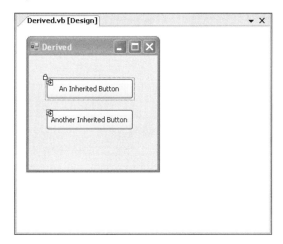

Figure 6-6: An inherited form in the designer

What's more, any time you make changes to BaseForm, DerivedForm will be updated automatically (although you may have to build the project before Visual Studio will update the display). None of the code will be repeated in the DerivedForm form class code, but it will all be available. For example, if you include a button click event handler in BaseForm, it will take effect in DerivedForm as well.

The only difference between BaseForm and DerivedForm is that you won't be able to move or alter the controls on DerivedForm. However, you can still add new controls to DerivedForm, and you can also change form-level properties (like the form caption or dimensions).

If you're curious to take a look behind the scenes (and confirm that inheritance really is at work), you need to dive into the designer code file for the form. First, select Project ▶ Show All Files to reveal it in the Solution Explorer. Then, expand the DerivedForm.vb node to show the DerivedForm.Designer.vb code file. (Chapter 4 has more on the designer code file, which has the automatically generated code that Visual Studio creates.)

In the DerivedForm.Designer.vb file, check out the class declaration. Instead of seeing this:

```
Public Class DerivedForm
  Inherits System.Windows.Forms.Form
```

you'll see this:

```
Public Class DerivedForm
  Inherits BaseForm
```

In other words, the DerivedForm class inherits from the BaseForm class (which itself inherits from the Form class). As a result, the DerivedForm is a DerivedForm, a BaseForm, and a plain old Form, all rolled into one.

Visual inheritance is a strict and somewhat limiting tool. However, if you need to create several extremely similar windows, such as a series of windows for a custom wizard, you can make good use of it.

Subclassing a Control

You can use a similar technique to extend a .NET control. The following example creates a customized text box that accepts only numeric input. (It's included as the NumericTextBox project with the samples.) To create it yourself, add the following class to a Windows application:

```
Public Class CustomTextBox
  Inherits System.Windows.Forms.TextBox

    ' Override the OnKeyPress method, which fires whenever
    ' a key is pressed.
    Protected Overrides Sub OnKeyPress(ByVal e As KeyPressEventArgs)
        ' Call the base method (which raises the KeyPress event).
        MyBase.OnKeyPress(e)

        ' Check if the just-typed character is numeric
        ' or a control character (like backspace).
        If Char.IsControl(e.KeyChar) = False And _
          Char.IsDigit(e.KeyChar) = False Then
            ' If it isn't, set the Handled property to
            ' tell the TextBox to ignore this keypress.
```

```
            e.Handled = True
        End If
    End Sub
End Class
```

This is a customized version of the common text box. It inherits everything that the TextBox control has to offer, and overrides one of the existing methods, OnKeyPress(). The OnKeyPress() method is always called when a key is pressed, just before the character appears in the text box. Here you have the chance to examine the character that was typed, and (optionally) refuse it by setting the KeyPressEventArgs.Handled property to True.

TIP   *How did we know there was an OnKeyPress() method to override? By .NET, all Windows controls provide an OnXxx() method for each event they provide. For example, a button has a Click event, so you can assume it also has an OnClick() method that fires just before the event is raised. If you want to react to this action, you can create an event handler (as you saw in Chapter 4), or you can derive a new class and override the related method (as with the custom text box example). Both approaches are functionally equivalent. The difference is in where you place the code and how you can reuse it.*

To use this class, begin by compiling your application. Then, switch to the design surface of a form. You'll see the CustomTextBox control appear in the Toolbox automatically (see Figure 6-7). This is a convenience that Visual Studio provides automatically—it searches your code for all classes that derive (directly or indirectly) from System.Windows.Forms.Control and makes them readily available.

Now you can drop your custom text box on a form and run your application. You'll notice that you can only type numeric characters into the text box. Letters and symbols are ignored.

This raises an interesting question. If you want to create a text box that rejects certain characters, is it a better idea to handle an event like KeyPress in your form, or to create a whole new custom control? Generally, it's better to prevent cluttering your application with extra classes, so it's simpler to keep all your code in the form. However, if you have any complex keystroke-handling logic that you need to share in several different forms, the custom control approach becomes a lot more attractive. Using this technique, you write the code once, and reuse it to your heart's content. You can even share your control in several separate applications by placing your class in a class library (.dll) project and sharing the component with other programmers.

Figure 6-7: A custom control in the Toolbox

Interfaces

The *interface* is a cornerstone of object-oriented design, particularly for large-scale applications that need to be deployed, maintained, and enhanced over long periods of time. Interfaces require a bit of extra effort to use, and they are often avoided because they provide few immediate benefits. However, over the long term, they help solve common problems that make an application difficult to extend and enhance.

The goal of an interface is to allow you to separate a class's definition from its implementation. An interface defines a small set of related properties, methods, and events. By convention, interfaces always start with the capital letter *I*.

For example, you could create an interface that collects common file access operations:

```
Public Interface IFileAccess

    Property IsFileOpen() As Boolean

    Sub Open(ByVal FileName As String)
    Sub Close()

    Sub LoadData()
    Sub SaveData()

End Interface
```

Note that interfaces don't use the `Public` or `Private` keyword in the declarations of their members. All the elements in an interface are automatically public. You'll also notice that interfaces don't define their members—in particular, they leave out the `End` statement and only include the signatures of properties and methods.

An interface contains absolutely no real code. It's a bare skeleton that describes the members needed to support a specific feature or procedure. The `IFileAccess` interface requires a class to provide its functionality—opening and closing a file, and loading and saving data. In that respect, an interface is very similar to an abstract `MustInherit` class that is entirely composed of empty `MustOverride` methods.

To use an interface in a class, you use the `Implements` statement. A class can implement as many interfaces as it needs. However, the class needs to provide its own code for every member of the implemented interface. Consider this example:

```
Public Class PersonData
  Implements IFileAccess
End Class
```

As soon as you enter this information in Visual Studio, the IntelliSense feature will underline the word IFileAccess to indicate that your class cannot be considered complete, because one or more member declared in the IFileAccess interface has not been defined in PersonData (see Figure 6-8).

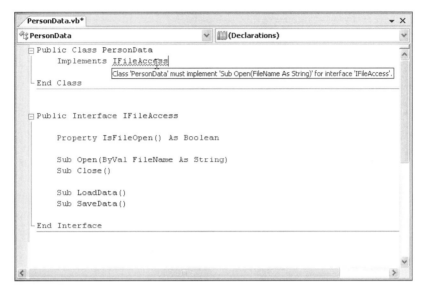

```
PersonData.vb*                                                    ▾ ✕
PersonData                         ⌄  (Declarations)              ⌄
 ☐ Public Class PersonData
      Implements IFileAccess
              Class 'PersonData' must implement 'Sub Open(FileName As String)' for interface 'IFileAccess'.
    End Class


 ☐ Public Interface IFileAccess

      Property IsFileOpen() As Boolean

      Sub Open(ByVal FileName As String)
      Sub Close()

      Sub LoadData()
      Sub SaveData()

    End Interface
```

Figure 6-8: An unimplemented interface

To fully implement an interface, you need to provide code for every method. Here is an example of how you would implement the Open() method:

```
Public Sub Open(ByVal FileName As String) Implements IFileAccess.Open
    ' (Code omitted.)
End Sub
```

NOTE *Visual Studio has a fantastic shortcut for implementing interfaces. Just type in the Implement... line, and then press ENTER. It will automatically fill in every required method for you, with the correct accessibility, data types, and so on. Of course, it's still up to you to add the code.*

Inheritance Versus Interfaces

The difference between inheritance and interfaces is that inheritance is used to share code, whereas interfaces are used to standardize it. Interfaces guarantee that several classes all present a standard set of methods to their clients, even when the implementation details are class-specific. In the IFileAccess example, interfaces are a good idea, because while saving data to and loading data from a file is a common operation that several classes need to support, the code for the SaveData() and LoadData() methods will depend on the type of data being saved and loaded, and vary from class to class. (Of course, these methods might themselves use a common .NET component or a custom file access class to take care of some of the heavy lifting and reuse some code.)

Using Interfaces

If you are new to interfaces, you're probably wondering why you should use them at all when they clearly require so much work. Unlike inheritance, interfaces do not let you reuse blocks of code; in order to share code, you have to make careful use of utility functions or inheritance in addition to interfaces. Interfaces also have the drawback of inflexibility (you always have to implement *every* member of the interface) and extra syntax (every member definition requires an additional `Implements` statement to match it to the method, property, or event that it implements). So what benefit does an interface provide?

In fact, interfaces aren't nearly as crazy as they look. First of all, you need to understand that interfaces are not designed to solve problems of code reuse. Instead, an interface is a contract that guarantees that a class offers a certain set of features. A client program may not know anything about a new `SalesInfo` class, but as long as it knows that the class implements the `IFileAccess` interface, it knows that the class provides `LoadData()` and `SaveData()` methods (and how they are used). Or, consider a `Microwave` and a `ToasterOven` object, both of which use a similar control panel to cook food. This could be modeled as an interface (`ICookFood`), which would allow a client to make dinner without necessarily needing to use any microwave-specific or toaster oven–specific functions.

Inheritance provides a similar standardization mechanism. As you learned earlier, you can cast an object to its parent's type to provide a get access to a basic set of functions and features. (For example, you can treat any `Person`-derived class as a `Person`.) The same is true with interfaces.

Imagine the following class, which implements the `IFileAccess` interface:

```
Public Class SalesInfo
  Implements IFileAccess
    ' (Code omitted.)
End Class
```

The `SalesInfo` class is standardized according to the `IFileAccess` interface. As a result, you could pass a `SalesInfo` object to any method that understands the `IFileAccess` interface. Here's an example:

```
Public Sub PrintFileInfo(DataObject As IFileAccess)
    ' Interact with the object (which is a SalesInfo in this example)
    ' through the IFileAccess interface.
    DataObject.Open()
    DataObject.LoadData()

    ' (Printing code omitted.)
    DataObject.Close()
End Sub
```

In other words, objects of any class that implements IFileAccess can be cast to IFileAccess. This allows generic functions to be created that can handle the file access features of any class. For example, the PrintFileInfo() method could handle an EmployeeInfo, CustomerInfo, or ProductInfo object, as long as these classes all implement the IFileAccess interface.

Interfaces and Backward Compatibility

Interfaces are designed as contracts. Therefore, once you specify an interface, you must be extremely careful how you change it. One fairly innocent change is to add a new method. Although you'll need to track down all the classes that implement the interface and add the new method, you won't need to change the code that *uses* these objects, because all the original methods are still valid.

However, it's much more traumatic to remove existing methods from an interface or to change their signatures. For example, if you decide you need to replace the LoadData() and SaveData() methods with versions that require different parameters (for example, a version that takes an additional parameter specifying a key for data encryption), existing programs that use the original IFileAccess interface may stop working. The problem is that the original version of the method—the one the code is attempting to use—won't be around anymore. (To avoid this problem, keep to the first rule—add new methods, but don't remove the original versions of the method.)

Some developers choose to *never* change anything about an interface once it's released into the wild. They won't even make "safe" changes (like adding new methods). If they absolutely have to modify the interface, they will create a whole new interface, like IFileAccess2. Your classes can implement both, and clients will have a choice of which to use:

```
Public Class SalesInfo
  Implements IFileAccess, IFileAccess2
    ' (Code omitted.)
End Class
```

In such a situation, when two interfaces overlap (i.e., they each declare a method with the same name and signature), you can create a single method that satisfies both interfaces:

```
Public Sub Open(ByVal FileName As String) _
  Implements IFileAccess.Open, IFileAccess2.Open
    ' (Code omitted.)
End Sub
```

All this interface-based programming may seem like a lot of extra work, and it sometimes is. You may therefore be tempted to forget about backward compatibility and just recompile all the programs that use a class whenever you change one of the interfaces it uses. In truth, that isn't such a bad idea. In many cases it may even be the best idea. However, this is only valid when you are developing a class for use in programs over whose development and maintenance you have total control. Once your class is distributed as a stand-alone component and used in third-party applications, you can't modify it without possibly breaking client applications.

Using Common .NET Interfaces

Interfaces aren't just used for backward compatibility. They also allow a class to standardize a range of feature sets from which clients may choose. Remember, a class can only inherit from one parent class, but it can implement all the interfaces it needs.

NOTE *Interfaces allow you to standardize how classes interact. Taken to its extreme, this allows different developers to code each class independently. As long as developers of the class and of its clients both stick to the rules of the interfaces and interact only through these interfaces, their code is guaranteed to be compatible.*

Interfaces are used extensively in the .NET Framework, and they represent the handiwork of master OO designers. For example, arrays implement the ICloneable interface (to provide every array with a Clone() method that copies the elements of an array), the IList and ICollection interfaces (which allow the array to act like a collection), and the IEnumerable interface (which allows the array to provide For Each enumeration support). The next few sections present some of .NET's most useful interfaces.

NOTE *To see these interfaces in action, try out the InterfaceTester project with the code for this chapter.*

Cloneable Objects

Each instance of every class that you create has the built-in intelligence to create a copy of itself. It acquires this feature from the MemberwiseClone() method, which every class inherits from the base System.Object class.

However, client code can't access this method directly, because it is marked as Protected, which means it's available to code *inside* the class, but not to code *using* the class. This is designed to impose some basic restrictions on object copying. As you'll see, the way the MemberwiseClone() method works isn't suitable for all classes, so .NET forces you to go through a little bit of extra work to enable it.

You could create your own public class method that uses MemberwiseClone(). The recommended approach, however, is to use the ICloneable interface, which is designed for just this purpose. By using the ICloneable interface, you guarantee that other pieces of code will know how to copy your objects, even if they've never seen them before.

The ICloneable interface defines a single method, Clone(). Your object provides the code for this method, which should use the internal MemberwiseClone() method to perform the copy (and possibly add some additional logic).

Here's a `Clone()` method that could be used for the `Person` class:

```
Public Class Person
  Implements ICloneable
    ' (Other code omitted.)

    Public Function Clone() As Object Implements ICloneable.Clone
        ' Return a duplicate copy of the object using the
        ' MemberwiseClone() method.
        Return Me.MemberwiseClone()
    End Function

End Class
```

Clients of a `Person` object can then call its `Clone()` method and use the `CType()` function to cast the result to the appropriate type.

NOTE *The `ICloneable` interface and the `Clone()` method need to be flexible enough to work with any class. For that reason, the `Clone()` method returns a generic `Object`. This design allows it to support every type of object, because no matter what object you create, you can always cast it to the `Object` type. However, it also forces the client using the `Clone()` method to do a little extra work and cast the object back to the correct type. It's a small price to pay to have a standardized object-cloning system.*

```
Dim CurrentPerson As New Person("Matthew", "MacDonald")
Dim NewPerson As Person

' Clone the author.
NewPerson = CType(CurrentPerson.Clone(), Person)
```

Cloning Compound Objects

One reason the `MemberwiseClone()` feature is hidden from client use is the difficulty involved in cloning a compound object. For example, consider the following cloneable `Family` class:

```
Public Class Family
  Implements ICloneable
    ' (Other code omitted.)

    Public Mother As Person
    Public Father As Person

    Public Function Clone() As Object Implements ICloneable.Clone
        Return Me.MemberwiseClone()
    End Function

End Class
```

When this object is cloned, the Mother and Father object references will be copied. That means that a duplicate Family class will be created that refers to the same Mother and Father. To modify this behavior so that the contained Mother and Father objects are also cloned (as shown in Figure 6-9), you would need to add additional code:

```
Public Function Clone() As Object Implements ICloneable.Clone
    Dim NewFamily As Family
    ' Perform the basic cloning.
    NewFamily = Me.MemberwiseClone()

    ' In order for this code to work, the Person object
    ' must also be cloneable.
    NewFamily.Father = Me.Father.Clone()
    NewFamily.Mother = Me.Mother.Clone()

    Return NewFamily
End Function
```

Here's an example that tests the Family.Clone() method:

```
' Create the family, with two parents.
Dim TestFamily As New Family()
TestFamily.Mother = New Person("Lucy", "Smith")
TestFamily.Father = New Person("Joe", "Xamian")

' Clone the family. This also duplicates the two referenced
' Person objects (the mother and father).
Dim FamilyCopy As Family = CType(TestFamily.Clone(), Family)
```

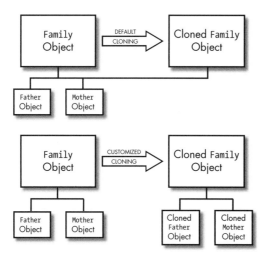

Figure 6-9: Two ways to clone

In this example, it's fairly obvious that the Family *class is a compound object. Compound objects are not always this recognizable. For example, an object might store information in a collection or an array. Collections and arrays are both reference types, which means that* MemberwiseClone() *will copy the reference, not duplicate the object. You need to be extra vigilant when adding cloning capabilities to a class in order to avoid this sort of subtle error.*

Disposable Objects

You'll remember from the last chapter that because of the nondeterministic nature of garbage collection, you can't count on code that runs when an object is destroyed to be executed immediately. If your class uses a limited resource (like a file or a database connection) that should be released as soon as an object is done using it, you should provide a method that allows this resource to be released explicitly. The recommended, standardized way to do this is to implement the IDisposable interface, which contains a single method called Dispose().

```
Public Class PersonFile
  Implements IDisposable

    Public Sub New()
        ' (Add code here to open the file.)
    End Sub

    Public Sub Dispose() Implements IDisposable.Dispose
        ' (Add code here to release the file.)
    End Sub
    ' (Other code omitted.)
End Class
```

There's not much to using IDisposable. Just remember that the calling code needs to call the Dispose() method. It will not be invoked automatically. A good safeguard is to use VB's new Using block with any disposable object. Here's an example:

```
Dim PFile As New PersonFile()
Using PFile
    ' Perform normal tasks with the PFile object here.
End Using
' When your code reaches this point, PFile.Dispose() is
' called automatically.
```

The nice thing about the Using block is that it guarantees Dispose() will be called (if the object implements IDispose; otherwise, the Using block doesn't do anything). Even if an unhandled exception occurs inside the Using block, the Dispose() method is still called, ensuring proper cleanup. This is a great way to make sure limited resources (like database connections or file handles) are always released, even in the event of an unexpected error.

The only disadvantage to the Using block is that if you have several objects you need to dispose of, this can lead you to write a stack of confusingly nested Using statements. In this case, a better solution is to use the Finally section of an exception-handling block (see Chapter 8) to perform your disposal.

For even more compact code, you can create an object at the same time you start your Using block:

```
Using PFile As New PersonFile()
    ' Perform normal tasks with the PFile object here.
End Using
```

Comparable Objects

By implementing the IComparable interface, you allow .NET to compare objects based on your class. One common reason that you might want to implement IComparable is to allow your classes to be sorted in an array or collection.

The IComparable interface has a single method called CompareTo(). In the CompareTo() method, your code examines two objects based on the same class and decides which one is greater. The CompareTo() method then returns one of three numbers: 0 to indicate equality, –1 to indicate that the compared object has a value less than the current object, or 1 to indicate that the compared object is greater than the current object. It's up to you to decide what it means for one class to be "greater" than another. For example, you might compare numeric data, strings, some other data, or a combination of variables.

Following is an example that shows how you can implement custom comparisons involving Person objects. In this case, the programmer decided that the criterion for comparing Person objects would be their age. Thus, in a sorted Person list the youngest people would appear first, and the oldest would appear last.

```
Public Class Person
  Implements IComparable
    ' (Other code omitted.)

    Public Function CompareTo(ByVal Compare As Object) As Integer _
      Implements IComparable.CompareTo
        Dim ComparePerson As Person = CType(Compare, Person)
        If ComparePerson.BirthDate = Me.BirthDate
            Return 0    ' Represents equality.
        ElseIf ComparePerson.BirthDate < Me.BirthDate
            ' The compared object's age is greater than the current object.
            ' (Remember, the greater the birth date, the smaller the age.)
            Return 1
        ElseIf ComparePerson.BirthDate > Me.BirthDate
            ' The compared object's age is less than the current object.
            Return -1
        End If
```

```
    End Function

End Class
```

If you want, you can use the CompareTo() method directly in code. However, the built-in Sort() method in the Array class recognizes the IComparable interface and uses the CompareTo() method automatically. Here's an example that puts it to work:

```
' Define birth dates for a 45, 28, and 5 year old.
DateTime BirthDate1, BirthDate2, BirthDate3 As DateTime
BirthDate1 = DateTime.Now.AddYears(-45)
BirthDate2 = DateTime.Now.AddYears(-28)
BirthDate2 = DateTime.Now.AddYears(-5)

' Create an array with three people.
Dim GroupOfPeople() As Person = {New Person("Lucy", "Smith", BirthDate1), _
  New Person("Joe", "Xamian", BirthDate2), _
  New Person("Chan Wook", "Lee", BirthDate3)}
' Sort the array, so that the people are ordered from youngest to oldest:
Array.Sort(GroupOfPeople)
```

NOTE   *Sometimes you need to provide a class that can be sorted in several different ways. In this case, you need to create separate sorting classes (like SortByName, SortByDate, and so on). Each of these sorting classes will implement the IComparer interface. This interface is similar to IComparable and provides one method, CompareTo(), that compares two objects and returns an integer indicating 0, 1, or −1. To use a special sorting method with the Array class, use the overloaded Sort() method that allows you to specify an additional parameter with the appropriate IComparer object.*

Collection Classes

Inheritance is a relatively strict type of relationship, referred to as an *is-a* relationship. For example, most would agree that a Politician is a Person. However, there are many other types of relationships in the world of objects. One of the most common is the *has-a* relationship—and as many can attest, in the materialistic world of today, what a person has is often more important than who they are. The same is true for classes, which can contain instances of other classes, or even entire groups of classes. This section discusses the latter case, and introduces the *collection class*, which is an all-purpose tool for aggregating related objects, particularly for inclusion in a class.

A collection is similar to an array, but much more flexible. An array requires that you specify a size when you create it. A collection, on the other hand, can contain any number of elements, and allows you to add or remove items as you see fit. An array requires that you specify the data type of the information it will contain (or specify Object, if you want the array to hold variables of different data types). A collection can contain any type of object. Lastly, while an array uses an index to identify its elements, a numeric index is of little use for a collection, because items can be added and removed arbitrarily. Instead, when you need to find a specific item in a collection, you either search through the collection until you find it or refer to it by a key that you specified for the item when you added it to the collection.

NOTE *A* key *is a short, unique string description. Collections that use keys are sometimes called* dictionaries, *because they store information under specific key headings, like a dictionary.*

A Basic Collection

Here's a code snippet that creates and uses a simple collection:

```
' Create a Person object.
Dim Person1 As New Person("Lucy", "Smith")

' Create a collection.
Dim People As New Collection()

' Add the Person to the collection with the key "First"
People.Add(Person1, "First")

' Display the number of items in the collection (currently 1).
MessageBox.Show(People.Count)

' Retrieve the Person from the collection
Dim RetrievedPerson As Person = People("First")
```

A NuclearFamily Class

Now it's time to jump right into a full-fledged example: the NuclearFamily class. I'll break down the elements of this example to explain how it uses a collection.

Here is the definition for our NuclearFamily class:

```
Public Class NuclearFamily
    Public Father As Person
    Public Mother As Person
    Public Children As New Collection()

    Public Sub New(ByVal Father As Person, ByVal Mother As Person)
        Me.Father = Father
        Me.Mother = Mother
    End Sub

    Public Function FindYoungestChild() As Person
        Dim Child As Person
        Dim Youngest As Person

        For Each Child In Children
            If Youngest Is Nothing Then
                Youngest = Child
            ElseIf Youngest.BirthDate < Child.BirthDate Then
```

```
                Youngest = Child
            End If
        Next

        Return Youngest
    End Function

End Class
```

Here's the rundown:

- The NuclearFamily class *has a* Father and a Mother variable, which point to corresponding Person objects. These variables are defined without the New keyword. This means that blank Father and Mother objects aren't created when you create a NuclearFamily. Instead, you must assign preexisting Person objects to these variables. (In the interest of shorter code, our example takes a shortcut by using variables instead of full property procedures.)

- All the children are contained in a collection called Children. This collection is defined with the New keyword, because it needs to be created before any Person objects can be added to it.

- A single constructor is used for the class. It requires parameters identifying both parents. In other words, you won't be able to create a NuclearFamily without a Father and Mother. Notice that the names of the parameters in the constructor are the same as the names of the variables in the class. This may seem confusing, but it's actually a common convention. In this case, the parameter name has priority over the class name, so you need to use the Me keyword to refer to the class in order to directly access the instance variables from within the function.

- A FindYoungest() function searches through the Children collection and compares each child until it finds the one with the most recent BirthDate (and hence, the youngest age).

To use the NuclearFamily class, you need to create and add family members:

```
' Create four distinct people.
Dim Lucy As New Person("Lucy", "Smith", 43)
Dim John As New Person("John", "Smith", 29)
Dim Anna As New Person("Anna", "Smith", 17)
Dim Eor As New Person("Eor", "Smith", 15)

' Create a new family.
Dim TheFamily As New NuclearFamily(John, Lucy)

' Add the children.
TheFamily.Children.Add(Anna)
TheFamily.Children.Add(Eor)

' Find the youngest child.
MessageBox.Show("The youngest is " & TheFamily.FindYoungestChild.FirstName)
```

The result of all this is shown in Figure 6-10.

There isn't much new material in this example. What's important is the way everything comes together. The NuclearFamily class is a compound class that contains two Person objects and its own collection.

Figure 6-10: Finding
the youngest member

A traditional structured program would probably model a family by creating a bunch of different information. Maybe it would keep track of only the children's birthdays, or even hard-code a maximum number of children. Along the way, a structured program would probably also introduce fixed assumptions that would make it difficult to expand the program and keep it clear. The NuclearFamily class, on the other hand, is built out of Person objects. Every family member is treated the same way, and the family is broken down into equivalent objects. You could even create multiple NuclearFamily classes that assign the same family member (Person object) different roles—for example, as a child in one class and a parent in another.

In short, everything is consistently well organized. We change the Person class, and any part of our code that uses it automatically benefits. Code that deals with people is contained inside the Person class, so we always know where to find it. Life is good.

To try out the NuclearFamily class, run the CollectionTester project from the sample code (see Figure 6-11).

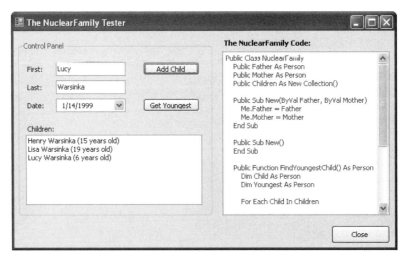

Figure 6-11: The NuclearFamily test utility

Specialized Collections

The basic Collection class is really a holdover from Visual Basic 6. However, .NET developers often use one of several more specialized collections, which can be found in the System.Collections namespace. Some popular collection classes include:

ArrayList

This is similar to the Collection class, but it doesn't support keys. It's just a collection that dynamically grows (when you use the Add() method) and shrinks (when you call the Remove() method).

Hashtable

This is similar to the Collection class, but it *requires* that each item have a key.

SortedList

This is like a Hashtable, but it automatically sorts itself (based on key values) whenever you add or remove an item.

Queue and Stack

A Queue is a first-in, first-out collection. You call Enqueue() to insert an item at the end of the queue, and Dequeue() to retrieve the oldest-added item. A Stack uses the same principle, but in reverse. You call Push() to add an item to the top of the stack and Pop() to get the item that's currently topmost.

Hold on—before you head off to the System.Collections namespace to check out these specialized collection classes, it's worth noting that .NET 2.0 added yet *another* set of collections, this one in the System.Collections.Generic namespace. You'll learn about these collections in the following section.

Generic Collections

One drawback with our NuclearFamily.Children collection is that it isn't type-safe. Though our respectful program only adds children into the collection, poorly written code could easily throw in strings, numbers, and other objects, which could cause all sorts of problems. Remember, when creating a component, you should always imagine that it is a separate program that may be thrust out into the world on its own and used by a variety of programmers, who may have little knowledge about its inner workings. For that reason, a class has to carefully protect itself against incorrect input.

One way to do this is through property procedures, as you saw in Chapter 5. In the NuclearFamily class, we could create a property procedure or a special method that accepts an object, checks its type, and then adds it to the Children collection if it is a Person. However, this approach has a significant drawback. Because the collection is no longer directly exposed, the client doesn't have any way to iterate through it. (*Iteration* is the handy process that allows a programmer to use a For Each block to move through all the items in a collection without worrying about indexes or keys.) Another solution is to create a custom collection class. This is fairly easy because .NET provides a System.Collections.CollectionBase class from which you can derive subclasses. It has all the tricky stuff built in, so you have relatively little code to add. In fact, *The Book of VB .NET* (No Starch Press, 2002) demonstrated a custom collection class for Person objects, which you can examine with the downloadable code for this chapter.

In VB 2005, you don't need to take either of these steps. That's because .NET 2.0 adds a new feature called *generics* that allows developers to build more flexible classes. One of the first beneficiaries of this change are the collection classes.

Thanks to generics, it's possible to create collections that can support any data type but are instantly "locked in" to the data type you choose when you create them. The only trick is that you need to specify that data type using a slightly unusual syntax. For example, imagine you want to use the generic List collection class. You would change the NuclearFamily class by modifying this line:

```
Public Children As New Collection()
```

to this:

```
Public Children As New System.Collections.Generic.List(Of Person)
```

The Of Person part in parentheses explains that you want your Children collection to only accept Person objects. From this point on, you won't be able to add any other type of object. For example, if you write this code:

```
Children.Add("This is some text, not a Person object.")
```

You'll get an error. Best of all, you'll receive the error when you try to compile your application (not later on, when it's running merrily). That way, your invalid code is stopped cold before it can cause a problem.

Another benefit is that you can pull a Person object out of the List collection without needing to use CType() to cast the object. For example, with an ordinary collection you need the following code to get the first Person object:

```
Dim FirstPerson As Person
FirstPerson = CType(Children(0), Person)
```

But with a generic collection, the following simpler code works fine, because the compiler knows your collection is limited to Person objects:

```
Dim FirstPerson As Person
FirstPerson = Children(0)
```

The List class is the generic version of the ArrayList class—it's a collection that doesn't use keys. You'll also find a few more generic collections in the System.Collections.Generic namespace. They include:

Dictionary

This is a name-value collection that indexes each item with a key, similar to the Hashtable collection.

SortedList

This is the generic version of the System.Collections.SortedList class (a perpetually sorted key-value collection).

Queue

This is the generic version of the System.Collections.Queue class (a first-in, first-out collection).

Stack

This is the generic version of the System.Collections.Stack class (a last-in, first-out collection).

What Comes Next?

This chapter has discussed a wide range of object-oriented techniques. However, now that you have the knowledge, you still need the experience to learn how to implement object-oriented designs.

A substantial part of the art of using objects is deciding how to divide a program into classes. That question has more to do with the theory of application architecture than with the Visual Basic 2005 language.

For example, you may be interested in learning the basics about *three-tier design*. Three-tier design is the idea that applications should be partitioned into three principal levels: the user interface, known as the *presentation tier*; the business objects or data processing procedures, known as the *business tier*; and a back-end data store (a relational database or a set of XML files, for example), known as the *data tier*. Figure 6-12 shows a diagram of this model.

Three-tier design has caught on because it allows extremely scalable applications. With clever design, all three levels can be separated, upgraded or debugged separately, and even hosted on different computers for a potential performance boost. The concepts of three-tier design are also important when you are creating simpler client-server or desktop applications. By remembering that database access, data processing, and user interface are three different aspects of a program, you can get into the habit of separating these functions into different groups of classes. For example, your form classes all reside at the user interface level. This means that they shouldn't contain any code for processing data; instead, they should make use of a business object. Similarly, a business object shouldn't display a message directly on the screen, or access a form. It should be completely isolated from the user interface, and should rely on receiving all the information it needs through method parameters and properties. Understanding three-tier design can help you ensure that even your most straightforward programs are more encapsulated and easier to enhance and troubleshoot.

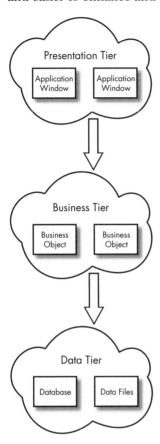

Figure 6-12: Three-tier design

7

ASSEMBLIES AND COMPONENTS

Some of the most remarkable changes to the way VB developers do business in the .NET world stem from the introduction of *assemblies*, .NET's catch-all term for executable application files and compiled components. In Visual Basic 6, creating and reusing a component was often tricky, especially if you wanted to share your work with applications coded in other programming languages. Registration hassles and versioning conflicts—which occur when two programs expect different versions of the same component—appear when you least expect them and can take hours to resolve. In this chapter, you'll learn how .NET clears out these headaches and offers a better model for sharing components. You'll also learn enough to prepare yourself for Chapter 14, which explores how you can create customized setup programs to deploy your applications.

New in .NET

Could the end of versioning headaches, deployment struggles, and multiple-application conflicts finally have arrived? In this chapter you'll see the changes in Microsoft's new deployment philosophy. Some of these changes include:

Assemblies

If you are an experienced developer, you've seen how COM can simplify code reuse by allowing programmers to create and share distinct components. You've probably also seen how much trouble can be caused when different shared components conflict, and installing one program breaks another. Assemblies are Microsoft's replacement to components and traditional application files, and they include built-in metadata designed to help you avoid "DLL Hell."

No more registration

The advent of assemblies means that you no longer have to rely on the registry to maintain important information about your component. Instead, it's all stored directly in your program files, making it easy to copy applications and components from computer to computer, and allowing you to share components in your programs without worrying about messy configuration details.

Versioning policies

.NET puts you in complete control over versioning. Only you have the power to decide which version of a component your application will use. If another application is given an upgraded version of a shared component, you're free to keep using the original version your application was built and tested with, guaranteeing rock-solid stability.

Resources

Need to use a binary image in your application, but you're worried about what happens if someone deletes, moves, or tampers with your image file? In this chapter, you'll learn how to embed the image within your application assembly as binary data, where no one can touch it. Best of all, Visual Studio will still let you update it easily.

Introducing Assemblies

An *assembly* is a .NET version of a .dll or .exe. Quite simply, an assembly is some grouping of program functionality that corresponds to a single component or application. In the programs you've seen so far, all the functions and features have been coded inside a single assembly, which becomes a .exe file when you compile it. If, however, you wanted to make separately distributable components, you would divide your program into several distinct units of functionality, which would then become individual assemblies.

Assemblies Versus Components That Use COM

At this point, you are probably wondering why developers need assemblies when we already have COM—a system for creating and sharing components that's baked into the Windows operating system. Once again, .NET is making a clean break. With the introduction of assemblies, the versioning headaches that developers have suffered through for years are finally at an end. That's not just hot air—assemblies have a few unique features that make them completely unlike anything Windows programmers have used before.

Assemblies Are Self-Describing

The most revolutionary aspect of assemblies is the fact that they are self-describing. Every assembly you create contains one or more program files and a *manifest*. The manifest includes additional information called *metadata*. (Metadata is "data about data." Essentially, your program code is the data, and the metadata is the information about your program, such as its name, version, publicly available types, and dependencies.) The manifest replaces the type library and registry information used with COM components. That brings us to the next point.

Assemblies Don't Need the Registry

All the information needed to use a component or to run an application is contained in the assembly's manifest, which is embedded right inside the corresponding .dll or .exe file. It is impossible to create a program in .NET without automatically generating a manifest and a proper assembly. This means that you can copy your applications and components to any other computer using .NET, and they will work automatically. There's no need to fiddle around with regsvr32.exe or other awkward tools to add information to the registry.

In Visual Basic 6, you can transfer a simple application from computer to computer easily enough. But as soon as your application uses other COM components or ActiveX controls, you face several new problems. Namely, you need to register these files on every computer that uses them, and the registration process can cause a conflict with other installed applications. But in .NET, you can simply identify and copy the needed files—no registration is required. Of course, if you forget a dependent file, you'll still run into trouble.

Assemblies Can Be Privately Shared

A Visual Basic 6 application can use two broad types of components: those that have been developed in-house to share company-specific functionality, and those that have been developed (and may even be sold) by third-party component developers or by Microsoft. The latter type of component requires some kind of central repository. In traditional COM programming, that's the Windows system directory, where all the files are piled in a somewhat disorganized mess. In .NET development, the Global Assembly Cache (GAC) serves much the same purpose, and we'll explore it later in this chapter.

In the other scenario—company-specific code modules—components don't need to be shared across the computer. They may be used by only a single application, or by a few applications created by the same developers. In COM development, there was no easy way to implement this approach. Private components still had to be tossed into the system directory with everything else, which meant extra registration steps, unnecessary information added to the registry (such as a global unique identifier, or GUID), and a clutter of components that couldn't be reused by other programs.

If you've ever tried to explore the full list of COM components and add some of them to your Visual Basic projects, you've surely discovered that many of the items that appear on the list aren't thoughtful examples of shared procedures and resources provided by other application developers. Instead, they are designed for use with a specific application that is installed on your computer and are essentially useless outside that program. They may even have licensing restrictions that prevent you from creating an instance of a component in your applications.

In .NET, private assemblies are private. You store these components in your application directory or in an application subdirectory.

Assemblies Are Rigorous Version Trackers

The manifest also records information about the current versions of all the included files. Whenever you compile a VB 2005 program, this version information is written into the manifest automatically, meaning that there's no possibility for it to become out of date, or not be synchronized with the underlying application code. The manifest also contains a short block of cryptographic hash code based on all the files in the assembly. Whenever you run an assembly, the Common Language Runtime verifies that the hash code is valid. If a change is detected that isn't reflected in the manifest (which is impossible, unless the file is corrupted or has been modified by a malicious user with a low-level tool), it won't let you run the application.

This is a stark difference from the way that COM components and ActiveX controls work. With COM components, you have to trust that the information in the registry and any associated type library is up to date—and this trust may not be rewarded.

Assemblies Support Side-by-Side Versioning

How many times have you installed a new application only to discover that it overwrote a file required for another application with a newer version that broke backward compatibility? No matter how hard developers struggle, the ideal of backward compatibility will never be universally achieved, and any system that uses a single component and a single version for dozens of different applications will run into trouble (or DLL Hell, as it is affectionately known).

.NET sidesteps this problem in two ways. The first solution is with private assemblies. Because each application has its own separate copy of a component, you're free to update the .dll files whenever you wish. It's up to you whether to roll out a change for a single application or a dozen.

Of course, that separation won't help you if you decide to share components across a computer by placing them in the GAC. Fortunately, .NET avoids trouble here as well with a landmark feature called *side-by-side execution*. Under this system, you can install multiple versions of a single component in the GAC. When you run an application, .NET uses the version of the component that it was developed with. If you run another program at the same time that uses the same component, the Common Language Runtime will load the appropriate version for that program as well. No unexpected behavior or incompatibilities will appear, because every application uses the set of components that it was designed for.

Why Haven't We Seen These Features Before?

It wasn't just shortsightedness that led Microsoft to create the COM we know, love, and hate, with its obvious versioning nightmares. Some of the features that assemblies use just weren't practical in the past. For example, side-by-side execution can multiply the amount of memory required when several applications are running. Each application may use a different version of the same component, which is effectively the same as if each application were using a completely separate component. Today, it's fairly easy to buy a few hundred megabytes more of RAM to prevent this problem, but in the past, an operating system designed without code sharing in mind would quickly grind to a standstill. Similarly, allowing multiple versions to be tracked and stored separately on a computer (or giving each application its own copy of a component with private assemblies) just wasn't efficient with the limited disk space of the past. Today, with physical space so absurdly cheap, the overhead is much less severe.

In other words, COM and the entire Windows platform were created with the vision of a single, centralized component repository. The emphasis was on saving space and memory to provide better performance, rather than on the relative luxury of making applications (and the life of a developer) easier, more convenient, and more consistently reliable. Today, more and more mission-critical applications are being designed in the Windows environment, which has shifted from a home user's toy to a professional business platform. The current emphasis is on reliability and on structured, fail-safe designs, even if a few megabytes have to be wasted in the process. After all, modern computers have resources to spare. It all comes back to one principle—.NET programming is *modern* programming.

Looking at Your Program as an Assembly

As mentioned earlier, all the applications you've created up to this point are genuine .NET assemblies. If they weren't, the Common Language Runtime would refuse to execute them. To see what your program looks like as an assembly, you can use an interesting program called ILDasm.exe

(IL Disassembler), which can be found in a directory like C:\Program Files\ Microsoft Visual Studio 8\SDK\v2.0\Bin, depending on where you have installed the .NET Framework and what version of Visual Studio you're using. The easiest way to launch ILDasm is to first start the Visual Studio command prompt (choose Programs ▶ Visual Studio 2005 ▶ Visual Studio Tools ▶ Visual Studio 2005 Command Prompt) and then type ildasm at the command line.

Once you run ILDasm, you can choose to open any .NET assembly (.exe or .dll file). Just choose File ▶ Open and browse to the file. In the following example, you'll see the ObjectTester utility from Chapter 5.

ILDasm uses a tree to show you information about your program. All the types that are defined in your projects are automatically defined in metadata in your program's assembly. This makes it easy to browse through a specific definition of our Person class, as shown in Figure 7-1.

Figure 7-1: Dissecting the Person class

If you double-click a method or property, you'll see the list of related .NET instructions that was created based on your program code, as shown in Figure 7-2.

If you've ever used any other disassembling tools, you probably realize that .NET code is quite different. Usually, the best you can hope for when looking at a compiled program is to find a list of low-level machine instructions. .NET, on the other hand, compiles programs to a special intermediary language called IL. IL instructions don't look the same as normal VB 2005 code, but they retain enough similarities that you can often get a general idea of what is happening in a section of code.

Because the IL instructions retain so much information about your program, the Common Language Runtime can perform optimizations, guard against illegal operations, and protect memory when running an application. However, retaining all this information also makes it fairly easy for other programmers to peer into some of the internal details about how a competing program works. This is a problem that has plagued Java for a while, and the .NET solution is similar to the Java solution. Namely, if readable code is a security concern, you need to use a third-party *obfuscation* tool that allows you to scramble your code so that it's difficult for humans to interpret. (For example, one technique is to give all variables meaningless numeric identifiers in the compiled program file.) The full version of Visual Studio ships with a scaled-down version of one popular obfuscator, called Dotfuscator.

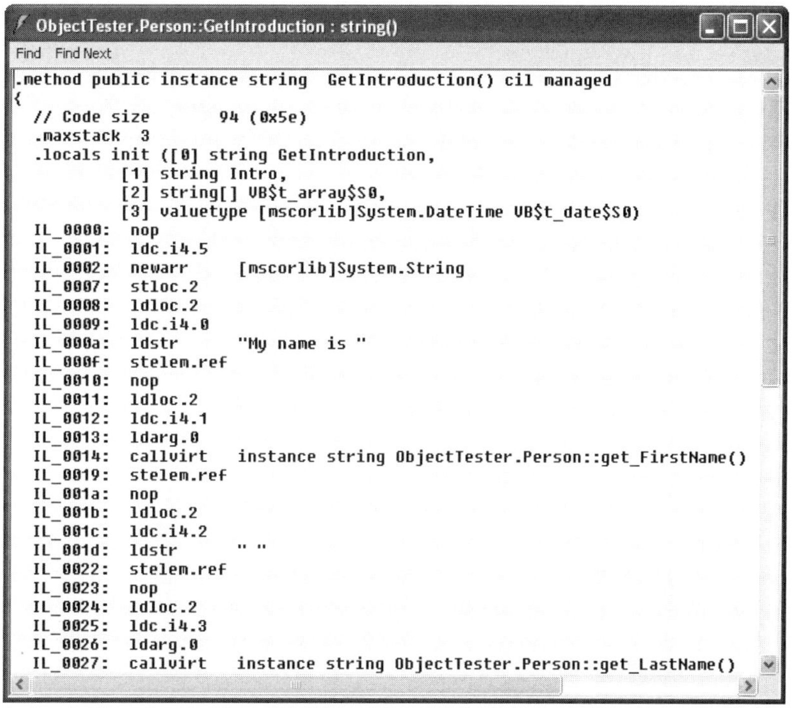

```
ObjectTester.Person::GetIntroduction : string()

Find  Find Next

.method public instance string  GetIntroduction() cil managed
{
  // Code size       94 (0x5e)
  .maxstack  3
  .locals init ([0] string GetIntroduction,
           [1] string Intro,
           [2] string[] VB$t_array$S0,
           [3] valuetype [mscorlib]System.DateTime VB$t_date$S0)
  IL_0000:  nop
  IL_0001:  ldc.i4.5
  IL_0002:  newarr       [mscorlib]System.String
  IL_0007:  stloc.2
  IL_0008:  ldloc.2
  IL_0009:  ldc.i4.0
  IL_000a:  ldstr       "My name is "
  IL_000f:  stelem.ref
  IL_0010:  nop
  IL_0011:  ldloc.2
  IL_0012:  ldc.i4.1
  IL_0013:  ldarg.0
  IL_0014:  callvirt     instance string ObjectTester.Person::get_FirstName()
  IL_0019:  stelem.ref
  IL_001a:  nop
  IL_001b:  ldloc.2
  IL_001c:  ldc.i4.2
  IL_001d:  ldstr       " "
  IL_0022:  stelem.ref
  IL_0023:  nop
  IL_0024:  ldloc.2
  IL_0025:  ldc.i4.3
  IL_0026:  ldarg.0
  IL_0027:  callvirt     instance string ObjectTester.Person::get_LastName()
```

Figure 7-2: IL code for the GetIntroduction() method

Dependency Information

Looking back at Figure 7-1, at the top of the ILDasm tree you'll see an item that represents the manifest for your assembly. If you double-click it, you will see such information as your assembly's version and locale settings. Most importantly, you can see information about dependencies, which will appear as .assembly extern statements that look like this:

```
.assembly extern System.Data
{
  .publickeytoken = (B7 7A 5C 56 19 34 E0 89 ... )
  .ver 2:0:2411:0
}
```

This example indicates that in order to function correctly, the current assembly requires the System.Data assembly included with .NET. There is also additional information that specifies the required version of the System.Data assembly: 2.0.2441.0. This number is in the format *major.minor.build.revision.* When you run this application, it will look for an application with this exact version number. By default, if this version doesn't exist the application simply refuses to run. Later versions won't be used automatically unless you explicitly configure a different versioning policy by creating a configuration file (as discussed later in this chapter). The risk for breaking code with components that claim to be backward compatible but aren't is just too great.

Setting Assembly Information

The dependency information is added automatically to the manifest when you create an assembly. But what about other information, such as product name and version number? All of these details are specified in a special file that every Visual Basic 2005 project contains. It's called AssemblyInfo.vb.

Ordinarily, the AssemblyInfo.vb file is hidden. But if you're truly curious, choose Project ▶ Show All Files, and then look for the file under the My Project node in the Solution Explorer (see Figure 7-3). Inside this file, you'll see a number of assembly attributes.

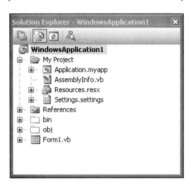

Figure 7-3: The hidden AssemblyInfo.vb file

Each of the attributes in the AssemblyInfo.vb file embeds a single piece of information into your compiled assembly. Here's what the attributes look like (with some sample information added):

```
<Assembly: AssemblyTitle("FileIOTester")>
<Assembly: AssemblyDescription("Test VB 2005 I/O features.")>
<Assembly: AssemblyCompany("No Starch Press, Inc.")>
<Assembly: AssemblyProduct("The No Starch VB 2005 Examples")>
<Assembly: AssemblyCopyright("Copyright 2006")>
<Assembly: AssemblyTrademark("No Starch(TM)")>
```

You can change all of these details by hand, but you don't need to; the same information is available in a Visual Studio designer. Just double-click the My Project node in the Solution Explorer, choose the Application tab, and then click the Assembly Information button. Figure 7-4 shows what you'll see.

Figure 7-4: Modifying assembly metadata the easy way

Taken together, these options replace the project properties used in classic versions of Visual Basic. If you're curious to see where this information ends up, just compile your application and fire up Windows Explorer. Browse to your file, right-click it, and choose Properties. You'll see a window like the one shown in Figure 7-5.

Figure 7-5: The assembly information

If you scroll to the bottom of the AssemblyInfo.vb file (or look at the bottom of the Assembly Information dialog box in Figure 7-4), you'll find the most important piece of information. It's the version number, and by default it looks like this in a new project:

```
<Assembly: AssemblyVersion("1.0.0.0")>
<Assembly: AssemblyFileVersion("1.0.0.0")>
```

Try to ignore the fact that the version number is actually specified twice. The reason for this quirk is that the first (the AssemblyVersion attribute) gives the official .NET version number, while the second (the AssemblyFileVersion attribute) gives the version older Windows applications, including Windows Explorer, will see in the file. Unless you're planning a truly strange joke (or have a particular backward-compatibility problem you're trying to solve), these version numbers should always stay the same. In the .NET world, the first version number is the most important.

If you take no action, the version of your application will be perpetually locked at 1.0.0.0, no matter how many times you recompile it. If you want to create a new version, you need to open the AssemblyInfo.vb file and modify this value to something else. For example, after making a new version with fairly minor changes, you might change the version to 1.1.0.0.

No one likes changing version numbers for each build, whether you do it by editing the AssemblyInfo.vb file or by using the Assembly Information dialog box. It's just too cumbersome (and it's too easy to forget to do it, leading to different versions with the same version number). Most programmers prefer to have some sort of auto-incrementing number. That way, each assembly has a unique version number.

In .NET, it's easy to use an auto-incrementing version number. You just need to use the asterisk (*) in your version number, as shown here:

```
<Assembly: AssemblyVersion("1.0.*")>
<Assembly: AssemblyFileVersion("1.0.*")>
```

This tells Visual Studio that your application will always be version 1.0 (these are the major and minor components of the version number), but it should increment the build and revision properties every time you compile a new .exe file (even when you do so for testing purposes by clicking the run button in the IDE). Note that these numbers increment by more than one. A typical version number using this system might be something like 1.0.594.21583.

Once you've finished your testing, you would typically change the major or minor version number component to create a file that will be clearly distinguishable as a new release. But in the meantime, the build and revision numbers can help keep multiple versions distinct.

Retrieving Assembly Information

Sometimes it's useful to be able to retrieve assembly information programmatically. The most obvious example is an About box, where your program displays such information as its current version. This information can't be hard-coded into the program, because it would need to be altered with every build and would not have guaranteed accuracy. Instead, the information can be retrieved via the `System.Windows.Forms.Application` class, which is similar to the `App` object in previous versions of Visual Basic. (The same information is also available through the `My` object.)

```
lblProductName.Text = Application.ProductName
lblProductVersion.Text = Application.ProductVersion
lblPath.Text = Application.ExecutablePath
```

In most cases, this class provides the basic features that you need. However, you can also delve into more interesting territory with the `System.Reflection.Assembly` class. This class uses reflection to retrieve information about an assembly. *Reflection* is a feature that allows you to peer into an assembly at runtime, and retrieve information about the structure of the code inside. For example, you can use reflection to find out what classes are in an assembly, or what methods are in a class, although you can't retrieve the actual code. In a nutshell, reflection is the slightly mind-bending trick of examining one piece of code with another piece of code.

To get started, you can use the `GetExecutingAssembly()` method to return a reference to the current assembly for the project. Our next example uses the assembly and retrieves all the defined types (including classes and other constructs, such as enumerations). Then, the code searches each class for a list of its methods, events, and properties. Along the way, a `TreeView` is constructed.

```
Dim MyAssembly As System.Reflection.Assembly
MyAssembly = System.Reflection.Assembly.GetExecutingAssembly()
lblAssemblyInfo.Text = MyAssembly.FullName

' Define some variables used to "walk" the program structure.
Dim MyTypes(), MyType As Type
Dim MyEvents(), MyEvent As System.Reflection.EventInfo
Dim MyMethods(), MyMethod As System.Reflection.MethodInfo
Dim MyProperties(), MyProperty As System.Reflection.PropertyInfo

' Iterate through the program's classes.
MyTypes = MyAssembly.GetTypes()
For Each MyType In MyTypes
    Dim nodeParent As TreeNode = treeTypes.Nodes.Add(MyType.FullName)

    ' Iterate through the events in each class.
```

```
        Dim node As TreeNode = nodeParent.Nodes.Add("Events")
        MyEvents = MyType.GetEvents
        For Each MyEvent In MyEvents
            node.Nodes.Add(MyEvent.Name)
        Next

        ' Iterate through the methods in each class.
        node = nodeParent.Nodes.Add("Methods")
        MyMethods = MyType.GetMethods()
        For Each MyMethod In MyMethods
            node.Nodes.Add(MyMethod.Name)
        Next

        ' Iterate through the properties in each class.
        node = nodeParent.Nodes.Add("Properties")
        MyProperties = MyType.GetProperties
        For Each MyProperty In MyProperties
            node.Nodes.Add(MyProperty.Name)
        Next
Next
```

The end result is a `TreeView` control that maps out a crude picture of the program's structure, showing every class in the application and its members (Figure 7-6). In this case, you'll find a few automatically generated classes (used to support the `My` objects), and the custom form class. You'll find this project (named Reflection) with the examples for this chapter.

Figure 7-6: Reflection information

Reflection is useful in countless unusual scenarios, but it's usually not a part of day-to-day development. Sometimes, it's interesting to experiment with reflection just to get a better idea of how the .NET engine works and how it classifies and organizes types and metadata.

You may find it interesting to explore reflection in more detail. Use the `Assembly` class as a starting point, and let it lead you to the other "info" classes in the `System.Reflection` namespace. Each one is customized to provide information about a special type of code construct and its metadata (for example, the preceding code uses the `EventInfo` class, which provides detailed information about the signature of an individual event).

Creating a .NET Component

A good way to understand .NET assemblies is to create a simple component of your own. As in earlier versions of Visual Basic, a *component* is a collection of one or more classes that contains a set of related functions and features. These classes are provided in a .dll file, and the client can create objects based on these classes as though the class definition were part of the current project.

NOTE   *In many cases, .NET developers use the terms* component *and* assembly *interchangeably. Technically, an assembly is a compiled .NET component. However, the term* component *is also used in a looser, less formal sense to refer to any package of related code.*

Creating a Class Library Project

The `Person` and `NuclearFamily` classes you saw in Chapters 5 and 6 could form the basis of a logical component. Currently, these class definitions are located inside the Windows Forms project that was designed to test them. By extracting these classes into a separate component, we acquire a separately distributable, shareable component that can be used in any type of application, including an ASP.NET website or a web service (see Chapters 12 and 13 for more about these project types). In small-scale projects, this pattern—where a class is developed inside a project and later made into a separate component—is a common one.

To create a component, choose File ▶ New ▶ Project from the Visual Studio menu. Then choose the Class Library project type from the Visual Basic project group (Figure 7-7).

An ordinary VB 2005 project will be created, without any graphical components such as Windows forms. You can use as many files as you want for creating classes. In our example, the class library will use code that has already been developed in another project. To transfer the code, you can import the existing .vb files into the project, or you can open another instance of Visual Studio, open the source project, and cut and paste the appropriate class definitions for the `NuclearFamily` and `Person` classes.

Once the code has been copied, you only need to build the project. You can build it by clicking the standard Start button. A .dll file with the project name will be compiled in the bin directory, and you will receive a warning message informing you that the project can only be compiled, not executed. Unlike stand-alone applications, components need a client that uses them, and they can't accomplish anything on their own. To skip the error message, just right-click the project in the Solution Explorer, and click Build whenever you want to generate the assembly.

Figure 7-7: Creating a class library

Creating a Client

To create a client, begin by either opening an existing project or starting a new Windows Forms application. Then, right-click the project in the Solution Explorer, and choose Add Reference.

To add your reference, click the Browse tab, and hunt for the .dll file from your class library project, as shown in Figure 7-8. You'll find the .dll file in the bin directory inside the project folder (for example, PersonComponent). Select the file, and click OK.

TIP *The approach demonstrated here (adding a reference using the compiled file) is a good way to learn about .NET components, because it's clear exactly what's taking place. However, if you plan to develop a client and a component at the same time, there's an easier way to debug them both. Begin by adding both projects to the same solution. (Make sure you set your client as the startup project, by right-clicking it in the Solution Explorer and choosing Set As StartUp Project.) This keeps all of your code together for easy editing. Now, when you add your reference, choose it from the Projects tab. That way, whenever you change anything in the component, a new version will be compiled for the client automatically.*

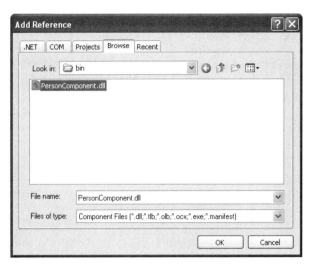

Figure 7-8: Referencing PersonComponent.dll

Once you have chosen the right file, click OK to continue. Visual Studio will copy the .dll file to the bin directory of the current project. The classes defined in your class library project will now automatically be available in your current project, just as though you had defined them in that project. The only difference is that you need to use the namespace of your project library in order to access its classes, as shown in Figure 7-9.

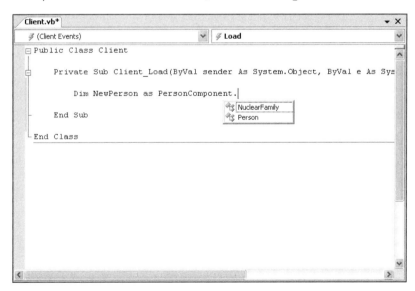

Figure 7-9: Using PersonComponent.dll

TIP   *To confirm that the component has been added as you expect, you can select Project ▶ Show All Files from the menu, and check the References group in the Solution Explorer. Your component should be listed as one of the references that's linked to your project.*

This is code sharing at its most efficient, and it easily crosses language barriers. You can work with C# classes in VB 2005 and vice versa, without even being aware of the difference. You can even inherit from and extend a class in a .dll file, using any .NET language. The actual .dll assembly is language-neutral and has its code stored in special IL instructions, like those you saw in the ILDasm program.

When you decide to deploy your new client project, you will once again notice how dramatic the differences are between COM and .NET. In COM development, you would need to first copy the custom component to the Windows system directory on the new computer, register it, and then use the client program. In .NET development, no registration is required. The class library .dll and client .exe files can be copied to any directory on the new computer, and they will work automatically. The .exe file has all the information that .NET needs in its manifest about dependencies. It will automatically locate the class library .dll, as long as it is present in the same directory.

The Global Assembly Cache

Not all assemblies are private. For example, no one would want to install a separate version of the .NET class library in the directory for each .NET application. For these situations, Microsoft still includes a central component repository. This time, instead of tossing files into a system directory shared with drivers and other system devices, Windows uses a dedicated area called the Global Assembly Cache (GAC). The GAC differs from the Windows system directory in a number of other important respects as well. For example, it allows—in fact, encourages—multiple versions of the same component to be installed. It doesn't lock files so that they can't be updated when in use; instead, it phases out existing users and provides the updated version for new users (or when the program is restarted). Finally, it allows you to put customized versioning policies into place that dictate exactly which version of a component an application will use.

Even with all these advances, you should resist the urge to start throwing components into the GAC. Many of the factors that required a global component store in the past simply don't apply in the .NET world. With COM, a component had to be part of the global registry in order to be used. In .NET, this isn't the case. If you develop your own component, there's no reason to use the GAC. In fact, even if you purchase a third-party component to use with your applications, there may still be no reason to put it in the GAC. You'll probably be better off just copying the file into your application directory. Remember, the .NET philosophy values easy, painless deployment over a few dozen extra megabytes of disk space. When in doubt, use a local, private assembly.

On the other hand, if you are developing your own components for other developers to use in their applications, or some other type of assembly that you want to make globally available on an entire system, the GAC may be exactly what you need. To take a look at the GAC, browse to the Windows directory in Windows Explorer, and then head to the Assembly subdirectory. Thanks to a dedicated plug-in within Windows Explorer, you'll see assemblies with their name, culture, and version information. Figure 7-10 shows a partial list of what you'll see on a computer that has both .NET 1.0 and 2.0 installed.

NOTE   Culture *is a technical term for a group of settings that apply to specific region or language. For example, a culture groups together information like the date and time formatting conventions, the language, sorting and text display rules, and so on. An example of a culture is zh-TW, which represents Chinese (Taiwan). You'll find .NET support for localization in the* System.Globalization *namespace.*

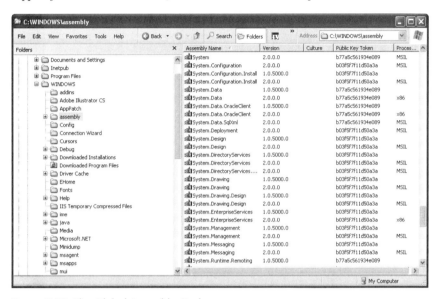

Figure 7-10: The Global Assembly Cache

The GAC is slightly less intimidating than the world of COM, because it has fewer components. More components and controls are bundled together in single assemblies. Also, the only assemblies that will be present initially are part of the .NET Framework.

The GAC "Under the Hood"

The appearance of a single list of files in the GAC is slightly deceptive. If what you see was really what you get, this simple approach would lead to two obvious problems:

Name collision
What would happen if you installed another assembly with the same filename as an existing assembly?

Versioning problems
One of .NET's greatest advances is its ability to store more than one version of an assembly in the GAC, so that every program uses exactly the version for which it was designed. But how is that possible if assemblies use the same filename?

The GAC reality is a little more surprising. What you see in Explorer is the product of a thoughtful Explorer plug-in. If you use a low-level utility to view directories, or a command prompt listing, you'll see a very different picture of the GAC (Figure 7-11).

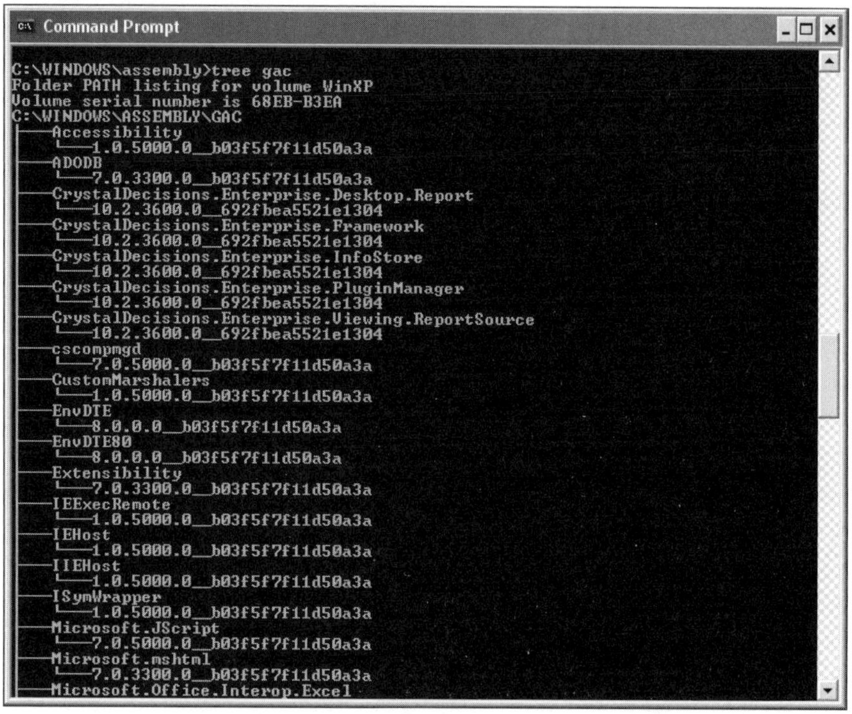

Figure 7-11: A partial listing of GAC directories

Instead of a simple list of assembly files, the GAC is really a complex directory structure. This structure allows multiple versions of any assembly, and uses special strong names to ensure that a name collision is impossible. The actual assembly file is given the name you see in the GAC plug-in, but it's stored in a special directory that uses the version number and a uniquely generated ID (such as C:\[WinDir]\Assembly\GAC\System.Web\ 2.0.2411.0__b03f5f7f11d50a3a, which could be used to store a version of the System.Web.dll assembly).

Creating a Shared Assembly

Now that you know the truth about the GAC, it probably won't come as a surprise to find out that you can't copy a private assembly directly into it. (In Windows Explorer, the Paste command is disabled.) Instead, you have to create a *shared assembly*.

Before you can copy a file to the GAC, you need to create a *strong name* for it. A strong name is a special concept introduced by .NET to help ensure that DLL Hell is never an issue. The idea is that all the assemblies you create are signed with a special key that only you possess. This system makes it impossible for anyone else to create an assembly that pretends to be a new version of your component. The strong name you use for a shared assembly also includes an ID that is guaranteed to be statistically unique (much like a GUID).

To make a long story short, you need to follow four steps:

1. Create a key.
2. Add the key to your assembly.
3. Then compile your assembly.
4. Install the assembly into the GAC.

In earlier versions of .NET, you had to resort to command-line tools to get the job done. In Visual Basic 2005, however, you can perform the first two steps right inside the design environment.

Creating a Key

The first step is to double-click the My Projects node in the Solution Explorer. Then click the Signing tab. This tab is a little intimidating, because its options include both the strong naming feature we're interested in right now and a signing feature for ClickOnce (which is discussed in Chapter 14). For now, stick to the strong naming feature, and check the Sign The Assembly check box. Next, in the Choose A Strong Name Key File list, choose New, supply a filename, and (optionally) a password, and click OK (see Figure 7-12). You'll see the key file appear in the Solution Explorer.

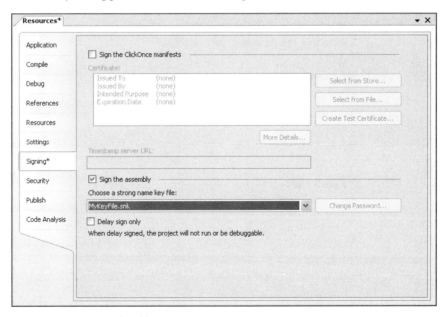

Figure 7-12: Setting a key file

TIP *.NET actually provides two types of key files: ordinary key files, which have the file extension .snk, and password-protected key files, which have the file extension .pfx. As you probably guessed, Visual Studio decides which one to create based on whether or not you supply a password when you create the key file. Although the security isn't ironclad, .pfx files add an extra layer of protection, because other developers won't be allowed to use them to sign applications unless they can supply the password.*

Each key file has a combination of a private and a public key. The public key is typically made available to the world. The private key is carefully guarded and should never be released to more than a selected few people in a specific organization. Private and public keys provide a special type of encryption. Anything encrypted with a private key can be read only with the corresponding public key. Anything encrypted with the public key can only be read with the corresponding private key. This is a time-honored encryption system used in email and other Internet applications.

In .NET use, the private key is used when the assembly is created, and the public key is stored in the assembly's manifest. When someone runs the assembly from the GAC, the Common Language Runtime uses the public key to decode information from the manifest. If a different key was used to sign, the operation will fail. In other words, by using a key pair, you can be sure that only a person with access to the key file can create an assembly with your identity. On the other hand, anyone can run a properly signed file, thanks to the included public key.

TIP *Once you have a key file, you can reuse it in as many projects as you want. You can even create a key file outside of Visual Studio, by using the sn.exe tool that's included with .NET. The magical command line to create a new key file with sn.exe is* sn -k KeyFileName.snk.

Installing the Assembly into the GAC

You now have a variety of options for installing the assembly into the GAC. You can use a dedicated setup program (see Chapter 14) or the GACUtil.exe utility, or you can drag and drop the assembly using the Windows Explorer GAC plug-in. Either way, the directory structure is created for you automatically, your assembly is copied, and your component will appear in the GAC list.

Policy Files

One of the most exciting features with strongly named assemblies is that you can configure their versioning settings. You do this by creating a file with the same name as the corresponding .dll or .exe file and adding the extension .config. This file will be automatically examined by the Common Language Runtime for additional information about where to search for assemblies and which versions to allow.

The information in the .config file is stored in a readable XML format. However, we're not going to discuss the format of the .config file. If you're curious, you can explore the Visual Studio Help. Instead, I recommend that you use a convenient management snap-in provided by Microsoft and shown in Figure 7-13. To run the .NET Framework Configuration utility, select Settings ▶ Control Panel ▶ Administrative Tools ▶ Microsoft .NET Framework 2.0 Configuration from the Start menu.

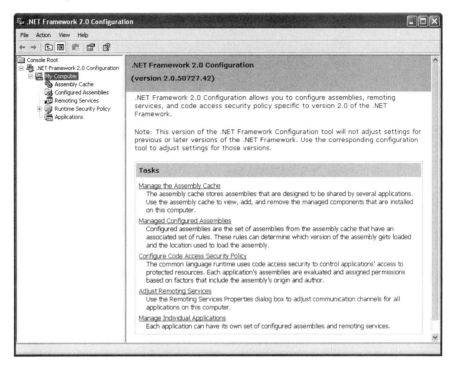

Figure 7-13: The .NET Framework Configuration utility

The configuration utility is filled with a dizzying number of options for everything from setting computer-wide security settings to viewing assembly dependencies. In this section, you'll consider how to use the configuration utility for a single purpose: to set a version policy.

To understand why this is necessary, consider the following scenario. You have installed a newer assembly to the GAC that is still backward compatible and improves performance. However, because it uses a new version number, it won't be used by existing applications. The solution? On an application-by-application basis, you can instruct programs to use the new version.

Creating a Version Policy

Here's how to change the version policy for an assembly. First, browse to the Configured Assemblies node in the tree, and click Configure An Assembly, which brings up the window shown in Figure 7-14.

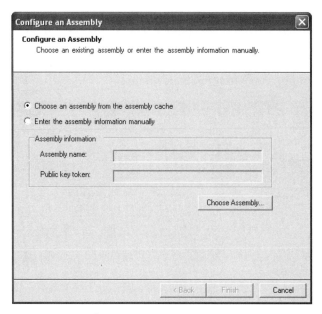

Figure 7-14: Configuring an assembly

Click the Choose Assembly button, and select the appropriate assembly from the GAC. Once you have confirmed your selection, you'll see a tabbed Properties window that allows you to change assembly options:

- The General tab provides basic information about the assembly.
- The Binding Policy tab allows you to configure version policies, which is our focus in this example.
- The Codebases tab allows you to specify a path for automatic downloading and updating of assemblies.

To set a new version policy, you need to add entries to the Binding Policy tab. Each entry links a requested version (or a range of requested versions) to a new version number. The requested version is what the client application attempts to access. The new version is the assembly that the Common Language Runtime decides to use instead. Essentially, .NET forwards the request for the assembly to another version of the same assembly.

In the following sample configuration (Figure 7-15), the component will use the version 2.0.0.0 when a request is received for any version between 0.0.0.0 and 1.9.9.9. This version is known to be backward compatible and to provide the best performance. A similar specification is made for versions between 3.0.0.0 and 3.9.9.9. However, a request for any other version (like 2.5.0.2, for example) will not be forwarded, and the requested assembly version will be used, if it exists.

NOTE   *The binding policy only applies to strongly named assemblies, and it only makes sense when you're dealing with shared assemblies in the GAC (where more than one version can coexist). When you create an ordinary private assembly without a strong name, the client application will simply use whatever version of the component is in the current directory.*

Figure 7-15: Creating a version policy

Resources

Many applications have related resources—ingredients like sound files, bitmaps, and large blocks of help text (which are occasionally translated into multiple languages). You could store all this information in separate files, but that complicates your deployment, and it opens the door to all kinds of insidious problems, like strange errors when these files go missing or are modified outside your program.

.NET has always had a solution for this type of problem, but in Visual Basic 2005 it finally has the convenient design-time support you need to use it effectively. The basic idea is that you'll take these separate files and embed them as binary data directly inside your compiled assembly (.dll or .exe file). That keeps them safe from prying eyes and tampering. When your program needs the resource, it can pull it out of the assembly, and hand it back to your program as a stream of bytes (or some more convenient data type).

Adding a Resource

To try this out, create a new Windows application. Then, double-click the My Project node in the Solution Explorer, and select the Resources tab. The Resources tab is the central place where you can add, remove, and manage all your resources. Resources are grouped into separate categories based on the type of content—for example, there's a separate section for string text (which you can edit by hand), images, icons, audio, and any other type of file. You choose the type of resource you want to see from the Category drop-down list (see Figure 7-16).

In this case, we're interested in images, so select the Images category. Each category has a slightly different view—the Images category shows a thumbnail of each picture. Of course, in a new application you'll start off without any image files.

To add a new picture, select Add Resource ▸ Add Existing File from the toolbar. Browse to an image file, select it, and click OK. If you don't have an image file handy, try using one from the Windows directory.

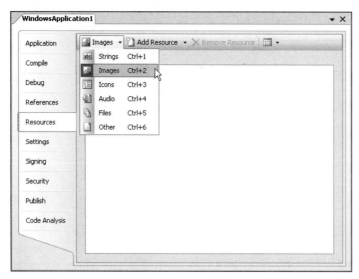

Figure 7-16: Viewing a type of resource

When you add a new resource, Visual Studio gives it the same name as its current filename (minus the extension, and with slight changes if the name isn't valid as a VB variable name). However, you can rename the resource after adding it by right-clicking the label and choosing Rename. Figure 7-17 shows an example with two sample images that have been added as resources.

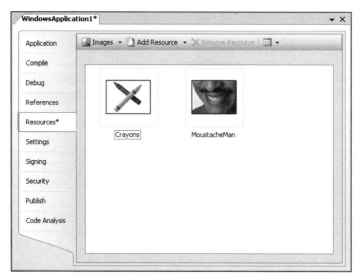

Figure 7-17: Adding image resources

Something interesting happens when you add a resource. Visual Studio creates a Resources subdirectory in your project directory and copies the file there. You can see this directory, along with all the resources it contains, in the Solution Explorer (see Figure 7-18).

Figure 7-18: Resource files in your project

In other words, the source files for your resources are kept around as part of your project. However, when you compile your application, each one of these resources is embedded into the assembly. The beauty of this model is that it's easy to update a resource—all you need to do is overwrite the file in the Resources folder and then recompile your application. In other words, you can safely use a resource in dozens of different code files and still update that resource with a single copy and paste operation. This is a much better approach than in previous programming frameworks. For example, Visual Basic 6 programmers often stored resources in separate files, which made their applications vulnerable if these files went missing or were tampered with.

Using a Resource

The only remaining step is to actually use the resource in the project. Because it's embedded in the assembly when your program is compiled, you don't need to fish it out from the file. In fact, the file won't even be deployed with your application. Instead, you need the help of a dedicated .NET class called the ResourceManager.

You don't need to use the ResourceManager directly. Instead, Visual Basic exposes all of your resources as dedicated properties of the My.Resources object. For example, imagine you've added the Crayons resource shown in Figure 7-17. You can retrieve it as an Image object from My.Resources using the automatically generated My.Resources.Crayons property. Here's an example of how you might take the image and assign it to the background of a form:

```
Private Sub Form1_Load(ByVal sender As System.Object, _
  ByVal e As System.EventArgs) Handles MyBase.Load
    Me.BackgroundImage = My.Resources.Crayons
    Me.BackgroundImageLayout = ImageLayout.Tile
End Sub
```

Figure 7-19 shows the result.

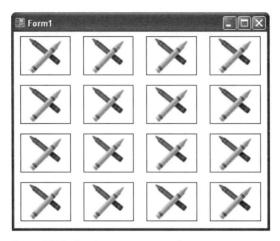

Figure 7-19: Displaying an image from a resource

In most cases, you won't resort to code to use a resource, unless you're planning to do some custom drawing or you want to use a dynamic effect (like an image that appears when the mouse moves over a portion of your form). The Visual Studio designer gives you great support for attaching image resources to other controls. For example, if you drop a PictureBox control onto your Windows form, you can click the ellipsis (. . .) in the Properties window next to the Image property to bring up the designer shown in Figure 7-20. It allows you to choose an image from any resource in your project.

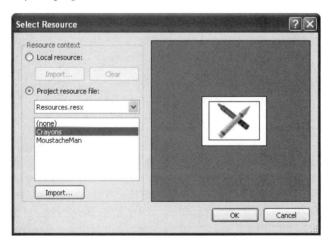

Figure 7-20: Attaching an image to a resource at design time

NOTE   *You can use the Local Resource option in the top portion of this window to import a picture and add it as a resource for just the current form. This mimics the behavior of earlier versions of Visual Basic. It gives you the benefit of embedding the resource in your assembly, but it has a serious drawback—namely, the image file isn't copied to the Resources subdirectory, so there's no easy way to update it. You also won't be able to use the same image resource with multiple forms.*

Incidentally, if you're curious you can see the automatically generated code for the `My.Resources` class (although you should never attempt to change it). To see this code, choose Project ▶ Show All Files and look for the Resources.Designer.vb file under the My Project node in the Solution Explorer.

Resources are used for other tasks in .NET. For example, you can experiment with different types of resources, like sounds and files, which you can retrieve in you program as byte arrays and stream objects. Resources also allow you to *localize* forms, a process by which you define control text in different languages and the proper version is applied automatically depending on the locale settings of the current computer. You can find out much more about localization in the Visual Studio Help.

What Comes Next?

This chapter has explored the heart of .NET versioning and how it differs radically from the COM way of life. You also you took a look at how you can embed resources (useful bits of binary information) directly into your assemblies, so your component never has to go looking for the data it needs.

Much of the complexity explored here won't affect you—thanks to .NET's planning, deploying an application is often just as easy as copying a directory. But if you want a deeper understanding of the .NET Framework, you can play with such tools as reflection, ILDasm, and the .NET Framework Configuration tool, all of which were introduced here.

Overall, .NET assemblies lay the groundwork for a new way to deploy applications. You already know enough to get a .NET application working on another computer. After all, as long as the .NET Framework is installed it's just a matter of transferring files. In Chapter 14, you'll go one step further and learn how you can create customized setup programs with a few more frills.

8

BUG PROOFING

Bugs—flaws in a program's logic, design,
or syntax—have crashed everything from
personal computers to a $125 million Mars
orbiter. This chapter examines how you can
code defensively, restrict possible problems, and protect yourself from bugs. You'll also learn how to handle
common problems by using Visual Basic 2005's structured exception handling,
which replaces the well-worn On Error Goto statement of classic VB. This
error-handling infrastructure allows you to filter out specific errors, pass
error information in exception objects, and deal with exceptions in
deeply nested code.

Traditional VB error handling used a sort of "traffic redirection" to deal
with problems. That made it very difficult to isolate error-handling code from
application code, and the resulting spaghetti-like tangle could actually make
errors more likely. VB 2005 exception handling works like a handcrafted net.
You design this net to catch specific error types, and then handle them
appropriately if they occur.

Of course, even the best error-handling methods won't stop every
potential problem. Eventually a bug will slip into your program, producing

an error that you can't fix, or generating results that just don't make sense. VB 2005 continues to offer the wide range of debugging tools found in earlier versions of Visual Basic, with some additional refinements. In this chapter, you'll learn how to use these tools to track down and exterminate any bug that's loose in your software. You'll also learn some debugging techniques that will help you peer into the low-level gears and wires of your applications and uncover what's really taking place while your code executes.

New in .NET

Visual Basic has always provided a rich set of debugging tools, and these tools are still available in VB 2005, with a few helpful tweaks and improvements. The real story, however, is the error-handling syntax that modernizes VB to match other .NET languages.

Some of the changes you'll see in this chapter include:

Structured exception handling
Finally, you can remove the last Goto statement from your application and clean out spaghetti code for good. Visual Basic 2005's structured exception handling helps you ensure that your application's error recovery logic is as clean and well organized as the rest of your code.

Error highlighting
Visual Basic has always been famous for catching errors as you type, and with the .NET platform, its intelligence has grown. Now troublesome code will be automatically underlined, identifying where you've tried to use a method or variable that doesn't seem to exist, or where you've performed an illegal data conversion. VB 2005 even flags code that isn't an error but might indicate an unintentional slip-up, like defining a variable but never using it.

Type safety
Accidental conversion errors are no longer a silent killer. VB 2005 allows you to forbid dangerous conversions, thus giving you tighter control over your code.

Improved debugging tools
With Visual Basic 2005, the great gets better. Enhanced debugging tools, including an improved Call Stack display and a Breakpoints window, make it a breeze to hunt down troublesome code. You can even set different debugging options (like break or continue) for different types of errors.

The return of the "run-edit-and-continue" pattern
Visual Basic .NET 1.0 lost the indispensable run-edit-and-continue feature due to the dramatic change in the way .NET applications are compiled (as compared to classic VB). But in the time since, Microsoft has been hard at work on the problem, and starting with Visual Basic 2005 you will once again be able to modify your programs on the fly while you're running them in the debugger. In fact, in several respects this feature has even been *improved* from classic VB.

Understanding Errors

Bugs exist in many different varieties—some exotic, others as well known as the common housefly. Some of the species you'll see include:

Editor mistakes

Mistyped words and syntax errors are source-code mistakes that are best caught as early as possible. The Visual Basic 2005 editor includes a sophisticated error checker that finds these errors as you type. This tool is your first defense against errors, and it's one of the best ways to catch minor mistakes and save time.

Compile-time errors

Compile-time errors can result when you ignore an editor mistake, or if you make some other type of error—such as trying to perform a math operation with a string—that may not be caught until the program is being built. When you run a program from the Visual Studio IDE, any compile-time errors are reported to you in the Output window and on the Error List.

Runtime errors

Runtime errors are problems that occur while the program is being used. Usually, a runtime error is an unhandled error that propagates back to the user and ends the program. For example, if you try to open a file that doesn't exist and don't provide any error-handling code, the Common Language Runtime will provide an error message and your code will stop abruptly. A compile-time error usually cannot become a runtime error, because Visual Basic 2005 will refuse to compile the offending code. (When you try to launch it, Visual Studio will explain the problem and give you the option to continue with the previously compiled version of your program.) However, a code statement that is syntactically correct may still result in a runtime problem. For example, trying to access a web page on a computer that may or may not have an Internet connection can cause a runtime error.

Logic errors

This is the most insidious type of bug, because it is often difficult to determine what part of the code is responsible. Code containing a *logic error* runs without generating any warning or error messages. However, the information or behavior that results is clearly not what is expected. A good example is an investment program that automatically *subtracts* 1.5 percent interest on existing balances.

Errors that can't happen

One of the goals of the .NET platform is to make your life easier. There are entire classes of errors that have troubled generations of earlier programmers but are now impossible. Memory leaks, pointer errors, and other types of fiendish problems that have plagued our programming ancestors are carefully defended against in the .NET world.

The Principles of Bug Proofing

The following rules will guide you in creating high-quality applications.

The earlier an error is detected, the better.

You should celebrate when Visual Basic 2005 generates a build error and refuses to compile your code. When a compile-time error occurs, it means that Visual Basic 2005's automatic error checking has found a potential problem that you've missed and has identified it so that you don't have to spend hours trying to troubleshoot a mystery in the future. Visual Basic 2005 improves on Visual Basic 6 by detecting many common errors earlier—finding missing variables while you type, for instance, instead of when you compile, and flagging data-type conversion problems with compile-time errors before they create runtime errors.

Expect the unexpected.

Later in this chapter, we'll consider some basic techniques for coding defensively. Once you start expecting users to enter strange and possibly illogical input, you are ready to prepare and prevent possible catastrophes. Often you can tell the novice programmer from the expert not by how fast an application is completed, but by how well the application stands up after a few months of intensive use in the field.

Don't ignore the compiler.

Once your program gets into the hands of users, and inexplicable errors start to occur, a trivial problem that once seemed to be fixed by a randomly changed line may keep you awake for a few sleepless nights.

Test early and test often.

I won't spend much time in this chapter talking about testing, because it really is a straightforward process. Still, it is amazing how many programmers don't try out their own creations, thus missing mistakes that can hurt their pride and careers once they deliver the code. None of the great tools in Visual Basic 2005 can remove the inevitability of human error, so be thorough, and make use of the debugging tools discussed in this chapter. Some programmers even insist that they won't let any code out of their hands until they've single-stepped through every line in every function.

Errors at Compile Time

Visual Basic 2005's treatment of errors is straightforward, but slightly different than in previous releases. In Visual Basic 6, the editor would interrupt you every time you made a mistake with an intrusive message box (as seen in Figure 8-1).

Visual Basic 2005 takes a friendlier approach, working as your partner, not your prosecutor. The process works like this:

- First, if you've made an obvious, clear-cut mistake, the editor tries to correct it for you automatically. For example, you'll notice that if you start an If block and leave out the word Then, the editor will add it for you. It will also add certain details (such as the closing End If, in this case) to prevent you from making other possible mistakes.

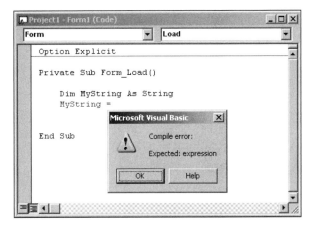

Figure 8-1: The intrusive editor in Visual Basic 6

- If the editor can't correct the mistake, it will underline the offending code. Common reasons for underlining include using a variable, method, or property that's not defined, calling a method with the wrong number of arguments, or using a language construct with syntax that just doesn't make sense (for example, writing If End instead of End If). If you have Option Strict enabled (and you should; see the next section for details), invalid variable assignments and conversions will also be highlighted. If you're wondering why a line is underlined, place the mouse over the line and read the corresponding tooltip text (see Figure 8-2).

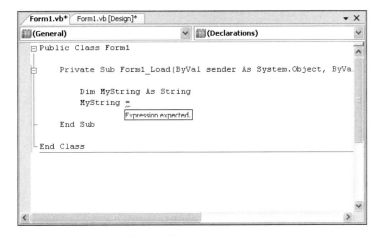

Figure 8-2: The polite editor in VB 2005

- When you compile a program, either for debugging or as a release, any editor errors you've ignored will become compile-time errors, and you'll be asked if you want to continue (Figure 8-3). If you continue, your application will not be recompiled, and you'll end up testing the previously compiled version of your code, without your recent changes.

Figure 8-3: A failed build

- Instead of continuing with compile-time mistakes, you should cancel the build process and review the contents of the Error List window (see Figure 8-4). This window appears automatically when you build an application that contains at least one compile error. Visual Basic 2005 makes it easy for you: Just double-click on an entry in the Error List, and you'll be brought to the appropriate spot in your code, with the error highlighted. This is a big improvement over Visual Basic 6, where you were told about errors one by one, and you had to fix the current error before finding out about the rest. Once you've corrected these errors, you can successfully launch your application and get to work.

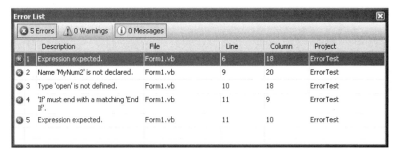

Figure 8-4: Problems in the error list

Option Explicit and Option Strict

These two lifesaving options should always be enabled. Option Explicit stops you from using a variable without creating it, and thus prevents the mistakes that can occur when a new, empty variable is automatically created after you misspell the name of an existing variable. Option Explicit is enabled by default.

Option Strict is new to the .NET versions of Visual Basic. It prevents errors that can result from attempted automatic variable conversions. For example, converting an Int32 into an Int16 is a "narrowing" conversion, and it may or may not succeed. With Option Strict off, you are free to try. . . .

```
Option Strict Off

Private Sub SwapNumbers(BigNumber As Int32, SmallNumber As Int16)
    Dim Swap As Int32
    Swap = BigNumber

    ' This is a widening conversion; it always works.
    BigNumber = SmallNumber

    ' This is a riskier narrowing conversion.
    SmallNumber = Swap
    ' Sure, it works now, but it could become a fatal
    ' runtime error under the right circumstances.
End Sub
```

In this example, Visual Basic won't complain, and you'll be blissfully unaware of the potential time bomb—until you submit a value for BigNumber that is larger than 32,767.

With Option Strict on, it's a different story. The code will be underlined, and an error will be generated at compile time. You won't be allowed to use the code without modifying it to perform an explicit (manual) conversion. At that point, you'll probably realize the potential problem, and either change SmallNumber to an Int32 or rewrite the code with an extra safeguard:

```
Option Strict On

Private Sub SwapNumbers(BigNumber As Int32, SmallNumber As Int16)
    Dim Swap As Int32
    Swap = BigNumber

    ' This is a widening conversion; it always works.
    BigNumber = SmallNumber

    If BigNumber > SmallNumber.MaxValue Then
        MessageBox.Show "Sorry, this number doesn't fit."
    Else
        ' The CType function manually converts the number.
        SmallNumber = CType(Swap, Int16)
    End If
End Sub
```

This example makes use of the MaxValue constant that is built into many simple data types, including integers. It indicates the largest number that the current variable can hold (which is 32,767 in this case). By using the MaxValue constant, you can avoid coding the number directly into the program, and you allow the program to continue working even if you change the data type of SmallNumber.

If you suspect that Option Strict or Option Explicit is not enabled for your project, right-click your project in the Solution Explorer, and select Properties. Now click the Compile tab (shown in Figure 8-5). You can use this tab to set both the Option Strict and Option Explicit settings. You can also configure a list of warnings that work in addition to these settings. For example, you can allow implicit conversions but ask the compiler to warn you when you inadvertently rely on this behavior.

Although the Option Explicit and Option Strict settings are the best defense, the warnings are also helpful. In fact, some of the warnings catch potential error conditions that would otherwise pass unnoticed, like declaring a variable but not using it, creating a function that doesn't provide a return value, or creating recursive code (for example, properties that refer to themselves, and are likely to tie your code up in an endless loop of self-referencing).

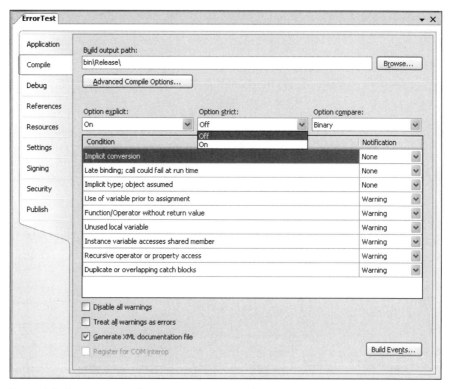

Figure 8-5: Project settings for Option Explicit and Option Strict

Line Numbers

Line numbers were once the hallmark of old-fashioned programming languages—such as the original DOS version of BASIC. In Visual Basic 6, you were able to optionally add numbers to specific lines. In Visual Basic 2005, you can't even do that. Line numbers have vanished. Or have they?

One well-kept secret is that you can enable a line number display for your code by selecting Tools ▶ Options to display the Options window, and then selecting the Text Editor ▶ Basic ▶ General tab. Click the Line Numbers check box, and Visual Studio will display a margin that numbers every line in the file, including blank ones (see Figure 8-6).

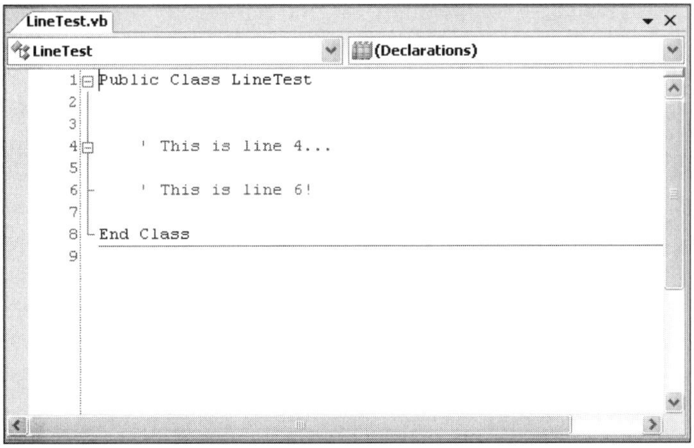

Figure 8-6: Line numbers return from the past

You can't directly enter or change these numbers. So why use them? As you'll see later in this chapter, Visual Basic errors include line number information that pinpoints where an error has occurred. If an unhandled error occurs at a client site, you can customize your error message to display or record the corresponding line number. Then you can track down the corresponding code at your desk, without needing to re-create the problem.

Visual Studio's Debugging Tools

It's bound to happen eventually. Illogical data appears. Strange behavior occurs. It looks as though information that you've never entered is appearing out of thin air, and code is being executed in a different order or in a different way than you expected. In other words, you've got a bug. So what should you do about it?

This section walks you through Visual Basic 2005's debugging tools, including *breakpoints* that let you study code flow, *watch windows* that let you examine variables in action, and the *call stack history*, which gives additional information about your program's place in the overall order of procedures.

Watching Your Program in Action

One of the greatest tools in any programming language is the ability to *step through* an application. This feature allows you to watch the action and study the flow, or the path, of execution your program takes, through the classes and functions that you provide it with. When you step through your code, you test the assumptions that you have about how it will work. You determine the order in which statements are executed, and the values that are recorded in your variables. Single-stepping allows you to spy on what your program is really up to.

To single-step through a Visual Basic 2005 program, follow these steps:

1. Find a convenient spot in your code where you want to pause execution and start single-stepping. Click in the gray margin next to the appropriate line to insert a red breakpoint (Figure 8-7). (You can put a breakpoint on any *executable* line of code. If you put it on a blank line, comment, or variable declaration, Visual Basic will quietly move your breakpoint down to the next executable line when you run your application.)

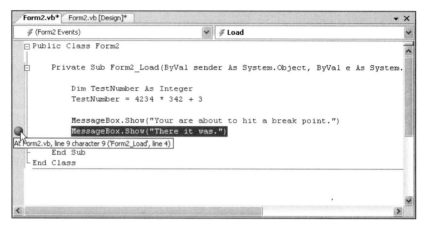

Figure 8-7: Setting a breakpoint

2. Run your program. When it reaches the breakpoint, execution will pause. The statement with the breakpoint will not be executed. This line will have a yellow arrow next to it, indicating that it is the next instruction that will be executed when the program resumes.

3. You can now hover over any variable to see its current value in a pop-up tooltip (see Figure 8-8).

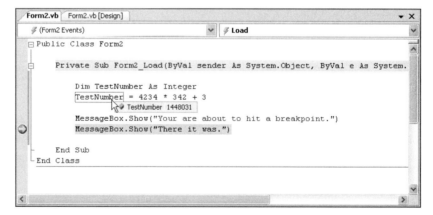

Figure 8-8: Checking out the contents of a variable

4. This a great way to test your assumptions about your code, and find out if there's a subtle disconnect between the information you think you're manipulating and the actual contents of your variables. To continue your investigation, you can run your program one line at a time by pressing F8.

Commands Available in Break Mode

While your program is paused, you can use the following commands. All of these commands have useful shortcut keys, and some are found in the Debug menu.

Step Into (F8)

> This command executes the currently highlighted line and then pauses again. If the currently highlighted line calls a method or a function, execution will pause at the first executable line *inside* the method or function (which is why this feature is called *stepping into*).

Step Over (SHIFT+F8)

> This command works the same as Step Into, except that it runs methods and functions as though they are a single line. If you press Step Over while a procedure call is highlighted, the entire method or function will be executed, and execution will pause at the next executable statement in the current procedure.

Step Out (CTRL+SHIFT+F8)

> This command executes all the code in the current procedure, and then pauses at the statement that immediately follows the one that called the executed method or function. In other words, it allows you to *step out* of the current procedure in one large jump.

Continue (F5)

> This command resumes the program and continues to run it normally, without pausing until another breakpoint is reached or you click the Pause button.

Run To Cursor (CTRL+F8)

> This command lets you run all the code up to a specified location (where your cursor is currently positioned). Run To Cursor is often used to skip a time-consuming loop, and is a little bit like creating a temporary breakpoint. You can also use this feature by right-clicking a line of code in break mode and choosing Run To Cursor from the context menu.

Set Next Statement (CTRL+F9)

> This command causes your program to mark the line where your cursor is positioned as the current line for execution. When you resume execution, that line will be executed, and the program will continue from that point. Essentially, Set Next Statement allows you to change your program's path of execution while you are debugging. This useful feature allows you to repeat a section of code, or to skip a section that is

potentially problematic or requires some sort of validation that would ordinarily prevent you from continuing. For example, you may have code that only runs in a certain situation. Rather than trying to re-create this situation, you can use the Set Next Statement command to jump directly to the appropriate section and run it.

TIP *There's another way to change the next statement to be executed. You can also click and drag the yellow arrow that points to the next line of code in break mode. Just drag it to where you want the code to resume, and then hit F8 or F5 to start it up.*

Show Next Statement

This command displays the current statement, which will be executed when you next press F8 or F5. The line will be marked by a yellow arrow. Show Next Statement is useful if you lose your place while editing, and you can choose it quickly from the right-click context menu.

The Breakpoints Window

You can take a quick look at all your breakpoints by using the Breakpoints window (Figure 8-9). Simply choose Debug ▶ Windows ▶ Breakpoints. In the Breakpoints window you will see a list of all the breakpoints defined in your project. You can jump to the corresponding location in code by double-clicking a breakpoint.

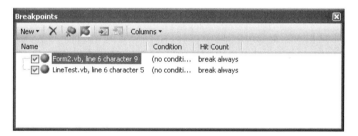

Figure 8-9: The Breakpoints window

If you uncheck a breakpoint, it appears in the code editor as a transparent gray circle with a red outline. This means that the breakpoint is disabled and will be ignored. However, you can quickly re-enable it from the Breakpoints window when it is needed again. The Breakpoints window also provides the hit count, showing the number of times a breakpoint has been encountered. The hit count is reset every time the program is stopped and restarted.

Unlike earlier versions of Visual Basic, VB 2005 automatically saves your breakpoints with your application. This means that you can insert breakpoints at important debugging points, temporarily disable them, and quickly enable them from the Breakpoints window when they are needed at a later time.

You can also configure breakpoint properties from this window by right-clicking an individual breakpoint. The following sections describe your options.

Condition

Sometimes you'll want to place a breakpoint in a heavily trafficked piece of code to hunt down an error. The problem is that this error might only happen in certain circumstances, whereas the breakpoint stops your code every time it's hit, which can be an annoying waste of time. Fortunately, there's a solution. You can set a condition that will be used to decide whether or not execution should pause at the breakpoint. To set a condition, right-click your breakpoint (either in the code margin or in the Breakpoints window), and select Condition.

For example, the condition shown in Figure 8-10 will stop execution at the specified point when the variable Animal contains the string "horse." Otherwise, the breakpoint will be ignored. You can use a condition to filter out a problem and then halt the program immediately when a specific piece of invalid data appears.

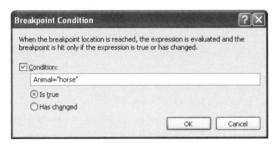

Figure 8-10: A sample breakpoint condition

Hit Count

The Hit Count window allows you to specify whether or not execution should pause at a breakpoint, depending on how many times the program has executed the line of code. This feature is useful when you create a breakpoint on a frequently executed line, such as one inside a loop. In this case, you may want to stop execution after a certain number of passes through the loop, rather than every time the statement is encountered.

Depending on the hit count options you set, you can configure your program to pause only after a breakpoint has been encountered a certain number of times, after a certain multiple of times (for example, every third time), or when the hit count is exactly equal to a specified number. To set the hit count, right-click the breakpoint and select Hit Count. Figure 8-11 shows a breakpoint that triggers every fifth time it's hit.

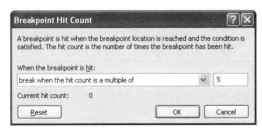

Figure 8-11: A Hit Count breakpoint condition

The Autos, Locals, and Watch Windows

When Visual Basic 2005 is in break mode, several additional tabbed windows are provided at the bottom of your screen. If any of these is not visible, you can display it using the Debug ▶ Windows menu.

The Autos, Locals, and Watch windows show you the contents of variables in break mode. As you have learned earlier in this chapter, you can inspect the current contents of a variable by finding it in your code and hovering your mouse cursor above it. However, the Autos, Locals, and Watch windows provide a more convenient way to peer "under the hood" at the contents of your variables.

- The Autos window is automatically set to variables that Visual Basic 2005 determines are probably important for the current breakpoint. Usually, these include only the variables that were accessed or changed in the previous line.

- The Locals window displays all the variables that are in scope in the current procedure. This window offers a quick summary of important variables.

- The Watch window is quite similar to the Autos and Locals windows. However, its list contains only variables that you have specifically added. This makes the Watch window well suited for prolonged testing, when you want to keep track of a specific variable or object during the lifetime of an application. Watches are even saved with your project, so you can pause testing and continue at a later time. You can add a watch quickly by double-clicking the last blank row in the Watch window and typing in an appropriate variable name, or by right-clicking a variable in your code display and selecting Add Watch.

Each row in the Autos, Locals, and Watch windows provides such information as the type or class of the variable or object, and its current value.

Object Structure

One of the most impressive features of the Autos, Locals, and Watch windows is that you can see the object structures of the classes and procedures in your program. For example, in the Locals window you'll see the term Me, which is a reference to the current class. Next to the word Me is a box with a plus sign (+), indicating that more information is available. Click this box to expand the Me reference and display all of its properties.

NOTE *The Watch window also shows information about nested objects. For example, an ordinary Form class contains a variable for each control displayed in the window. You can expand these variables to find out information about the properties of your text boxes, buttons, and labels.*

Figure 8-12 shows a good example of how to use a Watch window with an object. Using the Watch window on a Person object, it's possible to spot a potential mistake: The LastName property has not been initialized.

Figure 8-12: Examining the object structure of a Person

Notice that the Watch window knows no boundaries—it fearlessly displays both public data (properties such as `FirstName`, `LastName`, and `BirthDate`) and private data (the internal member variables, whose names are preceded with an underscore in this example).

Modifying Variables in Break Mode

The Autos, Locals, and Watch windows don't just display variables; they also allow you to change them while a program is in break mode. This allows you to easily re-create specific scenarios. For example, you might run a test to determine what happens when an invalid value is set in one of your variables.

To set a value, double-click the value in the `Value` column, and type the new value.

The Immediate Window

Longtime Visual Basic developers may remember the Immediate window, which is alive and well in VB 2005. Using the Immediate window, you can dump out the full contents of an object using the `Debug.Print` command (or the handy question mark shortcut), as shown in Figure 8-13.

Figure 8-13: Printing an object's contents

You can also use the Immediate window for more drastic actions, like assigning a new value to any variable that's currently in scope, or calling a method to trigger specific code in your application.

Errors at Runtime

As you've seen, you can switch your application into break mode at any time using breakpoints, and begin taking a closer look at your application's behind-the-scenes work. But breakpoints aren't the only way to get your program into break mode—Visual Studio also pauses your program when an error occurs.

When a runtime error occurs, .NET searches your code for an error handler that can deal with the problem. (You'll learn how to create these handlers later in this chapter.) If none is found, your program switches into break mode, and Visual Studio highlights the offending line, with a window that offers some tips for correcting the problem. Figure 8-14 shows an example. In this case, `Option Strict` is not enabled, so Visual Basic cheerily attempts to convert a string into a number. However, this string contains pure text, so the move is destined to fail.

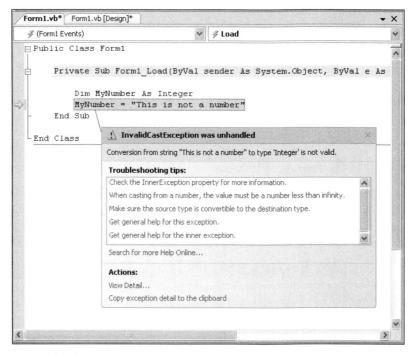

Figure 8-14: A runtime error

There are several steps you can take at this point. You can dodge the error, by dragging the yellow arrow to another line of code and then pressing F5 to resume running your application starting at that line. However, it's easy to skip over something you need, so this approach is likely to lead to another error.

Alternatively, you can try to resolve the error by editing the code. You don't need to stop your application to do this—Visual Basic allows you to tweak statements, refine your logic, and insert entirely new blocks of code while your application is paused. For example, replacing the string shown in Figure 8-14 with a number will take care of the problem, and you can resume execution by pressing F5.

Of course, there are some changes that will derail your debugging session. For example, deleting the current method where your code is running will put an end to your application. You can dig up a full list of unsupported changes in the Visual Studio Help (look under the "Edit and Continue" index entry). Visual Basic flags changes that will force a restart by underlining them with a squiggly line (similar to how it shows a compile error). You can hover over the line to get a full description, as shown in Figure 8-15.

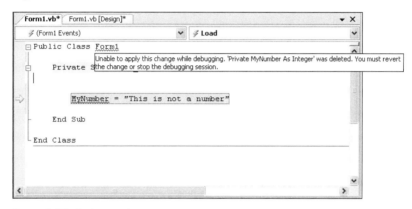

Figure 8-15: A change that requires a restart

NOTE   *If an error occurs while your application is running in the real world (instead of Visual Studio) debugging won't take place. Instead, the user will see a message explaining that an unhandled error occurred, with some fairly cryptic details. The program will then end. To prevent this rude ending, use exception handling, as described in the next section.*

Structured Exception Handling

Not every bug can be tracked down and removed from your program. In fact, there are some cases where an error can occur through no fault of your own. For example, if your program uses file input, when you open a file you are assuming that it is accessible to you, that the disk has not been corrupted by media failure or a virus, and that the file won't be deleted between the time the user selects it and the time your code attempts to read it.

Your application can and should handle basic verification procedures, such as checking that the file exists before attempting to open it, and checking that it contains the header that your program created to indicate that the file is valid. However, you can't defend yourself against all the possible problems that might occur. This is why Visual Basic 2005 provides *structured exception handling.*

Here's an example of structured exception handling in a file access routine:

```
Dim FileLine As String
Dim FileStream As System.IO.StreamReader

Try
    ' This code could cause a problem...
    FileStream = System.IO.File.OpenText("does_not_exist.txt")
    FileLine = FileStream.ReadLine()
Catch MyError As Exception
    ' We end up here if an error occurred.
    MessageBox.Show(MyError.Message)
Finally
    ' We end up here no matter what!
    If Not FileStream Is Nothing Then
        FileStream.Close()    ' Close the file.
    End If
End Try
```

The foundation of structured error handling is the Try/Catch/Finally block, which replaces certain patterns of use of Goto statements with a more modern structured construct, much as the If/End If or For/Next statements do.

In the preceding example, the portion of the code after the Try statement is the code that is being watched for errors. If an error occurs, the Catch portion of the code is executed. And either way, whether a bug occurs or not, the Finally section of the code is executed next. The Finally code allows you to perform some basic cleanup. Even if an unrecoverable error occurs that prevents the program from continuing, the Finally code will still be executed.

NOTE   *Along with this new method of error handling comes some new lingo. You've probably already noticed that it's not an error anymore, but an "exception." Also, exceptions aren't generated or raised but "thrown" by misbehaving code. Your Try/Catch block then "catches" the thrown exception.*

Understanding the Error Call Stack

When an error occurs in your application, Visual Basic 2005 tries to find a matching Catch statement in the current procedure. If none is found, the search continues through any Catch statements in the code that has called the current procedure. This process continues through the entire calling stack until a Catch block is found that can handle the current error, or until the search reaches the uppermost level of the application—at which point a runtime error will be generated, ending the program.

The Evolution from On Error Goto

Up until now, I've glossed over an ugly secret. Visual Basic 2005 still supports the `On Error Goto` command for backward compatibility. All your old programs can continue using it. However, you should adopt the new structured exception handling as soon as you start a new project. Why?

`On Error Goto` has a number of problems. Almost every other language, from Pascal to C++, has been using more advanced error handling for years. I hate to revisit ancient history, but here is a quick summary of what you are leaving behind when you enter the .NET world:

Spaghetti code

Error routines in Visual Basic 6 were clear and readable, as long as you were checking for only one type of error in one block of code. If you needed to handle multiple errors, you had to juggle numerous `On Error Goto` statements directing control to different sections of your program. Otherwise, you could determine the type of error, but not where it occurred.

Error monogamy

Visual Basic 6 has exactly one error object: the built-in `Err`. If an error occurs in your error-handling routine, or if you try to examine the error information in another routine, you'll find that all of the error information disappears immediately, leaving you empty-handed. Visual Basic 2005 exceptions are full-featured objects that you can catch and throw on your own, and pass from routine to routine.

Language limitations

Exceptions are built into the .NET runtime. This means that you can throw an exception in Visual Basic 2005 and catch it in C# without having to worry about writing compatibility code.

Limited diagnostic ability

The `Err` object just doesn't provide enough information. However, even the most basic exceptions contain a `StackTrace` property that gives you specific low-level information about where the error originated.

The Exception Object

The cornerstone of structured exception handling is the *exception object*. The basic exception class is `System.Exception`, and that's the type that we caught in the preceding example. Exceptions also exist in many different, more specialized versions that inherit from `System.Exception`. When an error is thrown, it's usually one of these more specific varieties. For example, in the previous file-handling example, the exception that occurred might have been `System.IO.EndOfStreamException` if the file existed but had no content, or it might have been `System.IO.FileNotFoundException` if the file had not been found.

To gain some insight into what an exception object is, it helps to examine one close up. A tool you can use for such an examination is the Locals window. To try it out, create a Windows Forms application, and enter the code from the previous file access example in the `Form.Load` event handler. This code is sure to fail, because the file does_not_exist.txt is not present on your computer. Now, place a breakpoint after the `Catch` line, on the `MessageBox.Show()` statement. When you run your program, the bug will be triggered, and the program will enter break mode. You can now take a closer look at the object structure of the exception you've caught in a Watch window (see Figure 8-16).

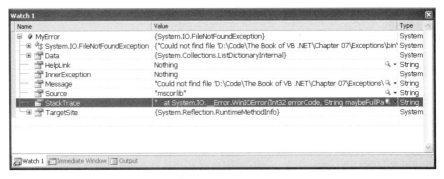

Figure 8-16: The internal structure of an exception

What does this tell us about the error object?

- Its type is indeed `System.IO.FileNotFoundException`.

- It comes with a `Message` property that contains explanatory text such as "Could not find file D:\does_not_exist.txt."

- It has a `Source` property that tells us which class or application the error occurred in.

- It has a `StackTrace` property that contains a whole list of information about the recent history leading up to the error. (The easiest way to see this information is usually to display it in the label of a message box.) The last line contains this important piece of information: "at ExceptionsAndAssertions.BasicExceptions.cmdThrow_Click(Object sender, EventArgs e) in D:\Code\The Book of VB .NET\Chapter 08\ Exceptions\BasicExceptions.vb:line 111".

- The last part of the `StackTrace` property indicates a line number that tells us where the problem occurred. This can be a very useful piece of information. For example, you might create a simple logging routine that automatically stores the `StackTrace` property in a text file when an error occurs. Then, if you have enabled line numbering as described earlier in this chapter, you can easily find the corresponding problem.

You can replace the `MessageBox.Show()` statement in the previous example with the following block of code. It reports more information about the exception (see Figure 8-17).

```
Dim Spacer As New String("-", 150)
Spacer = vbNewLine & Spacer & vbNewLine

' Use a StringBuilder, as this is the most efficient way
' to paste together a string.
Dim Message As New System.Text.StringBuilder()
Message.Append("Exception Type")
Message.Append(Spacer)
Message.Append(MyError.GetType().ToString() & vbNewLine & vbNewLine)
Message.Append("Message")
Message.Append(Spacer)
Message.Append(MyError.Message & vbNewLine & vbNewLine)
Message.Append("Stack Trace")
Message.Append(Spacer)
Message.Append(MyError.StackTrace)

MessageBox.Show(Message.ToString(), "Exception Occurred")
```

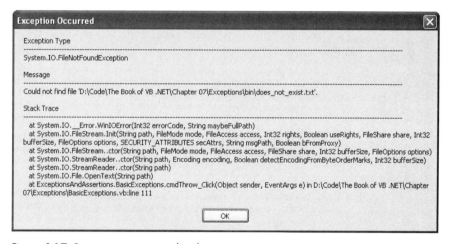

Figure 8-17: Reporting exception details

NOTE   *There are some other, less frequently used properties. For example, exceptions automatically have an* HResult *error code associated with them for backward compatibility with COM, and they can store a reference to a specific help file and topic in the* HelpLink *property.*

InnerException

One interesting property, InnerException, doesn't appear in the preceding example. InnerException is used when more than one error happens in quick succession. For example, a FileNotFoundException could trigger a higher-level data processing error, say a NullReferenceException, when you try to access a class that hasn't been initialized because the data couldn't be loaded from the file. In Visual Basic 6, you would lose track of all previous errors whenever a new error occurred. In Visual Basic 2005, however, you can preserve a previous error by putting it into the `InnerException` property of a new error object.

In the file access example, a custom class might return a `NullReferenceException` with a `FileNotFoundException` in the `InnerException` property, thus identifying the exception that started the whole problem. There's no limit to the number of errors you can chain together in this way. However, your code needs to perform this task manually, by creating a new exception object, and assigning the original exception to the `InnerException` property of this new object. (We'll consider how you can create your own exceptions a little later in this chapter.)

Filtering by Exception

The file access example used a generic error-handling routine that dealt with any error, regardless of the cause. The `Try/Catch/Finally` construct also allows you to identify specific types of exceptions and handle them separately. To do so, you would write several `Catch` statements, each designed to handle a different type of exception.

Consider the more sophisticated file access example here, which stores information read out of a file in a collection:

```
Dim FileLines As Collection
Dim FileStream As System.IO.StreamReader

Try
    FileStream = System.IO.File.OpenText("does_not_exist.txt")
    Do
        FileLines.Add FileStream.ReadLine()
    Loop
Catch MyError As System.IO.EndOfStreamException
    ' All the information has been read out of the file.
    ' No other action needs to be taken.
Catch MyError As System.IO.FileNotFoundException
    ' The file was not found.
    ' Add code to request a different file name from the user.
Catch MyError As Exception
    ' Some other error occurred.
    MessageBox.Show(MyError.Message)
Finally
    If Not FileStream Is Nothing Then
        FileStream.Close()   ' Close the file.
    End If
End Try
```

In this case, Visual Basic 2005 will automatically use the first matching exception when an error occurs. If an exception occurs, but it is not an `EndOfStreamException` or a `FileNotFoundException`, the final, generic `Catch` statement will handle it.

Exception Types

When writing code, you'll find it helpful to know what types of exceptions you can expect. You can get a nice overview from the Exceptions window (select Debug ▶ Exceptions). Expand the Command Language Runtime Exceptions item, and you'll see all the exceptions in the .NET class library, organized by namespace (as shown in Figure 8-18).

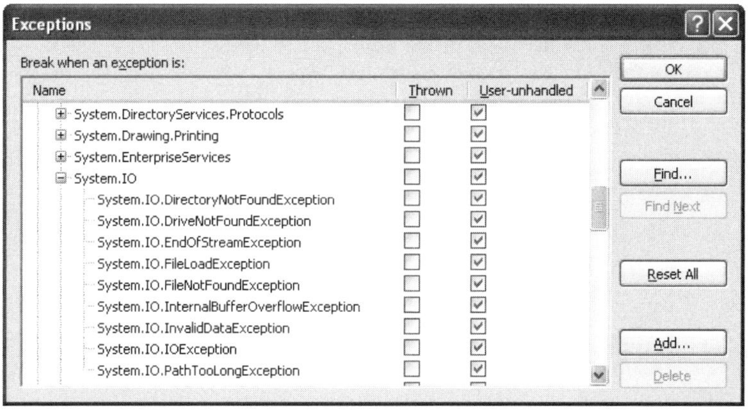

Figure 8-18: The .NET exception hierarchy

This window doubles as an extremely useful debugging tool. You probably remember how Visual Basic 6 provided two basic error-handling options: breaking on unhandled errors only, or breaking on all errors. The latter option allowed you to bypass your program's error-handling code when debugging, and be immediately alerted about an error. That meant you didn't need to disable your error-handling code to troubleshoot a problem.

VB 2005 goes one step further: It allows you to set this option individually for each type of exception. That means you could choose to allow your program to handle a common FileNotFoundException (which might just be the result of an invalid user selection), but cause it to enter debug mode if it encounters an unexpected EndOfStreamException (which might indicate a more serious error in your file access code). To set this up, you would add a checkmark in the Thrown column next to the EndOfStreamException. This tells Visual Studio to always enter break mode when this exception is thrown, regardless of whether you've included error-handling code that can deal with it. However, you could still provide error-handling code for both situations. This error-handling code would run in a non-debugging scenario to alert the end user of the problem or to abort the action.

Filtering by Conditions

Filtering out different types of exception objects is the most common way of filtering errors. However, you can also filter your code based on a specified conditional expression by using the When keyword. This is most useful in higher-level code where you might be dealing with a business object, rather than directly with a file. In the following example, a business object is used to create a new record in the database:

```
Dim NewSale As SaleItem
Try
    NewSale.ID = "sale220"
    NewSale.AddOrderItems(MyCustomOrderCollection)
    NewSale.AddToDatabase()
Catch When NewSale.Items = 0
    ' Error must have occurred when we tried to add the items.
Catch When NewSale.DBConnection = Nothing
    ' For some reason, the database connection couldn't be established.
Finally
    NewSale.Close()
End Try
```

Instead of looking for specific exception objects, this error routine examines properties of the NewSale object. You can accomplish the same sort of higher-level logic by creating your own exceptions, as explained in the next section.

Throwing Your Own Exceptions

In your own classes, you should throw an exception whenever a problem occurs. Remember, a business object should never present an error message directly to the user. Instead, it should alert the calling procedure when invalid data has been supplied, and let the procedure decide how to handle the problem. This is a principle of encapsulation, and it allows your code components to be flexible and highly reusable.

To throw your own exception, you must instantiate a valid exception object and then use the Throw keyword:

```
Public Sub UpdateFile()
    If IsFileOpen = False Then
        ' There is no currently open file to update!
        Dim MyError As New System.InvalidOperationException()
        Throw MyError
    End If
End Sub
```

Each exception object also provides a constructor that allows you to specify a string with a user-friendly text message that describes the problem:

```
Dim MyError As New InvalidOperationException( _
  "You have made a terrible mistake.")
Throw MyError
```

You can also create your own custom exception classes that can assist in providing more detailed information. For example, consider this custom exception, which is designed to identify invalid database information:

```
Public Class ConflictingDBDataException
    Inherits System.ApplicationException

    Public InvalidFields As New Collection()

End Class
```

This custom exception would be useful when, for instance, a user attempts to add a record to a database that contains conflicting information. The following block shows the action that the code will take when the user attempts to create a record that has two conflicting fields: an IsPetOwner flag set to False, but a PetBreed name set to Daschund, indicating that there really is a pet. The code responds by creating an instance of the ConflictingDBDataException and adding information about both fields to the InvalidFields collection:

```
Dim MyError As New ConflictingDBDataException()
MyError.InvalidFields.Add("IsPetOwner", IsPetOwner)
MyError.InvalidFields.Add("PetBreed", PetBreed)
Throw MyError
```

You can then catch this exception in the same way you would a natural .NET exception:

```
Try
    ' Try to add a database record here with your data.
Catch MyError As ConflictingDBDataException
    MessageBox.Show("Operation failed. You had " & _
      MyError.InvalidFields.Count & "conflicting data fields.")
End Try
```

There's really no limit to what you can do with custom exceptions. In highly componentized systems, you might create your own exceptions with special helper functions for performing additional diagnosis, troubleshooting, or cleanup. You can also use the InnerException property to add additional information—for example, to include a more basic exception type representing the origin of the problem.

TIP *All custom exceptions inherit from the ApplicationException class, not the basic Exception class. By inheriting from ApplicationException, you identify that your exception does not represent a Common Language Runtime error. Instead, it represents an application-specific problem.*

Perfecting a Custom Exception Class

In order to make your exception respectable, you should follow the design pattern specified by the .NET Framework. All exceptions require two special constructors: one that allows a custom exception message to be specified, and one that allows a nested exception to be inserted. In addition, you need to explicitly add the default parameterless constructor.

```
Public Class ConflictingDBDataException
    Inherits System.ApplicationException

    Public InvalidFields As New Collection()

    Public Sub New()
        MyBase.New()
    End Sub

    Public Sub New(Message As String)
        MyBase.New(Message)
    End Sub

    Public Sub New(Message As String, Inner As Exception)
        MyBase.New(Message, Inner)
    End Sub

End Class
```

All these constructors do is call the base class constructor with the supplied information. The base class performs the required initialization.

The UnhandledException Event: The Line of Last Defense

As described earlier, if an exception occurs and you fail to catch it, your program is finished. If you're debugging the application in Visual Studio, you'll enter break mode. If you're running your application outside the design environment, .NET will provide a message box identifying the problem, and then it will rudely terminate your program.

For this reason, it's always a good idea to catch any possible exceptions whenever you perform risky operations. However, there is a final recourse that you can take advantage of even if you fail to catch an exception: the UnhandledException application event.

Application events were first introduced in Chapter 4. They're useful for controlling what your program does when it's first launched. However, the UnhandledException also allows you to respond when an unhandled exception has sidelined your application. UnhandledException occurs just before .NET shuts down your application. This gives you a chance to log the cause of the error. (Logging is described later in this chapter.) And if you're feeling a little reckless, you can even ask your program to continue and ignore the exception.

To create an event handler for the `UnhandledException` event, double-click the My Project node in the Solution Explorer, select the Application tab, and then click the View Application Events button in the project properties window. The first time you do this, Visual Studio creates a new code file named ApplicationEvents.vb. You can choose the `UnhandledException` event from the drop-down lists at the top of the code window, and Visual Studio will add the event handler method you need to the autogenerated `MyApplication` class.

The `UnhandledException` event receives an `UnhandledExceptionEventArgs` object. You can use the properties of this object to retrieve the exception that wasn't handled (through the `Exception` property) and tell .NET whether your application should be allowed to carry on (through the Boolean `ExitApplication` property). By default, `ExitApplication` is false, and your application will end after your event handler finishes its work.

Here's an example that shows a message that indicates the type of exception and keeps the program alive, so long as it was an `ApplicationException` that occurred and not something else:

```
Private Sub MyApplication_UnhandledException(ByVal sender As Object, _
  ByVal e As UnhandledExceptionEventArgs) Handles Me.UnhandledException

    MessageBox.Show("An exception was not handled by your application.", _
      e.Exception.GetType.Name)

    If TypeOf e.Exception Is ApplicationException Then
        e.ExitApplication = False
    End If
End Sub
```

To test this code you'll need to build your program and then run it directly from Windows Explorer, outside the Visual Studio environment. Otherwise, Visual Studio will catch any unhandled errors and enter break mode, expecting you'll want to fix the problem.

NOTE   *Be very cautious about using the `ExitApplication` property. It may be that your program is not in a recoverable state, or that carrying on from the current point could cause more damage or just leave the application idling quietly in the background, without any visible windows for the user to actually* do *anything. In a well-written program, you should always catch the exception close to where it occurs.*

Defensive Coding

Defensive coding arises out of the philosophy that it's better to prevent an error than to try and compensate for it in your code or fix it afterward with an update to your application. The goal of defensive coding is to restrict the ways that an error can occur and to make sure that when an error does occur, it is confined to a limited, diagnosable area in your code.

The Principles of Defensive Coding

A few basic principles can guide you to code defensively:

Garbage in, garbage out.
This is a cliché in today's world, but it highlights an important programming truth. One of the most common sources of error is invalid user input. To compensate for this, many programmers write involved validation routines that verify submitted input and alert the user if an entry is invalid. If you've tried this approach, you know that it can be labor intensive. A better solution is just to restrict input so that invalid options can't be entered. Make the user choose from preselected lists whenever possible, disable invalid options by setting the Enabled property to False, and restrict input in text boxes using such properties as MaxLength and CharacterCasing. If numeric input is required, use the KeyPress event to check the character before it appears, and disallow it if it's invalid.

Reduce your assumptions.
Assumptions make your code fragile and result in code that may work properly at your site, but will break when run by a user in a different environment. A typical example is division. When dividing numbers, it's a good rule of thumb to check to make sure that the divisor doesn't equal zero, which would cause the infamous divide-by-zero error. Don't assume that just because the variable *must* be greater than zero; it will be. An error or oversight in your code may create a problem that you can easily protect against—*if* you take the time.

Build your code out of independent units.
You learned in Chapters 5 and 6 that if you structure your program as multiple, independent components, you will simplify the processes of enhancing, troubleshooting, and sharing your code. You will also make it easier to contain your errors. For example, a database error should be caught and trapped in a database access class, so it won't propagate into the rest of your program, where it might metamorphose into a data or logic error.

Testing Assumptions with Assertions

One reason why bugs are so difficult to eliminate from applications is that our code often contains easily overlooked assumptions. For example, you may assume that a certain object is always initialized when used or that a variable is always greater than zero, and so fail to see that a potential error lurks ahead.

Visual Basic 2005 includes an assertions feature that forces your code to test these assumptions. *Assertions* are statements that you guarantee must be true; otherwise something serious has gone unexpectedly wrong in your application. If Visual Basic 2005 tests an assertion and finds out that it is, in fact, false, it will provide an intimidating error message with a pile of diagnostic code, and give you the option to either halt the execution of your program, or ignore the problem and continue. Using assertions is a good way to train yourself to look for assumptions your code makes. They also allow you to halt problems (such as invalid data) before they cause more serious damage (such as a corrupted file or out-of-sync database).

There's one catch. Assertions only work in debug mode. Once you compile and distribute your program, all the assertions disappear. This means that assertions are designed to help you spot problems while testing your application. They do not take the place of error-handling code; rather, they let you know when your error-handling code has failed and something has gone wrong.

To include an assertion in your code, you use the `Assert()` method of the `Debug` class from the `System.Diagnostics` namespace. Here's an example:

```
Debug.Assert(Balance > 0)
```

If this assertion evaluates to `False` (that is, if the `Balance` variable is less than or equal to zero), an error message will be displayed, which will look something like Figure 8-19.

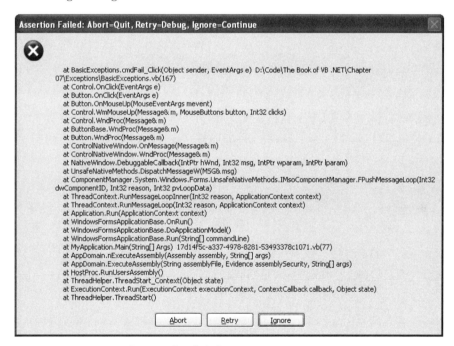

Figure 8-19: Pure intimidation with a failed assertion

Remember, assertions cannot take the place of error-handling code. If it is possible, for example, that the user might attempt to specify a balance less than zero in some way and then handle that error appropriately. If, however, you restrict the user from specifying a negative balance, then an assertion is a good place to double-check that the limitation really is in effect. Think of assertions as a form of quality control.

Debug assertions are completely removed from the final release of your program, so you don't have to worry about these checks slowing down your code. You do have to make sure that a debug assertion doesn't call a procedure that might somehow modify a value in your program, because then there might be unintended side effects when you remove it.

Debug.WriteLine()

Another useful tactic for reporting error information while debugging is to use the Debug class (from the System.Diagnostics namespace). Using Debug, you can write out diagnostic information to the Output window (as shown in Figure 8-20). For example, you could use the WriteLine() method to explain what your code is doing in a loop:

```
' Leaving out the code to define variables and open the file.
Dim i As Integer
For i = 0 to 100
    Info(i) = TextFile.ReadLine()
    Debug.WriteLine("Iteration number " & i.ToString() & _
      ". Read " & Info(i))
Next i
```

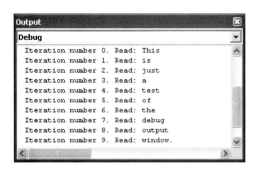

Figure 8-20: Writing debugging information

The nice thing about this method is that the information will be there if you need it, but can be easily ignored if you don't need it.

This kind of information can save a lot of time when you are testing your application, because you can see very clearly what data was being used and what point the application reached when a given error occurred. It can provide a shortcut to solving your problem when manually single-stepping through your code might take a little longer. As with the Debug.Assert() method, Debug.WriteLine() statements are removed from your code in the final release version, so they won't slow your application down.

Using Logging and Traces

Picture this situation: A client is having a problem with your Visual Basic program. You could probably fix it, if you could only figure out what it is. The client's memory is a little hazy . . . maybe the trouble occurred when he or she clicked the Submit button, or maybe just after . . . and no one thought to copy down the specific error message or error number that you created.

As you might guess, this scenario is quite common. The best solution is often to create a log file. When an error occurs, you can simply instruct the client to email the log file to you for technical review. Depending on your needs, you may want to create your own system for creating text log files, but you can also use the built-in features in the .NET class library. One of these features is *tracing*.

To use tracing, you use the Trace class in the System.Diagnostics namespace. It works very similarly to the Debug class, but trace writes and assertions are performed even in the release build of your program. To capture trace information to a file, you have to start off by adding a *listener*. In order for tracing to be useful, you will usually use a text file as a listener. This is the file where all output will be stored.

```
Dim FileListener As New TextWriterTraceListener( _
   System.IO.File.Create("output.txt"))
Trace.AutoFlush = True
Trace.Listeners.Add(FileListener)
```

You can now use the methods of the Trace class to write to the text file.

```
Trace.WriteLine("Starting application")
Trace.Indent    ' This is a nice touch to make well organized output.
Trace.WriteLine("Doing some task...")
' Add some code here.
Trace.WriteLine("Finished task")
Trace.Unindent()
Trace.WriteLine("All done")
```

The output.txt file would look like this:

```
Starting application
    Doing some task...
    Finished task
All done
```

Even if you don't use Trace.WriteLine() statements very often, make sure that you use them every time an error occurs. It's a good idea to develop a generic procedure that will take an exception object and write all of its properties to the Trace object (including the properties of any exception stored in the InnerException property). Here is an example:

```
Try
    ' Some code here.
Catch MyError As Exception
    WriteTraceInfo(MyError)
End Try
```

The generic routine would look something like this:

```
Public Sub WriteTraceInfo(CaughtError As Exception)

    Trace.Write(CaughtError.Message)
    Trace.Write(CaughtError.StackTrace)
    ' And so on...

    ' Use recursion to get all the information in the entire
    ' exception chain.
    If Not CaughtError.InnerException = Nothing Then
        ' Call this subroutine again, with the nested exception.
        WriteTraceInfo(CaughtError.InnerException)
    End If

End Sub
```

Keep in mind that a log file really can't contain too much information about an error, and information such as StackTrace and InnerException can really help track down the root of the problem.

What Comes Next?

In this chapter, you've seen how to maintain complete control of your code in .NET, and how to watch its flow, monitor the contents of its variables, and track its performance in the field. The key to successfully using these features is just to use them. Take the extra time to add logging instructions to your code. You will more than make up for that time when you are solving the inevitable bugs later on.

You've also learned how to use Visual Basic 2005's structured exception-handling feature to catch exceptions and to throw your own. You'll find that once you get comfortable dealing with exception objects, you won't ever feel the same thrill of fear when an error occurs. Instead, you'll be ready for it.

To really master exception handling, you should become familiar with the exception classes that .NET uses to notify you about common problem types. It's always better to specifically catch different types of exceptions than to just catch a generic System.Exception object. A good tool for learning about exceptions is the .NET class library reference in the Visual Studio Help. Start with the System.Exception class, and browse through any of its descendants that you think may be related to the tasks you are performing.

9

DEALING WITH DATA: FILES, PRINTING, AND XML

Most programs consist of a series of operations that retrieve, process, and display data. A typical example is a reporting program that reads information from a database, chews through it to produce interesting summary information according to the user's selections, and returns a result that can be displayed in a window or sent to a printer. More complicated applications might add considerably more sophisticated interfaces, and they might use other .NET features. They might also support various environments, from traditional desktop applications to interactive Internet sites. In the end, however, everything is about data.

This chapter examines some of the nuts and bolts of dealing with data. You'll learn how to store information in the registry and retrieve it as needed, how to display and print formatted documents, and how to interact with files in a completely object-oriented way. You'll also learn about .NET tools that let you work with XML files so easily and painlessly that you might make XML the native format for all your applications. (You won't learn how to retrieve information from a database yet—that subject is the focus of Chapter 10.)

Most of these capabilities aren't new to the .NET Framework. However, pre-.NET versions of Visual Basic provided a variety of different ways to access files—some more flexible than others—and required separate components for dealing with XML. By contrast, VB 2005 uses a unified model that suits everything from the simplest to the most sophisticated scenarios.

New in .NET

Data access in Visual Basic 2005 provides more refinement than revolution. However, if you are a longtime Visual Basic developer, you'll find many enhancements to be happy about.

Object-oriented file access

You may have already seen it with the FSO (File System Object) model in Visual Basic 6. Or, you may be an unredeemed user of `Open` and `Input #` commands. Either way, you'll discover that the .NET class library offers easy and consistent ways to access your computer's file system as a collection of interrelated objects.

Zip compression

Are your files getting too large to handle? VB 2005 adds a new data compression feature that lets you zip up files into small packages. Best of all, it plugs right into the ordinary file access model.

Asynchronous printing

In .NET, lengthy print operations can't drain the life out of your applications. Pages are sent to the printer one at a time, using a separate thread that triggers the `PrintPage` event.

Print preview

Once you've created a print routine in VB 2005, you have all the code you need to show a print preview—even though you might not realize it at first. All you need to do is pass your `PrintDocument` object to the `PrintPreviewDialog` control that .NET provides for you. If you've ever struggled to create a print preview with a third-party component or tried to draw a dynamic print preview on your own, this feature will be a welcome addition.

Unrestricted access to the registry

The built-in registry features in Visual Basic 6 limited you to a small branch of the registry, under the heading "VB and VBA Program Settings." This made life difficult when you wanted to read settings from a third-party program or use a more professional (and standardized) location. Visual Basic 2005 now makes it easy for you to read and write to any area of the registry.

XML access

In Visual Basic 6, reading XML files was one more activity that required the help of an additional component, which you had to distribute with your application and register on any computer that used it. VB 2005 fills the void with several different classes that allow you to write and read XML with the exact level of sophistication and complexity that you need. For quick and easy XML, you can use the straightforward XmlTextWriter class. For more advanced applications, you can manipulate XML files with the full XML Document Object Model (DOM), which treats XML data as a collection of interrelated objects.

Interacting with Files

Before we go ahead, it's worth surveying the .NET landscape to find out what tools are available for dealing with files. As in the previous chapters of this book, we want to do this the ".NET way"—which means using objects and the class library, of course!

The key namespace for files is System.IO. It contains all the classes you need to deal with files, directories, and drives. It also includes writer and reader classes that convert .NET data types into string or binary representations that you can send straight to a file. So to get off to a good start with the sample code you'll see in this chapter, import the System.IO namespace so you'll have all of its classes at your fingertips:

```
Imports System.IO
```

As you've seen throughout this book, VB 2005 adds a grab bag of useful features with the built-in My object. Some of these features aim to simplify file access. You'll find these under the My.Computer.FileSystem branch.

So what does the My object have in store for file manipulation? Essentially, you'll find two things:

- Methods for quickly reading and writing text and binary files

- Methods and properties that allow you to explore the file system and to manage files and folders (for example, you can use them to delete, copy, and move files)

All of these features are available directly through the classes in the System.IO namespace, but the My approach aims to streamline the process. However, while the My object works well for file management, it isn't nearly as useful when it comes to reading and writing files. As you'll see, the My object doesn't give you all of the features that you'll need. In this chapter, you'll see how you can use My to quickly perform basic tasks with files, and then you'll learn how to go further and dive into the class library on your own.

Reading and Writing Files

Many programs store some information in a file, whether it's a collection of user-configured settings or a document with data that you'll need to process later on. Reading and writing a file in VB 2005 is refreshingly easy, and there are two ways to do it: using the My object, and using the FileStream class.

Creating a File with the My Object

The `My.Computer.FileSystem` object gives you a few methods for creating or reading a file in one step. The centerpiece is the `WriteAllText()` and `ReadAllText()` pair of methods. `WriteAllText()` creates a file, copies a string into the file, and then neatly closes the file. You supply the full path and filename, the content, and a Boolean append parameter that indicates what you should do if the file already exists. You have the choice of overwriting it (`False`), or adding your content to the end of the file (`True`).

Here's the `WriteAllText()` method in action:

```
My.Computer.FileSystem.WriteAllText("c:\myfile.txt", _
  "Here is some sample content.", False)
```

As you can probably guess, this creates a text file named myfile.txt that contains a single line of text.

The logical partner to `WriteAllText()` is `ReadAllText()`, which extracts the contents of a file and provides it to your code as a single string:

```
Dim FileContents As String
FileContents = My.Computer.FileSystem.ReadAllText("c:\myfile.txt")
MessageBox.Show(FileContents)
```

Any guess what you'll see in the message box?

NOTE *Rather than hard-code a full path like c:\myfile.txt, you can use the shared `Application.StartupPath` property to find out where your application currently resides and create the file there.*

The `WriteAllText()` and `ReadAllText()` methods are great for one-off jobs, but they suffer from a few problems. First of all, they don't use the elegant stream model that you'll learn about next. (As you'll see, the stream model allows you to add more features, like automatic compression and encryption.)

Another problem is that these methods only work for small files. If you have a lot of data, you don't want to place all of it in memory at once as a single clunky string. Even if you use the appending feature of `WriteAllText()`, performance will suffer, because you're repeatedly opening and closing the file. And no matter what you do, `ReadAllText()` always gets you a string containing the full file. Parsing a string (huge or even not-so-huge) into logical sections isn't elegant or easy.

Finally, the `WriteAllText()` and `ReadAllText()` methods work only with text files. If you want binary data, you're out of luck. You can try to use the corresponding `WriteAllBytes()` and `ReadAllBytes()` methods, but then it's up to you to translate an intimidating byte array into the data types you really want. As you'll see, .NET makes it much easier for you when you use the `FileStream` class.

All in all, the file reading and writing features in the `My.Computer.FileSystem` object won't be suitable for purposes other than quick, simple file I/O.

Creating a File with the FileStream Class

As you might expect, the class library approach is a little more involved, but much more powerful. It all revolves around the `FileStream` class.

The `FileStream` class is your gateway to file access. Each instance of this class represents a file on your computer. Creating one is easy:

```
Dim fs As FileStream
fs = New FileStream("c:\myfile.txt", FileMode.CreateNew)
' You could also do this in one line like so:
' Dim fs As New FileStream("c:\myfile.txt", FileMode.CreateNew)
```

`FileMode` is an enumeration whose values are used to specify the type of file access you require. As you might have guessed, passing the `FileMode.CreateNew` value to the stream constructor tells Visual Basic 2005 that your program expects this file to be created anew; if the file already exists, you will receive an error (an `IOException` object, to be precise). Alternatively, you can instruct Visual Basic 2005 to open an existing file (`FileMode.Open`) or to append data to an existing one (`FileMode.Append`). You can even use `FileMode.OpenOrCreate`, which opens the file if it exists, and creates it if it doesn't. Finally, you can use `FileMode.Create`, which create a new file and quietly overwrite any existing file with the same name. This matches the behavior of the `WriteAllText()` method you saw earlier.

Before you can do anything with a file stream, you have to attach a stream reader or writer to it. Why the extra step? Even though you have already specified whether to read or write information using the new `FileStream` object, you still haven't specified the format that will be used to transmit data *through* that stream. Without this format information, your stream can't be used for any practical purpose.

At this point, you have two main options: You can work with binary data using the `BinaryWriter` and `BinaryReader` classes, or with plaintext using the `StreamWriter` and `StreamReader` classes. The `Writer` classes are for sending information *to* a file, while the `Reader` classes retrieve information *from* a file.

The StreamWriter and StreamReader Classes

It's easier to get the hang of streams if you begin with plaintext data. That way, you can examine the file you're using in Notepad to ensure that your program is working correctly.

Here's an example that uses a `StreamWriter` object to send two lines of information to a file:

```
' Create the file stream.
Dim fs As New FileStream("c:\myfile.txt", FileMode.CreateNew)

' Create a StreamWriter that uses this file stream.
Dim w As New StreamWriter

' Send some data.
```

```
w.WriteLine("First line")
w.WriteLine(40023)  ' Integers work as well as strings.

' Tidy up.
w.Close()
```

If you look at the resulting myfile.txt file in Notepad, you will see the following information:

```
First line
40023
```

Notice that there are no quotation marks around the data in the text file. A StreamWriter object outputs an entire line of text, not a quote-delimited string.

The StreamWriter object provides a reasonably straightforward approach to saving your data. Using a StreamReader object is just as easy. It has a ReadLine() method that returns a string containing a line of information that you placed in the file.

```
' Create the file stream.
Dim fs As New FileStream("c:\myfile.txt", FileMode.Open)

Dim r As New StreamReader(fs)
Dim FirstLine As String, SecondLine As Integer
FirstLine = r.ReadLine()
SecondLine = CType(r.ReadLine(), Integer)

r.Close()
```

The StreamWriter class is smart enough that it can handle any simple data type, including numbers, strings, and Booleans (which become the text *True* or *False* when written to a file). When you are retrieving information, though, it always comes out of the stream in the form of a string. You then have to convert this string to the appropriate type using the CType() function.

The BinaryWriter and BinaryReader Classes

The BinaryWriter class works in a similar fashion to the StreamWriter, except that it only works with bytes in an encoded binary format. If you need to convert data into byte arrays, you can use some of the shared methods of the System.BitConverter class, or you can just use the Write() method of the BinaryWriter class, which is smart enough to do all the work for you, as long as you are only using simple data types.

In many programs, binary files are the standard way of storing information (although XML is also gaining ground as a popular standard for hierarchical text-based information). One of the advantages of binary information is that it is not easily readable. While the information is still visible in the file (if you hunt for it), novice users are less likely to accidentally change it in Notepad or some other editor. Binary storage also makes the best use of space. The only thing you have to remember is that, as with the `StreamWriter` and `StreamReader` class, you must read information in the same order that you wrote it in.

The next example is slightly more sophisticated. It presents a custom Person class that has the built-in features it needs to serialize itself to a file. You can find the full code for this example in the SimpleSerializablePerson project.

NOTE Serialization *is the process of converting an object to a stream of bytes that can be written to another data source, like a file. As you'll see, .NET has several different options for serializing data.*

```
Public Class Person
    Public Name As String
    Public Age As Integer
    Public Height As Integer

    Public Sub New()
    End Sub

    Public Sub New(ByVal Name As String, ByVal Age As String, _
      ByVal Height As String)
        Me.Name = Name
        Me.Age = Age
        Me.Height = Height
    End Sub

    Public Sub SaveToFile(ByVal Filename As String)
        Dim fs As New FileStream(Filename, FileMode.CreateNew)
        Dim w As New BinaryWriter(fs)
        w.Write(Name)
        w.Write(Age)
        w.Write(Height)
        w.Close()
    End Sub

    Public Shared Function LoadFromFile(ByVal Filename As String) As Person
        Dim fs As New FileStream(Filename, FileMode.Open)
        Dim r As New BinaryReader(fs)
        Dim NewPerson As New Person()
        NewPerson.Name = r.ReadString()
        NewPerson.Age = r.ReadInt32()
        NewPerson.Height = r.ReadInt32()
        r.Close()
        Return NewPerson
    End Function
End Class
```

This class provides the following elements:

- Three pieces of information—a name, age, and height—all of which would be implemented as property procedures in a more sophisticated example, but are here represented as public variables for the sake of simplicity.

- Two constructors: a basic parameterless one that creates an empty `Person` object, and a more useful constructor that takes arguments to initialize the name, age, and height.

- A `SaveToFile()` method that stores the current `Person` object in a specified file as binary information. (Note that both this and the following `LoadFromFile()` function are simplified examples that do not incorporate the error checking that you would require in a production-level application.)

- A `LoadFromFile()` method that creates a `Person` object based on the information stored in a file. One interesting feature of this function is that it's declared with the `Shared` keyword, which means that you can use it even if you haven't created a `Person` object. It will then return an instantiated, fully initialized `Person` object for you to work with. This is a common object creation technique. Another option would be to supply a constructor that accepts a string specifying the name of the file containing the initial values and then loads this data into the new `Person` object.

To determine whether the class works as expected, we test it with this code:

```
' Create Bob and clone a copy of him into a file.
Dim Bob As New Person("Bob", 34, 5.25)
Bob.SaveToFile("c:\bob.dat")

' Erase the current copy of Bob.
Bob = Nothing

' Revive Bob by using the file, and check that his data is correct.
Bob = Person.LoadFromFile("c:\bob.dat")
MessageBox.Show(Bob.Name)
```

This verifies that we have created an intelligent, self-storing object. The only drawback to this method is that the binary format reflects the structure of each data type. As a result, when retrieving information in the `LoadFromFile()` method, you need to know the data type of each variable so that you can use the appropriate method to retrieve it (for example, `ReadString()` or `ReadInt32()`, in this case). This raises two potential problems. First of all, if other programmers want to use your binary files in their programs, there are a lot of data type details they need to know. Secondly, if you change a data type in your `Person` code (for example, switching from an `Integer` to a `Long`), you'll break your serialization routine. (And even if you fix it, you'll lose the ability to retrieve old files serialized with the previous version of your code.) You won't face these problems when you use the StreamWriter with plaintext data, because all types of numeric values are converted to a string representation before they're stored in the file.

TIP *A more powerful but time-consuming approach might use XML to describe the data and implement more intelligent storage and retrieval routines, which could allow Bob to be revived from older files even if the class is modified. You'll learn more about using XML later in this chapter.*

Figure 9-1 shows what the bob.dat file looks like in Notepad.

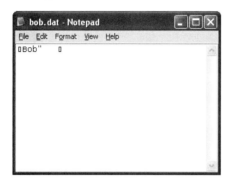

Figure 9-1: The contents of bob.dat

The string is still readable, but the conversion of our integers is quite unintuitive. All the information is packed together, with no spaces.

NOTE *.NET automatically adds information to the beginning of the string that indicates its length in characters. This lets the ReadString() method know how much information it should retrieve (and once again shows us the built-in cleverness of the .NET Framework).*

The last thing you should know about binary files is that you can use the Seek() method to move directly to a specific byte position in the file. However, this technique isn't used very much these days. It used to be important when processing files that hold distinct records, but now databases provide a much more powerful and flexible alternative to this type of data storage. The process of navigating through binary information in a file is frustrating, time-consuming, and prone to error.

Visual Basic–Style File Access

There is one ugly secret I should admit. VB 2005 still provides Visual Basic's old-fashioned file access routines—in a slightly recast form. The Open statement was removed because its name is potentially confusing: Why assume that the only thing that can be opened is a file? The new equivalent is the FileOpen statement, which closely parallels the archaic Open. The Input statement remains (along with LineInput), and Get and Put have been renamed FileGet and FilePut.

If you are an experienced Visual Basic developer, your first instinct may be to return to these familiar functions. I strongly discourage it. The file access classes in the System.IO namespace provide all the benefits of modern object-oriented programming. In addition, they settle issues of scope and code readability, make it easier to send information from procedure to procedure, and help you catch errors. If you want your program to have the greatest standardization, and you are thinking the .NET way, then you will use the compatibility functions I have just mentioned sparingly, for reasons of compatibility *only*.

A Little More About Streams

Our discussion so far has focused on the practical steps you need to follow when accessing a file. However, there are also some interesting concepts at work that aren't immediately obvious.

You'll remember that to access a file, you first create a stream, and then attach the appropriate writer and reader. Streams are an important concept in .NET, and they aren't just limited to files. Streams represent a generic way to access different data sources (also known as *backing stores*). This philosophy means that you can read information from a memory stream, a network stream, or a file stream using conceptually similar techniques. The .NET Framework even uses streams behind the scenes for tasks like saving a bitmap.

For most programmers, file access will be the most common use of streams. But consider the next example, which retrieves a web page (the eBay home page) and displays the resulting HTML text stream in a text box (see Figure 9-2). You'll find this example in the sample code as the NetReader project.

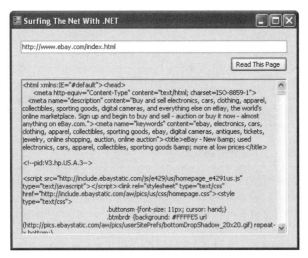

Figure 9-2: Reading a web page

The nice thing about this application is that it uses streams to do its work, with a little help from the System.Net namespace. And, because you now understand streams, you can probably already interpret the code.

```
Me.Cursor = Cursors.WaitCursor

Dim PageRequest As HttpWebRequest = WebRequest.Create(txtURL.Text)
Dim PageResponse As WebResponse = PageRequest.GetResponse()
Dim PageReader As New StreamReader(PageResponse.GetResponseStream())
Dim PageString As String = PageReader.ReadToEnd()
PageReader.Close()
txtHTML.Text = PageString

Me.Cursor = Cursors.Default
```

The basic steps are as follows:

1. Use the shared Create() method of the System.Net.WebRequest class to specify the page that you want to retrieve. You'll get an HttpWebRequest object that will do the job for you.

2. Use the GetResponse() method of the HttpWebRequest object to return the page as a WebResponse object. The WebResponse class exposes a GetResponseStream() method that allows you to access the underlying stream.

3. Create a StreamReader for the WebResponse object's stream.

4. Now you have a familiar stream object from which to read, and you can perform whatever additional steps you want, such as writing the information to a file or copying it to a variable.

NOTE *Retrieving a web page as a stream isn't as useful as it might seem at first. For one thing, it's next to impossible to retrieve any useful information from the page without making assumptions about how it is laid out. The moment the page is slightly changed, your application will fail to get the right data. Instead, a better way to communicate information over the Web is to use web services, which you'll examine in Chapter 13.*

Compressing Files

One of the neatest parts of the stream model is the way you can wrap streams to get extra features. For example, you've already seen how one class—the StreamReader—can work with files and web pages, because it has the ability to wrap any stream. The same is true with other classes, including the GZipStream class from the System.IO.Compression namespace. It can also wrap any stream, giving you the ability to compress or decompress data no matter what the backing store.

For example, the following code compares two approaches to data storage. It opens two files for writing, one with compression, and one without. To perform the compression, the code uses a GZipStream. This GZipStream sits between the `BinaryWriter` object and the underlying `FileStream`. As a result, every time you write a number through the `BinaryWriter`, it actually passes through the `GZipStream`, where it gets compressed, and is then passed to the `FileStream`. The no-compression approach works in the same way as the previous examples you've seen.

Once both streams are open and ready, the code writes 1,000 random strings, each of which is 30 characters long, to both files. (The private `GetRandomString()` helper method that generates the strings isn't shown in the code.)

```
' First, create a file that doesn't use any compression.
Dim fsNoCompress As New FileStream("c:\nocompress", FileMode.Create)
Dim rNoCompress As New BinaryWriter(fsNoCompress)

' Now create a file that will use compression.
Dim fsCompress As New FileStream("c:\compress", FileMode.Create)

' You need to create a GZipStream in Compress mode. It wraps the FileStream.
Dim CompressStream As New GZipStream(fsCompress, CompressionMode.Compress)

' The BinaryWriter writes to the GZipStream, not the FileStream.
Dim rCompress As New BinaryWriter(CompressStream)

' Write 1,000 random strings (each 30 characters long) to both files.
For i As Integer = 1 To 1000
    Dim RandomString As String = GetRandomString(30)
    rNoCompress.Write(RandomString)
    rCompress.Write(RandomString)
Next

' Close both files.
rNoCompress.Close()
fsNoCompress.Close()

rCompress.Close()
fsCompress.Close()
```

To test this code, you might want to compare the sizes of the compressed and non-compressed files it creates. Here's a snippet of code that does this for you, using the `GetFileInfo()` method you'll learn about later in this chapter:

```
MessageBox.Show("Compressed data from " & _
  My.Computer.FileSystem.GetFileInfo("c:\nocompress").Length & _
  " bytes to " & _
  My.Computer.FileSystem.GetFileInfo("c:\compress").Length & _
  " bytes.")
```

As you might expect, the compressed file is smaller. In this example, the difference is dramatic—the uncompressed file is a hefty 310,000 bytes, while the compressed file weighs in just under 41,000 bytes.

Of course, you'll need to adjust your code for reading the compressed file. Once again, it needs to use a GZipStream to wrap the FileStream, but this time you specify CompressionMode.Decompress.

```
Dim fsRead As New FileStream("c:\compress", FileMode.Open)
Dim DecompressStream As New GZipStream(fsRead, CompressionMode.Decompress)
Dim r As New BinaryReader(DecompressStream)

' (Read the data here.)

r.Close()
fsRead.Close()
```

To see the end-to-end code in action, look for the Compress project that's included with the sample code.

Managing Files and Folders

If you try to use the original Bob program twice in a row, you will receive an error indicating that your program is trying to create a file that already exists. To get around this problem, you could specify FileMode.Create instead of FileMode.CreateNew when creating the FileStream object. As described earlier, this instructs Visual Basic 2005 to erase the current file, if it exists. However, this is only a partial solution. What if the existing Bob file contains important information that you'll need to retain in a backup file? In order to handle that situation, you'll need a way to manage directories and files programmatically.

The FileInfo Class

Once again, the System.IO namespace in the .NET class library provides all the tools you need. This time, the class you need to work with is named FileInfo. You can create a FileInfo object by calling the My.Computer.FileSystem.GetFileInfo() method and passing it the full path to the file you want. You can also create a FileInfo object directly—the only difference in this case is that you would pass the path as a constructor argument.

```
' This works.
Dim Info1 As FileInfo = My.Computer.FileSystem.GetFileInfo(Filename)

' This also works.
Dim Info2 As New FileInfo(Filename)
```

A FileInfo object represents a single file. Often, you'll create a FileInfo object that corresponds to a file on your computer and then manipulate that file through the FileInfo object (retrieving properties, settings attributes, copying or deleting it, and so on). You can also create a FileInfo object for a file that doesn't exist. You might do this for one of two reasons—either you aren't sure that it exists and you want to check, or you want to create the file yourself. When you create a FileInfo object for a file that doesn't exist yet, its Exists property will return False.

You can use the FileInfo class to fix the Bob program so that it deals with duplicate files appropriately. For example, you could use code like the following to check for a previous copy of the file and then delete it. Simply add this code to the beginning of the Person.SaveToFile() method.

```
Dim BobFile As New FileInfo(Filename)
If BobFile.Exists Then
    BobFile.Delete()
End If
```

This example shows how easy it is to manipulate files with FileInfo objects. It's just a matter of finding the specific method that does what you need. There are methods for copying a file (the CopyTo() and MoveTo() methods) and an Attributes property for examining and changing file attributes. There are even shortcuts you can use to create the file (such as Create(), which returns a FileStream, and CreateText(), which returns a StreamWriter) or to read the file (such as OpenRead(), which returns a FileStream, and OpenText(), which returns a StreamReader).

NOTE *The information that's returned from the FileInfo properties is filled the first time you access a property. It's then cached in memory for best performance. That means if you've held onto a FileInfo object for a long time, you'll need to make sure you're getting the latest, most up-to-date information about the file by calling the FileInfo.Refresh() method before reading another property value.*

The following program shows another example of how a FileInfo object might be used. This program retrieves information for an existing file when a button is clicked. A subroutine called Out allows the program to quickly add information to a read-only text box.

```
Private Sub cmdGetInfo_Click(ByVal sender As System.Object, _
  ByVal e As System.EventArgs) Handles cmdGetInfo.Click
    Dim MyFile As New FileInfo("c:\myfile.txt")

    ' We can now access some of the following properties.
    Out("Length in bytes: " & MyFile.Length)
    Out("Attribute list: " & MyFile.Attributes.ToString)
    Out("Stored in: " & MyFile.DirectoryName)
    Out("Created: " & MyFile.CreationTime)

    ' Any property we can get, we can also change.
    MyFile.LastWriteTime = DateTime.Today.Add(TimeSpan.FromDays(100))
End Sub

' Utility for displaying information.
```

```
Public Sub Out(ByVal NewText As String)
    txtDisplay.Text &= vbNewLine & NewText
End Sub
```

After running this example (shown in Figure 9-3), you can check the
c:\myfile.txt file in Windows Explorer. You will see that it claims to have been
last updated 100 days in the future. (This example is available with the sample
code as the FileInformation project.)

Figure 9-3: Testing the `FileInfo` *class*

The `FileInfo` class is quite versatile. You can also work with directories by
using analogous `DirectoryInfo` class. Much as the `FileInfo` class has functionality
for creating, moving, and deleting files, the `DirectoryInfo` class has the built-in
smarts for copying, moving, and deleting directories. There is also a `DriveInfo`
class for working with drives.

TIP   *Some directories have a special meaning to the operating system. These include the*
Program Files directory, My Documents directory, Desktop directory, Temp directory,
and others. You can retrieve the physical paths for these special directories using the
`My.Computer.FileSystem.SpecialDirectories` *object. For each special directory, there's*
a property that returns the full path to the directory as a string.

File Attributes

There is one interesting trick you should understand when working with
files, and it has to do with file attributes. File attributes are accessed through
the `FileInfo.Attributes` property (or the `GetAttributes()` and `SetAttributes()`
methods of the `File` class). This property can be set using the `FileAttributes`
enumeration, whose values denote the various properties that a file can
possess (hidden file, system file, read-only file, and so on).

However, a file can have a *combination* of these attributes. To evaluate
or set a combination of enumerated values, you need to use what is called a
bitwise comparison or assignment.

To understand this better, let's consider the following fatally flawed code.

```
If MyFileInfo.Attributes = FileAttributes.Hidden Then
    ' The file is hidden, but has no other attributes.
End If
```

The problem here is that a file may have several attributes, including hidden, system, read-only, and so on. This code only succeeds if the file is hidden but doesn't have any other attributes applied, which probably isn't what you want.

The correct approach is to use the And keyword to filter out just a single attribute. You can then examine if this attribute is set. Here's the code:

```
If (MyFileInfo.Attributes And FileAttributes.Hidden) =
FileAttributes.Hidden Then
    ' You have successfully filtered out the hidden attribute, and found
    ' that it is set.
End If
```

The same rule applies with assignment. Here's an assignment to the FileInfo.Attributes property done the wrong way:

```
' A dangerous mistake that accidentally clears all other attributes:
MyFileInfo.Attributes = FileAttributes.ReadOnly
```

The correct solution uses the Or keyword to combine an additional attribute to the current set of attributes.

```
' This adds a read-only attribute, and leaves the other attributes intact.
MyFileInfo.Attributes = MyFileInfo.Attributes Or FileAttributes.ReadOnly

' This removes a read-only attribute, and leaves the other
' attributes intact.
MyFileInfo.Attributes = _
  MyFileInfo.Attributes And Not FileAttributes.ReadOnly
```

File and Directory Relationships

Another nice feature is the way that the file and directory objects link up with each other. A FileInfo object provides a Directory property, which returns a DirectoryInfo object that represents the directory where the file resides. Each DirectoryInfo object also has methods, such as GetFiles() and GetDirectories(), that return arrays of FileInfo and DirectoryInfo objects, representing files and subdirectories in that directory.

```
' Make a DirectoryInfo for c:\
Dim RootDrive As New DirectoryInfo("c:\")

' Get all the files.
Dim FileArray() As FileInfo
FileArray = RootDrive.GetFiles()
```

```
' Display every file's name.
Dim i As Integer
For i = 0 To FileArray.GetUpperBound(0) - 1
    Out(FileArray(i).Name)
Next i
```

It's simple but powerful. You can access your computer's file system as a collection of interrelated objects, and you can manipulate attributes and names just by changing properties.

A Simple Directory Browser

The next example recursively traverses the file system on a drive and fills a TreeView control with a complete directory listing. The user can click any directory to see the list of files it contains (as shown in Figure 9-4).

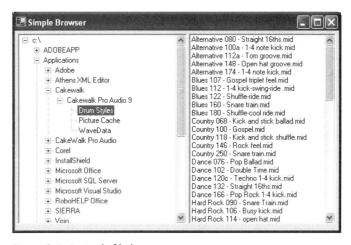

Figure 9-4: A simple file browser

The program begins by filling the TreeView with all the subdirectories on drive C: at startup. It does this with the help of a Fill() method that calls itself recursively to burrow down the levels of the directory tree.

```
Private Sub Browser_Load(ByVal sender As System.Object, _
  ByVal e As System.EventArgs) Handles MyBase.Load

    Dim RootDir As New DirectoryInfo("c:\")
    Dim RootNode As New TreeNode("c:\")
    treeFiles.Nodes.Add(RootNode)
    Fill(RootDir, RootNode)
End Sub

Private Sub Fill(ByVal Dir As DirectoryInfo, ByVal DirNode As TreeNode)
    For Each DirItem As DirectoryInfo In Dir.GetDirectories()
        ' Add node for the directory.
        Dim NewNode As New TreeNode(DirItem.Name)
        DirNode.Nodes.Add(NewNode)
```

```
        ' Use a recursive call here to get all subdirectories.
            Fill(DirItem, NewNode)
        Next
    End Sub
```

When a node is selected, a DirectoryInfo object is created and used to retrieve a list of the contained files, which is then added to the list box:

```
Private Sub treeFiles_AfterSelect(ByVal sender As System.Object, _
  ByVal e As TreeViewEventArgs) Handles treeFiles.AfterSelect
    Dim Dir As New DirectoryInfo(e.Node.FullPath)
    lstFiles.Items.Clear()
    lstFiles.Items.AddRange(Dir.GetFiles())
End Sub
```

NOTE *It can take quite a long time for the program to start and fill the initial tree on startup. A better approach would be to fill the first level of nodes and to fill in subdirectories "just in time" as the nodes are expanded. You could do this by responding to the* TreeView.BeforeExpand *event. For an example of this technique, see the online code (look for the DirectoryTree project).*

"Watching" the File System

Another interesting feature introduced with .NET is the ability to "watch" folders for any changes, deletions, or additions. This technique can come in quite handy. For example, you could create a sales fulfillment program that waits for a new order file to be saved in a directory (perhaps after it is received by a sales associate as an email attachment), and then automatically springs into action to process the new file. This technique replaces some of the ugly tricks that programmers resorted to in the past, which include continuously examining a directory for changes, and thereby wasting precious CPU cycles with unproductive checks.

To add this functionality to your applications, you just need to use the FileSystemWatcher class, which, like all our file access tools, is found in the System.IO namespace. You set the Path property to indicate the directory to monitor (here, d:\Orders), and set the Filter string to specify the file types (here, .xls files).

```
Dim Watch As New FileSystemWatcher()
Watch.Path = "d:\Orders"
Watch.Filter = "*.xls"

' You can also allow the FileSystemWatcher to search subdirectories.
' Watch.IncludeSubdirectories = True
```

The FileWatcher produces four events: Changed, Created, Deleted, and Renamed. If needed, you can disable its events by setting the EnableRaisingEvents property to False.

```
' Add an event handler dynamically.
AddHandler Watch.Created, AddressOf NewFile
```

The subroutine below reacts when a new file is added to the monitored directory, retrieving its name using the supplied parameters. Figure 9-5 shows this code in action.

```
Public Sub NewFile(ByVal sender As Object, _
  ByVal e As System.IO.FileSystemEventArgs)

    lstNewFiles.Items.Add("New file: " & e.Name)
End Sub
```

Figure 9-5: Monitoring the file system

NOTE *To make this example more robust, you need a dash of multithreading smarts. That's because the FileWatcher fires events on another thread, not the thread that's controlling your application. To prevent a conflict, consider the code shown in the FileWatcher project (included with the sample code), which uses the Control.Invoke() method. This technique is explained in detail in Chapter 11.*

File System Change Events

It's easy to handle the Created, Deleted, and Renamed events of the FileSystemWatcher. However, the Changed event is a little trickier, because there are a huge number of types of possible changes that can be detected as Windows performs its ordinary housekeeping.

In order to handle the Change event properly, you need to set the types of changes you want to monitor in the NotifyFilter property (specifying each one using a value from the NotifyFilters enumeration). You can combine several different types of monitored actions using the bitwise Or keyword.

```
' Watch for changes to file size or file name.
Watch.NotifyFilter = NotifyFilters.FileName Or NotifyFilters.Size
```

Object Serialization

The Bob program we looked at earlier used a relatively crude (but effective) mode of handmade *serialization*. The .NET platform also introduces an automatic form of serialization that you can use to store the information in an object (see Figure 9-6). This technique can be used in your own applications, and the .NET Framework also relies on it to transmit a class to a remote component on another computer if you are designing a distributed application.

Figure 9-6: .NET serialization

Implementing this type of serialization in one of your classes is extremely easy. All you need to do is flag your class as serializable with a special attribute. The client code (the code using your class) can then decide what type of serialization it wants to use, and store the object as a binary file, as an XML file, or as something else.

Here is the Person class, simplified and remade to support automatic serialization.

```
<Serializable> Public Class SerializablePerson
    Public Name As String
    Public Age As Integer
    Public Height As Integer

    Public Sub New()
    End Sub

    Public Sub New(ByVal Name As String, ByVal Age As String, _
      ByVal Height As String)
        Me.Name = Name
        Me.Age = Age
        Me.Height = Height
    End Sub
End Class
```

Did you notice the differences? There are exactly two modifications:

- The SaveToFile() and LoadFromFile() methods were removed. This time, .NET will do the serialization for us automatically.

- The Class now has a <Serializable> attribute in the first line, where it is declared. This tells .NET that it is allowed to persist and restore instances of this class to and from any type of stream.

Storing and Retrieving a Serializable Object

To serialize the class, you need to use a serializer from the System.Runtime .Serialization branch of the class library. The best choice is the BinaryFormatter class, which is found in the System.Runtime.Serialization.Formatters.Binary namespace. To get off to a good start, we'll import the namespace:

```
Imports System.Runtime.Serialization.Formatters.Binary
```

The BinaryFormatter class has two important, straightforward methods: Serialize() and Deserialize(). Serialize() takes an object, converts it to a compact binary format, and sends it to the specified stream.

```
Dim Bob As New SerializablePerson("Bob", 34, 5.25)
Dim fs As New FileStream("c:\bob.dat", FileMode.Create)
Dim bf As New BinaryFormatter()

' Store Bob with the help of the BinaryFormatter.
bf.Serialize(fs, Bob)

fs.Close()
```

Deserialize() retrieves the information from the stream and reconstructs the object. The object is returned to life as the generic System.Object type, so you need to use the CType() function to give it back its proper identity.

```
Dim fs As New FileStream("c:\bob.dat", FileMode.Open)
Dim bf As New BinaryFormatter()

' Retrieve Bob with the help of the BinaryFormatter.
Dim Bob As SerializablePerson
Bob = CType(bf.Deserialize(fs), SerializablePerson)

' Verify Bob's information.
MessageBox.Show(Bob.Name)

fs.Close()
```

That's really all you need. It's very simple (although some error-handling code would be nice to guard against any possible file access errors). You can try out this code with the SerializablePerson2 project.

Fine-Tuned Serialization

In some cases, you might have a class that can be partly but not entirely serialized. For example, you might have certain member variables that correspond to information that won't have any meaning on another computer or at another time, such as a low-level *handle* to a Window. (A handle is a number that the operating system uses to uniquely identify a currently running window. It's abstracted away by .NET, but it's heavily used by the Windows API.) To deal with this case, just mark the nonserializable information with a <NonSerialized> attribute. This indicates to .NET that it should ignore this value when persisting instances of the class. When the serialized object is reconstructed, this variable will return to its default uninitialized value.

In the PartlySerializablePerson class shown below, any information about Height will not be retained. When a PartlySerializablePerson is deserialized, its Height will return to zero.

```
<Serializable> Public Class PartlySerializablePerson
    Public Name As String
    Public Age As Integer
    <NonSerialized> Public Height As Integer
End Class
```

A more interesting situation occurs with serializable objects that contain references to other objects. In this case, the referenced object must *also* support serialization, or the whole process will fail. The .NET Framework will store and restore all the subobjects automatically. This can end up persisting a large amount of information. For example, if you have a SerializablePerson object that contains a reference to another SerializablePerson object, which in turn references a third ScrializablePerson object, you will end up with three times the data you expected. If you don't want to serialize a linked object, you can always mark the as appropriate variables with <NonSerialized>.

Cloning Objects with Serialization

Serialization also provides us with an interesting way to clone an object. You may remember (from Chapter 6) that cloning an object is not always easy, particularly if the class contains multiple subobjects.

Cloning an object with serialization basically consists of copying the object into a memory stream and then retrieving it from the stream as a new object. You can insert this cloning code directly into your object, as shown here.

```
<Serializable> Public Class ClonableSerializablePerson
  Implements ICloneable
```

```
    Public Name As String
    Public Age As Integer
    Public Height As Integer

    Public Function Clone() As Object Implements ICloneable.Clone
        Dim ms As New MemoryStream()
        Dim bf As New BinaryFormatter()

        ' No more MemberwiseClone()!
        bf.Serialize(ms, Me)
        Clone = bf.Deserialize(ms)
        ms.Close()
    End Function

End Class
```

This code will duplicate *every* contained object. In some cases this will be too much, and you'll need a more controlled approach that involves manually copying some objects, as shown in Chapter 6.

Printing and Previewing Data

Printing in Visual Basic 2005 is quite different than it was before .NET. The main difference is that the printing process is now asynchronous. In Visual Basic 6, the computer would be temporarily frozen while output commands were sent to the printer. While this worked fine for most applications, programs that required lengthy print operations would be unresponsive while the information was being sent.

Visual Basic 2005 introduces an event-based printing model. Here's how it works. First, you create a `PrintDocument` object. You then start printing by calling the `Print()` method. At this point the `PrintDocument` begins firing the `PrintPage` event, once for each page that needs to be printed.

The `PrintPage` event provides your code with a `PrintPageEventArgs` object which contains information about the printer, together with methods you can use to print text and pictures. Your code handles the `PrintPage` event in an event handler, outputs the next page, and then decides whether or not another page is required. If it is, the event handler sets `PrintPageEventArgs.HasMorePages` to `True`, and the `PrintPage` event is fired again a short time after. If not, it sets `PrintPageEventArgs.HasMorePages` to `False`, and the process ends.

Because pages are printed one at a time, your program remains responsive. However, another consequence of the page-by-page printing model is that your code needs to keep track of where it currently is in the printout, so that the next time the `PrintPage` event is fired, the printing resumes at the proper position.

How can you keep track of your position? This part is up to you, but a common way is to use a variable that stores the current page. Then, each time the `PrintPage` event fires you can check the variable in a conditional block (an `If/End If` statement or a `Select Case` statement) and print the corresponding text. In many programs, a printout actually consists of a single large block of information that spans as many pages as needed, in which case it makes more sense to store an offset into that block. For example, if you are printing rows of report information from a database, you might store the current row number. If you are printing a text stream, you might keep track of the character position.

Printing Data from an Array

The following example uses a simple array. The reference to the PrintDocument object and the code for the PrintPage event are contained in a form class named PrintStatus.

```
Imports System.Drawing.Printing

Public Class PrintStatus
    Private WithEvents MyDoc As PrintDocument
    Private PageNumber As Integer
    Private Offset As Integer
    Private PrintData(100) As String
    Private PrintFont As New Font("Arial", 10)

    Private Sub PrintStatus_Load(ByVal sender As System.Object, _
      ByVal e As System.EventArgs) Handles MyBase.Load
        ' Fill PrintData array with bogus information.
        Dim i As Integer
        For i = 0 To 100
            PrintData(i) = "This is line number " & i + 1 & ". "
            PrintData(i) &= "It originates from the array element number "
            PrintData(i) &= i & "."
        Next
        MyDoc = New PrintDocument()
    End Sub

    Private Sub cmdPrint_Click(ByVal sender As System.Object, _
      ByVal e As System.EventArgs) Handles cmdPrint.Click
        PageNumber = 0
        Offset = 0
        MyDoc.Print()
    End Sub

    Private Sub MyDoc_PrintPage(ByVal sender As Object, _
      ByVal e As PrintPageEventArgs) Handles MyDoc.PrintPage
        ' (Printing code left out.)
    End Sub

End Class
```

This form contains member variables that store the current page number and print offset, as well as the actual print data. In the Load event, the print data array is filled with sample information, and a printer is selected. Asynchronous printing is started when the user clicks the `cmdPrint` button.

The actual printing takes place once the `PrintPage` event occurs. The first `PrintPage` event will occur almost instantaneously (as you can verify by inserting a breakpoint). Inside the event handler, you use the `PrintPageEventArgs` object to perform the actual printing:

```
Private Sub MyDoc_PrintPage(ByVal sender As Object, _
  ByVal e As PrintPageEventArgs) Handles MyDoc.PrintPage

    ' Determine the line height.
    Dim LineHeight As Single = PrintFont.GetHeight(e.Graphics)

    ' Create variables to hold position on page.
    Dim x As Single = e.MarginBounds.Left
    Dim y As Single = e.MarginBounds.Top

    ' Increment global page counter and refresh display.
    PageNumber += 1
    lblStatus.Text = "Print Page " & PageNumber

    ' Print all the information that can fit on the page.
    Do
        e.Graphics.DrawString(PrintData(Offset), PrintFont, _
          Brushes.Black, x, y)
        Offset += 1
        y += LineHeight
    Loop Until (y + LineHeight) > e.MarginBounds.Bottom Or _
      Offset > PrintData.GetUpperBound(0)

    ' Determine if another page is needed.
    If Offset < PrintData.GetUpperBound(0) Then e.HasMorePages = True

End Sub
```

In our example, the `PrintPage` event will occur twice—once for each of the two required pages. The event handler code begins by defining a font that will be used for printing and determining how large the line spacing should be to accommodate that font. The next two lines create variables to track the current position on the page. By default, printing begins at the page margin border. Remember, with printing routines, you need to take care of all the details; for example, you have to break up long strings into multiple lines of text, and explicitly set the position on the page every time you print a new line.

The following two lines increment the page counter and display the page information in a label control in the window. This keeps the user informed about print progress. The `Do/Loop` block contains the actual printing code. This code uses the `DrawString()` method to print out a single line of text at the indicated coordinates. The code then increments our `Offset` value (which represents the line number) and moves the *y* coordinate down one full line space. (Coordinates are measured from zero, starting at the upper left corner.) Before continuing to print the next line, the event handler checks for two possible conditions:

```
Loop Until (y + LineHeight) > e.MarginBounds.Bottom Or _
   Offset > PrintData.GetUpperBound(0)
```

In order to continue, there must be space left on the current page for the next line, and there must be data left to print. (The value of `PrintOffset` can't be larger than the upper boundary of our array, because then it would indicate a row that doesn't exist.)

The final line of our event handler determines whether there is still unprinted data left in the array. If there is, the `e.HasMorePages` property must be set to `True`. Otherwise, .NET will assume that our printing is completed and won't bother to call the `PrintPage` event again.

Printing Wrapped Text

Some applications print out extremely long strings of text that break over more than one printed line. There are several different ways to handle this scenario. You can split the text into a series of separate lines before printing and then load the information into an array or collection. Alternatively, you can split the information into lines as you print it, depending on the width of the current page. This approach, known as "wrapping" the text, is often the required solution if you are printing mixed information that combines text, graphics, and other data, or if you allow the user to select the font size you use.

.NET has a handy shortcut that handles this job. You simply need to use the `Graphics.DrawString()` method with *x* and *y* coordinates *and* a bounding rectangle. The rectangle represents the bounds inside of which you want the text to be printed. The *x* and *y* coordinates tell .NET where the top-left corner of the rectangle should be placed on the page. The text is automatically wrapped to fit the rectangle.

The online samples for this chapter include a WrappedPrinting example that demonstrates the difference between wrapping and not wrapping (Figure 9-7).

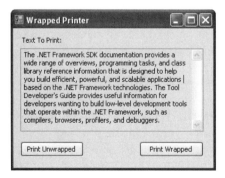

Figure 9-7: The WrappedPrinting project

When printing text that doesn't need to wrap, you simply specify the top-left coordinate where printing should start. The line extends to the right indefinitely and will continue off the edge of the page without causing an error.

```
e.Graphics.DrawString(txtData.Text, MyFont, Brushes.Black, _
  x, y, StringFormat.GenericDefault)
```

To print wrapped text, you supply a Rectangle object instead of the coordinates. (The Rectangle object is defined in the System.Drawing namespace.) You can create a rectangle by hand, but this example simply uses the already available rectangle that represents the page margins, e.MarginBounds. The default page margins are set according to the printer settings. You'll learn how to tweak these details in the next section.

```
e.Graphics.DrawString(txtData.Text, MyFont, Brushes.Black, _
  e.MarginBounds, StringFormat.GenericDefault)
```

Figure 9-8 shows the result.

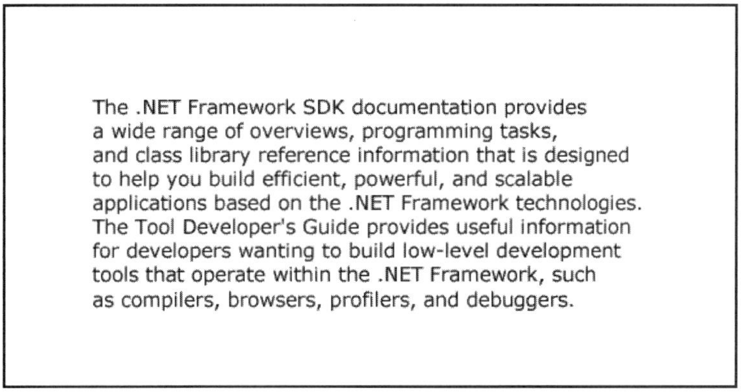

The .NET Framework SDK documentation provides a wide range of overviews, programming tasks, and class library reference information that is designed to help you build efficient, powerful, and scalable applications based on the .NET Framework technologies. The Tool Developer's Guide provides useful information for developers wanting to build low-level development tools that operate within the .NET Framework, such as compilers, browsers, profilers, and debuggers.

Figure 9-8: The wrapped printout

You can also modify the StringFormat parameter that you use with the DrawString() method to specify different options for the text alignment. For example, you can create a new StringFormat object and configure it to automatically center the printed text with this code:

```
Dim CustomFormat As StringFormat = StringFormat.GenericDefault

' Center the block of text on the page (vertically).
CustomFormat.LineAlignment = StringAlignment.Center

' Center the individual lines of text (horizontally).
CustomFormat.Alignment = StringAlignment.Center

e.Graphics.DrawString(txtData.Text, MyFont, Brushes.Black, _
  e.MarginBounds, CustomFormat)
```

Printing Pictures

The previous example demonstrates how to print the most common type of information: formatted text. You can also use other methods from the Graphics object with equal ease to print different types of information, including basic shapes (through methods like DrawRectangle), lines (DrawLine), and even pictures:

```
e.Graphics.DrawImage(Image.FromFile("c:\MyFolder\MyFile.bmp"), x, y)
```

When you use the Graphics object, you are actually making use of the GDI+ technology in the .NET Framework. The interesting part is that this standard Graphics object is reused in more than one place. For example, you use DrawImage() and DrawString() to place output on a printed page in exactly the same way that you use them to place output onto a Windows form. Even though you are less likely to use GDI+ to manually create window output, it's good to know that the skills you use in printing can be reused with on-screen graphics if required.

NOTE   *If you don't want to store the graphic in a separate file, you can embed it directly into your application assembly using the resource techniques described in Chapter 7.*

Print Settings

The previous printing examples use the default margin and page size settings. However, this approach is rarely flexible enough for a real application. Most users expect to have control of at least some basic printing options, including the ability to choose the specific printer they want to use. In Visual Basic 6, this was a fairly straightforward but manual task that involved presenting the user with a Print Options window, retrieving the settings they chose, and applying them to the Print object before beginning a print operation. In .NET, the process has been made much easier.

All the tools you need for displaying standard Print Options and Page Settings windows are provided in convenient classes from .NET's class library. Before you display a Printer Settings window, you associate it with the PrintDocument object that you are using. Then, any configuration that the user performs will be automatically incorporated in the appropriate object (MyDoc in our example) and in the PrinterEventArgs object (called e) provided in the PrintPage event.

```
Private Sub cmdConfigure_Click(ByVal sender As System.Object, _
 ByVal e As System.EventArgs) Handles cmdConfigure.Click

    Dim dlgSettings As New PrintDialog()
    dlgSettings.Document = MyDoc
    dlgSettings.ShowDialog()
End Sub
```

With this simple code, you allow the user to set the standard printer options such as Printer and Number of Copies. These settings will be stored in the supplied `PrintDocument` object. For example, that means the `MyDoc.PrinterSettings.PrinterName` property will be automatically updated to reflect the selected printer.

For simplicity, this example creates the `PrintDialog` object entirely in code. You could also use the component tray to add it to your form and set its properties at design time. Of course, the end result would be the same. The only difference is that Visual Studio will automatically add the corresponding code for the `PrintDialog` object to the hidden designer code file.

Similar code can be used to give the user a chance to modify page settings:

```
Dim dlgSettings As New PageSetupDialog()
dlgSettings.Document = MyDoc
dlgSettings.ShowDialog()
```

These changes will also be reflected automatically throughout related areas of the program. For example, margin selections will affect the `e.MarginBounds.Top` property used in the `PrintPage` event.

Print Preview

Visual Basic 2005's print preview feature is almost an example of getting something for nothing. With a few simple lines, you can create a Print Preview screen that displays the printed information and its pagination, complete with controls for zooming and options for displaying multiple pages at a time.

Here is the code needed to incorporate the print preview feature in our current example:

```
Private Sub cmdPreview_Click(ByVal sender As System.Object, _
  ByVal e As System.EventArgs) Handles cmdPreview.Click

    Dim dlgPreview As New PrintPreviewDialog()
    dlgPreview.Document = MyDoc
    dlgPreview.Show()

End Sub
```

Once again, rather than add the `PrintPreviewDialog` control to the component tray at design time (which would work just as well), this code creates the `PrintPreviewDialog` control manually at runtime. When your users click the `cmdPreview` button, a new nonmodal window will appear, as shown in Figure 9-9.

Figure 9-9: The Print Preview screen

The amazing aspect of the print preview feature is that it uses all your prewritten printing code, both saving you trouble and eliminating differences in appearance between the Print Preview display and the actual printed copy. Various third-party components attempt to implement this simple but tricky concept, but none do so as simply or as successfully as the .NET Framework.

The print preview feature also provides a substantial amount of flexibility and customization. Before you display your `PrintPreviewDialog` object, you can tweak various form properties, including such standards as `WindowState`, `Size`, `MaximumSize`, `MinimumSize`, and `StartupPosition`. You can even set its `MdiParent` property to make it become an MDI child window inside your program!

The PrintPreview Control

.NET also gives you the ability to create a custom Print Preview window or integrate the Print Preview display into one of your application windows. This allows you to combine print preview information with other components of the user interface. For example, you could create a program with a customized Print window that lets your users set special options, such as footer and page numbering style. Whenever a change is made, you would update the Print Preview display automatically to provide a *dynamic preview*.

To incorporate a Print Preview display inside one of your windows, you use the `PrintPreview` control and draw it on your form at design time. Figure 9-10 shows an example (available in the samples as the PrintTest project). This application uses a custom form that includes three buttons, a label with status information, and a preview window (courtesy of the `PrintPreview` control) on the right side.

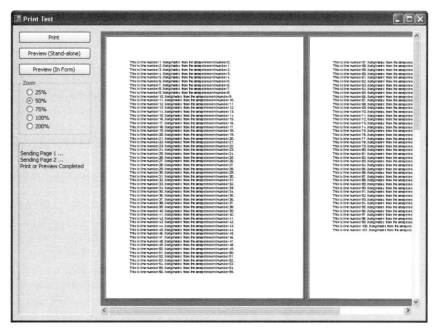

Figure 9-10: Incorporating the print preview feature in a form

To display the preview inside the `PrintPreview` control, just set its `Document` property, as you would with the `PrintPreviewDialog`. You can also tweak the `Zoom` property to specify how large the pages should be and the `Columns` or `Rows` property to set the number of pages that can be displayed side by side.

```
' The default size zoom is 0.3. 1 is full-size.
Preview.Zoom = 0.2

' The Rows and Columns settings mean 6 pages can be displayed at once
' (2 x 3).
Preview.Columns = 2
Preview.Rows = 3

Preview.Document = MyDoc

' The next line triggers the actual preview.
Preview.InvalidatePreview()
```

To recalculate the Print Preview display, call the `InvalidatePreview()` method again.

Working with the Registry

As long as we're on the subject of data, it's worth slipping in a quick discussion of the Windows registry, which is the central repository for storing application settings on a Windows computer. It wasn't hard to use the registry in Visual Basic 6, but you were forced to put your settings into a special area designated for VB programmers. To escape this bizarre (and somewhat insulting) restriction and access the full registry, you had to resort to the Windows API. Thankfully, VB 2005 has improved the picture once again.

To access the Windows registry in .NET, you use two classes from the Microsoft.Win32 namespace: Registry and RegistryKey. Registry provides your starting point into one of the main divisions of the registry. Typically, you will use the Registry.CurrentUser property to work with the registry settings that affect the currently logged-on user. Less often, you might use another branch, such as Registry.LocalMachine, which allows you to configure settings that will affect all users.

The registry is a hierarchical repository, containing keys and many levels of subkeys. The usual practice for an application is to store information in either the CurrentUser (HKEY_CURRENT_USER) or LocalMachine (HKEY_LOCAL _MACHINE) branch, in the path Software*CompanyName*\ *ProductName*\ or Software*CompanyName**ProductName**Category*. This location is the organizational equivalent of a file folder on a hard drive. The actual information about the application is stored in string values.

The following example shows a generic RegistryReader class that receives a reference to a form, and then either saves its current size and position attributes (SaveSize) or retrieves another set of attributes and applies them instead (SetSize). The path name is hard-coded for this application as Software\AcmeInsurance\PolicyMaker. A key is added to the path using the name of the form, to help group the settings for different forms (as in Software\AcmeInsurance\PolicyMaker\Main). Depending on how your application works, this may not be an appropriate way to store information. For example, if you create different forms dynamically, and are in the habit of giving them the same name, their settings will overwrite each other in the registry.

Inside each form-specific key, four values are specified: Height, Width, Top, and Left.

```
Imports Microsoft.Win32

Public Class RegistryReader

    Public Shared Sub SaveSize(ByVal frm As System.Windows.Forms.Form)
        ' The next line creates the key only if it doesn't already exist.
        Dim rk As RegistryKey
        rk = Registry.LocalMachine.CreateSubKey( _
          "Software\Acme\TestApp\" & frm.Name)
        rk.SetValue("Height", frm.Height)
        rk.SetValue("Width", frm.Width)
        rk.SetValue("Left", frm.Left)
        rk.SetValue("Top", frm.Top)
    End Sub

    Public Shared Sub SetSize(ByVal frm As System.Windows.Forms.Form)
        Dim rk As RegistryKey
        rk = Registry.LocalMachine.OpenSubKey( _
```

```
                "Software\Acme\TestApp\" & frm.Name)

            ' If the value isn't found the second argument is used.
            ' This leaves the size and location unchanged.
            frm.Height = CType(rk.GetValue("Height", frm.Height), Integer)
            frm.Width = CType(rk.GetValue("Width", frm.Width), Integer)
            frm.Left = CType(rk.GetValue("Left", frm.Left), Integer)
            frm.Top = CType(rk.GetValue("Top", frm.Top), Integer)
        End Sub

End Class
```

NOTE   *Registry settings are not case-sensitive, so differences in the capitalization of a key or value name will be ignored. As you've seen in the preceding examples, you don't need to worry about missing values. You can use the same command to add a new value or to replace an existing one. When retrieving a value, you can supply a default, which will be returned if the specified value does not exist.*

To use this class, just call the appropriate subroutine with the form that you want to save or reset. The following example shows two button event handlers that can be used to make a form automatically save and restore its size and position. (You can run the included RegistryTester program to try this out.)

```
Private Sub cmdSave_Click(ByVal sender As System.Object, _
  ByVal e As System.EventArgs) Handles cmdSave.Click
    RegistryReader.SaveSize(Me)
End Sub

Private Sub cmdLoad_Click(ByVal sender As System.Object, _
  ByVal e As System.EventArgs) Handles cmdLoad.Click
    RegistryReader.SetSize(Me)
End Sub
```

NOTE   *For more convenient access to the registry, you can use the* My.Computer.Registry *branch of the* My *object.*

XML Files

The real story with XML and Visual Basic 2005 is how the .NET platform uses XML behind the scenes to accomplish a variety of tasks. You'll discover in Chapters 10 and 13 how .NET uses XML to provide communication between web services and clients, and to store relational data in ADO.NET. In these cases, the use of XML is automatic and transparent. You won't need to deal with the XML information directly. For many programmers, this will be the closest they get to XML. Sometimes, however, you may want to read or write XML files manually. You might be interacting with data stored by another program, or you may want to use XML to store your own application's data.

For example, you might create a special sales ordering program that allows customers to choose the items they want to order out of a database, and to save their choices to a file if they don't want to order right away. This file will probably contain little more than a list of product IDs that identify the selected items. The corresponding price and product information will reside in corresponding records in the full product database, which is stored on your company's website. In this case, it would make sense to store the local list of product IDs in a simple format, such as a text file rather than a separate database. An XML file, which is really a text file with an enhanced, standardized organization, may be exactly what you need.

What Is XML, Anyway?

XML code is stored on your computer in a text file, but it looks more like HTML. That's because XML uses elements to "mark up" content. A very basic XML document might look a little like this:

```
<?xml version="1.0"?>
<mydocument>
    <person>
        <name>Matthew</name>
        <phone>555-5555</phone>
    </person>
</mydocument>
```

This XML document has four *elements*. As with most XML files, the whole document is contained in a *root element*, which in this case is called mydocument. This element contains a single person element, which in turn contains two additional pieces of information—a name and a phone number—in separate element called name and phone. Elements come in starting and ending pairs (known as *tags*) that look the same, except that the ending tag has a slash (/) character in front. In between the two tags is where the element content goes.

As in an HTML document, extra whitespace is collapsed. The different levels of indentation are used to indicate structure, but they have no effect on how the document is read. If this were a text file, you would read it line by line. However, with an XML document you will read it element by element. Even if the document above were condensed to a single line, its elements would be read separately.

Content, Not Format

The preceding example illustrates the primary difference between HTML and XML. In an HTML document, tags indicate formatting. For example, <h1>The Title!</h1> tells an Internet browser to place a line of text in a bold font with a larger size than normal body text. An XML document, on the other hand, indicates absolutely nothing about how to format data for presentation. In fact, if you open an XML document in Internet Explorer, you'll see everything in the same size text, with the tags displayed (Figure 9-11).

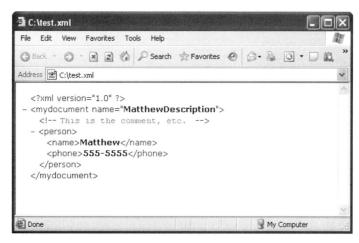

Figure 9-11: XML in Internet Explorer

XML tags indicate content, not format. In fact, XML documents are used almost exclusively for storing data, because the data is described in a way that makes it easy for other programs (and even humans) to interpret it.

Part of the complexity of using XML is understanding the many standards for writing XML documents. As you can see, the underlying concept behind XML is pretty general. You can create an XML document pretty much any way you want. Different standards are used to ensure some consistency, but we won't have a chance to review them in this book.

Attributes and Comments

One other thing you should know about XML is that it doesn't just use elements, although those are its primary units for organizing content. You can also use *attributes* and *comments*. Comments go anywhere and are ignored for data processing purposes. Usually, they just provide additional information that might help a human being understand something about a file. Comments are bracketed by <!-- and -->.

Attributes add extra information into an element. Attributes appear inside the opening tag of an element and are specified using a *Name*=*"Value"* syntax. A subject of great debate in the XML world is what information should go into an attribute, and what should go into an element. Generally, an element is preferred for storing the core information (like names and phone numbers in a customer list), while attributes are used to indicate extra descriptive information (like the version of the document, the time a change was made, a particular way the information should be processed or interpreted, and so on). Once again, there is no single all-encompassing standard.

Here is a modification of the previous XML document that includes two comments and an attribute:

```
<?xml version="1.0"?>
<mydocument title="MatthewDescription">
```

```
<!-- This is the comment. Right above us is the attribute, inside the
mydocument element (attributes are always part of a tag like this). It says
that mydocucment has the title "MatthewDescription". -->
    <person>
        <name>Matthew</name>
        <phone>555-5555</phone>
    </person>
    <!-- It would make sense to add more person tags here, as needed. -->
</mydocument>
```

Writing a Simple XML Document

The easiest way to write an XML document is to use the no-nonsense
XmlTextWriter class, which works a little like the StreamWriter class. This class is
designed to let you write a series of XML information from start to finish.
If your information needs to be edited, you need to perform the necessary
operations with the data in memory before you start writing it to the file.

Our next example shows a block of Visual Basic 2005 code that could
create the sample XML document we looked at in the previous section.
Before beginning, make sure you import the two required namespaces:

```
Imports System.IO
Imports System.Xml
```

The XML-writing code is shown below. This listing uses indentation to
help you see the structure of the corresponding XML document.

```
Dim fs As FileStream = New FileStream("c:\myfile.xml", FileMode.Create)
Dim w As XmlTextWriter = New XmlTextWriter(fs, Nothing)
w.WriteStartDocument()
w.WriteStartElement("mydocument")
    w.WriteAttributeString("name", "", "MatthewDescription")
    w.WriteComment("This is the comment, etc.")
    w.WriteStartElement("person")
        w.WriteStartElement("name")
            w.WriteString("Matthew")
        w.WriteEndElement()                 ' Close the name element.
        w.WriteStartElement("phone")
            w.WriteString("555-5555")
        w.WriteEndElement()                 ' Close the phone element.
    w.WriteEndElement()                     ' Close the person element.
' Could add more person elements here...
w.WriteEndElement()                         ' Close the mydocument element.
w.WriteEndDocument()
w.Close()
```

Notice that you need the root mydocument element. As soon as you close it,
the XML document is finished. .NET will not allow you to open another
mydocument element in the same file, nor will it allow you to write a file consisting
only of several person elements without any other element containing
them, because a document structured in this way would violate the XML

standard. (This is one of the benefits of using the XmlTextWriter class instead of StreamWriter for XML information: It proofreads your output and stops you if you try to create invalid XML.)

Reading XML

To read an XML file, you can use a simple text-reading class called, unsurprisingly, XmlTextReader, or you can use a combination of the XmlDocument and XmlNodeReader classes, which is what we will do here. XmlNodeReader is designed to read *nodes.* Each time you use the XmlNodeReader.Read() method, it loads the information for the next node in the XML file into the XmlNodeReader object (using the Name, Value, and NoteType properties). The Read() method returns True if the operation is successful, and False if the end of the file has been reached and another node couldn't be found. An XmlError is thrown if the XML file is discovered to contain invalid content, such as a starting tag that doesn't have a corresponding ending tag. If the read operation succeeds, you can then use the various properties of the XmlNodeReader object to access the content in the node.

By this point you may be wondering, "What exactly is a node?" and, "Is it any different than an element?" The easiest way to answer these questions is to show you what an XmlNodeReader will read from the sample myfile.xml file.

The following example uses a subroutine called Out to add some information to a label without overwriting it. (This simple procedure, which isn't shown here, was used earlier in this chapter.)

```
Dim doc As New XmlDocument()
doc.Load("c:\myfile.xml")
Dim r As XmlNodeReader = New XmlNodeReader(doc)
' Use a counter to keep track of how many nodes are found.
Dim ElementNumber As Integer = 0

' Loop until the file is finished.
Do
    ElementNumber += 1
    ' Display each node property, unless it's blank.
    Out(ElementNumber.ToString & ". " & r.NodeType.ToString)
    If Not (r.Name = "") Then Out("  Name: " & r.Name)
    If Not (r.Value = "") Then Out("  Value: " & r.Value)
    Out("")
Loop While r.Read() = True
```

This program performs the simple task of displaying information about each node in the label control. The information that is displayed will look like this:

```
1. XmlDeclaration
  Name: xml
  Value: version= "1.0"

2. Element
  Name: mydocument
```

```
 3. Element
    Name: person

 4. Element
    Name: name

 5. Text
    Value: Matthew

 6. EndElement
    Name: name

 7. Element
    Name: phone

 8. Text
    Value: 555-5555

 9. EndElement
    Name: phone

10. EndElement
    Name: person

11. EndElement
    Name: mydocument
```

From this listing, it's obvious that our XML file has 11 nodes. There is one node for every starting tag, every ending tag, every comment, and even the XML definition at the top of the file. Elements have names, but no values. The data inside an element has no name, but it does have a value. The only potential problem with this arrangement is that attributes don't appear. However, that's because attributes are actually *properties* of nodes—not nodes. To check for an attribute, examine the node's HasAttributes property or its AttributeCount property. If attributes are present, you can then use the MoveToAttribute() method to jump to the attributes, and the MoveToElement() method to get back to the element and continue on your way.

It works like this:

```
If r.HasAttributes Then
    Dim i As Integer
    For i = 0 To r.AttributeCount - 1
        r.MoveToAttribute(i)
        ' Display the attribute's properties.
        Out("   Attribute #" & (i + 1).ToString())
        Out("      Name: " & r.Name)
        Out("      Value: " & r.Value)
    Next i
    ' Go back to the start of the original element.
    r.MoveToElement()
End If
```

(Of course, you could also just refrain from using attributes altogether and make your life a little easier.)

The full code can be found in the online XmlTester application (shown in Figure 9-12).

Figure 9-12: The XmlTester utility

This should give you a little taste of what it's like to work with the full XML Document Object Model (DOM), in which you navigate through an XML file as a collection of objects.

Advanced XML

The techniques you've learned in this chapter are the most convenient ways to create and access XML documents. However, they are designed for quickly writing or reading from an entire XML file at once. For example, you might use an XmlNodeReader in some sort of FileOpen() routine that creates business objects and sets their properties based on the information that you read. You could then use these objects to manipulate the information, and possibly end by writing a new XML file (or overwriting the existing file) using an XmlTextWriter.

On the other hand, you might sometimes prefer that applications read XML data and work with the information *as* XML data, not as custom objects. This technique might be useful in a cross-platform project, for example, where XML data is going to be used in several different programming environments, and the features of those environments are known to be incompatible.

In order to work with XML data, you can use the XML DOM which treats your XML document as a collection of related objects, based on their element tags. This model is available in .NET through the XmlDocument class, which has methods for adding nodes in any location, and for navigating through your document. It's similar to working your way through a `TreeView` control, with properties like `FirstChild`, `NextSibling`, and so on.

In this book, we stick to basic XML reading and writing. If you need to store complex structured information, you should check out ADO .NET, which uses XML natively. If you are working on a cross-platform project that needs more in-depth XML features, refer to the reference in the Visual Studio Help class library for the `XmlDocument` class in the `System.Xml` namespace.

What Comes Next?

In this chapter, we've examined how to reach out from Visual Basic 2005 programs and manipulate the data in the registry, as well as in text, binary, and XML files. You have learned how to send data to the printer, build a logical printing framework, configure printing settings, and display a Print Preview window.

Now that you have a good understanding of the fundamental ingredients, it's up to you to discover how to best integrate these features in a live application. It's here where object-oriented design starts to come into play. For example, you might want to create your own class to represent a data file. This class would contain the appropriate `StreamReader` and `StreamWriter` objects, but it would expose an interface to the rest of your program that is specific to the type of information stored in the file. Your class might also take care of basic chores, such as writing a special identifying signature at the top of a file when creating the file, and then verifying the signature when reading the file to make sure that the file really does belong to your application. Or, it might calculate a checksum based on the data in the file. (A simple example would be adding together all the product numbers in a purchase order file and then storing this total at the end of the file. When reading the file, you could verify this checksum to make sure the data hasn't been accidentally corrupted.)

These are all examples of *abstraction* at work—your file class handles the low-level text stream features, and your program only has to understand higher-level operations like opening files, checking for error conditions, and reading the appropriate properties. This is where the real fun of .NET design begins.

10

DATABASES AND ADO.NET

If you've ever programmed internal projects for tracking customers, sales, payroll, or inventory, you've probably realized that data is the lifeblood of any company. For the Visual Basic programmer, this understanding is particularly relevant, because no other language is used as often to create database applications. In the early days of Windows programming, Visual Basic came to prominence as a simple and powerful tool for writing applications that could talk to a database and generate attractive reports. In some ways, this is still Visual Basic's most comfortable niche.

Over the years, Microsoft has given the world a confusing alphabet soup of database access technologies. Visual Basic programmers first started with something called Data Access Objects (DAO), later upgrading to Remote Data Objects (RDO) to access client-server database products such as SQL, and then migrating to Active Data Objects (ADO), which was supposed to provide the best of both worlds. In many ways, ADO fulfilled its promise, providing a flexible and powerful object model that could be used by programmers in just about any Windows-based programming language. However, it didn't take Microsoft long to throw in the towel once again and decide with .NET that what everyone needs is yet another entirely new way to access data.

And calling ADO.NET "entirely new" is only a modest exaggeration. While ADO.NET has some superficial similarities to ADO, its underlying technology and overall philosophy are dramatically different. While ADO was a connection-centered database technology that threw in some disconnected access features as an afterthought, ADO.NET is based on disconnected DataSets, with no support for server-side cursors. While ADO was a "best of breed" standard Microsoft component built out of COM, ADO.NET is an inhabitant of the .NET class library, designed for managed code, and integrated with XML. As you'll see in this chapter, ADO.NET is one more .NET revolution.

New in .NET

The .NET languages require a new database technology. ADO, the previous standard, was wedded to COM, and every interaction between .NET-managed code and COM-based code suffers an automatic performance hit. The surprise is that ADO.NET is not just a .NET version of ADO. Instead, ADO.NET has been redesigned from the ground up.

No server-side cursors
In ADO, a cursor tracks your current location in a result set, and allows you to perform updates on live data. Cursors have completely disappeared in ADO.NET. They are replaced by a new disconnected model that doesn't maintain connections.

DataSets and DataReaders replace Recordsets
ADO.NET introduces the DataSet, an all-in-one data storage object that replaces the more limited Recordset from classic ADO. The DataSet is the perfect container for relational data—it's able to store more than one table of data at a time, it supports table relations and column constraints, and it tracks changes seamlessly. For situations where you need fast read-only access, and you don't want to hold onto information for longer than a few seconds, ADO.NET provides a streamlined DataReader object.

The DataAdapter
In ADO, Recordsets were usually directly connected to a data source. In the connectionless world of ADO.NET, DataSets don't directly relate to any data source. Instead, you use a special DataAdapter to pull information out of the database and pop it into a DataSet. You also use the DataAdapter to submit DataSet changes back to the database when you're finished.

XML-based data storage
In ADO, XML data access is an afterthought. ADO.NET, however, uses XML effortlessly. Using this XML support, you can store data locally in a file or transfer XML data to a component on another computer or operating system (like a web service).

Introducing ADO.NET

There are essentially two ways you can use ADO.NET in your applications. First of all, you can use it entirely on its own to create tables and relations by hand. You can then easily store this information in an XML file using ADO.NET's built-in XML capabilities and retrieve it later to work with it again. This way of using of ADO.NET, with a dynamically created data file, is described later in this chapter. It provides a single user with a simple, no-frills approach to creating and storing information.

However, it's much more likely that you'll use ADO.NET to interact with an underlying database. This database might be a stand-alone Access database, or it might be a multiuser relational database management system (RDBMS) such as Microsoft SQL Server or Oracle. No matter what your data source, the way you use ADO.NET will be essentially the same. You can still write data to an XML file for temporary storage, but your ultimate goal is to commit any modifications back to the database.

Using Relational Data

ADO.NET excels at dealing with *relational data*: information that is conceptually organized as a set of tables, which are filtered and fused together in various ways by your application.

For example, consider an application that tracks the work records for different employees. You could try store all this information in a single table, but you'd end up duplicating the same employee information in multiple work records whenever an employee works on several jobs at different sites. Figure 10-1 shows a more efficient arrangement that models this data using three tables: Employee, Location, and WorkLog.

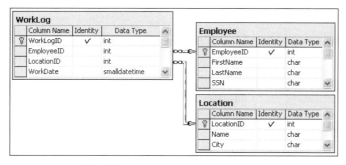

Figure 10-1: Table relations

In this example, the Employee table contains all the personnel information related to specific individuals. The Location table stores the information about the work sites. Finally, the WorkLog table records the number of hours worked by each employee at various sites. Each WorkLog record contains a reference to the appropriate record in the Employee table specifying who did the work (given in the EmployeeID field) and the appropriate record in the Location table specifying where the work was done (given in the LocationID field).

This carefully factored arrangement makes it easy to manipulate the data in many different ways. For example, you could generate a list of employees who worked at a specific location, or determine the total number of hours worked by a single employee, or calculate the total number of hours worked at a specific site by all employees. This arrangement is also lean on storage space, and it avoids potential conflicts that could occur if you were to store employee-specific information (such as the worker's name) or location-specific information (such as the site address) in the WorkLog table.

This example, of course, shows the standard way to store information in any relational database, whether it is SQL Server, Oracle, MySQL, or something else. The applications that need to access this information can use a combination of SQL statements and *stored procedures* (miniature programs stored in the database) to access and change this information. ADO and ADO.NET handle the processes of sending commands to the database and of retrieving results. Both ADO and ADO.NET allow you to connect to other data sources—even sources that are not relational databases. But in the majority of cases, you will use ADO or ADO.NET to access a relational database.

The Northwind Database

All the examples in this chapter use tables from the Northwind database, a sample database included with SQL Server to help you test database access code. If you have SQL Server but you don't have the Northwind database installed, you can use the script included with the online samples to install it automatically. You can also use this script to install the Northwind database for SQL Server 2005 Express Edition. (Consult the README file for specific instructions.)

If you have another database product or you don't want to install the Northwind database, you can tweak the examples to use another data source. Usually you'll only have to adjust the connection string and the names of the tables and fields. Bear in mind, however, that some data sources, such as Microsoft Access databases, don't support all the features we'll discuss (stored procedures, for instance).

SQL Server 2005 Express Edition

SQL Server 2005 Express Edition is one of Microsoft's best-kept secrets—it's essentially a scaled-down version of SQL Server 2005 that's bundled with full versions of Visual Studio and available separately for no cost. It's completely compatible with SQL Server (in fact, it *is* SQL Server) and free to use for anyone. There are just a few limitations that are designed to restrict it to smaller systems—for example, it's only able to use one CPU and 1 GB of memory, and it can't create a database larger than 4 GB. But even these restrictions shouldn't cause you too much worry—if a client installs SQL Server 2005 Express Edition and then wants to upgrade to a system that supports more simultaneous users, a full version of SQL Server 2005 can be easily installed, and your databases can be imported in a snap.

The only catch is that SQL Server 2005 Express Edition, on its own, doesn't provide the nice graphical tools that help you build tables and relations, monitor performance, and perform general database upkeep. To remedy this problem, Microsoft has added some helpful developer database utilities to Visual Studio. Using the Server Explorer window in Visual Studio, you can create a new connection to SQL Server 2005 Express Edition, and start creating databases, tables, and even stored procedures, without leaving the comfort of the design environment.

However, this is a chapter about *programming* with databases—not how to use database management tools. Although I don't have the space to tell you everything you need to know to install and configure SQL Server 2005 Express Edition, you can find more information at Microsoft's SQL Server 2005 Express site (www.microsoft.com/sql/express).

The Provider Model

ADO.NET uses a *provider* model. In this model, you use a different set of classes to connect to each type of database. Each of these sets is known as a *provider*. For example, if you want to connect to a SQL Server database, you use the SQL Server provider. If you want to connect to Oracle, you use the Oracle provider, which is also included with .NET. Altogether .NET 2.0 includes four providers (there is also one for OLE DB data sources and one for ODBC drivers), and you can find many more on the Web (or buy them from third-party component developers).

At first glance, this approach seems unnecessarily complicated. After all, wouldn't developers want a *single* database access framework that lets them write code that works for *any* database provider? It's actually not as bad as it seems, because all providers adopt the same strict model. For example, each provider must include a `Connection`, a `Command`, and a `DataAdapter` class, each of which must provide exactly the same set of methods. The only thing that changes is the prefix before the name. So SQL Server fans use the `SqlConnection.Open()` method, whereas Oracle mavens get an `OracleConnection.Open()` method. In other words, the data model is ruthlessly consistent, so if you learn to program ADO.NET with one provider's set of objects, you'll know most of what you need to write code for any other provider. And every provider uses the exact same `DataSet` class to store data once it's extracted from the database.

There are two reasons ADO.NET uses the provider-based model. First, it allows performance optimizations. That's because `OracleCommand` can use the fastest communication method known to Oracle databases. Behind the scenes, `SqlCommand` can use the best approach for SQL Server. Previous database access technologies, like classic ADO, forced everyone to go through a common layer, which necessarily slowed everything down (even if only by a bit). Second, the provider model also makes sense because individual database vendors are able to provide customized features. For example, SQL Server 2000 and later versions can perform an XML query that returns results as an XML document. Oracle databases provide specialized support for large data fields. These extra features can be accessed through additional provider-specific methods above and beyond the core methods that are part of the ADO.NET standard (which you will study in this chapter). All in all, ADO.NET bets that customized features and performance are more important than write-once, run-with-any-database coding.

However, if you *do* want to write code that can be adapted for any database, it is still possible. Because all the provider objects use the same interfaces, you can create code that uses these interfaces, instead of the objects directly. With a little care, you can create a program that chooses a provider based on a configuration file and then opens connections and performs queries entirely through the interfaces. In fact, there's an example of one such program in the downloadable code for this chapter (it's named GenericDataAccess).

However, you won't see this technique described here. Why? It just isn't practical for most applications. Different databases need different optimizations and data access strategies. Choosing a database product is a significant investment. Usually, companies want to stick with one database and get the best they can out of it. They don't flip to a different product on a whim, and if they do change, they're ready to rewrite some database code for optimum performance.

TIP   *Even if you decide to stick with one database, it's always a good idea to minimize the interdependencies between your database code and the rest of your application. You should be able to put your database code into one or more separate classes (and possibly even compile them separately into a component, as described in Chapter 7). That way, if you do choose to change your database later on, your changes will be confined to one section of your application. When you need to send data to the rest of your application, you should use the* DataSet, *which isn't provider-specific.*

The Basic ADO.NET Objects

All of the ADO.NET features are provided through types in the System.Data branch of the .NET class library. This includes the following namespaces:

System.Data
> Contains the fundamental classes for managing data, such as DataSet and DataRelation. These classes are totally independent of any specific type of database.

System.Data.Common
> Contains some base classes that are inherited by other provider-specific classes. The classes in this namespace specify the basic functionality, whereas the classes in the other namespaces are customized for particular data sources. Thus, you don't use the System.Data.Common classes directly.

System.Data.SqlClient
> Contains the classes you use to connect to a Microsoft SQL Server database using the optimized TDS (Tabular Data Stream) interface. This includes such classes as SqlCommand and SqlConnection.

System.Data.Oracle
> Contains the classes you use to connect to an Oracle database, including OracleCommand and OracleConnection. To use these classes, you must add a reference to the system.oracle.dll assembly.

System.Data.OleDb

Contains the classes you use to connect to an OLE DB provider, including `OleDbCommand` and `OleDbConnection`. These classes are useful if you still have OLE DB providers kicking around, and you don't have a pure .NET provider for that database. One example for which OLE DB is necessary is a Microsoft Access database.

System.Data.SqlTypes

Includes additional data types that aren't provided in .NET, but are used in SQL Server. These include `SqlDateTime` and `SqlMoney`. These types can be converted into the standard .NET equivalents, but the process introduces the possibility of a conversion or rounding error that might adversely affect data. Instead, you can create objects based on the structures defined in this class. It might even increase speed a bit, as no automatic conversions will be required.

This chapter uses SQL Server and the associated `System.Data.SqlClient` namespace. In most cases, the techniques described here are identical for Oracle and OLE DB providers.

To get off to a good start, you should import the two namespaces that you'll need for the examples that follow:

```
Imports System.Data           ' Provides common classes like DataSet.
Imports System.Data.SqlClient ' Contains the SQL Server provider.
```

Fast-Forward Read-Only Access

There are two ways you can access relational data with ADO.NET: as a read-only stream of information that wraps an underlying database connection or as a disconnected `DataSet` that you can examine and manipulate long after the database connection has been closed. In a sense, ADO.NET forces you to choose between two dramatically different approaches. The middle ground found in ADO programming—a live read-write cursor that maintains a connection—just isn't an option in ADO.NET.

In the first section of this chapter, you'll consider how to access data the easy way and temporarily avoid the thorny issues surrounding disconnected data. As you read ahead, you might want to refer to the diagram in Figure 10-2, which shows you the basic model for this simple type of data access.

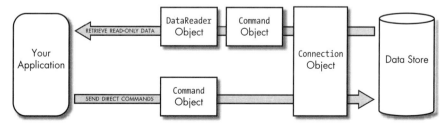

Figure 10-2: Using ADO.NET without disconnected data

Your first task is to explore the basic ingredients for any type of data access: connections and commands.

Connection Objects

You use a Connection object to establish a connection to a data source. The only trick is using the right connection string.

The Connection String

The connection string specifies, in a single line of text, all the information that the database needs to establish a client session. It consists of a string with pairs of named parameters and values (for example, user id=sa), each of which is separated by a semicolon.

Here's an example of a connection string:

```
Dim ConnectionString As String = _
  "Data Source=localhost;Initial Catalog=Northwind;" & _
  "Integrated Security=True"
```

This connection string supplies three pieces of information. First, it specifies a connection to the SQL Server database on the local computer (rather than a remote network server). Next, it identifies the database that you want to use (Northwind). Finally, it uses *Windows integrated security*, which means it attempts to connect using the current Windows user account.

This approach works only if your database supports Windows integrated security. SQL Server supports Windows integrated security and an older authentication model (called SQL Server authentication), but by default only Windows authentication is enabled.

If you've allowed the older SQL Server authentication model, you can connect by supplying a database-defined user ID and password. Commonly, you'll use the user sa (for system administrator), as shown here:

```
Dim ConnectionString As String = _
  "Data Source=localhost;Initial Catalog=Northwind;" & _
  "user id=sa;password=S5lt_o"
```

In order for this to work, you need to use the right password for the sa account, which you may have specified when installing SQL Server.

If you're using SQL Server 2005 Express Edition, you need to modify the Data Source value slightly, as shown here:

```
Dim ConnectionString As String = _
  "Data Source=localhost\SQLEXPRESS;Initial Catalog=Northwind;" & _
  "Integrated Security=True"
```

This change is required because SQL Server 2005 Express Edition installs itself as a *named instance* (with the name SQLEXPRESS). When connecting to a named instance of any SQL Server database, you need to supply the instance name in the connection string.

And just for variety, here's how a connection string might look for an OLE DB provider using the OleDbConnection object. The only real difference is the addition of the Provider setting, which identifies the appropriate OLE DB provider. In the following example, the connection string points to the SQL Server OLE DB provider, which you generally won't use because it's slower than the native SQL Server provider.

```
Dim ConnectionString As String = _
  "Provider=SQLOLEDB.1;Data Source=localhost;" & _
  "Initial Catalog=Northwind; Integrated Security=True"
```

Other providers include MSDAORA (the OLE DB provider for an Oracle database) and Microsoft.Jet.OLEDB.4.0 (the OLE DB provider for Access).

There are several other options you can set for a connection string, and they are all documented in the MSDN Help (look up the connection class, like SqlConnection or OleDbConnection). They include settings that specify how long you'll wait while trying to make a connection before timing out, and how long .NET should keep a connection in the connection pool for possible reuse later. If you're using SQL Server 2005, you also have the option to use the AttachDbFilename parameter, which allows you to open a database directly from a file (rather than the catalog of registered databases). Here's an example of this trick:

```
Dim ConnectionString As String = _
  "Data Source=localhost\SQLEXPRESS;" & _
  "AttachDbFilename='C:\SQL Server 2000 Sample Databases\NORTHWND.MDF';" & _
  Integrated Security=True"
```

Making a Connection

Once you have created the right connection string, it's easy to create a connection object and establish a live connection. For SQL Server, you use a SqlConnection object. It works like this:

```
Dim ConnectionString As String = "Data Source=localhost;" & _
  "Integrated Security=True;Initial Catalog=Northwind;"
Dim con As New SqlConnection(ConnectionString)
con.Open()
```

The Open() method is used to establish the connection. You can close your connection at any time by calling the Close() method.

NOTE   *As illustrated in the preceding example, you don't really use a Connection object. Instead, you use the appropriate derived class (such as SqlConnection or OleDbConnection). In cases where there is more than one flavor of a class, as with the Connection class, this chapter introduces them with a common (yet fictitious) object name.*

Storing Connection Strings

You should never hard-code a connection string. Doing so introduces several problems. First of all, if you need to move the database to another server, you need to edit your code and recompile the entire application. And if you're not careful, you'll be forced to make changes to database code throughout your application, making for a management nightmare.

Fortunately, VB 2005 provides a convenient solution—you can store the connection string in a configuration file. This technique works in any type of application (including Windows, web, and console projects). Best of all, you can edit the configuration file at any time without being forced to recompile anything.

To create a configuration file that contains a connection string, follow these steps:

1. Open or create a project in Visual Studio.
2. Double-click the My Project node in the Solution Explorer.
3. Click the Settings tab. You'll see a list of all the settings that are defined for this application. (By default, this list is empty.)
4. Add a new setting to the list. Give it a descriptive name (for example, Northwind), use Application for the scope (so that the setting is common for all users), and supply the full connection string as the value. Figure 10-3 shows an example of a completed connection string.

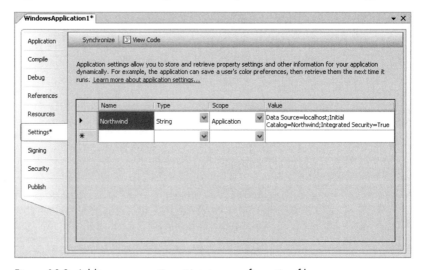

Figure 10-3: Adding a connection string to a configuration file

When you carry out this step, Visual Studio generates a new file named app.config, which contains your connection string. You'll see this file in the Solution Explorer. If you're curious, you can open the configuration file to see what it contains. You'll notice that it uses an XML format. You can edit this file using an ordinary text editor (such as Notepad) if you want to change the connection string after you've compiled the application.

When you compile your application, the app.config file is transferred to the bin folder (along with your compiled application). However, there's a twist: the configuration file is renamed to match your application. For example, if you create the application MyDatabaseChecker.exe, the config file is name MyDatabaseChecker.exe.config. This is how .NET recognizes that the configuration file and application are linked.

Retrieving a setting from the configuration file is easy, thanks to the My object. Here's the code you need to retrieve the setting shown in Figure 10-3:

```
Dim ConnectionString As String = My.Settings.Northwind
```

As you can see, using a configuration file makes for cleaner, more maintainable code.

Command Objects

Now that you've learned how to create connections and manage connection strings, you're ready to move on to the next step and execute database operations with Command objects.

Command objects represent SQL statements or stored procedures that you use to retrieve data or submit changes. In order to use ADO.NET, you should have a basic understanding of SQL. The following section provides a quick refresher.

SQL Statements

Here's a SQL statement at its simplest. It's used to retrieve data from a single table in the current database (in this case, the Orders table). The asterisk (*) indicates that you want to retrieve all the fields from the table (OrderID, CustomerID, and so on).

```
Dim SQLString As String = "SELECT * FROM Orders"
```

Seasoned database programmers will shudder when they see this statement, because it doesn't limit the number of returned records in any way. In other words, it selects all the records in the Orders table, whether there are fifty or five million of them. An application that includes this type of statement typically works well when it is first deployed, but gradually slows to a crawl as the number of records in the database climbs. Eventually, you may even receive timeout errors.

A safer SQL statement would look like this:

```
Dim SQLString As String = "SELECT * FROM Orders " & _
 "WHERE OrderDate < '2000/01/01' AND OrderDate > '1987/01/01'"
```

The Where clause ensures that only certain rows are retrieved. In this case, the OrderDate column must have a value between the two specified dates. (This example uses the international standard date format *yyyy/mm/dd*, which is typically the safest representation.) The values (dates) being compared to the OrderDate are enclosed in single quotes, unless they are numbers. The And keyword allows you to apply to criterion that the results must meet.

In a real application, SQL statements are often much longer and much more complex. For example, they will usually access several tables and specify only certain fields in each table (rather than using the asterisk, which can slow down your application by requesting data that it doesn't need).

Creating a Command

Once you have a connection, a command is easy to define. If you are using a SQL Server database, you will use the SqlCommand object, as shown here:

```
Dim SQLString As String = "SELECT * FROM Orders " & _
 "WHERE OrderDate < '2000/01/01' AND OrderDate > '1987/01/01'"
Dim cmd As New SqlCommand(SQLString, con)
```

This example creates a SqlCommand object using a constructor that lets you specify the connection that should be used and the SQL statement that it will execute. Like ADO, ADO.NET often provides many paths toward the same end, and you could accomplish the same thing in the more verbose form shown here:

```
Dim cmd As New SqlCommand()
cmd.CommandText = SQLString
cmd.Connection = con
' Strictly speaking, the next line isn't required because
' CommandType.Text is the default.
cmd.CommandType = CommandType.Text
```

Notice that these two examples don't actually read any data; each of them simply defines a command. In order to use the command, you have to decide whether to create a simple DataReader or a full-fledged disconnected DataSet.

DataReader Objects

A DataReader is a *firehose cursor*, which gets its name from the fact that it provides a steady one-way stream of data pouring from the database straight into your program. It provides few additional frills. A DataReader doesn't provide disconnected access or any ability to change or update the original data source. You should use a DataReader whenever you need fast, read-only data access, as its performance will always beat that of the full-fledged DataSet. On the other hand, the DataSet provides few features beyond simple read-only access (like the ability to navigate relationships and sort records on the fly).

Each provider includes its own DataReader class. For SQL Server, you use the SqlDataReader class. Once you've made a connection and created the appropriate Command object, you can access the data through a DataReader instance. The heart of ADO.NET DataReader programming is contained in a single line of code:

```
Dim reader As SqlDataReader = cmd.ExecuteReader()
```

This declares a SqlDataReader object and initializes it using the ExecuteReader() method of our Command object. Remember, we have already created the Connection object and the Command object that are being used here. Once you have the reader, you can use it to move through the records in the result set from start to finish, interacting with one record at a time, as shown below. Note that there is no way to move backward. This is similar to the way you interact with a Recordset in classic ADO, but instead of using the MoveNext() method you use the Read() method. This method returns True as long as there is a row of data at the current position. It returns False when an attempt is made to read a record following the last one.

```
Do While reader.Read()
    ' Process current row here.
Loop

reader.Close()
con.Close()
```

This loop invokes the reader.Read() method in each pass. When the reader has read all the available information, the Read() method returns False and the loop ends gracefully. Keep in mind that you have to call the Read() method before you start processing the first record. When the reader is first created, there is no "current" row.

TIP   *Remember, DataReaders maintain a live connection, so you should process the data and close your connection as quickly as possible.*

To access the data in the current record, you can use either a field name or an index number (which starts counting from zero). For example, if you want to add the contents of the OrderID field of each record processed into a list box named lstOrders, you would use this code in the body of the loop:

```
' Add the data from the OrderID field.
lstOrders.Items.Add(reader("OrderID"))
```

Alternatively, you could perform the same task using the field index:

```
lstOrders.Items.Add(reader(0))
```

Usually, a field name is the clearest option, but a numeric index provides an easy way for you to make sure you use every column in the row (as you'll see in the next section).

This is just about all that a DataReader allows you to do.

Using the DataReader to Fill a ListView

The next example uses a `SqlDataReader` object to move through the returned records and place some basic information into a `ListView` control (see Figure 10-4). The code looks more complicated than the previous snippets you've seen, because the `ListView` control requires a few special considerations. To see the complete code, refer to the ListViewDataReader project with the sample code for this chapter.

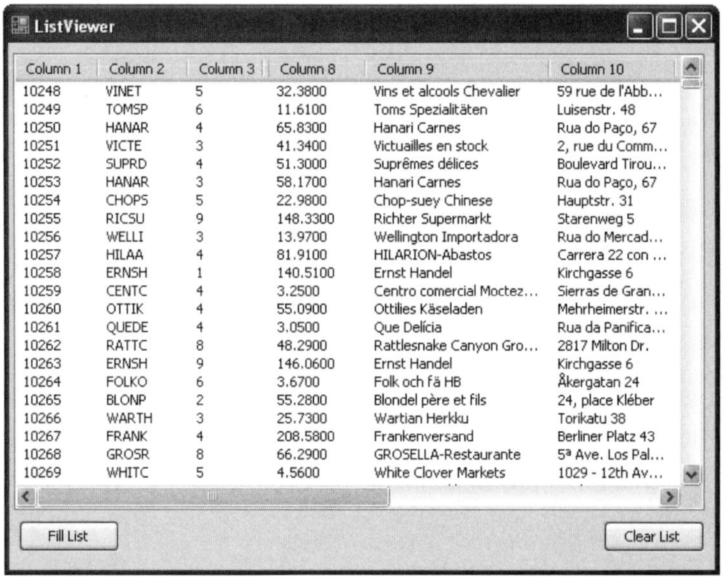

Figure 10-4: Filling a `ListView`

The first step is to set up the `ListView` control so that it displays a multi-column list:

```
lvOrders.View = View.Details
```

Now you can add a column for each field in the `DataReader`. There is no quick and easy way to get the field names, so this example sticks to index numbers. `FieldCount` is one of the few properties provided by the `SqlDataReader` object, so you can use that to determine how many columns are required:

```
Dim i As Integer
For i = 0 To reader.FieldCount - 1
    lvOrders.Columns.Add("Column " & (i + 1).ToString, 100, _
    HorizontalAlignment.Left)
Next
```

Now that the initial setup is complete, the data can be added:

```
Do While (reader.Read())
    Dim NewItem As New ListViewItem()
    NewItem.Text = reader(0)

    For i = 1 To reader.FieldCount - 1
        If reader(i) Is DBNull.Value Then
            NewItem.SubItems.Add("")
        Else
            NewItem.SubItems.Add(reader(i).ToString())
        End If
    Next i

    lvOrders.Items.Add(NewItem)
Loop
```

This example looks more complicated than it is. The code is divided into two portions because of the way the ListView control works. Every ListView control contains a collection of items. (In our example, each item represents an OrderID.) To put information into additional columns, you have to add subitems to each ListView item.

This example also checks for a null value in the field. In a database, a null value indicates only that the field is empty and that no information has been entered. You can't change a null value into a string, however, so the Add() method will fail if it's used to add a field that contain a null value.

If you can accomplish everything you need to do with a DataReader, it's always a good choice. If you need more sophisticated data manipulating abilities, like the ability to navigate table relations, dynamically sort data, or cache data for long periods of time, you'll need to step up to the DataSet object. The DataSet is described a little later in this chapter.

Updating Data with a Command Object

The DataReader object provides a simple way to pull a stream of data out of a database, but it doesn't allow you to make any changes.

In ADO.NET, you have two options for updating data:

- Updating it directly with a customized Command. This is the easiest and often the most practical solution, because it minimizes the chance of conflict between users. All other users will see your change the next time they query the database.

- Creating a DataSet, implementing the changes there, and then committing them to the original data source later on. This pattern (change-wait-commit) is a little trickier, because it increases the chance that multiple users will make conflicting changes at the same time. However, it may offer better performance, because you can group changes together in batches that are more efficient.

The next section examines the easier of these two methods: using a Command object directly.

NOTE *All the command examples in this section can be found in the SimpleDBCommandTester project with the sample code.*

Why Use a Command Object?

If your application makes relatively straightforward changes, the best way to update the data source is to use a Command object directly. The Command object can contain a SQL statement to perform the modification (such as Update or Delete), or it can run a stored procedure that exists in your database for this purpose.

Generally, a Command object provides the most straightforward and uncomplicated way to make a change. The drawback is that it can require some extra work (and code) if your application allows the user to make substantial, varied modifications. This approach—using a Command object to go straight to the data source—was available in ADO. However, ADO developers often fell back on the Recordset object because it was easier to code a solution on the fly. The advantages of using a Command object are as follows:

- No data is returned from the database. After all, why waste time creating a Recordset, and then using a Select statement to put some information into it, if you don't need to?

- If there's a problem following your update instruction, you'll know it right away. (With disconnected data and DataSets, however, several changes are usually made at the same time, and this makes it harder to track down what's failed and identify the cause.)

- Disconnected DataSets require extra planning to use properly. They can apply changes in an unpredictable order, which may cause problems with related tables. In these cases, it's often easier to perform updates through direct commands.

A Data Update Example

Here's an example that uses a Command object to perform an update operation, with the help of its ExecuteNonQuery() method:

```
' Create connection.
Dim ConnectionString As String = _
  "Data Source=localhost;Integrated Security=True;" & _
 "Initial Catalog=Northwind;"
Dim con As New SqlConnection(ConnectionString)
con.Open()

' Create a silly update command.
Dim SQL As String = "UPDATE Orders SET ShipCountry='Oceania' " & _
  "WHERE OrderID='10248'"
Dim cmd As New SqlCommand(SQL, con)

' Execute the command.
Dim NumAffected As Integer
```

```
NumAffected = cmd.ExecuteNonQuery()
con.Close()

' Display the number of affected records.
MessageBox.Show(NumAffected.ToString & " records updated", "Results", _
   MessageBoxButtons.OK)
```

This code creates the standard Connection and Command objects and then executes the command directly. The update command is a SQL Update statement that finds the record with the OrderID 10248 (which exists in the default Northwind database) and changes its ShipCountry value to Oceania. The matching record will be updated even if ShipCountry has already been changed (although in that case the modification won't produce any noticable effect). The message you'll see is shown in Figure 10-5.

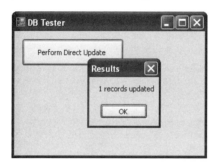

Figure 10-5: A simple update test

NOTE *The preceding example uses a fairly straightforward SQL Update statement. However, if you aren't familiar with SQL, it still may take a little getting used to. Unfortunately, SQL is beyond the scope of this book. You can get a basic SQL primer at the excellent tutorial site www.w3schools.com/sql.*

In a more realistic example, the Update statement would be created dynamically. Here's an example:

```
Dim SQL As String = "UPDATE Orders SET ShipCountry='" & lstCountry.Text & _
   "' WHERE OrderID='" & intCurrentOrder & "'"
```

Although this is a commonly used approach, writing a SQL statement like this in your program is extremely bad form. One of the key problems it introduces is the possibility of a *SQL injection attack*, where a malicious user tricks your application into doing something it shouldn't by using special characters (like the apostrophe) in the input text. When you combine these user-supplied values with the rest of your command template and execute the resulting query, you might unwittingly return confidential information or even end up launching an extra command that deletes records or performs arbitrary changes.

To avoid these problems, you have two choices. You can validate your data very carefully and remove special characters before you use it in SQL queries. This is hard to do accurately, and it gets more complicated if your input field needs to accept characters like the apostrophe. A better approach is to call a stored procedure, or use a *parameterized command*, which encodes user-supplied values in a much safer way. You'll learn how to use stored procedures and parameterized commands in the following sections.

Calling a Stored Procedure

Stored procedures are programs stored inside a relational database. A typical stored procedure consists of a number of SQL statements that perform some specific task (such as selecting, updating, inserting, or deleting data).

Here's an example of a stored procedure that to adds a new customer record to the Customers table. It's not present in the default SQL Server Northwind database, so before you can use the procedure, you have to use the Enterprise Manager or SQL Server to add it. (It will already be added if you used the script provided with this chapter's examples to install the database.)

```
CREATE PROCEDURE AddNewCustomer
    @CustomerID varchar(5), @CompanyName varchar(40),
    @ContactName varchar(30)
AS INSERT INTO Customers(CustomerID, CompanyName, ContactName)
    VALUES(@CustomerID, @CompanyName, @ContactName)
```

This code looks quite different from anything you could write in VB 2005. The basic details are as follows:

- The procedure is called AddNewCustomer.
- The procedure uses three variables, which are defined in the second and third lines. All SQL variables are identified by an at (@) symbol at the beginning of their names. The data types for these variables are also unfamiliar to the VB programmer. Varchar is the SQL Server–specific version of a string type (and the number in brackets specifies the maximum length).
- The fourth line features an Insert command, which adds a new row to the Customers table. It also inserts values for the three named fields (using the information on the next line, which is the list of variables). All other fields will be left empty—in fact, they will have null values.

You can use a Command object to execute a stored procedure in the same way you would execute a SQL statement. However, there are two differences. First of all, you should set the Command object's CommandType to CommandType.StoredProcedure:

```
' (Code to create a connection omitted).
Dim cmd As New SqlCommand("AddNewCustomer", con)
cmd.CommandType = CommandType.StoredProcedure
```

Secondly, if your stored procedure requires parameters with additional information (as the AddNewCustomer procedure does), you need to create a few Parameter objects. Here's how you would create parameters to use with the AddNewCustomer procedure:

```
' Declare a SqlParameter variable.
' We will use the Command object to actually create each
' SqlParameter object.
Dim param As SqlParameter

param = cmd.Parameters.AddWithValue("@CustomerID", "*TEST")
param = cmd.Parameters.AddWithValue("@CompanyName", "No Starch Press")
param = cmd.Parameters.AddWithValue("@ContactName", "Matthew MacDonald")
```

When you add a parameter, you must specify the corresponding stored procedure variable name and the value you want to supply. Based on the data type you supply, .NET is able to convert the information in your VB variable into a database-friendly data type. However, some restrictions apply. For example, database fields are usually size limited, and if you supply a string that's too long, part of your information will be truncated.

Once you've added the parameters and assigned the appropriate values, you can execute the stored procedure:

```
Dim NumAffected As Integer
NumAffected = cmd.ExecuteNonQuery()
con.Close()
```

The new record will be added, as shown in Figure 10-6.

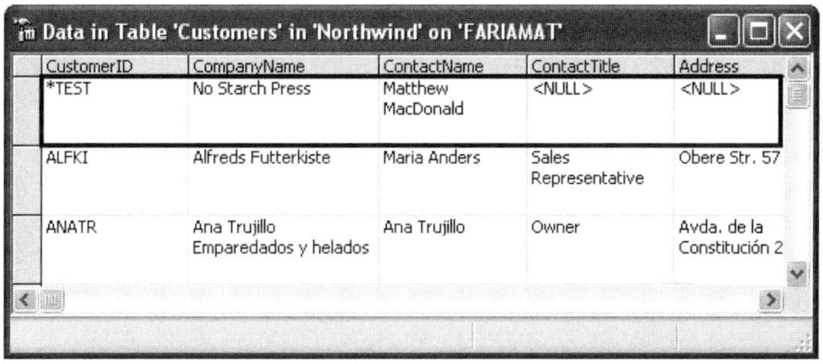

Figure 10-6: The inserted record

Stored procedures are quite handy. They let the application programmer remove database code from the application and the database administrator control security (by restricting direct access to the tables, but allowing access to permitted stored procedures) and improve performance. All of these advantages together mean that you will probably want to use stored procedures in any large, professional business application. However, stored procedure design can become quite complicated. A stored procedure might perform multiple tasks, and it may even return a result set. A stored procedure can also send additional information to your program using output parameters. By default, all the `Parameter` objects you add are for input parameters. However, this is easy to change:

```
param.Direction = ParameterDirection.Output
```

When using an output parameter, you use the `Add()` method instead of the `AddWithValue()` method. That's because you don't supply a value. Instead, you define the exact database data type.

```
' Define the parameter.
param = cmd.Parameters.Add("@OutputID", SqlDbType.VarChar, 5)
param.Direction = ParameterDirection.Output

' Execute the query.
cmd.ExecuteNonQuery()

' Get the result.
Dim Result As String = param.Value
```

After the command has been executed, you can read the output parameter from the `Parameter.Value` property to retrieve your results.

Using a Parameterized Command

When you call a stored procedure, your command supplies its information through parameters. This is a safer approach than dynamically constructing a SQL statement by pasting together bits of text. Because ADO.NET separates the command text from the parameter values, there's no possibility that malicious input could be used to launch a SQL injection attack.

Fortunately, you can take advantage of this higher level of security even if you aren't using stored procedures. The trick is to write parameterized commands—commands that use parameters even though they aren't linked to a stored procedure. Creating a parameterized command is surprisingly easy. All you need to do is replace the places where you would ordinarily put hard-coded values with parameter-name placeholders.

For example, imagine you want to execute a command like this one (from an earlier example) to update a record:

```
Dim SQL As String = "UPDATE Orders SET ShipCountry='" & lstCountry.Text & _
  "' WHERE OrderID='" & intCurrentOrder & "'"
```

The parameterized version of this query looks like this:

```
Dim SQL As String = _
  "UPDATE Orders SET ShipCountry=@ShipCountry WHERE OrderID=@OrderID"
```

Two points are worth noting. First, it doesn't matter what parameter names you use, so long as you're consistent when you refer to them later (when setting the parameter values), and @ is the first character. Of course, using the field name (as in @ShipCountry) usually makes most sense.

Second, different providers use different syntax for parameterized commands. For example, the OLE DB provider doesn't use named parameters. Instead, each parameter is indicated by a question mark. You need to supply the parameter values in exactly the same order as they appear in the command, and the OLE DB provider sets the values by position.

To supply parameter values, you add Parameter objects, exactly as you would with a command that calls a stored procedure. For example, here's the complete code required to execute a parameterized update statement:

```
' Define the connection.
Dim con As New SqlConnection(ConnectionString)
con.Open()

' Define the parameterized command.
Dim SQL As String = _
  "UPDATE Orders SET ShipCountry=@ShipCountry WHERE OrderID=@OrderID"
Dim cmd As New SqlCommand(SQL, con)
' Add the parameters.
cmd.Parameters.AddWithValue("@ShipCountry", lstCountry.Text)
cmd.Parameters.AddWithValue("@OrderID", intCurrentOrder)

' Execute the command.
Dim NumAffected As Integer
NumAffected = cmd.ExecuteNonQuery()
con.Close()
```

Remember, this approach is far more secure and error-proof than using dynamically created SQL. It's recommended that all database applications use parameterized commands.

A Transaction Example

A *transaction* allows you to execute several commands at once and to be guaranteed that they will all succeed or fail as a unit. The basic principle of a transaction is that if any of the actions in it fails, the whole process is "rolled back" to its initial state. You can appreciate the value of this system if you have ever used an instant bank machine. If, after requesting a withdrawal, the bank machine failed and could not give you any money, you would not be happy if it still deducted the amount from your bank account. In other words, withdrawing money is a transaction consisting of two steps: your bank account being debited and you receiving your money. Neither one of these steps should happen without the other.

A database often uses transactions in its stored procedures. They can save you the trouble of coding extra database logic inside your application and help separate the basic data management code from the rest of your application.

In some cases it is convenient to be able to create an ad hoc transaction programmatically in your VB 2005 code. To do this, you create a Transaction object and use the BeginTransaction() method of the Connection object.

To start the process, you need to create and initiate the transaction:

```
' (The code to create the standard Connection and Command objects
' is left out.)
' Don't need to use New, as this object will be created for us.
Dim tran As SqlTransaction

' Create the transaction and assign it to our Transaction object.
tran = con.BeginTransaction()
```

Now the transaction exists, but it includes no Command objects yet. To make a Command object a part of this transaction, you can set its Transaction property. Assuming that we've already created two Command objects (cmdOne and cmdTwo), this is done like so:

```
cmdOne.Transaction = tran
cmdTwo.Transaction = tran
```

These commands can now be executed in the normal way:

```
Dim NumAffected As Integer
NumAffected = cmdOne.ExecuteNonQuery()

' Add the rows affected for the second query to find the total number of
' rows affected by both statements.
NumAffected += cmdTwo.ExecuteNonQuery()
```

However, the changes won't be permanently made to the data source until you commit them:

```
tran.Commit()
```

If necessary, you can use the Rollback() method to reverse changes that have not been committed and set the data source back to its original state. Usually, you would use the Rollback() method in response to an error, as shown here:

```
' Define Connection, Command, and Transaction objects here.
Try
    ' Start the Transaction, execute the Commands, and perform any other
    ' related code here.
    tran.Commit()
Catch err As Exception
    tran.Rollback()
End Try
```

Using DataSet Objects

In many ways, the DataSet object is the focus of ADO.NET programming. Unlike the data reader, a DataSet is disconnected by nature. You can place information retrieved from a relational database into a DataSet or move information from a DataSet back into a relational database, but the DataSet itself never maintains a connection with a data source—in fact, it doesn't even have a connection property. To shuffle information back and forth between a DataSet object and a data source, you need to use a DataAdapter object. Figure 10-7 shows all the ADO.NET objects involved in disconnected access and how they interact.

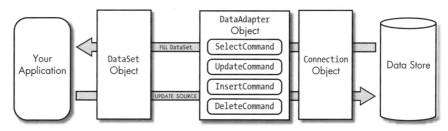

Figure 10-7: Disconnected data access with ADO.NET

When to Use a DataSet Object

A DataReader provides the best possible performance. In general, you should always use a DataReader unless you need the advanced capabilities of a DataSet. Some of these capabilities include the following:

- The ability to store data for long periods of time and transfer it as a neatly packaged object to other classes or components.
- The ability to perform complex updates and changes to the data, without needing to execute each change through a separate Command object.
- The ability to save or retrieve XML-formatted data to a file.
- The ability to bind your data to controls in a Windows form or an ASP.NET web page for quick, code-free display.
- The ability to sort and filter your results on the fly. (Dynamic sorting and filtering isn't discussed in this chapter, but you can learn all you need to know by searching for the DataView class in the Visual Studio Help.)
- Greater flexibility when reading data, such as the ability to move forward and backward through data and the ability to jump back and forth between distinct but related tables in the DataSet.

Filling a DataSet with a DataAdapter

As with a DataReader, you need to create a Connection and a Command object before you can retrieve the rows you need:

```
Dim ConnectionString As String = "Data Source=localhost;" & _
  "Integrated Security=True;Initial Catalog=Northwind;"
Dim con As New SqlConnection(ConnectionString)

Dim SQL As String = "SELECT * FROM Orders " & _
 "WHERE OrderDate < '2000/01/01' AND OrderDate > '1987/01/01'"
Dim cmd As New SqlCommand(SQL, con)
```

So far, these lines are the same as those used by the DataReader example you saw earlier.

Next, you need to create a DataAdapter. DataAdapters are another example of data source–specific objects in the provider model. There are several flavors, including SqlDataAdapter (shown here), OracleAdapter, and OleDbDataAdapter.

```
Dim adapter As New SqlDataAdapter(cmd)
```

This statement creates an adapter using a Command object. There are several other ways to accomplish the same task. For example, you could pass the SQL and ConnectionString strings to the SqlDataAdapter constructor, and coax it into creating an implicit Connection and Command on its own. However, the approach used in the preceding example is generally more flexible, particularly if you need to reuse the connection or to run more than one SQL query in a row with the same adapter.

The next step is to create a new DataSet and then fill it by calling the DataAdapter.Fill() method:

```
Dim dsNorthwind As New DataSet()
con.Open()
adapter.Fill(dsNorthwind, "Orders")
con.Close()
```

The Fill() method executes the command you've specified, takes the results, and inserts them into the dsNorthwind DataSet in a table named Orders. (In this case, the destination table name is the same as the table name in the data source, but it doesn't need to be.)

NOTE *The DataSet object is generic. Whether you are using an Oracle provider, SQL Server provider, or something else altogether, you always create and fill the same type of DataSet object.*

Accessing the Information in a DataSet

The information in a DataSet is stored in collections. This is quite different from a DataReader, which exposes only one row at a time, forcing you to use the Read() method to move from row to row. A DataSet, on the other hand, has a `Tables` property that contains a collection of `DataTable` objects. Each `DataTable` has a `Rows` property that contains a collection of `DataRow` objects. You access these `DataRows` by using the corresponding field names, much as you would with a `DataReader`. The diagram in Figure 10-8 shows the overall object model.

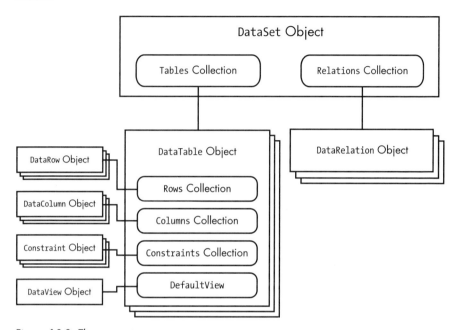

Figure 10-8: The DataSet

You'll notice that the discussion so far has left out a few of the details shown in this illustration. For example, a `DataSet` can also contain `DataRelation` objects (which link different `DataTables` together), and each `DataTable` can also contain `Constraint` objects (which specify restrictions on allowable column information) and `Column` objects (which contain information about the field name and data type of each column). These collections are generally less important, although later in the chapter we will return to the `DataRelation` object in more detail.

You move through the data in a table using the `Rows` collection, as shown here:

```
Dim row As DataRow
For Each row In dsNorthwind.Tables("Orders").Rows
    ' Here you can retrieve a value using the current row.
    lstOrders.Items.Add(row("OrderID"))
    ' Or you can change it.
    row("ShipCountry") = "Lilliput"
Next
```

NOTE *Of course, the* DataSet *object is always disconnected. This means that any changes you make will appear in your program but won't affect the original data source unless you take additional steps, which this chapter will delve into a little bit later.*

Deleting Records

You can also delete records from a DataSet using the Delete() method. The process is quite straightforward:

```
Dim row As DataRow
Dim colRowsToDelete As New Collection()

For Each row In dsNorthwind.Tables("Orders").Rows
    If row("ShipCountry") <> "Brazil" Then
        ' If the ShipCountry is not Brazil, mark it for deletion.
        row.Delete()
    Else
        ' Otherwise, add it to our list.
        lstOrders.Items.Add(row("OrderID") & " to " & row("ShipCountry"))
    End If
Next
```

However, when you use the Delete() method, the row is not actually removed, only marked for deletion. That's because ADO.NET needs to retain information about the record in order to be able to remove it from the original data source when you reconnect later. You need to be aware of this fact, and you need to include steps that prevent your programs from trying to use or display deleted rows. Here's an example that explicitly ignores deleted rows when adding items to a list:

```
For Each row In dsNorthwind.Tables("Orders").Rows
    If row.RowState <> DataRowState.Deleted Then
        lstOrders.Items.Add(row("OrderID"))
    End If
Next
```

NOTE *If your program tries to read a field of information from a deleted item, an error will occur. This error is meant to alert you that you are trying to access information that is scheduled for deletion.*

You can also use the Remove() method to delete an item completely. However, if you use this method, the record won't be deleted from the data source when you reconnect and update it with your changes. Instead, it will just be eliminated from your DataSet object.

Adding Information to a DataSet

You can also easily add a new row using the Add() method of the Rows collection. The trick is to use the NewRow() method first to get a blank copy of the row you want to create.

```
Dim rowNew As DataRow
' Create the row.
rowNew = dsNorthwind.Tables("Orders").NewRow()

' Set the information in the row.
rowNew("OrderID") = 12000
rowNew("ShipCountry") = "Lilliput"
' (And so on to add more fields...)

' Add the row to the DataSet.
dsNorthwind.Tables("Orders").Rows.Add(rowNew)
```

In a real application it might not be this easy, depending on your original data source. For example, the database may have other requirements for these columns (such as a maximum length, or a restriction against null values). In addition, most database designs use *auto-incrementing* identity columns. For example, if OrderID were an auto-numbering column, SQL Server would automatically give it a new value when you add a new record. This means that you shouldn't specify any value at all in the OrderID field while you are creating the record, or else you risk specifying a number that will conflict with an already generated value, thus causing a problem.

ADO.NET provides a tool that can help you in many cases. It's called the FillSchema() method, and you can use it to retrieve information about your database before invoking the Fill() method. The FillSchema() method generates an empty DataTable and preconfigures it with details like fields, column constraints, data types, and so on. However, no records are added.

```
adapter.FillSchema(dsNorthwind, SchemaType.Mapped, "Orders")
adapter.Fill(dsNorthwind, "Orders")
```

The FillSchema() method adds the DataTable and all the DataColumn objects, but it doesn't add the actual data. Unlike the Fill() method, FillSchema() completely configures each DataColumn object with such information as default value, whether it can be null, and maximum length. (For a full list, check the properties of the DataColumn object in the Visual Studio Help.) The primary key requirement is also added as a Constraint object. Foreign keys, which define relationships between tables, are not added, because ADO.NET has no way of knowing whether you have added the required linked tables. When you use the Fill() method, the information streams into the ready-made columns without a problem.

The specific details of how to create and modify column constraints and default values are beyond the scope of this chapter. Most programmers will use a visual database design tool (like SQL Server's Enterprise Manager) for this task. Also, keep in mind that it's often a better idea to add a new record directly by using a stored procedure rather than create a DataSet, add the record, and commit the update with a DataAdapter.

Working with Multiple Tables

Sadly, the Fill() method can add only one table at a time to a DataSet. If you want to add more than one table, you have to use the Fill() method more than once and create several Command objects (or change the Command.CommandText property in between). Here's an example:

```
Dim dsNorthwind As New DataSet()
adapter.Fill(dsNorthwind, "Orders")

' This command is still linked to the DataAdapter.
cmd.CommandText = "SELECT * FROM Customers"
adapter.Fill(dsNorthwind, "Customers")

cmd.CommandText = "SELECT * FROM Employees"
adapter.Fill(dsNorthwind, "Employees")
```

After these commands, there will be three tables in the DataSet, each of which can be accessed individually by specifying the appropriate table name (for example, dsNorthwind.Table("Customers") accesses the Customers table).

DataTable Relations

There is no way to import information about linked tables from the data source. Instead, you need to add this information manually if you want to make use of it. To link two tables together, you need to create a DataRelation object.

Our multiple-table example uses three tables that are related. For example, the Orders table has a CustomerID field that corresponds to a CustomerID in the Customers table. To specify this relationship in a DataSet, you can use the following code:

```
' Define the relation.
Dim relCustomersOrders As New DataRelation("CustomersOrders", _
 dsNorthwind.Tables("Customers").Columns("CustomerID"), _
 dsNorthwind.Tables("Orders").Columns("CustomerID"))

' Add the relation to the DataSet.
dsNorthwind.Relations.Add(relCustomersOrders)
```

This code defines a relationship in which the Customers table is the *parent* and the Orders table is the *child*. This is because one customer record can have multiple children (orders), but every order has only one parent (customer). This parent-to-child relationship is just another way of describing a *one-to-many relationship*, which is a basic ingredient in database theory. Once the relationship is defined, our example adds it to the DataSet to put it to work.

As with any relational database, using a relation here implies certain restrictions. For example, if you add a relation to the DataSet and then try to create a child row that refers to a nonexistent parent, ADO.NET will generate an error. Similarly, you can't delete a parent that has child records linked to it.

These requirements will be enforced by your data source, but by adding them to the DataSet, you ensure that your application will catch any errors as soon as they occur, rather than when it tries to commit an entire batch of changes to the data source later on only to have them rejected.

You can also use your relation to better navigate through records. This technique, shown in the following code, allows you to combine information dynamically from several linked tables, without having to use a join query. It works using the GetChildRows() method of a DataRow object. The results are shown in Figure 10-9 (and are available in the RelationalDataNavigation project).

```
Dim rowParent, rowChild As DataRow
For Each rowParent In dsNorthwind.Tables("Customers").Rows
    For Each rowChild In rowParent.GetChildRows(relCustomersOrders)
        ' Display combined information using both rows.
        lstOrders.Items.Add(rowParent("CompanyName") & _
          " ordered on " & rowChild("OrderDate"))
    Next
Next
```

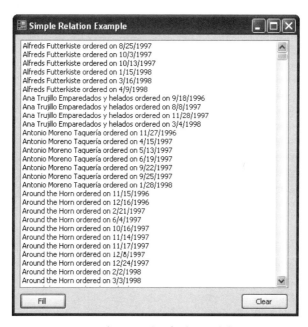

Figure 10-9: A simple example of relational data

An even more useful way to use this relational ability would be to construct a hierarchical TreeView display. The only difference in the code is that you need to make sure to store a reference to the current customer node so that you can add subnodes for orders. The following code demonstrates with a tree named treeDB.

```
Dim nodeParent, nodeChild As TreeNode
Dim rowParent, rowChild As DataRow

For Each rowParent In dsNorthwind.Tables("Customers").Rows
    ' Add the customer node.
    nodeParent = treeDB.Nodes.Add(rowParent("CompanyName"))

    ' Store the disconnected customer information for later.
    nodeParent.Tag = rowParent

    For Each rowChild In rowParent.GetChildRows(relCustomersOrders)
        ' Add the child order node.
        nodeChild = nodeParent.Nodes.Add(rowChild("OrderID"))

        ' Store the disconnected order information for later.
        nodeChild.Tag = rowChild
    Next
Next
```

As an added enhancement, this code stores a reference to the associated DataRow object in the Tag property of each TreeNode. When the node is clicked, all the information is retrieved from the DataRow, and then displayed in the adjacent text box. This is one of the advantages of disconnected data objects: You can keep them around for as long as you want.

NOTE *You might remember the Tag property from Visual Basic 6, where it could be used to store a string of information for your own personal use. The Tag property in VB 2005 is similar, except you can store any type of object in it.*

```
Private Sub treeDB_AfterSelect(ByVal sender As System.Object, _
  ByVal e As System.Windows.Forms.TreeViewEventArgs) _
  Handles treeDB.AfterSelect

    ' Clear the textbox.
    txtInfo.Text = ""
    Dim row As DataRow = CType(e.Node.Tag, DataRow)

    ' Fill the textbox with information from every field.
    Dim Field As Object
    For Each Field In row.ItemArray
        txtInfo.Text &= Field.ToString & vbNewLine
    Next

End Sub
```

This sample program (featured in the chapter examples as the RelationalTreeView project and shown in Figure 10-10) is also a good demonstration of docking at work. To make sure all the controls stay where they should, and to allow the user to change the relative screen area given to the TreeView and text box, a SplitContainer control is used along with an additional Panel along the bottom.

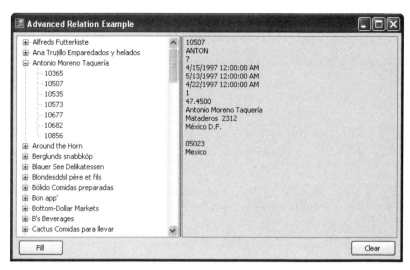

Figure 10-10: An advanced example of relational data

Using a DataSet Object to Update Data

The DataSet object stores additional information about the initial values of your table and the changes that you have made. You have already seen how deleted rows are left in your DataSet with a special "deleted" flag (DataRowState.Deleted). Similarly, added rows are given the flag DataRowState.Added, and modified rows are flagged as DataRowState.Modified. This allows ADO.NET to quickly determine which rows need to be added, removed, and changed when the update is performed with the DataAdapter.

For example, in order to commit the update for a changed row, ADO.NET needs to be able to select the original row from the data source. To allow this, ADO.NET stores information about the original field values, as shown in this example:

```
Dim rowEdit As DataRow
' Select the 11 row (at position 10).
rowEdit = dsNorthwind.Tables("Orders").Rows(10)

' Change some information in the row.
rowEdit("ShipCountry") = "Oceania"

' This returns "Oceania".
lblResult.text = rowEdit("ShipCountry")

' This is identical.
lblResult.text = rowEdit("ShipCountry", DataRowVersion.Current)

' This returns the last data source version (in my case, "Austria").
lblResult.text = rowEdit("ShipCountry", DataRowVersion.Original)
```

Ordinarily, you don't need to worry about this extra layer of information, except to understand that it is what allows ADO.NET to find the original row and update it when you reconnect to the data source.

The whole process works like this:

1. Create a Connection object, and define a Command object that will select the data you need.

2. Create a DataAdapter object using your Command object.

3. Using the DataAdapter, transfer the information from the source into a disconnected DataSet object. Close the Connection object.

4. Make changes to the DataSet (modifying, deleting, or adding rows).

5. Create another Connection object (or reuse the existing one).

6. Create Command objects for inserting, updating, and deleting data. Alternatively, to save yourself some work, you can use the special CommandBuilder class.

7. Create a DataAdapter object using your Command or CommandBuilder objects.

8. Reconnect to the data source.

9. Using the DataAdapter, update the data source with the information in the DataSet.

10. Handle any concurrency errors (for example, if an operation fails because another user has already changed the row after you've retrieved it) and choose how you want to log the problem or report it to the user.

You can see why using a simple command containing a SQL Update statement is a simpler approach than managing disconnected data!

Using the CommandBuilder Object

Assuming that you have already created a DataSet, filled it with information, and made your modifications, you can continue on with Step 5 from the preceding list. This step involves defining a connection, which is straightforward:

```
Dim ConnectionString As String = "Data Source=localhost;" & _
  "Integrated Security=True;Initial Catalog=Northwind;"
Dim con As New SqlConnection(ConnectionString)
```

The next step is to create the Command objects used to update the data source. When you selected information from the data source, you needed only one type of SQL command—a Select command. However, when you update the data source, up to three different tasks could be performed in combination, depending on the changes that you have made: Insert, Update, and Delete. In order to avoid the work involved in creating these three Command objects manually, you can use a CommandBuilder object.

NOTE *In this chapter, we use the* CommandBuilder *for quick, effective coding. However, the commands the* CommandBuilder *creates may not always be the ones you want to use. For example, you might want to use stored procedures. Or, you might not like the fact that* CommandBuilder-*generated commands try to match records* exactly *when they perform updates. That means if someone else has modified the record since you queried it, your change won't be applied. (You'll learn how to handle the resulting concurrency error later in this chapter.) Although this is generally the safest option, it might not be what you want, or you might want to implement that strategy in a different way, such as with a timestamp column. In any of these cases, you must give the* CommandBuilder *a pass and create your own* Command *objects from scratch.*

The CommandBuilder takes a reference to the DataAdapter object that was used to create the DataSet, and it adds the required additional commands.

```
' Create the Command and DataAdapter representing the Select operation.
Dim SQL As String = "SELECT * FROM Orders " & _
 "WHERE OrderDate < '2000/01/01' AND OrderDate > '1987/01/01'"
Dim cmd As New SqlCommand(SQL, con)
Dim adapter As New SqlDataAdapter(cmd)
```

At this point, the adapter.SelectCommand property refers to the cmd object. This SelectCommand property is automatically used for selection operations (when the Fill() and ExecuteReader() methods are called). However, the adapter.InsertCommand, adapter.DeleteCommand, and adapter.UpdateCommand properties are *not* set. To set these three properties, you can use the CommandBuilder:

```
' Create the CommandBuilder.
Dim cb As New SqlCommandBuilder(adapter)

' Retrieve an updated DataAdapter.
adapter = cb.DataAdapter
```

Updating the Data Source

Once you have appropriately configured the DataAdapter, you can update the data source in a single line by using the DataAdapter.Update() method:

```
Dim NumRowsAffected As Integer
NumRowsAffected = adapter.Update(dsNorthwind, "Orders")
```

The Update() method works with one table at a time, so you'll need to call it several times in order to commit the changes in multiple tables. When you use the Update() method, ADO.NET scans through all the rows in the specified table. Every time it finds a new row (DataRowState.Added), it adds it to the data source using the corresponding Insert command. Every time it finds a row that is marked with the state DataRowState.Deleted, it deletes the corresponding row from the database by using the Delete command. And every time it finds a DataRowState.Modified row, it updates the corresponding row by using the Update command.

Once the update is successfully complete, the DataSet object will be refreshed. All rows will be reset to the DataRowState.Unchanged state, and all the "current" values will become "original" values, to correspond to the data source.

Reporting Concurrency Problems

Before a row can be updated, the row in the data source must exactly match the "original" value stored in the DataSet. This value is set when the DataSet is created and whenever the data source is updated. But if another user has changed even a single field in the original record while your program has been working with the disconnected data, the operation will fail, the Update will be halted, and an exception will be thrown. In many cases, this prevents other valid rows from being updated.

An easier way to deal with this problem is to detect the discrepancy by responding to the DataAdapter.RowUpdated event. This event occurs each time a single update, delete, or insert operation is completed, regardless of the result. It provides you with some additional information, including the type of statement that was just executed, the number of rows that were affected, and the DataRow from the DataTable that prompted the operation. It also gives you the chance to tell the DataAdapter to ignore the error.

The RowUpdated event happens in the middle of DataAdapter.Update() process, and so this event handler is not the place to try to resolve the problem or to present the user with additional user interface options, which would tie up the database connection. Instead, you should log errors, display them on the screen in a list control, or put them into a collection so that you can examine them later.

The following example puts errors into one of three shared collections provided in a class called DBErrors. The class looks like this:

```
Public Class DBErrors
    Public Shared LastInsert As Collection
    Public Shared LastDelete As Collection
    Public Shared LastUpdate As Collection
End Class
```

The event handler code looks like this:

```
Public Sub OnRowUpdated(ByVal sender As Object, ByVal e As
  SqlRowUpdatedEventArgs)

    ' Check if any records were affected.
    ' If no records were affected, the statement did not
    ' execute as expected.
    If e.RecordsAffected() < 1 Then
        ' We add information about failed operations to a table.
        Select Case e.StatementType
```

```
        Case StatementType.Delete
            DBErrors.LastDelete.Add(e.Row)
        Case StatementType.Insert
            DBErrors.LastInsert.Add(e.Row)
        Case StatementType.Update
            DBErrors.LastUpdate.Add(e.Row)
    End Select

    ' As the error has already been detected, we don't need the
    ' DataAdapter to cancel the entire operation and throw an exception,
    ' unless the failure may affect other operations.
    e.Status = UpdateStatus.SkipCurrentRow
End If

End Sub
```

The nice thing about this approach is that it allows you the flexibility to decide how you want to deal with these errors when you execute the Update() method, rather than hard-coding a specific approach into the event handler for the RowUpdated event.

To bring it all together, you need to attach the event handler before the update is performed. The next example goes one step further, and examines the error collections and displays the results in three separate list controls in the current window.

```
' Connect the event handler.
AddHandler(adapter.RowUpdated, AddressOf OnRowUpdated)

' Perform the update.
Dim NumRowsAffected As Integer
NumRowsAffected = adapter.Update(dsNorthwind, "Orders")

' Display the errors.
Dim rowError As DataRow
For Each rowError In DB.LastDelete
    lstDelete.Items.Add(rowError("OrderID"))
Next

For Each rowError In DB.LastInsert
    lstInsert.Items.Add(rowError("OrderID"))
Next

For Each rowError In DB.LastUpdate
    lstUpdate.Items.Add(rowError("OrderID"))
Next
```

The ConcurrencyErrors project shows a live example of this technique. It creates two DataSets and simulates a multiuser concurrency problem by modifying them simultaneously in two different ways (see Figure 10-11). This artificial error is then dealt with in the RowUpdated event handler.

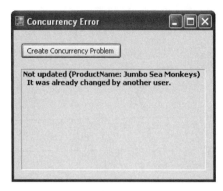

Figure 10-11: Simulating a concurrency problem

Updating Data in Stages

Concurrency issues aren't the only potential source of error when you update your data source. Another problem can occur if you use linked tables, particularly if you have deleted or added records. When you update the data source, your changes will probably not be committed in the same order in which they were performed in the DataSet. If you try to delete a record from a parent table while it is still linked to other child records, an error will occur. This error can take place even if you haven't defined relations in your DataSet, because the restriction is enforced by the database engine itself. In the case of the Northwind database, you could encounter these sorts of errors by trying to add a Product that references a nonexistent Supplier or Category, or by trying to delete a Supplier or Category record that is currently being used by a Product. (Of course, there are some exceptions. Some database products can be configured to automatically delete related child records when you remove a parent record, in which case your operation will succeed, but this might have more consequences than you expect.)

There is no simple way around these problems. If you are performing sophisticated data manipulations on a relational database using a DataSet, you will have to plan out the order in which changes need to be implemented. However, you can then use some built-in ADO.NET features to perform these operations in separate stages.

Generally, a safe approach would proceed in this order:

1. Add new records to the parent table, then to the child table.
2. Modify existing records in all tables.
3. Delete records in the child table, then in the parent table.

To perform these operations separately, you need a special update routine. This routine will create three separate DataSets, one for each operation. Then you'll move all the new records into one DataSet, all the records marked for deletion into another, and all the modified records into a third.

To perform this shuffling around, you can use the `DataSet.GetChanges()` method:

```
' Create three DataSets, and fill them from dsNorthwind.
Dim dsNew As DataSet = dsNorthwind.GetChanges(DataRowState.Added)
Dim dsModify As DataSet = dsNorthwind.GetChanges(DataRowState.Deleted)
Dim dsDelete As DataSet = dsNorthwind.GetChanges(DataRowState.Modified)

' Update these DataSets separately, in an order guaranteed to
' avoid problems.
adapter.Update(dsNew, "Customers")
adapter.Update(dsNew, "Orders")
adapter.Update(dsModify, "Customers")
adapter.Update(dsModify, "Orders")
adapter.Update(dsDelete, "Orders")
adapter.Update(dsDelete, "Customers")
```

Creating a DataSet Object by Hand

Incidentally, you can add new tables and even populate an entire `DataSet` by hand. There's really nothing tricky to this approach—it's just a matter of working with the right collections. First you create the `DataSet`, then at least one `DataTable`, and then at least one `DataColumn` in each `DataTable`. After that, you can start adding `DataRows`. This brief example demonstrates the whole process:

```
' Create a DataSet and add a new table.
Dim dsPrefs As New DataSet
dsPrefs.Tables.Add("FileLocations")

' Define two columns for this table.
dsPrefs.Tables("FileLocation").Columns.Add("Folder", _
  GetType(System.String))
dsPrefs.Tables("FileLocation").Columns.Add("Documents", _
  GetType(System.Int32))
' Add some actual information into the table.
Dim newRow As DataRow = dsPrefs.Tables("FileLocation").NewRow()
newRow("Folder") = "f:\Pictures"
newRow("Documents") = 30
dsPrefs.Tables("FileLocation").Rows.Add(newRow)
```

Notice that this example uses standard .NET types instead of SQL-specific, Oracle-specific, or OLE DB–specific types. That's because the table is not designed for storage in a relational data source. Instead, this `DataSet` stores preferences for a single user, and must be stored in a stand-alone file. Alternatively, the information could be stored in the registry, but then it would be hard to move a user's settings from one computer to another. This way, it's stored as a file, and these settings can be placed on an internal network and made available to various workstations.

Storing a DataSet in XML

To store and retrieve the custom data as an XML document, you use the built-in methods of the `DataSet` object:

```
Dim dsUserPrefs As New DataSet()
' (Code for defining and filling the DataTables goes here.)

' Save the DataSet to an XML file using the WriteXml() method.
dsUserPrefs.WriteXml("c:\MyApp\UserData\" & UserName & ".xml")

' Release the DataSet.
dsUserPrefs = Nothing

' And recreate it with the ReadXml() method.
dsUserPrefs.ReadXml("c:\MyApp\UserData\" & UserName & ".xml")
```

The XML document for a `DataSet` is shown in Figure 10-12, as displayed in Internet Explorer.

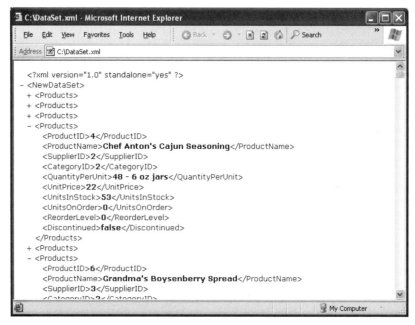

Figure 10-12: A partly collapsed view of a DataSet in XML

Of course, you will probably never need to look at it directly, because the ADO.NET `DataSet` object handles the XML format automatically. You can test XML reading and writing with the sample project XMLDataSet.

NOTE *It really is quite easy to use ADO.NET's XML support in this way. However, keep in mind that what you get is not a true database system. For example, there is no way to manage concurrent user updates to this file—every time it is saved, the existing version is completely wiped out.*

Storing a Schema for the DataSet

If you need to exchange XML data with another program, or if the structure of your DataSet changes with time, you might find it a good idea to save the XML schema information for your DataSet. This document (shown in Figure 10-13) explicitly defines the format that your DataSet file uses, preventing any chance of confusion. For example, it details the tables, the columns in each table, and their data types.

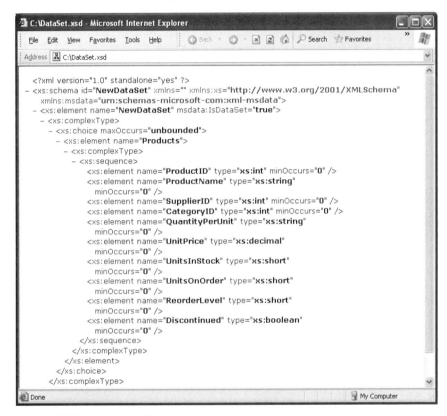

```
C:\DataSet.xsd - Microsoft Internet Explorer
File  Edit  View  Favorites  Tools  Help        Back  ·    ·       Search   Favorites    »
Address   C:\DataSet.xsd

<?xml version="1.0" standalone="yes" ?>
- <xs:schema id="NewDataSet" xmlns="" xmlns:xs="http://www.w3.org/2001/XMLSchema"
    xmlns:msdata="urn:schemas-microsoft-com:xml-msdata">
  - <xs:element name="NewDataSet" msdata:IsDataSet="true">
    - <xs:complexType>
      - <xs:choice maxOccurs="unbounded">
        - <xs:element name="Products">
          - <xs:complexType>
            - <xs:sequence>
                <xs:element name="ProductID" type="xs:int" minOccurs="0" />
                <xs:element name="ProductName" type="xs:string"
                  minOccurs="0" />
                <xs:element name="SupplierID" type="xs:int" minOccurs="0" />
                <xs:element name="CategoryID" type="xs:int" minOccurs="0" />
                <xs:element name="QuantityPerUnit" type="xs:string"
                  minOccurs="0" />
                <xs:element name="UnitPrice" type="xs:decimal"
                  minOccurs="0" />
                <xs:element name="UnitsInStock" type="xs:short"
                  minOccurs="0" />
                <xs:element name="UnitsOnOrder" type="xs:short"
                  minOccurs="0" />
                <xs:element name="ReorderLevel" type="xs:short"
                  minOccurs="0" />
                <xs:element name="Discontinued" type="xs:boolean"
                  minOccurs="0" />
              </xs:sequence>
            </xs:complexType>
          </xs:element>
        </xs:choice>
      </xs:complexType>
Done                                                              My Computer
```

Figure 10-13: A DataSet schema

Generally, storing the schema is a good safeguard, and it's easy to implement. You simply need to remember to write the schema when you write the DataSet, and read the schema information back into the DataSet to configure its structure before you load the actual data.

```
' Save it as an XML file with the WriteXmlSchema() and WriteXml() methods.
dsUserPrefs.WriteXmlSchema("c:\MyApp\UserData\" & UserName & ".xsd")
dsUserPrefs.WriteXml("c:\MyApp\UserData\" & UserName & ".xml")
dsUserPrefs = Nothing

' And retrieve it with the ReadXmlSchema() and ReadXml() methods.
dsUserPrefs.ReadXmlSchema("c:\MyApp\UserData\" & UserName & ".xsd")
dsUserPrefs.ReadXml("c:\MyApp\UserData\" & UserName & ".xml")
```

Data Binding

Data binding is a powerful way to display information from a DataSet by binding it directly to a user interface control. It saves you from writing simple but repetitive code to move through the database and manually copy content from a DataSet into a control. (The ListView example used this kind of code, but in that case, there was no other choice, because the ListView control doesn't support data binding.)

Binding a control in a Windows application is often just as easy as setting a DataSource property. Here's an example with the super-powerful DataGridView control:

```
DataGridView1.DataSource = dsNorthwind.Tables("Products")
```

This produces a display that includes every field in a separate column and all the rows of data, as shown in Figure 10-14.

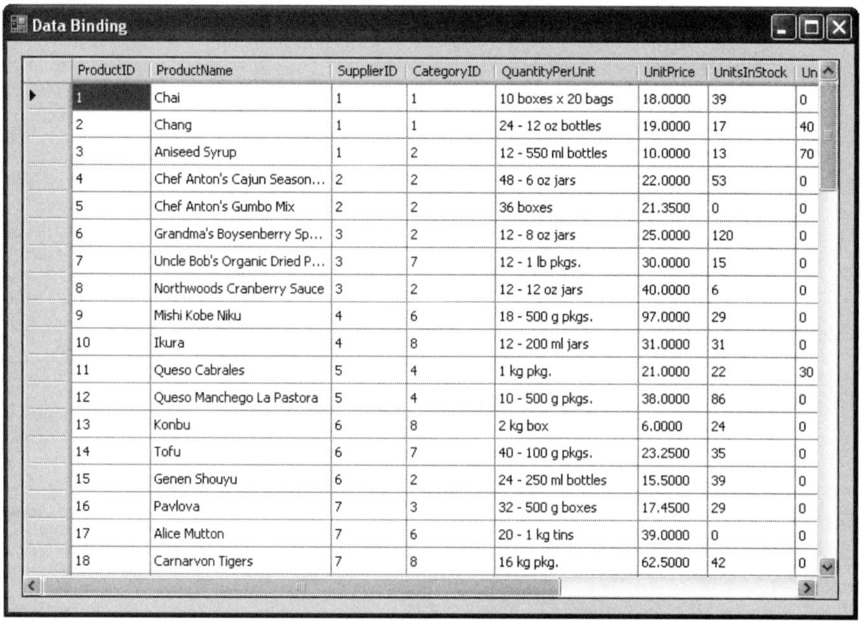

ProductID	ProductName	SupplierID	CategoryID	QuantityPerUnit	UnitPrice	UnitsInStock	Un
1	Chai	1	1	10 boxes x 20 bags	18.0000	39	0
2	Chang	1	1	24 - 12 oz bottles	19.0000	17	40
3	Aniseed Syrup	1	2	12 - 550 ml bottles	10.0000	13	70
4	Chef Anton's Cajun Season...	2	2	48 - 6 oz jars	22.0000	53	0
5	Chef Anton's Gumbo Mix	2	2	36 boxes	21.3500	0	0
6	Grandma's Boysenberry Sp...	3	2	12 - 8 oz jars	25.0000	120	0
7	Uncle Bob's Organic Dried P...	3	7	12 - 1 lb pkgs.	30.0000	15	0
8	Northwoods Cranberry Sauce	3	2	12 - 12 oz jars	40.0000	6	0
9	Mishi Kobe Niku	4	6	18 - 500 g pkgs.	97.0000	29	0
10	Ikura	4	8	12 - 200 ml jars	31.0000	31	0
11	Queso Cabrales	5	4	1 kg pkg.	21.0000	22	30
12	Queso Manchego La Pastora	5	4	10 - 500 g pkgs.	38.0000	86	0
13	Konbu	6	8	2 kg box	6.0000	24	0
14	Tofu	6	7	40 - 100 g pkgs.	23.2500	35	0
15	Genen Shouyu	6	2	24 - 250 ml bottles	15.5000	39	0
16	Pavlova	7	3	32 - 500 g boxes	17.4500	29	0
17	Alice Mutton	7	6	20 - 1 kg tins	39.0000	0	0
18	Carnarvon Tigers	7	8	16 kg pkg.	62.5000	42	0

Figure 10-14: A data-bound grid

In its default mode, the DataGridView even allows you to edit a data value by typing in a field and to add a new row by entering information at the bottom of the row (see Figure 10-15).

When you change or add information to the DataGridView, the linked DataSet is modified automatically, providing some very convenient basic data editing features.

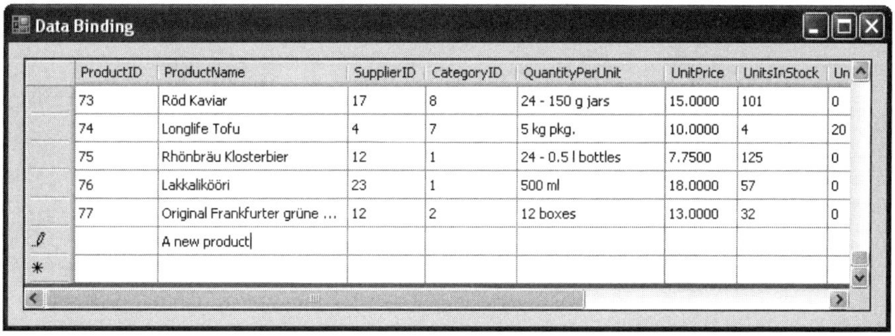

Figure 10-15: Adding a new record

Not all controls support data binding, and few can bind to multiple tables at once. Some, like `ListBox` controls, can only support binding to one field in a table. In this case, you have to specify two properties: the table data source, and the field that should be used for display purposes:

```
lstID.DataSource = dsNorthwind.Tables("Employees")
lstID.DisplayMember = "EmployeeID"
```

Just about every .NET control supports single-value data binding through the `DataBindings` property. This property provides a collection that allows you to connect a field in the data source with a property in the control. That means you could have a check box control, for example, that has several bound properties, including `Text`, `Tag`, and `Checked`.

The following code binds a generic text box:

```
' Bind the FirstName field to the Text property.
txtName.DataBindings.Add("Text", dsNorthwind.Tables("Employees"), _
  "FirstName")
```

You can bind a `DataSet` to as many controls as you want, all at the same time (as shown in Figure 10-16). However, only one record can be selected at a time. When you select a value in the `ListBox`, the corresponding full record row is selected in the `DataGridView`, and the corresponding values are filled into other bound controls like the text box.

This allows you to create windows that contain many different controls, each of which allows you to edit one property of the currently selected record. There's much more that you can do with data binding to configure advanced column display. For example, using such features as column mapping, you can rename or hide specific columns. ASP.NET even allows you to use templates to configure specifically how a column will look. Unfortunately, we won't get a chance to explore these topics in this chapter. Instead, refer to the Visual Studio Help.

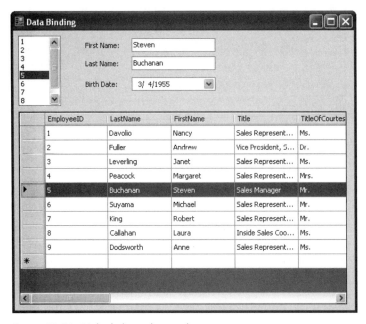

Figure 10-16: Multiple bound controls

What Comes Next?

This chapter has tackled a subject that can easily make up an entire book of its own. We've examined all the essentials, with a fairly in-depth look at the best way to organize database code, update information, and manage disconnected DataSet objects. You may want to take the time to work through this chapter again, as many of the insights contained here are the basis for "best practices" and other techniques that can ensure a robust, scalable database application.

There are still many more possibilities left for you to discover with ADO.NET. Here are some of them:

- If you don't already know SQL, now is the perfect time to learn. Although you don't need a sophisticated understanding of SQL to program with ADO.NET, the difference between a competent database programmer and an excellent one is often an understanding of the limitations and capabilities of SQL. Many excellent SQL resources are available online.

- It also helps to know a specific database product in order to create stored procedures and well-organized data tables. SQL Server provides Books Online, documentation which covers advanced tools such as stored procedures, views, column constraints, and triggers, all of which can help you to become a database guru. SQL Server 2005 even allows you to create these database ingredients using pure VB 2005 code!

- Data binding was a dirty word in traditional Visual Basic programming, because it was slow, inefficient, and extremely inflexible. In .NET, data binding has been improved so much that it finally makes sense. Using data binding with the `DataGridView`, for example, you can automatically provide a sophisticated number of data editing features.

- In the examples in this chapter, we updated our data source using a `DataSet` and the default `UpdateCommand`, `InsertCommand`, and `DeleteCommand` that ADO.NET generates automatically. You might be able to improve performance and provide additional options if you learn how to customize these properties with your own commands. For example, you might create a command that can update a record even if it has been changed in the meantime, by making the selection criteria less strict. (You might look the record up just using the `ID` column, for example.) Or, you could configure the `DataAdapter` to use a specific stored procedure you have created. See the Visual Studio Help for more information.

- To become a database programming expert, you might want to consult a dedicated book on the subject. Consider David Sceppa's relentlessly comprehensive *Programming Microsoft ADO.NET 2.0: Core Reference* (Microsoft Press, 2006).

11

THREADING

Threading is, from your application's point of view, a way of running various different pieces of code at the same time. Threading is also one of the more complex subjects examined in this book. That's not because it's difficult to use threading in your programs—as you'll see, Visual Basic 2005 makes it absurdly easy—but because it's difficult to use threading *correctly*. If you stick to the rules, keep your use of threads simple, or rely on the new all-in-one BackgroundWorker component, you'll be fine. If, however, you embark on a wild flight of multithreaded programming, you will probably commit one of the cardinal sins of threading, and wind up in a great deal of trouble. Many excellent developers have argued that the programming community has repeatedly become overexcited about threading in the past, and has misused it, creating endless headaches.

This chapter explains how to use threading and, more importantly, the guidelines you should follow to make sure you keep your programs free of such troubles as thread overload and synchronization glitches. Threading is a sophisticated subject with many nuances, so it's best to proceed carefully. However, a judicious use of carefully selected threads can make your applications appear faster, more responsive, and more sophisticated.

New in .NET

In Visual Basic 6, there was no easy way to create threads. Programmers who wanted to create truly multithreaded applications had to use the Windows API (or create and register separate COM components). Visual Basic 2005 provides these enhancements:

Integrated threads

The method of creating threads in Visual Basic 2005 is conceptually and syntactically similar to using the Windows API, but it's far less error-prone, and it's elegantly integrated into the language through the System.Threading namespace. The class library also contains a variety of tools to help implement synchronization and thread management.

Multithreaded debugging

The Visual Studio debugger now allows you to run and debug multi-threaded applications without forcing them to act as though they are single-threaded. You can even view a Threads window that shows all the currently active threads and allows you to pause and resume them individually.

The BackgroundWorker

As you'll learn in this chapter, multithreaded programming can be complicated. In .NET 2.0, Microsoft has added a BackgroundWorker component that can simplify the way you code a background task. All you need to do is handle the BackgroundWorker events and add your code— the BackgroundWorker takes care of the rest, making sure that your code executes on the correct thread. This chapter provides a detailed look at the BackgroundWorker.

An Introduction to Threading

Even if you've never tried to implement threading in your own code, you've already seen threads work in the modern Windows operating system. For example, you have probably noticed how you can work with a Windows application while another application is busy or in the process of starting up, because both applications run in separate processes and use separate *threads*. You have probably also seen that even when the system appears to be frozen, you can almost always bring up the Task Manager by pressing CTRL+ALT+ DELETE. This is because the Task Manager runs on a thread that has an extremely high priority. Even if other applications are currently executing or frozen, trapping their threads in endless CPU-wasting cycles, Windows can usually wrest control away from them for a more important thread.

If you've used Windows 3.1, you'll remember that this has not always been the case. Threads really came into being with 32-bit Windows and the Windows 95 operating system.

Threads "Under the Hood"

Now that you have a little history, it's time to examine how threads really work.

Threads are created by the handful in Windows applications. If you open a number of different applications on your computer, you will quickly have several different processes and potentially dozens of different threads executing simultaneously. The Windows Task Manager can list all the active processes, which gives you an idea of the scope of the situation (Figure 11-1).

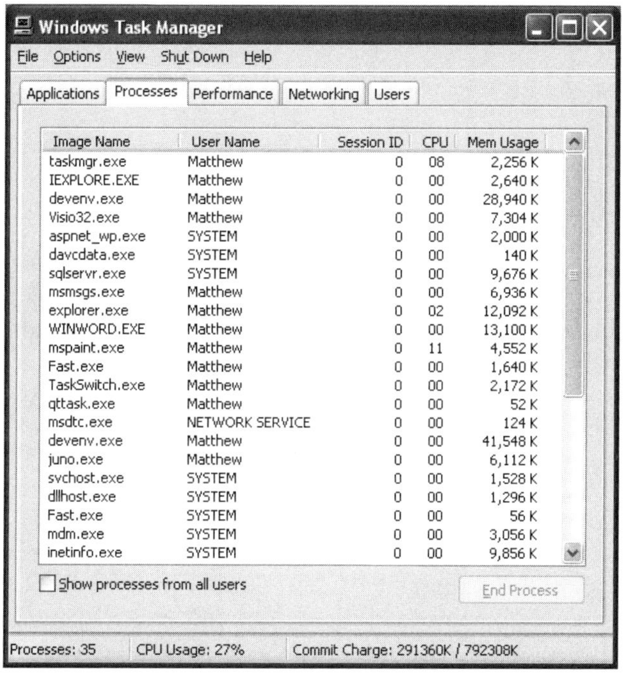

Figure 11-1: Active processes in Task Manager

In all honesty, there is no way any computer, no matter how technologically advanced, can run dozens of different operations literally at once. If your system has two CPUs, it is technically possible for two instructions to be processed at the same time, and Windows is likely to send the instructions for different threads to different CPUs. At some point, however, you will still end up with many more threads than CPUs.

Windows handles this situation by switching rapidly between different threads. Each thread *thinks* it is running independently, but in reality it only runs for a little while, is suspended, and is then resumed a short while later for another brief interval of time. This switching is all taken care of by the Windows operating system and is called *preemptive multitasking*.

Comparing Single Threading and Multithreading

One consequence of thread switching is that multithreading usually doesn't result in a speed increase. Figure 11-2 shows why.

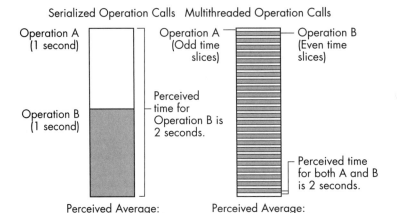

Serialized Operation Calls   Multithreaded Operation Calls

Operation A (1 second)

Operation A (Odd time slices)

Operation B (Even time slices)

Perceived time for Operation B is 2 seconds.

Operation B (1 second)

Perceived time for both A and B is 2 seconds.

Perceived Average: (1+2)/2 = 1.5 seconds

Perceived Average: (2+2)/2 = 2.0 seconds

Figure 11-2: Multithreading can make operations appear slower

This illustration compares a *single-threaded* and a *multithreaded* application. Both are performing the same two tasks, but the multithreaded program is working by dividing the two operations into numerous little intervals, and rapidly switching from one to the other. This switching introduces a small overhead, but overall, both applications will finish at about the same time. However, if a user is waiting for both tasks to end, they will both seem to be running more slowly, because both tasks will finish at more or less the same time—at the end of two seconds. With the single-threaded approach, Operation A will be completed sooner, after about a second of processing time.

So why use multithreading? Well, if you were running a short task and a long task simultaneously, the picture might change. For example, if Operation B took only a few time slices to complete, a user would perceive the multithreaded application as being much faster, because the user wouldn't have to wait for Operation A to finish before Operation B was started (in technical terms, with multithreading Operation B is not *blocked* by Operation A). In this case, Operation A would finish in a fraction of a second, rather than waiting the full one-second period (see Figure 11-3).

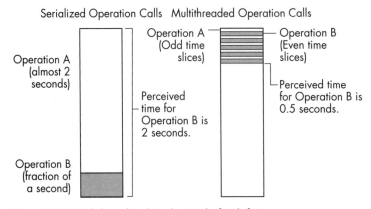

Serialized Operation Calls   Multithreaded Operation Calls

Operation A (Odd time slices)

Operation B (Even time slices)

Perceived time for Operation B is 0.5 seconds.

Operation A (almost 2 seconds)

Perceived time for Operation B is 2 seconds.

Operation B (fraction of a second)

Figure 11-3: Multithreading lets short tasks finish first

This is the basic principle of multithreading. Rather than speeding up tasks, it allows the quickest tasks to finish first; this makes an application appear more responsive and adds only a slight performance degradation (caused by all the required thread switching).

Multithreading works even better in applications where substantial waits are involved for certain tasks. For example, an application that spends a lot of time waiting for file I/O operations to complete could accomplish other useful tasks while waiting. In this case, multithreading can actually speed up the application, because it will not be forced to sit idle.

Scalability and Simplicity

There is one other reason to use threading: It makes program design much simpler for some common types of applications. For example, imagine you want to create an FTP server that can serve several simultaneous users. In a single-threaded application, you may find it very difficult to manage a variable number of users without hard-coding some preset limit on the number of users and implementing your own crude thread-switching logic.

With a multithreaded application, you can easily create a new thread to serve each client connection. Windows will take care of automatically assigning the processor time for each thread, and you can use exactly the same code to serve a hundred users as you would to serve one. Each thread uses the same code, but handles a different client. As the workload increases, all you need to do is add more threads.

Timers Versus Threads

You may have used Timer objects in previous versions of Visual Basic. Timer objects are still provided in Visual Basic 2005, and they are useful for a wide variety of tasks. Timers work differently than threads, however. From the program's standpoint, multiple threads execute simultaneously. In contrast, a timer works by interrupting your code in order to perform a single task at a "timed" interval. This task is then started, performed, and completed before control returns to the procedure in your application that was executing when the timer code launched.

This means that timers are not well suited for implementing long-running processes that perform a variety of independent, unpredictably scheduled tasks. To use a timer for this purpose, you would need to fake a multithreaded process by performing part of a task the first time a timer event occurs, a different part the next time, and so on.

To observe this problem, you can create a project with two timers and two labels, and add the following code.

```
Private Sub Form1_Load(ByVal sender As System.Object, _
  ByVal e As System.EventArgs) Handles MyBase.Load
    Timer1.Enabled = True
    Timer2.Enabled = True
End Sub
```

```
Private Sub Timer1_Elapsed(ByVal sender As System.Object, _
  ByVal e As System.EventArgs) Handles Timer1.Tick
    Dim i As Integer
    For i = 1 To 5000
        Label1.Text = i.ToString()
        Label1.Refresh()
    Next
    Timer1.Enabled = False
End Sub

Private Sub Timer2_Elapsed(ByVal sender As System.Object, _
  ByVal e As System.EventArgs) Handles Timer2.Tick
    Dim i As Integer
    For i = 1 To 5000
        Label2.Text = i.ToString()
        Label2.Refresh()
    Next
    Timer2.Enabled = False
End Sub
```

When you run this program, one timer will take control, and one label
will display the numbers from 1 to 5,000. The other timer will also perform
the same process, but only after the first timer finishes. Even though both
timers are scheduled to start at the same time, only one can work with the
application window at a time. (Indeed, if Visual Basic 2005 were to allow timer
events to execute simultaneously, it would lead programmers to encounter
all the same synchronization issues that can occur with threads, as you'll see
later this chapter.)

You'll also notice that while the timer is executing in this example (incrementing a label), the application as a whole won't be responsive. If you try to
have perform another task with your application or drag its window around
on the desktop, you'll find it performs very sluggishly.

Basic Threading with the BackgroundWorker

The simplest way to create a multithreaded application is to use
the BackgroundWorker component, which is new in Visual Basic 2005. The
BackgroundWorker handles all the multithreading behind the scenes and
interacts with your code through events. Your code handles these events to
perform the background task, track the progress of the background task, and
deal with the final result. Because these events are automatically fired on the
correct threads, you don't need to worry about thread synchronization and
other headaches of low-level multithreaded programming.

Of course, the BackgroundWorker also has a limitation—namely, flexibility.
Although the BackgroundWorker works well when you have a single, distinct task
that needs to take place in the background, it isn't as well suited when you
want to manage multiple background tasks, control thread priority, or maintain a thread for the lifetime of your application.

To use the BackgroundWorker, you begin by dragging it from the Components section of the Toolbox onto a form. (You can also create a BackgroundWorker in code, but the drag-and-drop approach is easiest.) The BackgroundWorker will then appear in the component tray (see Figure 11-4).

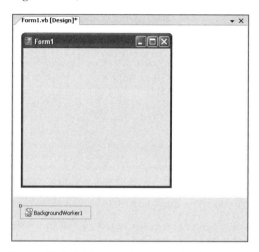

Figure 11-4: Adding the BackgroundWorker to a form

Once you have a BackgroundWorker, you can begin to use it by connecting it to the appropriate event handlers. A BackgroundWorker throws three events:

- The DoWork event fires when the BackgroundWorker begins its work. But here's the trick—this event is fired on a *separate* thread (which is temporarily borrowed from a thread pool that the Common Language Runtime maintains). That means your code can run freely without stalling the rest of your application. You can handle the DoWork event and perform your time-consuming task from start to finish.

NOTE *The code that responds to the DoWork event can't communicate directly with the rest of your application or try to manipulate a form, control, or member variable. If it did, it would violate the rules of thread safety (as you'll see later in this chapter), perhaps causing a fatal error.*

- The ProgressChanged event fires when you notify the BackgroundWorker (in your DoWork event handler) that the progress of the background task has changed. Your application can react to this event to update some sort of status display or progress meter.

- The RunWorkerCompleted event fires once the code in the DoWork handler has finished. Like the ProgressChanged event, the RunWorkerCompleted event fires on the main application thread, which allows you to take the result and display it in a control or store it in a member variable somewhere else in your application, without risking any problems. RunWorkerCompleted also fires when the background task is canceled (assuming you elect to support the Cancel feature).

To try out the BackgroundWorker, you can create a simple test. First, drop the BackgroundWorker component onto a form. Then attach the following DoWork event handler, which simply idles away ten seconds without doing anything. (We'll return to the Sleep() method later in the chapter.)

```
Private Sub BackgroundWorker1_DoWork(ByVal sender As System.Object, _
  ByVal e As System.ComponentModel.DoWorkEventArgs) _
  Handles BackgroundWorker1.DoWork

    ' This fires on a thread from the CLR thread pool.
    ' It's not safe to access the form here or any shared data
    ' (such as form-level variables).
    System.Threading.Thread.Sleep(TimeSpan.FromSeconds(10))

End Sub
```

WARNING   *If you do break the rule in the above code and manipulate a control or form-level variable, you might not receive an error. But eventually you will cause a more serious problem under difficult-to-predict conditions, as described later in this chapter.*

Next you need to handle the RunWorkerCompleted event, in order to react when the background task is complete:

```
Private Sub BackgroundWorker1_RunWorkerCompleted( _
  ByVal sender As System.Object, _
  ByVal e As System.ComponentModel.RunWorkerCompletedEventArgs) _
  Handles BackgroundWorker1.RunWorkerCompleted

    ' This fires on the main application thread.
    ' It's now safe to update the form.
    MessageBox.Show("Time wasting completed!")

End Sub
```

The only thing remaining is to set the BackgroundWorker in motion when the form loads. To do this, call the BackgroundWorker.RunWorkerAsync() method. Here's the code that launches the BackgroundWorker when the form loads:

```
Private Sub Form1_Load(ByVal sender As System.Object, _
  ByVal e As System.EventArgs) Handles MyBase.Load

    BackgroundWorker1.RunWorkerAsync()

End Sub
```

When you run this application, you'll see a message box appear after ten seconds have elapsed.

Although this example is trivial, it should be clear that if you were doing something truly time-consuming in the DoWork event handler (like performing a database query or calling a web service on a remote computer), there would be a clear benefit: Your application would remain responsive as this work is taking place in the background.

In the next section, you'll see how to extend this pattern to use the BackgroundWorker in a more realistic application.

Transferring Data to and from the BackgroundWorker

One of the main challenges in multithreaded programming is exchanging information between threads. Fortunately, the BackgroundWorker includes a mechanism that lets you send initial information to the background thread and retrieve the result from it without any synchronization headaches.

To supply information to the BackgroundWorker you pass a single parameter to the RunWorkerAsync() method. This parameter can be any object type from a simple integer to a full-fledged object. However, you can only supply a single object. This object will be delivered to the DoWork event.

For example, imagine you want to calculate a series of cryptographically strong random digits. Cryptographically strong random numbers are random numbers that can't be predicted. Ordinarily, computers use relatively well-understood algorithms to generate random numbers. As a result, a malicious user can predict an upcoming "random" number based on recently generated numbers. This isn't necessarily a problem, but it is a risk if you need your random number to be secret.

For this operation, your code needs to specify the number of digits and the maximum and minimum value. In this case, you might create a class like this to encapsulate the input arguments:

```
Public Class RandomNumberGeneratorInput

    Private _NumberOfDigits As Integer
    Private _MinValue As Integer
    Private _MaxValue As Integer

    ' (Property procedures are omitted.)

    Public Sub New(ByVal numberOfDigits As Integer, _
      ByVal minValue As Integer, _
      ByVal maxValue As Integer)
        Me.NumberOfDigits = numberOfDigits
        Me.MinValue = minValue
        Me.MaxValue = maxValue
    End Sub

End Class
```

The form should provide text boxes for supplying this information and a button that can start the asynchronous background task. When the button is clicked, you'll launch the operation with the correct information. Here's the event handler that starts it all off:

```
Private Sub cmdDoWork_Click(ByVal sender As System.Object, _
  ByVal e As System.EventArgs) Handles cmdDoWork.Click
```

```
' Prevent two asynchronous tasks from being triggered at once.
' This is allowed but doesn't make sense in this application
' (because the form only has space to show one set of results
' at a time).
cmdDoWork.Enabled = False
' Clear any previous results.
txtResult.Text = ""

' Start the asynchronous task.
Dim Input As New RandomNumberGeneratorInput( _
  Val(txtNumberOfDigits.Text), _
  Val(txtMin.Text), Val(txtMax.Text))
BackgroundWorker1.RunWorkerAsync(Input)
End Sub
```

Once the BackgroundWorker acquires the thread, it fires a DoWork event.
The DoWork event provides a DoWorkEventArgs object, which is the key ingredient for retrieving and returning information. You retrieve the input through
the DoWorkEventArgs.Argument property, and return the result by setting the
DoWorkEventArgs.Result property. Both properties can use any object.

Here's the implementation for a simple secure random number generator that's deliberately written to take almost 1,000 times longer than it
should (and thereby make testing easier).

```
Private Sub BackgroundWorker1_DoWork(ByVal sender As System.Object, _
  ByVal e As System.ComponentModel.DoWorkEventArgs) _
  Handles BackgroundWorker1.DoWork

  ' Retrieve the input arguments.
  Dim Input As RandomNumberGeneratorInput = CType( _
    e.Argument, RandomNumberGeneratorInput)

  ' Create a StringBuilder to hold the generated random number sequence.
  Dim ResultString As New System.Text.StringBuilder()

  ' Start generating numbers.
  For i As Integer = 0 To Input.NumberOfDigits - 1
      ' Create a cryptographically secure random number.
      Dim RandomByte(1000) As Byte
      Dim Random As New _
        System.Security.Cryptography.RNGCryptoServiceProvider()

      ' Fill the byte array with random bytes. In this case,
      ' the byte array only needs a single byte.
      ' We fill it with 1000 just to make sure this is the world's slowest
      ' random number generator.
      Random.GetBytes(RandomByte)

      ' Convert the random byte into a decimal from MinValue to MaxValue.
      Dim RandomDigit As Integer
```

```
        RandomDigit = Int(RandomByte(0) / 256 * _
          (Input.MaxValue - Input.MinValue + 1)) + Input.MinValue

        ' Add the random number to the string.
        ResultString.Append(RandomDigit.ToString())
    Next

    ' Return the complete string.
    e.Result = ResultString.ToString()
End Sub
```

TIP *In many cases, you'll want your* DoWork *event handler to call a method in another class to perform the actual work. This more extensively factored approach gives you greater flexibility—you can decide whether to perform the task synchronously, asynchronously, in multiple forms, or even in other applications (if you place the component in a separate class library assembly).*

Once the handler completes, the BackgroundWorker fires the RunWorkerCompletedEventArgs on the user interface thread. At this point, you can retrieve the result from the RunWorkerCompletedEventArgs.Result property and update the interface and access form-level variables without worry:

```
Private Sub BackgroundWorker1_RunWorkerCompleted( _
  ByVal sender As System.Object, _
  ByVal e As System.ComponentModel.RunWorkerCompletedEventArgs) _
  Handles BackgroundWorker1.RunWorkerCompleted
    ' Show the results.
    txtResult.Text = CType(e.Result, String)

    ' Allow another operation to be started.
    cmdDoWork.Enabled = True
End Sub
```

This code completes the simple asynchronous random number generator shown in Figure 11-5. You can find this example (complete with the refinements for cancellation handling and progress tracking that you'll consider in the following sections) in the BackgroundWorkerTest project.

This simple application really demonstrates the power of threading. When you run it, you have no idea that any work is being carried out in the background. Best of all, the user interface remains responsive, which is not the case when timers are used. The user can click other buttons and perform other tasks while the time-consuming random number calculation is performed without any noticeable slowdown.

One reason multithreading works so well is that modern computers are so fast. Slowing down an application to execute several operations at once is a performance degradation that most applications can easily afford. Also, there's a little human psychology involved—in a user's experience, perception *is* reality.

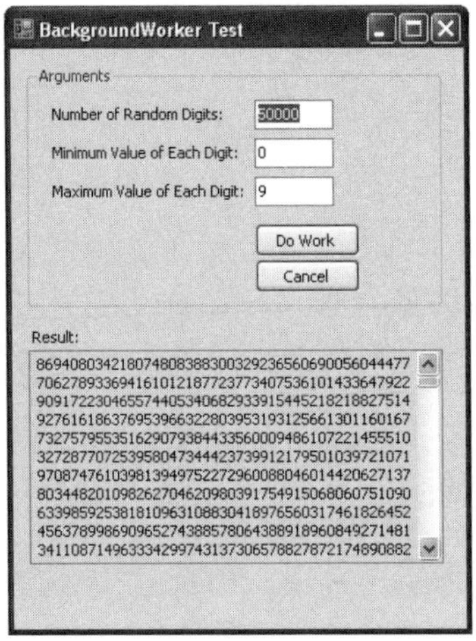

Figure 11-5: Generating random numbers asynchronously

Tracking Progress

There's no automatic way to report progress with the BackgroundWorker because it won't know how long your code will take to execute. However, the BackgroundWorker does provide built-in support for your DoWork code to read progress information and pass it to the rest of the application. This is useful for keeping a user informed about how much work has been completed in a long-running task.

To add support for progress reporting, you first need to set the BackgroundWorker.WorkerReportsProgress property to True. Then it's up to your code in the DoWork event handler to call the BackgroundWorker.ReportProgresss() method and provide an estimate of percentage complete (from 0% to 100%). You can do this as little or as often as you like. How is progress estimated? Each time you call ReportProgress(), the BackgroundWorker fires the ProgressChanged event. You can react to this event to read the new progress percentage and update the user interface. Because the ProgressChanged event fires on the user interface thread, there's no need for you to worry about marshalling your call to the correct thread.

Reporting progress usually involves a calculation, a call to another thread, an event, and a refresh of the form's user interface. Because of this overhead, you want to cut down the rate of progress reporting as much as possible. In our random number generator example, we do this by reporting progress in 1% increments only. Before the loop starts, a calculation is made to determine how many iterations must pass before a 1% progress change has occurred:

```
Dim ProgressIteration As Integer = Input.NumberOfDigits / 100
```

For example, if you are calculating 500 random numbers, progress will be reported every fifth iteration. This is a relatively quick calculation to make in the loop:

```
For i As Integer = 0 To Input.NumberOfDigits - 1
    If BackgroundWorker1.WorkerReportsProgress _
      And ProgressIteration > 0 Then
        If i Mod ProgressIteration = 0 Then
            BackgroundWorker1.ReportProgress(i / ProgressIteration)
        End If
    End If
    ...
Next
```

Now the only remaining step is to respond to the `ProgressChanged` event and update a `ProgressBar` control:

```
Private Sub BackgroundWorker1_ProgressChanged( _
  ByVal sender As System.Object, _
  ByVal e As System.ComponentModel.ProgressChangedEventArgs) _
  Handles BackgroundWorker1.ProgressChanged

    ProgressBar1.Value = e.ProgressPercentage
End Sub
```

Remember, you'll also need to reset the `ProgressBar.Value` at the beginning of each new operation. Figure 11-6 shows the revised program with a random number calculation in progress.

Figure 11-6: Tracking progress in an asynchronous task

Supporting a Cancel Feature

Another feature your users will appreciate is cancellation—the ability to halt an asynchronous task before it's complete if the information isn't needed. However, there's no generic way to support cancellation in the BackgroundWorker component. After all, your DoWork code might need to perform some cleanup before it can stop, or it might be in the middle of an operation that isn't safe to stop. However, the BackgroundWorker provides support for passing cancellation messages, which you can take advantage of. To enable this feature, first set the BackgroundWorker.WorkerSupportsCancellation property to True.

As long as WorkerSupportsCancellation is true, your form can call the BackgroundWorker.CancelAsync() method to request a cancellation. In this example, the cancellation is requested when a Cancel button is clicked:

```
Private Sub cmdCancel_Click(ByVal sender As System.Object, _
  ByVal e As System.EventArgs) Handles cmdCancel.Click

    BackgroundWorker1.CancelAsync()
End Sub
```

Nothing happens automatically when you call CancelAsync(). The code that's performing the task needs to explicitly check for a cancel request, set the DoWorkEventArgs.Cancel property to true, perform any required cleanup, and return. Here's how you can add this code to the loop in your DoWork code:

```
For i As Integer = 0 To Input.NumberOfDigits - 1
    If BackgroundWorker1.CancellationPending Then
        e.Cancel = true
        ' Return without doing any more work.
        Return
    End If
    ...
Next
```

Even when you cancel an operation, the RunWorkerCompleted event still fires. At this point, you can check whether the task was canceled and handle it accordingly.

```
Private Sub BackgroundWorker1_RunWorkerCompleted( _
  ByVal sender As System.Object, _
  ByVal e As System.ComponentModel.RunWorkerCompletedEventArgs) _
  Handles BackgroundWorker1.RunWorkerCompleted

    ' This fires on the main application thread.
    ' It's now safe to update the form.
    If e.Cancelled Then
        MessageBox.Show("Task canceled.")
    Else
        txtResult.Text = CType(e.Result, String)
    End If
```

```
        cmdDoWork.Enabled = True
        ProgressBar1.Visible = False
End Sub
```

Advanced Threading with the Thread Class

The BackgroundWorker is a great tool for implementing a single, straightforward background task. However, there are several situations in which you might want to use a more sophisticated (and more complex) approach. Here are some examples:

- You want to control the priority of a background task.
- You want to have the ability to suspend and resume a task (by suspending and resuming the thread that executes it).
- You want to reuse a thread over the lifetime of the application.
- You need to have a single thread perform multiple tasks and communicate with multiple forms or other classes.

Although there's no denying that the BackgroundWorker is a great tool for many common scenarios involving a single, asynchronously running background task, sooner or later nearly every Windows programmer is tempted to get his or her hands dirty with something a little more powerful. In the rest of this chapter, you'll get an overview of how you can use the Thread class from the System.Threading namespace to create and control threads at will.

A Simple Multithreaded Application

The first type of threaded program we will create using the Thread class is an *unsynchronized* multithreaded application. An unsynchronized application only spawns threads that perform independent tasks—that is, tasks that require no interaction with other parts of your application in order to do their work.

NOTE *The BackgroundWorker example obviously wasn't an example of unsynchronized multithreading—not only did it return a result after it finished its work, but it also reported progress along the way. However, in this scenario the distinction between unsynchronized and synchronized multithreading wasn't as important because the BackgroundWorker handles the messy plumbing without requiring any work from you.*

Before going any further, it makes sense to import the namespace that's used for threading so that its classes are easily accessible in your code:

```
Imports System.Threading
```

A thread runs a single method (technically, a procedure that takes no arguments and doesn't have a return value). Thus, before you can create a thread, you need to create a method and code the task you want to perform inside it. In this example, the method has a boringly simple task—every ten seconds, it writes a timestamp to a file named Alive.txt.

NOTE *There is no necessary relationship between a thread and an object. A single thread can run code that belongs to several objects. The methods of a single object can be executed by different threads.*

```
Private Sub WriteRegularTimeStamp()
    Dim LastUpdate As DateTime
    Do
        ' Write the file every 10 seconds.
        If DateTime.Now.Subtract(LastUpdate).TotalSeconds > 10 Then
            My.Computer.FileSystem.WriteAllText( _
                "c:\alive.txt", _
                DateTime.Now.ToLongTimeString + vbNewLine, True)
            LastUpdate = DateTime.Now
        End If

        ' You could use the following line of code to pause the thread,
        ' which makes the overall application more efficient.
        ' This example leaves it out, just to prove that
        ' multithreading works smoothly even with a CPU-intensive loop.
        'Thread.Sleep(TimeSpan.FromSeconds(10))
    Loop
End Sub
```

The thread is created and started in the handler for the Click event of a button:

```
Private Sub cmdStart_Click(ByVal sender As System.Object, _
  ByVal e As System.EventArgs) Handles cmdStart.Click

    Dim MyThread1 As New Thread(AddressOf WriteRegularTimeStamp)
    MyThread1.IsBackground = True
    MyThread1.Start()
End Sub
```

All of the threading logic is contained in just three lines. This code declares a thread for the appropriate procedure, and then sets its IsBackground property to True. This ensures that the thread will be a *background* thread. A background thread lasts only as long as another *foreground* thread is running (namely, the rest of your application). That way, the thread stops as soon as you exit the application. Another option would be to write some sort of termination condition in the loop, so that it only writes the timestamp a certain number of times before exiting. (Once the thread's method ends, the thread dies off.) Finally, you could also terminate a thread the hard way, by explicitly calling its Abort() method, as discussed later in this chapter. Generally, however, a background thread is a good choice for a noncritical task that can be shut down independently of any other application activity.

Once the thread is created, you simply need to call its Start() method to send it on its way.

The Start() method does not instantaneously start the thread. Instead, it notifies the Windows operating system, which then schedules the thread to be started. If your system is currently bogged down with a heavy task load, there could be a noticeable delay.

You'll have no obvious indication that the thread is at work while your application is running. But after it's been at its work for a while, you'll find a list of timestamps in the Alive.txt file that look something like this:

```
3:28:22 PM
3:28:32 PM
3:28:42 PM
3:28:52 PM
3:29:02 PM
...
```

Sending Data to a Thread

There's an obvious drawback with this application the way it stands. Namely, it hard-codes the file path. What if you want to move the Alive.txt file to another directory, or you want to run two threads, each of which will be working with its own Alive.txt file? You need a way to pass some date to your thread—namely, the full path of the file you want to use.

You might think that this modification would work:

```
Private Sub WriteRegularTimeStamp(filePath As string)
```

Here, the WriteRegularTimeStamp() method is modified to accept a string argument. Unfortunately, this isn't allowed. Thread objects can only point to a method that takes no parameters.

The best way to get around this limitation is to create a class that encapsulates the procedure that you want to use and any data that it needs. In this case, the only data required is the path to the file to be modified. The following class works well for the desired purpose:

```
Public Class TimeStamper
    Private filePath As String

    Public Sub New(ByVal filePath As String)
        Me.filePath = filePath
    End Sub

    Public Sub WriteRegularTimeStamp()
```

```
        Dim LastUpdate As DateTime
            Do
            ' Write the file every 10 seconds.
            If DateTime.Now.Subtract(LastUpdate).TotalSeconds > 10 Then
                My.Computer.FileSystem.WriteAllText( _
                    filePath, DateTime.Now.ToLongTimeString + vbNewLine, True)
                LastUpdate = DateTime.Now
            End If
        Loop
    End Sub
End Class
```

As a nice touch, each instance of this class receives its path string as an argument in its constructor, rather than forcing you to set it through a property.

You can now modify the code in the click event handler. Here's an example that starts two threads off, each with a different file:

```
Private Sub cmdStart_Click(ByVal sender As System.Object, _
  ByVal e As System.EventArgs) Handles cmdStart.Click

    Dim Stamper1 As New TimeStamper("c:\alive1.txt")
    Dim MyThread1 As New Thread(AddressOf Stamper1.WriteRegularTimeStamp)
    MyThread1.IsBackground = True

    Dim Stamper2 As New TimeStamper("c:\alive2.txt")
    Dim MyThread2 As New Thread(AddressOf Stamper2.WriteRegularTimeStamp)
    MyThread2.IsBackground = True

    ' Start both threads.
    MyThread1.Start()
    MyThread2.Start()
End Sub
```

If you run the program now, you'll find that it works more or less the same as before. Under the hood, however, the design is much more elegant and extensible. You can find this code in the ThreadTest project, with the samples for this chapter. (This sample project also uses the notification technique described in the following section, so it reports to the user every time the file is stamped.)

One of the reasons this works so well is that each thread has its own data. There's no need to worry about exchanging or synchronizing information, as each thread is independent. If you stick to this type of multithreading, you'll have little to worry about.

In many situations, unsynchronized multithreading can be very useful. For example, you might want to process a batch of data while waiting for the user to enter more information. Or, you might want to create something like a graphical arcade game, where the background music is handled by a separate thread that queues the appropriate music files.

Threading and the User Interface

One of the reasons our examples have worked so well is that the information the threads return is sent directly to the appropriate label control in the window. There is no need for the main program to determine whether a thread is finished, or to try to retrieve the result of its work. Most real-world programs don't work this way. It is far more common (and far better program design) for an application to use a thread to perform a series of calculations, retrieve the results once they are ready, and then format and display them in the user interface, if necessary.

This technique isn't as easy as it seems. For example, imagine you want to modify the previous threading example so that every time it writes a new timestamp to the Alive.txt file, it updates the text in a status bar. This seems like a trivial task—after all, you simply need to tweak the text in the WriteRegularTimeStamp() method, right?

Wrong. In fact, if you attempt to interact with a Windows control from another thread, the results could be disastrous. While you're debugging a prerelease version your application, most controls are kind enough to throw an exception to warn you when you've made this mistake, but when you compile a release version of your application, these checks disappear (for better performance). In this environment, you won't get an error, and your code might work fine in many cases. But under certain difficult-to-predict conditions, your application will lock up. Tricks that you might think would get you out of this mess won't help. For example, you might try to dodge the problem by firing an event from the code that's performing the background work (like the file stamping in the previous example). Then the form can handle that event and update the user interface safely, right? Not so fast. It turns out that it doesn't matter *where* you write the code—even if you place the event handler in your form, it's still going to be executed on the time stamper thread, because the time stamper thread fires the event. So this approach just creates the same problem in another location.

Fortunately, there is a solution. .NET provides a way to force a code routine to run on the user interface thread. You just need to follow these steps:

1. Put your otherwise unsafe code into a separate procedure.
2. Create an instance of the MethodInvoker delegate, and point it to this procedure.
3. Call the Invoke() method on any control or form in your application, and pass it the MethodInvoker delegate as an argument.

Invoke() is the only user interface method that's safe to call from another thread. It triggers the code you specify through the delegate to execute it on the safe user-interface thread. You can also check a control's InvokeRequired property to determine whether the current code is running on the user-interface thread or on another thread. This allows you to determine whether you need to call Invoke() when modifying the control.

Here is a revised `TimeStamper` example that uses the `Invoke()` solution and reports its last update in a label in a thread-safe manner (the changed lines are highlighted in bold):

```
Public Class TimeStamper
    Private filePath As String
    Private statusLabel As Control

    Public Sub New(ByVal filePath As String)
        Me.filePath = filePath
    End Sub

    Public Sub New(ByVal filePath As String, ByVal statusLabel As Control)
        Me.filePath = filePath
        Me.statusLabel = statusLabel
    End Sub

    Private LastUpdate As DateTime
    Public Sub WriteRegularTimeStamp()
        Do
            ' Write the file every 10 seconds.
            If DateTime.Now.Subtract(LastUpdate).TotalSeconds > 10 Then
                My.Computer.FileSystem.WriteAllText( _
                    filePath, DateTime.Now.ToLongTimeString + vbNewLine, True)
                LastUpdate = DateTime.Now

                ' Perform the update on the right thread.
                Dim method As New MethodInvoker(AddressOf UpdateStatusLabel)
                statusLabel.Invoke(method)
            End If
        Loop
    End Sub

    Private Sub UpdateStatusLabel()
        statusLabel.Text = "File updated at " + _
            LastUpdate.ToLongTimeString()
    End Sub
End Class
```

Figure 11-7 shows the revised application in action. This example is provided with the sample code as the ThreadTest project.

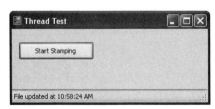

Figure 11-7: Updating the user interface from another thread (safely)

This example shows one way to get information out of a thread and back into the rest of your application. But directly updating a user interface element is not the only approach. In many cases, you want a way to transfer information to some sort of variable, where other code can access it later as needed. You'll see this issue later when we tackle synchronization.

Basic Thread Management

The previous example takes advantage of some simplifications. For one thing, it assumes that you can create a thread and then leave it to do its work without ever worrying about it again. In the real world, however, you often need to know when a thread has completed its work. You might even need to pause or kill a thread.

Thread Methods

You've already seen how to start a thread. You can also stop a thread by using the Abort() method, which will finish it off by raising a ThreadAbortException.

```
MyThread.Abort()
```

Your thread class can then handle this exception in order to try to end as gracefully as possible, performing any necessary cleanup in a Finally block. However, the ThreadAbortException can never be killed off. Even if you catch it, once the cleanup code finishes, the exception will be thrown again to end the code in the thread procedure.

Using the Abort() method is a relatively crude way to stop a thread. You might use it to reign in an otherwise unresponsive thread, but it's not an ideal mechanism. It's more typical for a long-running thread to take the responsibility of polling a variable that indicates whether or not it should continue, as shown below. This relies on the thread being well behaved, but it also allows processing to be interrupted at a natural stopping point, as opposed to being unpredictably interrupted with an exception. If you wrap your thread in a class, it makes sense for this to be a public class variable or property.

```
Private Sub ThreadFunction()
    Do Until ThreadStop = true
        ' Do some work here.
    Loop
End Sub
```

You can also pause and resume a thread with the Suspend() and Resume() methods:

```
MyThread.Suspend()
' Do something in the foreground that requires a lot of CPU work.
MyThread.Resume()
```

As you've already seen, you can pause a thread for a preset amount of time using the shared Sleep() method:

```
Thread.Sleep(TimeSpan.FromSeconds(1))
```

This is a common method to use in a CPU-intensive or disk-intensive process to provide a bit of time during which other threads can get their work done. The example here uses the TimeSpan class to send the thread to sleep for one second, which makes the resulting code very readable.

Another commonly used method is Join(). It waits for a thread to complete.

```
MyThread.Join()
```

When you use the Join() method, your code becomes *synchronous,* meaning that the thread executing the Join() will not progress until the waited-for thread is finished. In the above example, the code won't continue until MyThread finishes its work. The Join() method can also be used with a TimeSpan that specifies the maximum amount of time that you will wait before continuing.

And how do you know what a thread is up to? You can examine its ThreadState property and compare it against the possible enumerated values. Here's an example:

```
MyThread.Join(TimeSpan.FromSeconds(10))
If (MyThread.ThreadState And ThreadState.Stopped) = _
  ThreadState.Stopped Then
    MessageBox.Show("We waited with Thread.Join, and the thread finished.")
ElseIf (MyThread.ThreadState And ThreadState.Running) = _
  ThreadState.Running Then
    MessageBox.Show( _
      "We waited 10 seconds, but the Thread is still running.")
End If
```

Figure 11-8 shows the different stages in a thread's execution.

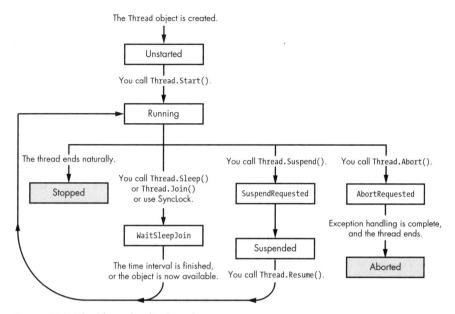

Figure 11-8: The life cycle of a thread

Thread Priorities

All threads are created equal, but they don't have to stay that way. *Priorities* allow you to make sure that some threads are always executed preferentially. Threads with low priorities, on the other hand, may not do much work if the system is heavily bogged down with other, higher priority tasks.

You can set a thread's priority to various values: AboveNormal, BelowNormal, Highest, Lowest, and Normal, which is the default. These priorities are relative; they are significant only in the way that they compare with the priorities of other currently executing threads in your program or in other programs. If all of your application's threads have the same priority, it doesn't make much difference whether that priority is Normal or Highest (assuming, for the moment, that there aren't any other programs or processes competing for the CPU's attention).

Setting a thread's priority is straightforward:

```
MyThread.Priority = ThreadPriority.Lowest
```

A thread with a high priority may need to use the Sleep() method to allow other threads a chance to get their work done. Fine-tuning this sharing of the CPU is an art that requires significant trial-and-error experimentation.

When Is Too Much Not Enough?

As just mentioned, you must be careful about using high priorities. If you have too many aggressive threads, some threads may not receive enough CPU time to be able to perform their work properly. The sorry state that results when too many threads compete for too few resources is called *thread starvation*, and it can make an application perform poorly, or render some functions inoperable.

TIP *When using threads, it's a good idea to test them on the minimum system configuration that your application will support.*

Thread Priority Example

The online chapter sample code provides a project named ThreadPriorities that allows you to satisfy your curiosity and create as many simultaneous threads as you want (see Figure 11-9). These threads "compete" to increment their individual counter variables. The ones that receive the most CPU time will increment their counters the fastest.

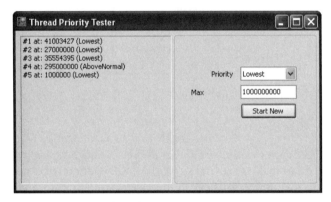

Figure 11-9: Testing threads

A separate thread class, ThreadCounter, provides this counter functionality and incorporates a Boolean "stop signal" variable named ThreadStop:

```
Public Class ThreadCounter

    Public LoopCount As Integer
    Public MaxValue As Integer
    Public Priority As String
    Public ThreadStop As Boolean

    Public Sub New(ByVal MaxValue As Integer, ByVal Priority As String)
        Me.MaxValue = MaxValue
        Me.Priority = Priority
    End Sub

    Public Sub Refresh()
        ' Increment the counter.
        For LoopCount = 0 To MaxValue - 1
            ' Check for the signal to stop abruptly.
            If ThreadStop = True Then Exit For
        Next
```

```
        End Sub

End Class
```

The interesting part about this program is that it uses a collection called ActiveCounters to store references to all the objects that are running on the various threads (and another collection called ActiveThreads to store references to the Thread objects). Periodically, a timer fires, and a routine in the form code loops through the ActiveCounters collection and prints out the status of every thread in a label.

```
Private Sub tmrThreadMonitor_Tick(ByVal sender As System.Object, _
  ByVal e As System.EventArgs) Handles tmrThreadMonitor.Tick

    lblThreads.Text = ""
    Dim Counter As ThreadCounter
    Dim i As Integer

    For Each Counter In ActiveCounters
        i += 1
        lblThreads.Text &= "#" & i.ToString() & " at: "
        lblThreads.Text &= Counter.LoopCount.ToString() & " ("
        lblThreads.Text &= Counter.Priority & ")"
        lblThreads.Text &= vbNewLine
    Next

End Sub
```

The ThreadPriorities program allows you to set the priority of each thread when you create it. This allows you to verify that a high-priority thread will increment its counter much faster than a low-priority one. You'll also notice that when you create a thread with a high priority, your application (and your computer) will become noticeably less responsive until the thread is finished incrementing its counter.

When you end the program, it performs some graceful cleanup by iterating through the ActiveThreads collection and stopping each thread. Rather than use the Abort() method, this program does things the nice way, setting the ThreadStop member variable of each ThreadCounter object, and then waiting on each thread's termination with the Join() method to verify that it has stopped. This is actually much faster than aborting each thread, because it avoids the overhead of wresting control of the thread and throwing an exception.

Here's the code:

```
Private Sub ThreadPriorityTester_Closing(ByVal sender As Object, _
  ByVal e As System.ComponentModel.CancelEventArgs) Handles MyBase.Closing

    ' Signal each thread to stop.
    Dim Counter As ThreadCounter
    For Each Counter In ActiveCounters
        Counter.ThreadStop = True
```

```
    Next

    ' Wait to verify that each thread has stopped.
    Dim CounterThread As Thread
    For Each CounterThread In ActiveThreads
        CounterThread.Join()
    Next

End Sub
```

Thread Debugging

One very useful technique when debugging a multithreaded project is to
assign each thread a name. This allows you to distinguish one thread from
another and to verify which thread is currently executing. It's not unusual
when debugging a tricky problem to discover that the thread you thought
was at work actually isn't responsible for the problem.

To name a thread with a descriptive string, use the `Thread.Name` property:

```
CounterThread.Name = "Counter 1"
```

To check which thread is running a given code procedure at a specific
time, you can use code like this, which uses the shared `CurrentThread()`
method of the `Thread` class:

```
MessageBox.Show(Thread.CurrentThread.Name)
```

Visual Studio also provides some help with a Threads debugging window
(Figure 11-10). This window shows all the currently executing threads in
your program and indicates the thread that currently has the processor's
attention with a yellow arrow. The `Location` column even tells you what code
the thread is running.

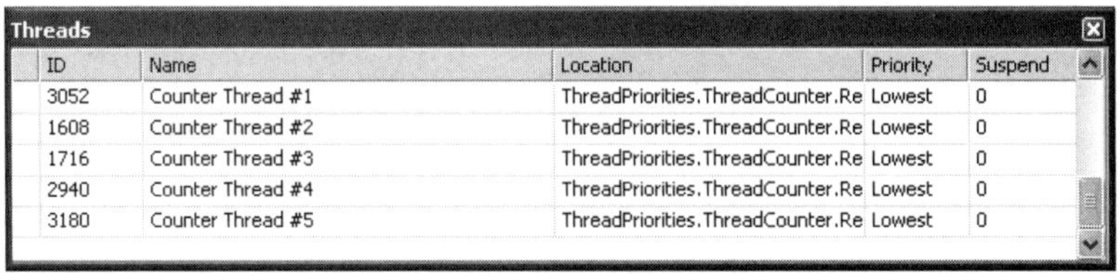

	ID	Name	Location	Priority	Suspend	
	3052	Counter Thread #1	ThreadPriorities.ThreadCounter.Re	Lowest	0	
	1608	Counter Thread #2	ThreadPriorities.ThreadCounter.Re	Lowest	0	
	1716	Counter Thread #3	ThreadPriorities.ThreadCounter.Re	Lowest	0	
	2940	Counter Thread #4	ThreadPriorities.ThreadCounter.Re	Lowest	0	
	3180	Counter Thread #5	ThreadPriorities.ThreadCounter.Re	Lowest	0	

Figure 11-10: Controlling threads at runtime

NOTE *To access the Threads window, you need to pause your program's execution and choose
Debug ▶ Windows ▶ Threads. You can then use some advanced features for controlling
threads. For example, you can set the active thread by right-clicking a thread and selecting
Switch to Thread. You can also use the Freeze command to instruct the operating system
to ignore a thread, giving it no processing time until you select the corresponding Thaw
command to restore it to life. This fine-grained control is ideal for isolating problematic
threads in a misbehaving application. The Threads window includes other threads that
you haven't created, but are a part of .NET. As a general rule of thumb, you should
assign names to all the threads you create so that you can identify each one in the list.*

Thread Synchronization

The mistake that most novice programmers make when they start creating multithreaded applications is simple: They assume that everything they want to do is thread-safe. In other words, they assume that any action that can be performed by a synchronous piece of code can be moved into a thread. This is a dangerous mistake that ignores the effects of concurrency.

Potential Thread Problems

Remember, threads work almost simultaneously as Windows switches from one thread to another. This means that each time you run the application, the relative order of execution of the multithreaded code may vary. Sometimes Thread A might perform a given action before Thread B, but at other times Thread B might take the lead. You can configure the priorities of individual threads, as you've seen, but you can never be absolutely sure when a thread will act, or what the order will be for operations on different threads.

What's more, if you have more than one thread manipulating the same object, eventually at least two of them will try to use it at once. Consider a situation where you have a global counter used by multiple threads for keeping track of the number of times an operation takes place. Sooner or later, Thread A will try to increment the value from, say, 10 to 11 at the same time that Thread B is also trying to increment the value from 10 to 11. The result? In this case, the count will be set to 11, even though the final value should really be 12. The more threads there are (and the greater the delay between reading and updating the counter variable), the worse the problem will become.

Concurrency and synchronization problems are particularly tricky because they often don't show up when an application is being tested, but only lead to bugs later in unpredictable situations, after the application has been deployed. If you neglect giving adequate consideration to synchronization issues at design time, there is no way to know when a problem could appear. Many programmers don't realize the dependencies of the objects they are using. Trying to use an object concurrently when that object has not been designed to be thread-safe is likely to cause a runtime exception in the best case, and a more insidious data (and more difficult to spot) data error in the worst case.

NOTE *Most classes in the .NET Framework are not thread-safe, because adding the required synchronization code would dramatically slow down their performance.*

Basic Synchronization

The best approach to avoiding data synchronization problems is often to refrain from modifying variables that are accessible to multiple threads. If this isn't possible, the next best thing is to use synchronization (which is also known as *locking*). The idea behind synchronization, as mentioned earlier, is to acquire a lock on a resource before you access it so that other threads that try to access the resource will be forced to wait. This process prevents collisions, but it also slows down performance.

All you need to do is place code that uses shared objects inside a SyncLock/End SyncLock block. The first line of this block identifies the data item that is being synchronized. This item must be a reference type, such as an object or an array; it can't be a simple value type.

When you use the SyncLock statement, your application waits until it has exclusive access to the object you've specified before performing the commands in the SyncLock block. While these commands are being executed, any other thread that tries to access the synchronized object will be temporarily suspended by the operating system. When the final End SyncLock statement is reached the lock is released and the operating system gives other threads the opportunity to access that object. Again, although this guarantees thread safety, performance can suffer, because all threads trying to access a locked object are blocked.

A Sample Synchronization Problem

To demonstrate how synchronization works, we will use a variant of a global counter program. There are many different ways to observe the effects of thread synchronization problems, but this one gives a quick demonstration of the potential hazards.

The first ingredient is a GlobalCounter class:

```
Public Class GlobalCounter
    Public Counter As Integer
End Class
```

An instance of this class is provided as a public variable in the form class:

```
Public MyGlobalCounter As New GlobalCounter()
```

There is also a class that wraps our threaded operations, as before:

```
Public Class IncrementThread

    Private Counter As GlobalCounter
    Private LocalCounter As Integer
    Private ThreadLabel, GlobalLabel As Label

    Public Sub New(ByVal Counter As GlobalCounter, _
      ByVal ThreadLabel As Label, ByVal GlobalLabel As Label)
        Me.Counter = Counter
        Me.ThreadLabel = ThreadLabel
        Me.GlobalLabel = GlobalLabel
    End Sub

    Public Sub Increment()
        Dim i As Integer
        Dim GlobalCounter As Integer
```

```
        For i = 1 To 1000
            LocalCounter = LocalCounter + 1
            GlobalCounter = Counter.Counter
            Thread.Sleep(TimeSpan.FromTicks(1))
            Counter.Counter = GlobalCounter + 1
        Next i

        ' Assume that ThreadLabel and GlobalLabel are on the same window.
        Dim Invoker As New MethodInvoker(AddressOf UpdateLabel)
        ThreadLabel.Invoke(Invoker)
    End Sub

    Private Sub UpdateLabel()
        ThreadLabel.Text = LocalCounter.ToString()
        GlobalLabel.Text = Counter.Counter.ToString()
    End Sub

End Class
```

This threading class wraps two counters—a local counter (stored in an integer) and a global counter, which is stored in an object so it can be shared between several different IncrementThread objects. When IncrementThread finishes its work (coded in the Increment() method), it uses the thread-safe MethodInvoker described earlier to update the user interface with information based on both its local and global counters.

A deliberate feature of this example is the way that the global counter is incremented. Instead of doing it in one instruction (GlobalCounter = Counter.Counter + 1), our example uses two lines, pausing the thread for one tick (a small interval of time equal to 100 nanoseconds) in between the time that the counter value is read and the time that the counter is updated. This pause is meant to simulate thread latency and therefore increase the likelihood that synchronization issues will occur when this example is run. In realistic scenarios, synchronization issues occur only when many more threads than are at work here compete for the CPU. (Remember, one of the most devious aspects of synchronization problems is that they often don't come out of the woodwork when you are testing under simple conditions.)

As before, the threads are created and started in a Click event handler for a button on the form. The following code is used:

```
Private Sub cmdStart_Click(ByVal sender As System.Object, _
 ByVal e As System.EventArgs) Handles cmdStart.Click
    MyGlobalCounter.Counter = 0
    Dim Increment1 As New IncrementThread(MyGlobalCounter, _
      lblThread1, lblGlobal)
    Dim Increment2 As New IncrementThread(MyGlobalCounter, _
      lblThread2, lblGlobal)
    Dim MyThread1 As New Thread(AddressOf Increment1.Increment)
    Dim MyThread2 As New Thread(AddressOf Increment2.Increment)
    MyThread1.Start()
    MyThread2.Start()
End Sub
```

The result is shown in Figure 11-11.

Each thread has kept track of its own private local counter value, so that much is accurate. However, the global counter is completely wrong. It should be 2,000, reflecting that each of the two threads incremented it 1,000 times. Instead, the competing threads performed overlapped edits that didn't take each other's actions into account. Here's an example of how the problem occurs (assuming the counter's current value was 12):

1. MyThread1 reads the value 12.
2. MyThread2 reads the value 12.
3. MyThread1 sets the value to 13.
4. MyThread2 sets the value to 13—instead of 14.

Figure 11-11: A flawed global counter

Using SyncLock to Fix the Problem

In this case, the fix is quite easy. Because GlobalCounter is a full-fledged object, you can use SyncLock while your thread is executing to gain exclusive access to the global counter. (If GlobalCounter was only a variable, this solution wouldn't be possible.)

In fact, all you need to do is to add two lines to the Increment() method, as shown here:

```
Public Sub Increment()
    Dim i As Integer
    Dim GlobalCounter As Integer
    For i = 1 To 1000
        LocalCounter = LocalCounter + 1
        SyncLock Counter
            GlobalCounter = Counter.Counter
            Thread.Sleep(TimeSpan.FromTicks(1))
            Counter.Counter = GlobalCounter + 1
        End SyncLock
    Next i

    Dim Invoker As New MethodInvoker(AddressOf UpdateLabel)
    ThreadLabel.Invoke(Invoker)
End Sub
```

Now the result, as shown in Figure 11-12, will be correct. You can see the complete code in the ThreadingSynchronization project.

If you timed the application, you might notice that it has slowed down. All of the automatic pausing and resuming of threads creates some overhead. But when you consider the frustrating problems that SyncLock can help you avoid, you'll be eager to put it to work in your applications.

Figure 11-12: A successful global counter

What Comes Next?

This chapter has endeavored to give you a solid understanding of the fundamentals of threading, and a knowledge of the issues involved. Mastering all the aspects of threading could almost be a life's work, and many books and articles have been written on the subject.

If you're in search of more threading information, the best place to start is the documentation. Both the Visual Studio Help and the MSDN website provide white papers describing the technical details of threading, along with code examples that show it in action in live applications.

12

WEB FORMS AND ASP.NET

Creating web applications with Visual Basic 6 was a bit of a mess. To start with, there were a dizzying number of different options. Visual Basic 6 shipped with a "kitchen sink" of competing web technologies, including templates for applications built out of Dynamic HTML, ActiveX documents, and Active Server pages (in which case you had the additional choice of Web Classes, Visual Interdev, Notepad with VBScript, or a good stiff drink and a new career).

In .NET, Microsoft has an ambitious strategy for web development, and this time it's not going to cost you a few months of sleepless nights. With ASP.NET, life for the web developer gets a whole lot simpler. You're able to take care of your application's business logic (that is, what your program actually accomplishes) while using Microsoft's class infrastructure to handle all the messy Internet-specific details. The long-promised dream—being able to create software for the Web as easily as for Windows—has finally come true.

New in .NET

The ASP.NET toolkit is a new .NET innovation with no parallel in the VB 6 world. The web technologies you had to choose from in VB 6 are completely gone in Visual Basic 2005.

- Programs based on Dynamic HTML (DHTML) and ActiveX documents were just too restrictive in their browser requirements, and they suffered from a substantial learning curve. These technologies have been removed from Visual Basic 2005.
- Active Server Pages (ASP) technology has been transformed into ASP.NET. Along the way, such tools as Web Classes and Visual Interdev have disappeared, replaced by the much more flexible and straightfoward Web Form Designer.

With Visual Basic 2005, programming an Internet application automatically means creating an ASP.NET application.

A Web Development Outline

In this chapter, you'll learn how to create a server-side web application. Server-side web applications have a few basic characteristics. They appear to users as a collection of web pages. Users move through these pages, entering information in forms and clicking buttons and other graphical widgets. The information they enter is handled by pure VB code that runs on the server. This code tracks what's important, interacts with other resources (such as databases), and dynamically configures the web page content before sending it to the user.

If you're like many Visual Basic programmers, you've never created a web application before. This chapter will teach you the basics and help you understand the special considerations that apply to Internet programming.

The development plan for an ASP.NET project goes something like this:

1. You design your web application's interface, using the web forms you need.

2. You write the code behind your forms and add any classes you need, just as you would with an ordinary Windows application. The only difference is that you have to spend some time thinking about maintaining *state*, that is, how your program remembers information in between user requests. This chapter spends a large amount of time examining different methods of state management.

3. You upload your completed web application to a web server.

4. Using a web browser, a user navigates to one of your application's web forms. Behind the scenes, the web server examines the settings of the user's browser in order to tailor its responses to make the most of the features that browser supports. As the user selects options and clicks on buttons, the web server runs the appropriate web application code, creating the appearance of a fully integrated application.

What Was Wrong with Classic ASP?

Quite simply, a lot. ASP made it all too easy to create disorganized, inefficient programs that mixed together HTML markup code and programming logic. It was possible to create a world-class ASP application, but the lack of structure in ASP led to—and even encouraged—poor programming.

- ASP programs emphasized an old-fashioned, script-based style of programming. ASP.NET is completely component-based, and as you know from Chapter 6, component-based programs are more elegant, efficient, and easy to maintain.

- ASP programs provided part of the infrastructure you needed in order to create a web application, but some tasks were still a chore. ASP.NET provides a host of addictive frills, including graphically rich controls, an easy way to validate user input, and painless state management.

- Well-designed ASP applications were generally built out of ASP pages and ActiveX components created in Visual Basic. This was a good system, but it imposed additional headaches when you configured, installed, and versioned your applications. We won't get into the details here, except to note that ASP.NET applications are a breeze to install and update.

- ASP applications were notoriously difficult to debug if you didn't have a spare web server in the office. With ASP.NET, you can use all of Visual Basic's debugging tools while running the application from a browser on your local computer.

- ASP pages used VBScript, a stripped-down flavor of Visual Basic with its own quirks and idiosyncrasies. ASP.NET no longer supports VBScript and now uses Visual Basic as its native language.

- ASP.NET compiles your pages automatically the first time they are used and every time they are updated. That may seem like a small detail, but it's one of a series of performance improvements that makes ASP.NET the fastest version of ASP yet.

Still the Same: IIS

If you've programmed with ASP before, you'll find that not everything has changed. If you look hard enough, you'll even find familiar objects, such as Request and Response, although you won't need to use them nearly as much this time around. One detail that hasn't changed is that ASP.NET applications are hosted by Internet Information Services (IIS), a built-in service that's included with Windows 2000, Windows XP Professional, and Windows Server 2003 (although it's not installed by default). IIS can't run on non-Microsoft platforms. While site visitors using your web application are free to work with any type of browser or operating system, you still need to host your application on a Windows web server.

Web Application Basics

It used to be that you needed a special computer to act as a web server. These days, any computer with a modern Windows operating system can install the necessary IIS hosting software from the Windows setup CD.

Of course, in most cases you won't develop an ASP.NET application directly on the web server that will host it. Doing so could hamper the performance of the server, or even lead to crashes that would make your website unavailable (not to mention the fact that the web server is often located at a different site). Instead, you will generally perfect your web application on another computer, and copy the project directory to the web server when all your work is complete.

The trick is that in order to debug your web application, your computer needs to act as a web server. Fortunately, Visual Studio 2005 includes its own built-in web server that's limited to testing on the local computer. That means when you debug an ASP.NET application, you will actually be making requests through HTTP to a virtual web server, which then instructs ASP.NET to run the code in the corresponding web page. You can use all the same debugging tricks that you learned about in Chapter 8, like breakpoints and variable watches.

In other words, there is no difference between the way you interact with your web application while testing, and the way a site visitor will use it over the Internet. The only distinction between your local testing and the final deployed application is that your test website is not visible or accessible to other web clients on the Internet. At the end of this chapter, you'll get a quick primer that shows you how to deploy a finalized web application to a web server.

NOTE *To create web projects, you need a full version of Visual Studio 2005 (Standard, Professional, and Team editions work fine) or the Visual Web Developer 2005 Express Edition (which can* only *create web applications). The scaled-down Visual Basic 2005 Express Edition doesn't support the Web.*

Creating a Web Application

Before going any further, let's dive right into our first ASP.NET application. To get started, select File ▸ New Web Site from the Visual Studio menu. The New Web Site dialog box (shown in Figure 12-1) will appear.

The New Web Site dialog box allows you to choose from several basic templates—use the ASP.NET Web Site template to start out with an ordinary website. Here are some of the templates you may see:

- ASP.NET Web Site creates a new web application with one default web page (named Default.aspx).

- ASP.NET Web Service creates a new web application with one default web service (named Service.asmx). You'll learn about web services in Chapter 13.

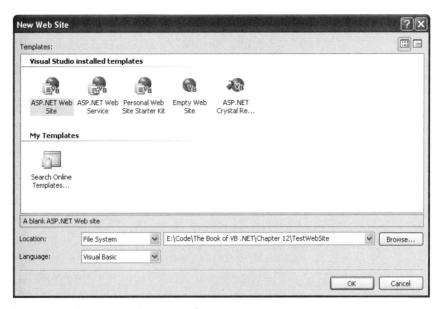

Figure 12-1: Creating an ASP.NET website

- Empty Web Site creates a new web application with no files at all. Of course, you can easily add new web pages and web services as you see fit.

- Personal Web Site Starter Kit creates a full-fledged personal website, complete with a standardized look and feel, an integrated navigation system, and some basic web pages (like Resume.aspx, Download.aspx, and Links.aspx). You can use this project to learn more about ASP.NET after you've finished this chapter.

- ASP.NET Crystal Reports Web Site creates a new web application with a Default.aspx page that's designed to show a database-driven report using the Crystal Reports. This is a rarely used specialty feature.

The Location box is more important. It allows you to tell Visual Studio where you'll store your website files. Typically, you'll choose File System (as in Figure 12-1), and then use a directory somewhere on your computer. That's sufficient for creating and testing an application. When you're ready to make your work available to a crowd of eager web surfers, you'll then upload your files to a web server. Unlike other types of Visual Basic projects, you can't create a new website project without saving it.

NOTE   *The other location options allow you to create your application directly on a web server. You can use HTTP if you want to directly connect to an IIS web server and create your website. (This might be the case if you're working with a test web server on your computer or local network.) You can also use FTP if you want to upload your files to a remote web server. Neither option is commonly used at the development stage. As mentioned earlier, it's always better to create a test version of your website, perfect it, and only then upload it to a live web server that other people can access.*

Once you've chosen your location, click OK to create your website. You'll start out with a relatively small set of files, as shown in Figure 12-2.

Figure 12-2: Initial files for a web application

Ingredients of an ASP.NET Project

Every web project is made up of the following files:

web.config

> This file allows you to fine-tune advanced settings that apply to your entire application, including security and state settings. These options are outside the scope of this chapter, but you can read up on them in the Visual Studio Help.

.aspx files

> These files are the ASP.NET web pages. Each web form you create will have an .aspx file that contains controls and formatting information. The .aspx file is sometimes called the *presentation template* of a web form. When you start a new website, Visual Studio adds one file—a Default.aspx page that represents your *home page* (the default starting page for your web application).

.vb files

> These files are used to hold the code "behind" each web form. For example, a typical web form named HelloWorld would have its visual layout stored in the file HelloWorld.aspx, and its event-handling code in the Visual Basic file HelloWorld.aspx.vb. The Web Form Designer links these files together automatically.

NOTE *You might think that it is a serious security risk to have your source files located in a publicly accessible place, like a folder on a web server. However, ASP.NET is configured to automatically reject browser requests for configuration files like web.config and requests for any .vb file. ASP.NET also includes deployment tools that let you precompile your source code so that it won't be readable to anyone, even the administrators managing the website.*

You can add a new web page to your application by selecting Website ▶ Add New Item. The most common type of item you'll add is a web form. It's recommended that you always keep the Place Code In Separate File check box selected, as in Figure 12-3. This tells ASP.NET to create an .aspx file for the page design (which contains HTML markup and ASP.NET control tags) and a separate .vb file with your event handler code. This separation makes it easier to program your page without worrying about the HTML details, and it's the approach used in this chapter.

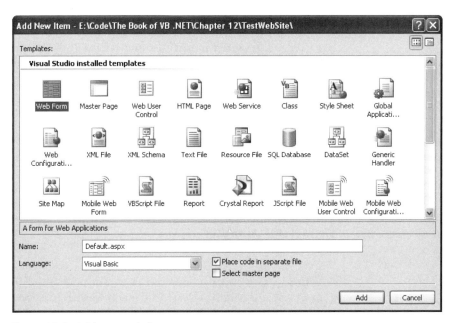

Figure 12-3: Adding a web form

TIP   *The Select Master Page option allows you to create web forms that are based on other web form templates, similar to the way that visual inheritance works with forms. Master pages aren't covered in this chapter, although you can learn more in the Visual Studio Help (look for the index entry "master pages").*

You can also add other types of resources to a web project, like ordinary HTML pages, style sheets (.css files), images to which you plan to link, and so on.

When you create a web application, Visual Studio doesn't place project (.vbproj) and solution (.sln) files in your website directory (as it does with other project types). Instead, it stores these files in a user-specific location in the Visual Studio projects directory (which is typically something like c:\My Documents\Visual Studio 2005\Projects). This keeps your website directory clean and uncluttered, containing only the files you actually need. It also simplifies deployment. Best of all, the project and solution files aren't required for deployed web applications, so if you accidentally delete them (or you don't copy them when you transfer a website to another development computer), Visual Studio will quietly re-create new ones.

NOTE   *The only important data that's stored in the project and solution files are your debug settings (for example, any breakpoints you create) and a list of other projects that you want to load in the same solution for testing purposes (such as additional components that your website uses).*

Designing Web Forms

Web forms are designed to work as much like Windows forms as possible. However, there are still some basic differences between the two. There is no direct way to display a Windows-style dialog box from a web page, so throw away any ideas about using floating tool windows, message boxes, and multiple-document interfaces. A web form's ultimate destination is an HTML page, to be delivered to a user working on an Internet browser. The ASP.NET engine may make use of JavaScript or Dynamic HTML to improve the appearance of your page if it detects that the client's browser supports these enhancements, but every web form ultimately boils down to basic HTML.

That said, you'll find that web forms aren't programmed like static web pages. Unlike ASP pages, which were often created with cryptic `Response.Write()` commands, a web form can (and usually should) be composed entirely of web controls that have properties and events, just like the controls in a Windows form.

ASP.NET provides this kind of magic by using *server-side controls*. The basic idea behind a server-side control is that the display of the control is sent to the user in HTML, but the user's interaction with the control is handled at the server. All of the web controls in ASP.NET are server-side controls.

The Basic Controls

To add a web control, you drag the control you want from the Toolbox (on the left) and drop it onto your web page. The controls in the Toolbox are grouped in a number of categories based on their function. Here's a quick overview of the different groups:

Standard
> This group has all the essentials, including web controls like labels, buttons, and text boxes, all of which closely resemble their Windows counterparts. You'll use this group most often.

Data
> This group contains controls for ASP.NET data binding, including controls for rich grid data display.

Validation
> This group contains validators—controls that automatically display error messages when the input in another control (usually a text box) is invalid.

Navigation
> This group contains controls that can help surfers navigate through all the pages of a website, including the snazzy TreeView control.

Login
> This group contains security-related controls that allow you to add pages for logging in, creating users, and retrieving passwords.

WebParts
> This group contains specialized controls that work with WebParts, ASP.NET's model for portal sites.

HTML

This group contains plain HTML tags that don't have any server-side interactivity.

NOTE *You can convert any piece of static HTML into a server control by right-clicking it and choosing Run As Server Control. This transforms the HTML tag into an HTML server control, which is a more limited type of server-side control than the other control types in the Toolbox. HTML server controls are primarily useful for backward compatibility when migrating an HTML page or a classic ASP page to ASP.NET.*

The arsenal of ASP.NET controls is truly impressive—in fact, there are many more controls for ASP.NET than for Windows Forms applications.

Adding Controls to a Web Form

The Web Form Designer provides many of the same controls as the Windows Form Designer, including labels, text boxes, and buttons. Unlike the Windows Form Designer, the Web Form Designer uses *flow layout*, which means elements are positioned relative to each other, rather than in absolute coordinates.

In a Windows application, every control is lined up according to an invisible grid. In a web application, controls are positioned one after another, like in a word processor. That means if you add more content to one element and it gets larger, the following elements are bumped down the page to make room, which is a clear advantage when dealing with large, variable amounts of content (as often found in web pages).

NOTE *Flow layout can be just as useful in a Windows application, although it's not as often used for this purpose. In Chapter 4, you took a quick look at layout controls like the FlowLayoutPanel that use this system of arranging controls. The future holds even more—the next-generation framework for Windows user interface (named Windows Presentation Foundation, or WPF) makes flow layout the new standard. WPF is currently an early alpha technology that will feature in Windows Vista, the next version of the Windows operating system.*

Flow layout also has a disadvantage: namely, you can't place controls exactly. Instead, you need to add spaces and hard returns to position them on the page. You also need to drag and drop controls onto the page instead of drawing them on the page. This approach can take a little getting used to.

TIP *Technically, it is possible to position elements using absolute coordinates in a web page, but in order to do it you need to use the advanced formatting muscle of cascading style sheets (CSS). Usually flow layout is easier and more flexible, but if you want to learn more about grid layout with CSS, see www.w3schools.com/css/css_positioning.asp. Style sheets are also a great way for formatting entire web pages (without having to set font and color settings for each individual control).*

Getting pages to look right in flow layout mode takes a little bit of practice. To see the potential problem, take a look at the MetricConverter page shown in Figure 12-4. It has all the necessary controls, but getting them to line up properly using nothing but spaces and hard returns is iffy at best.

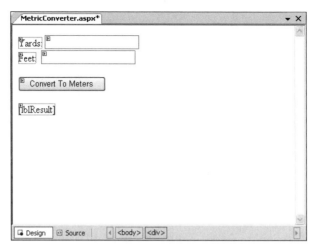

Figure 12-4: A first crack at designing a page

Fortunately, a few simple tricks can save a lot of trouble:

- Use invisible tables to line up columns (for example, a series of text labels with text boxes). To add a table to your page, use the Table control from the HTML group. You can then add or remove columns and rows, resize it, and so on.

NOTE *Don't use the table from the Standard group. This is a dynamic table that you can interact with in code. However, it's not as convenient for layout because you can't edit it using the Web Form Designer.*

- Use panels to get a nice border around a group of controls, separating them from the rest of page. The easiest way to do this is to use the Div control (which stands for division) from the HTML group or the Panel control in the Standard group.

- You can format web controls using properties like Font, ForeColor, BackColor, and so on. However, this is tedious. In Windows applications, you had a shortcut—you could adjust these properties in the main form, and they'd automatically apply to all contained controls, unless the controls explicitly overrode them. A similar trick is possible in web pages using the Div and Panel controls. Any formatting you apply to the Div or Panel controls affects everything inside. However, the Properties window isn't the way to format the Div control—instead, right-click it, and choose Style to set border, color, margin (external spacing), padding (internal spacing), and font options.

NOTE *If you're a web guru, it may interest you to know that ASP.NET performs almost all its formatting using CSS. However, you don't need to learn the details—instead, you simply configure the controls, and the appropriate style tags are set automatically.*

Figure 12-5 shows the revamped MetricConverter page. Now it has a Div that applies a background color, the well supported Verdana font, and a border. Inside the Div is a table that keeps the labels and text boxes properly aligned.

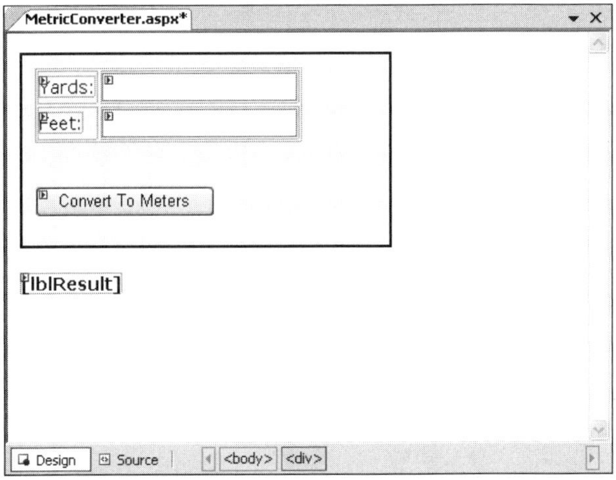

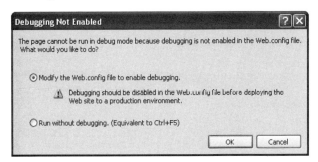

Figure 12-5: Designing a better page

Before continuing, try creating this page yourself so that you can follow through the rest of the example.

Running a Web Page

You can try out your simple MetricConverter web page, and see what it looks like in a browser, by running it. Just click the Start button in Visual Studio as you would with a Windows application. When you run a web application, Visual Studio starts up its integrated web server to handle the requests and launches your default web browser to show you the web page output.

The first time you run a web application, Visual Studio will inform you that it needs to edit the web.config file to add a setting that allows debugging (see Figure 12-6). Choose OK to make the change and continue.

Figure 12-6: Allowing debugging

When you're ready to deploy your final application, you'll want to remove this setting for the sake of optimum performance. To do so, find this line in the web.config file:

```
<compilation debug="true" strict="false" explicit="true">
```

and remove the debug="true" attribute.

In a Windows application, you always know which window you'll see first. A web application is a little different, because there are multiple points of entry. A user could surf to your site by typing a URL (or clicking an external link) that points to any page in your site. Similarly, when you debug your application, you can start running any page you want to test. All you need to do is select that page in the Solution Explorer before you run the application.

Visual Studio's behavior changes if you don't select a web page (for example, if you select the application name or another file that can't be executed, like the web.config settings file, in the Solution Explorer). In this case, Visual Studio runs the Default.aspx page (if your website includes it). If your website doesn't have a Default.aspx page, the integrated web server in Visual Studio generates a list of all files in your web application (see Figure 12-7). You can then click any .aspx page to launch it.

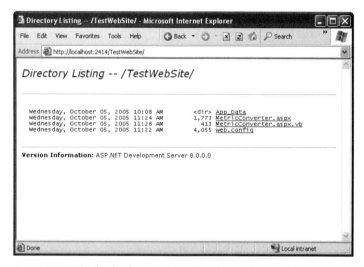

Figure 12-7: The file list for a web application with one web page

TIP   *Because the compilation model is for a web application is different from that for other types of applications, you can't use run-edit-continue debugging. Although you can make changes at debug time, the new code won't be used automatically. But there is one shortcut available. After you make changes, you can start working with the new version of a web page by saving the file (in Visual Studio) and then clicking the Refresh button in your web browser.*

When you run a page, ASP.NET compiles the code in your page behind the scenes, runs it, and then returns the final HTML to the browser. Of course, the MetricConverter page doesn't actually do anything yet, but you can still launch it and see all its controls.

Adding an Event Handler

Using Visual Studio, you can create event handlers for web forms exactly as you do in the Windows Form Designer (see Chapter 4 if you need a refresher). For example, you can add a Click event handler to the button in the MetricConverter program by double-clicking the button. Add the following code. (You may have to make slight modifications, depending on the names that you have given your controls.)

```
Protected Sub cmdConvert_Click(ByVal sender As System.Object, _
  ByVal e As System.EventArgs) Handles cmdConvert.Click
    Dim Inches, Meters As Single
    Inches = 36 * Val(txtYards.Text) + 12 * Val(txtFeet.Text)
    Meters = Inches / 39.37
    lblResult.Text = "Result in meters: " & Meters.ToString()
End Sub
```

You can now try running the program. Enter some sample values and click the Convert button. The label will be refreshed with the result of the conversion (see Figure 12-8).

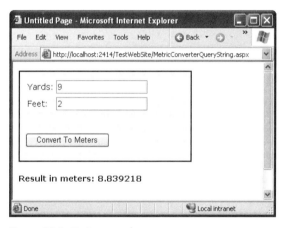

Figure 12-8: Testing a web page

How Does It Work?

What happens in our MetricConverter program is relatively simple: The server delivers an HTML page with a form submission button to your browser. When you click the button, the information entered by the user is transmitted back to the server, your code runs, and a new version of the page is delivered in response. This entire process unfolds automatically.

Every time a user interacts with a control that fires an event, a similar "round trip" occurs from the client to the server and back. This round trip is called a *postback*.

When you run a web page, you'll notice that the URL in the browser includes a port number. For example, in Figure 12-8 you can see that running the page named MetricConverter.aspx in a folder on my computer named TestWebSite displays the URL http://localhost:2414/TestWebSite/MetricConverter.aspx. The localhost part at the beginning of the URL indicates that the web server is running on your computer. The port number (in this case, 2414) is randomly chosen every time Visual Studio starts the web server, which ensures that web server requests won't conflict with any other applications that might be running on your computer and listening for network communication.

NOTE *When you deploy a website you won't need to use a port number to access it. That's because the IIS web server listens to port 80, which is the official port for all HTTP traffic. When a URL doesn't have a port number, port 80 is assumed by default.*

The AutoPostback Property

The button we've created is a special type of control that will always cause a postback when clicked. Other controls are not as straightforward. For example, consider the TextChanged event of a TextBox control. In the MetricConverter program, we don't use this event. However, another program might update the display dynamically as new text is entered, or as CheckBox or RadioButton controls are selected by the user. In this case, you would need to set the AutoPostback property for each of these controls to True.

Because a postback involves getting a new page from the server, it can slow things down a little, and the user may notice the page flicker as it is being refreshed. For that reason, the default AutoPostback setting is False. When AutoPostback is disabled, the control's events will be delayed until another control (like a button) triggers a postback. Thus, the code in the control's event handler will not execute immediately.

Web Control Events

Events in web form controls are slightly different from Windows Forms controls. For example, the CheckedChanged event occurs when a RadioButton selection is changed, not necessarily every time it is clicked.

Similarly, the TextBox event occurs when a user moves to a different control on the page after modifying the text box, not every time he or she presses a key. These changes are designed to minimize the number of postbacks. If a postback occurred every time the user pressed a key in a text box, the web page would be constantly reloading, the user would quickly become frustrated, and the web developer responsible would need to find a new line of employment. For similar reasons, events such as MouseMove and KeyPress aren't implemented at all.

In our MetricConverter example, we can leave AutoPostback set to False for all our controls, because a postback is triggered when the user clicks the button.

A Web Form "Under the Hood"

Here's an interesting question: What's the difference between Visual Basic 2005 and ASP.NET?

The answer is that ASP.NET defines the markup language you use to design your web pages. Ordinarily, you can rely on Visual Studio to help you out here, and simply drag-and-drop your way to success. However, as you do this Visual Studio quietly creates and modifies the control tags in the .aspx page.

We won't be examining the ASP.NET tags in this book because the Web Form Designer abstracts away these details. However, if you fall in love with ASP.NET and decide to devote yourself to web development, you might want to take a closer look under the hood. To do so, click the Source button at the bottom of the web form display. Figure 12-9 shows a portion of the ASP.NET markup that defines the controls and layout for the MetricConverter page, with one of the control tags highlighted. You can click the Design button to switch back to the graphical designer view.

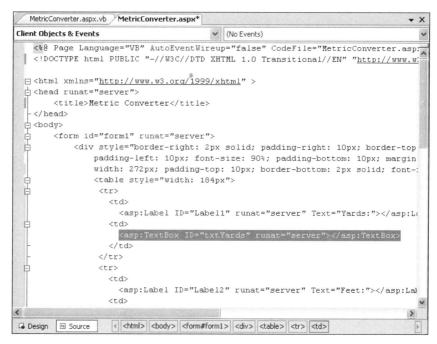

Figure 12-9: ASP.NET control tags for the MetricConverter page

Here's a sample ASP.NET control tag:

```
<asp:TextBox ID="txtYards" runat="server"></asp:TextBox>
```

This tag declares a TextBox control named txtYards. The runat="server" portion indicates that this is a dynamic server-side control that your code can interact with. If you were to set other properties for the text box, like a font, maximum length, and so on, those properties would also appear in the text box tag.

If you're familiar with HTML, you'll notice that the ASP.NET control tags use a syntax that looks suspiciously like HTML. In fact, the .aspx page *is* the HTML that will be sent to the client, with a few extra details—namely, the ASP.NET control tags. When a user requests a page, the ASP.NET engine scans the .aspx page. Each time it finds a control tag, it creates a control object that your page can interact with. This allows your code to read values out of the text boxes and change the text in the labels. After all your code has finished running, ASP.NET replaces each control tag with the HTML elements that are needed to display the control in the browser. For example, an Image control becomes an HTML <img> tag, and an ordinary text box will become an <input> tag.

To see the HTML *output* that the web server generates, try running the MetricConverter page again. Then, choose View ▸ Source from your browser menu to see the HTML your browser received.

Figure 12-10 shows a portion of the HTML output that ASP.NET sends to the client for the MetricConverter page. It's similar to but different from the original ASP.NET tags, which can only be understood by the ASP.NET engine and not by ordinary Internet browsers.

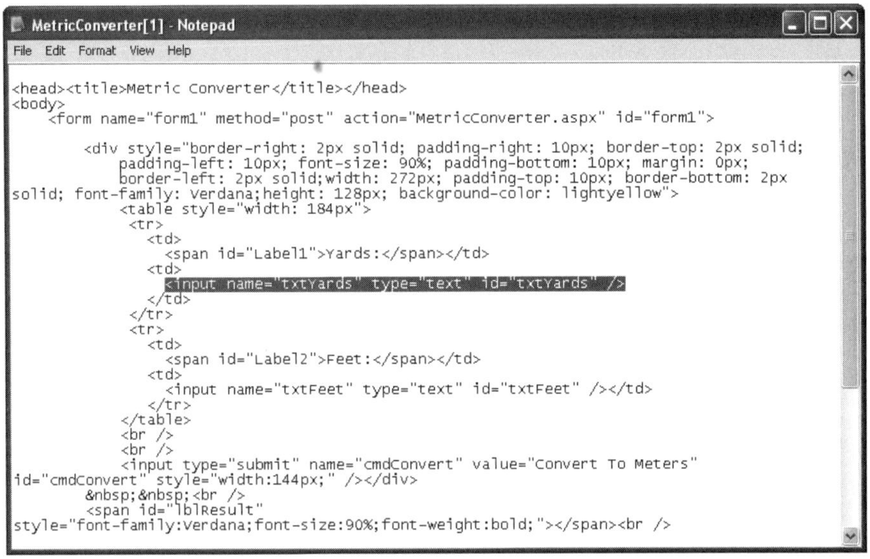

```
<head><title>Metric Converter</title></head>
<body>
    <form name="form1" method="post" action="MetricConverter.aspx" id="form1">

        <div style="border-right: 2px solid; padding-right: 10px; border-top: 2px solid;
            padding-left: 10px; font-size: 90%; padding-bottom: 10px; margin: 0px;
            border-left: 2px solid;width: 272px; padding-top: 10px; border-bottom: 2px
solid; font-family: Verdana;height: 128px; background-color: lightyellow">
            <table style="width: 184px">
             <tr>
               <td>
                 <span id="Label1">Yards:</span></td>
               <td>
                 <input name="txtYards" type="text" id="txtYards" />
               </td>
             </tr>
             <tr>
               <td>
                 <span id="Label2">Feet:</span></td>
               <td>
                 <input name="txtFeet" type="text" id="txtFeet" /></td>
               </tr>
            </table>
            <br />
            <br />
            <input type="submit" name="cmdConvert" value="Convert To Meters"
id="cmdConvert" style="width:144px;" /></div>
          <br />
        <span id="lblResult"
style="font-family:Verdana;font-size:90%;font-weight:bold;"></span><br />
```

Figure 12-10: HTML output for the MetricConverter

The best part about all of this is that you don't need to understand the quirky details of HTML, because the ASP.NET engine on the web server takes care of it for you. For example, if you create a TextBox web control, ASP.NET might use an HTML text box, password box, or text area element, depending on the properties you've set. Similarly, you can use advanced controls, such as the Calendar control, even though there are no direct equivalents in HTML code. In this case, the ASP.NET engine will use several HTML elements to create the control, and it will handle all the processing and redirecting of events.

NOTE *This point is so amazing that I have to repeat it. If you know anything about HTML elements, forget it now. Not only will the ASP.NET engine translate your web form flawlessly every time, it can also circumvent some the ugliest limitations of the HTML language.*

View State

You probably take it for granted that the values in the two text boxes in the MetricConverter program remain after you click the Convert button. This is intuitively how we expect an application to work—but it's not the way that traditional ASP pages worked.

Ordinarily, every time your web page makes a round trip to a web server (for instance, when an event occurs), all the information entered in the user interface controls is lost. This is because the web page is essentially recreated from scratch every time the user requests it. ASP.NET just loads the .aspx template to set up the initial page appearance, runs the appropriate event handler code to respond to the current action, and then returns the final HTML output.

Losing information can be a traumatizing experience for users, so ASP developers have traditionally toiled long and hard to make the controls store and reload data. The great news with ASP.NET is that the server can perform this chore by recording information about the current state of web page controls in a hidden field on the web page. This hidden field is then transmitted back to the server with each postback. ASP.NET automatically uses this information to fill your control objects with the appropriate data before it runs your event handling code. The end result is completely transparent, and your code can safely assume that information is retained in every control, as it would be in an ordinary Windows application.

You can see the information in this hidden field by looking at the HTML page in Notepad or another text editor. View state information is encoded to save space and prevent the casual user from being able to tell what it contains. Here's an example:

```
<input type="hidden" name="__VIEWSTATE" value="dDwyMzcOMTY5ODU7Oz4=" />
```

In order for a control to maintain its state, its `EnableViewState` property must be set to `True` (the default). This property doesn't apply just to user input controls, but to any control that you can modify in code, including labels, buttons, and lists. If you are absolutely sure that a control doesn't need to maintain state (for example, a label that always has the same text), you can set the `EnableViewState` property to `False`. This may speed up your web page a little, as there will be less information to be transmitted in each postback, but the effect is usually minor with simple controls.

The Page Processing Cycle

To make sure you understand view state, it helps to consider the actual life cycle of a web page.

1. The page is posted back whenever the user clicks a button or modifies an `AutoPostback` control.

2. ASP.NET recreates the page object using the .aspx file.

3. ASP.NET retrieves state information from the hidden view state field, and fills the controls. Any control that does not maintain state will be left with its initial (default) value.

4. The Page.Load event occurs.

5. The appropriate event-handling code runs (such as the Click event for a button or TextChanged event for a text box).

6. ASP.NET creates the HTML output for the final page and sends it to the client.

7. The Page.Unload event occurs and the web page object is unloaded from the server's memory.

Note that the Page.Load event occurs every time the page is posted back, because the page is essentially being recreated from scratch with each user request. If you use this event to do some page initialization on the first request, be sure your event handler checks the web form's IsPostBack property first, as shown here:

```
Protected Sub Page_Load(ByVal sender As System.Object, _
  ByVal e As System.EventArgs) Handles MyBase.Load
    If IsPostback Then
        ' Do nothing, this is a postback.
    Else
        ' The page is loading for the first time,
        ' so you can perform any required initialization.
        txtFeet.Text = "0"
        txtYards.Text = "0"
    End If
End Sub
```

Other Controls

As with the Windows Forms engine, Microsoft provides a full complement of controls for web forms. Table 12-1 provides a quick overview of some of the most useful controls in the Standard tab.

Thinking About State

There is one area where web programming is completely unlike Windows programming. HTTP, the protocol used to communicate over the Internet, is *stateless*, which means that the client (the browser) does not maintain a connection to the server (where your code is running). A Windows application, by contrast, is much simpler. It's always loaded and running on a single machine, with a dedicated amount of memory set aside.

Table 12-1: Essential Controls for Web Forms

Function	Control	Description
Text display (read-only)	Label	Displays text that users can't edit.
Text edit	TextBox	Displays text that users can edit.
Selection from a list	DropDownList	Allows users either to select from a list or to enter text as in a standard combo box.
	ListBox	Displays a list of choices. Optionally, the list can allow multiple selections.
Graphics display	Image	Displays an image.
	AdRotator	Displays a sequence (predefined or random) of images, which is often used in banner advertisements.
Value setting	CheckBox	Displays a standard check box.
	RadioButton	Displays a standard option button.
Date setting	Calendar	Displays a calendar that allows the user to select a date and browse from month to month. Extensively configurable (much more than the Windows DateTimePicker control)—you can even add text into individual date cells or make certain dates unselectable.
Commands	Button	Displays a button that the user can click to cause a postback and run some code.
	LinkButton	Like a button, but it has the appearance of a hyperlink.
	ImageButton	Like a button, but it incorporates an image instead of text.
Navigation control	HyperLink	Creates a web navigation link that gets your user to another page.
Grouping and list controls	CheckBoxList	Creates a collection of check boxes. From an HTML standpoint, these check boxes aren't obviously related, but ASP.NET lets you interact with them using a single control object.
	Panel	Creates a box (with or without a border) that serves as a container for other controls.
	RadioButtonList	Creates a grouping of radio buttons. Inside the group, only one button can be selected.
Data controls	Repeater	Displays information (usually from a database) using a set of HTML elements and controls that you specify, repeating the elements once for each record in the DataSet. A powerful tool for some custom database viewing/editing applications.
	DataList	Like the Repeater control, but with more formatting and layout options, including the ability to display information in a table. The DataList control comes with built-in editing capabilities.
	GridView	Like the DataList, but even more powerful, with the ability for automatic paging, sorting, and editing. It's designed to display information from a data source (like a DataSet).

Anatomy of a Web Request

In a typical web request, the client's browser connects to the web server and requests a page. As soon as the page is delivered, the connection is broken, and the web server immediately forgets everything it ever knew about the client. This method of communication is highly efficient. Because a client needs to be connected for only a few seconds, a typical web server can easily handle thousands of requests without a noticeable performance hit. However, life gets a little more interesting when you want your web server to not only display content, but also run a (stateful) web application.

In the world of classic ASP, every time a new web request was made, your program had to store every piece of information that it needed and reload it as required. In ASP.NET, there are some ready-made state management features that make the web application request-handling process a lot easier. You've already seen how view state manages the state of user controls for you automatically. The next step is to learn how to harness it for storing your own information, such as private form variables.

Witnessing the Problem

To see what can happen when your web server needs to display content and run a web application simultaneously, we'll return to our MetricConverter program and make the small enhancement shown in the following code. Our intention is to use the private variable Counter to keep track of how many times the user performs a conversion.

```
Private Counter As Integer

Protected Sub cmdConvert_Click(ByVal sender As System.Object, _
  ByVal e As System.EventArgs) Handles cmdConvert.Click
    Dim Inches, Meters As Single
    Inches = 36 * Val(txtYards.Text) + 12 * Val(txtFeet.Text)
    Meters = Inches / 39.37
    lblResult.Text = "Result: " & Meters.ToString() & " Meters. "

    Counter += 1
    lblResult.Text &= Counter.ToString() & " conversions performed."
End Sub
```

If you try this code out, you'll see that it doesn't work the way we intended. The counter never rises above a value of 1, because the Counter variable is recreated at the start of each new web request (and discard at the end).

Clearly, in order to keep track of the counter in between requests, the server will need to store the Counter variable in its memory. However, in a scenario with hundreds of users and operations that require a lot more persistence than a single integer, the server might quickly run out of memory (or at least start to show reduced performance). There are several ways to solve this problem. The easiest is to store the information in the page's view state.

Storing Extra Information in View State

You've already seen how view state allows controls to retain information between postbacks. When you switch on the EnableViewState property for a control, you're telling ASP.NET to keep track of the control's properties in a hidden field of the web page. However, you can also add your own information into view state, including simple data types, arrays, and even DataSet objects! As with ASP.NET controls, this information is encoded in hidden fields and sent back from the client with each round trip.

To store or retrieve information from the view state for the current page, you use the ViewState collection. Here's a code example that corrects the problem shown in the previous section:

```
Protected Sub cmdConvert_Click(ByVal sender As System.Object, _
  ByVal e As System.EventArgs) Handles cmdConvert.Click
    Dim Inches, Meters As Single
    Inches = 36 * Val(txtYards.Text) + 12 * Val(txtFeet.Text)
    Meters = Inches / 39.37
    lblResult.Text = "Result: " & Meters.ToString() & " Meters. "

    ' Retrieve the state information.
    Dim Counter As Integer = CType(ViewState("Counter"), Integer)

    ' Update the counter and display the result.
    Counter += 1
    lblResult.Text &= Counter.ToString() & " conversions performed."

    ' Store the new value.
    ViewState("Counter") = Counter
End Sub
```

As you can see, items in the ViewState collection are indexed by name. (This example uses the name Counter.) When you assign information to a state value that doesn't exist, it's created automatically. If you try to retrieve a state value that doesn't exist, you'll just end up with a null value (represented by the keyword Nothing). Figure 12-11 shows the page in action.

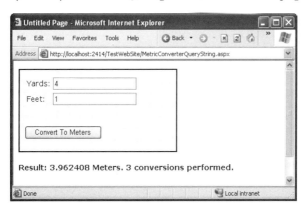

Figure 12-11: A MetricConverter with state management

If you mistype the name of an item in the ViewState collection, you won't receive an error; you'll just receive blank space. A good way to help safeguard yourself is to create properties for every item stored in the hidden field view state, as shown next, and add them to your page class. (To refresh your memory about properties, review Chapter 5.)

```
Private Property Counter() As Integer
    Get
        Return CType(ViewState("Counter"), Integer)
    End Get
    Set (ByVal Value As Integer)
        ViewState("Counter") = Value
    End Set
End Property
```

Are there any drawbacks to this method? Using view state is an excellent way to store information without adversely affecting web server performance. However, there are a few things you might want to consider:

- View state information is stored in the final rendered HTML page. That means if you store a lot of information in view state, it can slow down transmission times, both when receiving the page and when sending it as part of postback.

- ASP.NET uses a hash code to detect if anyone attempts to tamper with view state information (in which case it rejects the request). However, a malicious user can still take a look at the view state details, because they aren't encrypted. If you need to store sensitive information, consider using encryption by modifying the web.config file. Find the <pages> tag and change it to

```
<pages viewStateEncryptionMode="Always">
```

- View state relies on the hidden field in the current web form. If your user navigates to a different web form, you'll need a method of passing information from one form to another. This is the issue we'll discuss next.

Transferring Information

So far you've learned enough to create a basic, one-page web application. But what happens in a multiple-page project? Unlike the Windows Forms engine, you can't display a new web page by invoking a handy Show() method. In fact, you can't refer to another web page at all. Instead, you need to redirect the user to the right page.

There are two basic ways to navigate to another page:

- Use the HyperLink web control.
- Use the built in Redirect() method of the built in Response object, as in

```
Response.Redirect("WebPage2.aspx")
```

Because the new web form will be in the same directory as the current web form, you don't need to enter a full URL (such as http://www.mysite.com/myapplication/WebPage2.aspx).

The only problem is that the new page won't have the benefit of the hidden view state field of the previous page, and so they won't be able to access its ViewState collection. Even if the user navigates back to the original page by clicking the Back button or another hyperlink, the page still starts over again with no view state data.

There are several ways that you can resolve this problem. In the following section, you'll consider two common solutions—the query string and session state.

Passing Information in the Query String

If you've ever studied the URL bar in your web browser while exploring popular sites, you might have noticed the appearance of some extra information. For example, after you perform a search in Yahoo!, the URL looks a little like this:

```
http://search.yahoo.com/search?p=dogs
```

Clearly, the first part of this line is telling your browser where it should connect. The interesting part occurs after the question mark. The user in this case has entered a search looking for websites about dogs, and Yahoo! has stored this information in the URL, under the variable p. This type of augmentation is called a *query string*, and you can use it in ASP.NET.

Programming the Query String

The query string is similar to the ViewState collection in that it contains a list of name-value pairs that you can retrieve from a collection. However, the only way you can add to the query string is by supplying a new URL, with the appropriate values added at the end of the browser string. You can do this with a hyperlink, or by using the Response.Redirect() method.

For example, consider a modified MetricConverter that displays the conversion results in a separate page by passing the information in a query string. Here's the code that executes when the user clicks the Convert button:

```
Protected Sub cmdConvert_Click(ByVal sender As System.Object, _
  ByVal e As System.EventArgs) Handles cmdConvert.Click
    Dim QueryString As String
    QueryString = "?Yards=" & txtYards.Text & "&Feet=" & txtFeet.Text

    ' Send the information to the QueryStringResult page
    ' and redirect the user there.
    Response.Redirect("QueryStringResult.aspx" & QueryString)
End Sub
```

Note that to pass more than one value in the query string, you need to separate them with an ampersand (&) symbol.

The QueryStringResult.aspx page processes this information in a Page.Load event handler and displays the output shown in Figure 12-12.

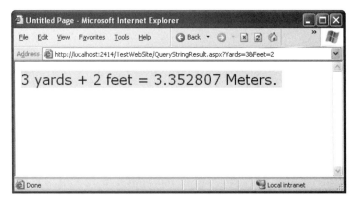

Figure 12-12: The QueryStringResult.aspx page

```
Protected Sub Page_Load(ByVal sender As System.Object, _
  ByVal e As System.EventArgs) Handles MyBase.Load
    ' Retrieve the query string information.
    Dim Feet, Yards As Single
    Feet = Val(Request.QueryString("Feet"))
    Yards = Val(Request.QueryString("Yards"))

    ' Perform the calculation
    Dim Inches, Meters As Single
    Inches = 36 * Yards + 12 * Feet
    Meters = Inches / 39.37

    ' Display the result
    lblResult.Text = Yards.ToString() & " yards + " & Feet.ToString()
    lblResult.Text &= " feet = " & Meters.ToString() & " Meters. "
End Sub
```

Best of all, like the view state, the query string stores information without affecting the performance of your web server.

TIP *The query string is often used to display detailed information about a specific item. For example, you might have a page that displays a catalog of products and allows the user to choose a product to view additional information about it. Upon selecting a product, the user would be redirected to the product's page, and a query string argument would be appended to specify the selected product (as in ?ProductID=34). The Page.Load event-handling code in the new page would open the file or database, retrieve the appropriate product information, and display it.*

Convenient as it is, there are some drawbacks to using the query string that you might want to consider.

- The amount of information you can store is limited. To ensure compatibility with all browsers, you shouldn't make the query string more than about 1,000 bytes.

- The information is extremely insecure. Not only it is transmitted in clear text over the Internet, but it's also clearly visible to the person using your application. In fact, it might be *too* visible . . . giving malicious users the opportunity to alter information by changing the query string manually, or just revealing too much about how your program works and what variables it stores.

- You can't store complex information in the query string. Everything is stored as a string, so arrays and objects won't work.

If you need to get around these limitations, you have another option. You can use session state to store information in the server's memory.

Using Session State

Session state is one of the most useful tools for tracking information. It stores user-specific information that's available to every web form in your application.

A session begins when a user navigates to a page in your web application. A session ends when you end it programmatically (by calling the Session.Abandon() method), or when it times out after the web server stops receiving requests from the user. The standard timeout is about 20 minutes, but you can configure this default using the web.config file. To do so, you need to insert the <sessionState> tag inside the <system.web> tag, assuming it isn't already there (by default, it isn't). You can use the <sessionState> tag specifically to set the timeout, in minutes. Here's an example:

```
<configuration>
    <!-- Other settings omitted. -->
    <system.web>
        <sessionState timeout="20" />
        <!-- Other settings omitted. -->
    </system.web>
</configuration>
```

Setting the right timeout interval is not as easy as it seems. You don't want to erase a user's information too quickly, in case the user returns and needs to start over again. However, you also don't want to waste memory on your server and potentially make life difficult for other users.

How Session State Works

Session information is stored on the server. Even after the client receives a web page and breaks its connection, session information remains floating in memory on the web server. When the client reconnects by clicking a control or requesting a new page, the web server looks up the user's session information and makes it available to your code. The whole process is automatic; it works because the browser stores a small scrap of information (known as a *cookie*) that uniquely identifies that user's session. ASP.NET automatically generates a session cookie with a unique session ID whenever a user requests a web page that accesses session state.

Programming Session State

To create a MetricConverter page that uses session state instead of view state doesn't take very much effort. You still need to use a collection of name-value pairs, except that this time they are stored in the built-in Session object. Remember, session information will be accessible from any web page in your web application (typically, any other .aspx file in the virtual directory).

```
Protected Sub cmdConvert_Click(ByVal sender As System.Object, _
  ByVal e As System.EventArgs) Handles cmdConvert.Click
    Dim Inches, Meters As Single
    Inches = 36 * Val(txtYards.Text) + 12 * Val(txtFeet.Text)
    Meters = Inches / 39.37
    lblResult.Text = "Result: " & Meters.ToString() & " Meters. "

    ' Retrieve the state information.
    Counter = CType(Session("Counter"), Integer)

    ' Update the counter and display the result.
    Counter += 1
    lblResult.Text &= Counter.ToString() & " conversions performed."

    ' Store the new value.
    Session("Counter") = Counter
End Sub
```

Because session information is stored on the server and is never transmitted to the client, session state is more secure than any of the other kinds of state management I've discussed. It also allows you to store just about any type of information you need, including objects. However, session state does come with one potential drawback: It consumes server memory. Even a small amount of session information can consume extensive server resources if hundreds or thousands of users are using the web application simultaneously. To help reduce problems, you'll have to follow these guidelines:

Acquire late, release early.
Store information only when you need it, and release it as soon as you don't need it anymore. In the preceding example, you could use the line Session("Counter").Remove() to release your state information.

Consider all state possibilities.
Before you store information in session state, consider whether it would be better suited for view state or one of ASP.NET's other state management options. Table 12-2 on page 415 summarizes and compares the various choices.

Reduce the amount of information you need.

Store only what you need. It sounds simple, but you would be amazed how many problems occur because a web application programmer decides to store multiple `DataSet` objects in server memory.

Using Application State

Application state is similar to session state, except that it applies to the whole application, not just a single user, and it never times out. Once you add something to the built-in `Application` object, it's available to all users for the entire lifetime of your web application. For example, if we stored our `Counter` in application state, we could track the total number of times that all users have clicked the Calculate button.

NOTE *Generally, your web application's lifetime is as long as the server is running. However, depending on the settings on the web server, web applications sometimes "recycle" themselves to clean up any stray memory and resources that might not have been released properly. If this takes place (typically when certain resource usage or time thresholds are reached), all application state is lost.*

Unfortunately application state isn't quite as simple as it seems. For one thing, you can run into problems if multiple users try to modify a variable stored in application state at the same time. To get around this, you can use the `Application` object's `Lock()` and `Unlock()` methods, as shown here, but this method can cause a significant slowdown in a multiuser scenario.

```
' Store the new value.
Application.Lock()
Application("Counter") = Counter.ToString()
Application.Unlock()
```

It's probably best to avoid using application state unless you absolutely need it. And don't try to improve performance by using application state to store important information. It's much better to use ASP.NET's caching features for this purpose. For more information, read up on the built-in `Response.Cache` object in the Visual Studio Help.

Where Do All These Built-in Objects Come From?

So far, you've tackled a number of problems using built-in objects. By this point, you're probably wondering where all these built-in objects come from. To get the lowdown on exactly how this works, you need to know a little bit about the object-oriented internals of an ASP.NET application. All the built-in objects are provided through references in the `System.Web.UI.Page` class, which is the basis for every ASP.NET page, as shown in Figure 12-13.

The `Page` class is fully described in the .NET class reference included in the Visual Studio Help.

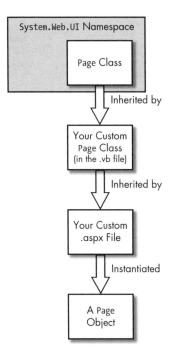

Figure 12-13: The System.Web.UI.Page class

A Summary of Different Types of State Management

So far, you've learned about view state, session state, application state, and the query string. It turns out there are actually several more possibilities for managing state in a web application. In fact, considering the tools ASP.NET gives you for this feature, you might conclude that ASP.NET is downright obsessed with state management. Table 12-2 compares your options.

We haven't discussed the last two options in this table, because they require more programming work than the others. They tend to be specialty items.

- Cookies are small files that are stored on the client's computer to remember items of information. They are similar in function and use to other state management methods, and, like the query string, they can only contain strings. The only difference is that every cookie includes an expiration date that you can use to store information for long periods of time (for example, a cookie can store customer preferences in between visits). You use a cookie by creating an instance of the HttpCookie class, and using the Response.AppendCookie() method to add it to the Response object's cookie collection.

- Server-side database storage requires custom programming. It's an extremely flexible approach, but you need to write the ADO.NET code that makes it work. If you've read Chapter 10 about databases, you already know everything you need.

Table 12-2: State Management Options in ASP.NET

Type of State Management	Scope	Storage Location	Lifetime	Security
View state	The current page and the current user.	A hidden field in the current page	Lost when you browse to another page.	Fairly secure (if you opt for automatic encryption).
Query string	The specified page and the current user, although it can be passed along from page to page if your code redirects the user.	The browser's URL string	Lost when you type a new URL or close the browser. However, can be stored between sessions in a bookmark.	Insecure, and can be modified by the user.
Session state	The entire application and the current user.	Server memory	Times out after a predefined period.	Secure
Application state	The entire application; shared with all users.	Server memory	Never times out; remains until you remove it (or the application is restarted).	Secure
Cookies	The entire application and the current user.	Client's computer	Set by the programmer, and can persist between visits.	Insecure, and can be modified by the user.
Database	The entire application; shared with all users.	Server hard drive	Permanent unless removed.	Secure

Displaying Data with Data Binding

ASP.NET is packed with impressive features that are impossible to cover completely in this chapter. But before you move on, it's worth introducing just one of these tools—automatic data binding.

Automatic data binding provides a convenient way to retrieve and display information from a database in an ASP.NET application. Data binding works quite a bit differently in ASP.NET than it does in a Windows application. When you use data binding with a web control, the information can only travel in one direction. It flows from the data source into the control, where it becomes ordinary content. Any modifications to the control do not affect the original DataSet—in fact, the original DataSet ceases to exist as soon as the operation is complete and the page is presented to the user.

Web controls work differently in this regard because they are designed for optimal web application performance. Even with this limitation, data binding still provides a very useful way for retrieving information from a database and displaying it in a web page with a minimum amount of coding. Best of all, the ADO.NET data access code is identical whether you are programming for the web or the desktop.

Basic ASP.NET Data Binding

The online examples contain a simple ASP.NET page called DataBinding.aspx that demonstrates data binding in action (Figure 12-14). It binds a drop-down list, a check-box list, and a GridView control.

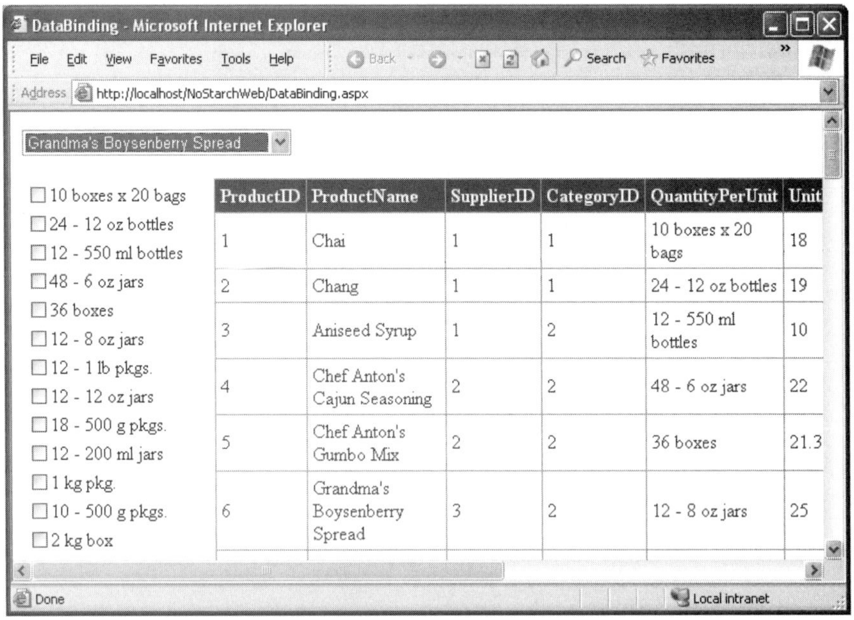

Figure 12-14: A data-bound web page

Basic ASP.NET data binding looks a lot like data binding in a Windows Forms application. The most noticeable difference in the code is that you must explicitly trigger data binding. You can bind a single control calling that control's DataBind() method, or you can bind the entire page at once by calling the page's DataBind() method. It's at this point that the web control is filled. If you forget to call this method, no data will appear in the bound control.

```
Protected Sub Page_Load(ByVal sender As System.Object, _
  ByVal e As System.EventArgs) Handles MyBase.Load

    Dim con As New SqlConnection(ConnectionString)
    Dim SQL As String = "SELECT * FROM Products"
    Dim cmd As New SqlCommand(SQL, con)
    Dim adapter As New SqlDataAdapter(cmd)
    Dim dsNorthwind As New DataSet()

    con.Open()
    adapter.Fill(dsNorthwind, "Products")
    con.Close()

    ' Bind the grid.
    gridDB.DataSource = dsNorthwind.Tables("Products")

    ' Bind the drop-down list to the ProductName field.
    lstName.DataSource = dsNorthwind.Tables("Products")
    lstName.DataTextField = "ProductName"
```

```
' Bind the check-box list to the QuantityPerUnit field.
lstQuantity.DataSource = dsNorthwind.Tables("Products")
lstQuantity.DataTextField = "QuantityPerUnit"

' Move the information from the DataSet into the controls.
Me.DataBind()
```

```
End Sub
```

NOTE *When you bind to multiple controls at once in a Windows application, the controls are automatically synchronized. If you select a record in one control, the corresponding information appears in all the other controls. This is not the case in ASP.NET, where the controls act as though they had been filled manually. That is because data binding in ASP.NET exists only while the page is being processed. When the final HTML output is received by the client, only ordinary HTML content remains.*

The Data Source Controls

Basic data binding gives you a quick way to get your information about a data object (like the DataSet) and into the controls on a page. But ASP.NET goes a step further, providing a whole set of data source controls that are designed to help you avoid writing any code at all!

Here's how it works. You drop one of the data source controls (found on the Data group in the Toolbox) onto a web page. You can choose one of several data source controls, depending on whether you want to extract data from a database or from a custom class that you've created with ADO.NET (the two most common options). You configure this data source control so it has all the information it needs to get the information you want. Then, you simply link it to your data control by setting the DataSourceID property. When you run the page, the control automatically asks the data source control for data, the data source control retrieves the data, and then the data binding happens automatically, without a single keystroke of code on your behalf.

NOTE *The data source controls appear on your form at design-time, so it's easier to select them and set their properties. However, they don't appear when you run the page.*

The easiest way to understand how this works is to consider a basic example. Imagine you want to simplify the data binding example from the previous section. Instead of writing the ADO.NET code to query the Products table, you want to get a data source control to do the work for you. In this case, the SqlDataSource is your man—it's the data source that's designed for working with an ADO.NET provider to get information from a relational database. Here's what you need to do:

1. Double-click the SqlDataSource control in the Toolbox to add it to your page. Select it so you can configure its properties in the Properties window.

2. Set the ID page to something descriptive, like sourceProducts (because we're returning product information).

3. Set the `ProviderName` property to the name of the ADO.NET provider you want the data source to use. You can use `System.Data.SqlClient` for the SQL Server provider, `System.Data.OracleClient` for Oracle, or `System.Data.OleDb` for the OLE DB provider.

4. The next step is to supply the required connection string through the `ConnectionString` property.

5. Now you need to define the query that the `SqlDataSource` will use. To do so, edit the `SelectCommand` to be `SELECT * From Products`.

6. Now your data source is fully configured for selecting records. Add another control that supports data binding to your page (such as the `GridView`), and then set its `DataSourceID` to match whatever name you chose in Step 2 (here, `sourceProducts`).

7. Run the page. The grid is filled with data automatically, even though you haven't written any code.

Professional ASP.NET developers are split on the data source controls. Clearly, they offer a nifty way to create data bound pages without much effort. However, if you rely heavily on the `SqlDataSource`, you'll end up embedding all kinds of database details into your web pages, and you'll lose the ability to customize how queries are performed in the same way that you can with pure ADO.NET code. Whether or not you dabble with the data source controls probably depends on how much flexibility you need and how quickly you need to create your pages.

TIP *This section has only scratched the surface of ASP.NET's data binding features. If you dig deeper, you'll find ways to commit updates automatically using advanced controls, such as the `GridView`, as well as ways to bind to custom classes. To get hard core, try the references provided at the end of this chapter.*

Deploying Your Website

Until you deploy them, the websites you create in Visual Studio are only available while Visual Studio is running. As soon as you shut Visual Studio down, the integrated web server disappears, and there's no way to surf to your pages. There's also no way to access a web page from another computer (at any time), because the integrated web server doesn't support remote connections.

This is all perfectly reasonable for testing applications, but there comes a time when you need to deploy your application so others can use it. If you're planning to upload your web application to the Internet, you're probably going to use a dedicated web host provider (like www.brinkster.com). In this case, all you need to do is to copy the contents of your website folder to your web host, usually by FTP.

On the other hand, if you secretly have a web server stashed in your basement, or you just want to run a web server on an ordinary computer to let other people on the same network access it (useful for a company intranet), than you'll need to know a little more about how IIS works. Keep reading.

IIS Setup

In order for your computer to become a web server, it needs to have the IIS software installed. Although IIS is a part of the Windows operating system, it isn't necessarily installed by default. To see whether IIS is installed, try typing the following request into an Internet browser:

```
http://localhost/localstart.asp
```

Localhost is the special "loopback" alias that always refers to the current computer. Localstart.asp is a traditional ASP file that is stored in the root directory of your computer's website home directory.

You should see the picture shown in Figure 12-15.

Figure 12-15: The Localstart.asp home page

You could also request the file using the specific name of your computer (as in http://MyComputer/localstart.asp). This is the approach you need to use if you want to request the localstart.asp file on your computer from another computer on the network.

If you receive an error message, check that you have IIS installed. If it's not already installed, click the Start button, and select Settings ▶ Control Panel. Then, choose Add or Remove Programs, and click Add/Remove Windows Components. Find Internet Information Services in the list (see Figure 12-16), select it, and click Next to install the appropriate files.

There's one catch. If you install IIS *after* you install the .NET Framework, IIS won't be correctly configured. The problem is that IIS doesn't won't know anything about the .aspx file type, and so it won't pass requests along to ASP.NET like it should. Fortunately, it's easy to correct this problem by repairing the IIS file mappings. Just run the Visual Studio command prompt (select Programs ▶ Visual Studio 2005 ▶ Visual Studio Tools ▶ Visual Studio 2005 Command Prompt), and then type this:

```
aspnet_regiis.exe -i
```

The aspnet_regiis tool will update IIS by registering the ASP.NET file types.

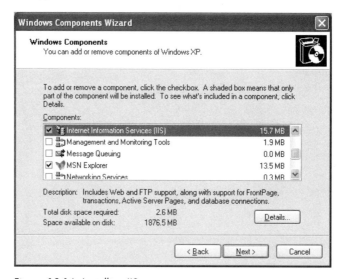

Figure 12-16: Installing IIS

Virtual Directories

By default, your website's home directory is the physical directory c:\ Inetpub\wwwroot, and the localstart.asp file is contained in this directory. If you try to double-click localstart.asp to run it directly from Windows Explorer, you will receive an error. This file can only be rendered by ASP, must be invoked by IIS in response to a web request. ASP processes the .asp page and returns an HTML page that can be displayed in the browser. This is essentially the same way that ASP.NET works with .aspx files.

When you create a new web page, you have two choices. You can place it in c:\Inetpub\wwwroot or in one of its subdirectories. For example, if you create a directory c:\Inetpub\wwwroot\MyFiles and place the file Test.html in it, you can request this page via HTTP by entering the URL http://localhost/MyFiles/Test.html in a browser.

A more flexible approach is to create your own *virtual directory*. A virtual directory represents a physical web directory, but it doesn't need to use the same name as the physical directory, and it doesn't need to be a subdirectory of c:\Inetpub\wwwroot. For example, you could expose the directory c:\WebApps\01 as the virtual directory Sales. Then you can request the Test.html file from the c:\WebApps\01 directory by entering the URL http://localhost/Sales/Test.html.

Virtual directories are easy to create, but you don't use Visual Studio to do the work. Instead, you have to use the IIS Manager utility. You can run IIS Manager by selecting Settings ▶ Control Panel ▶ Administrative Tools ▶ Internet Services Manager from the taskbar (Figure 12-17).

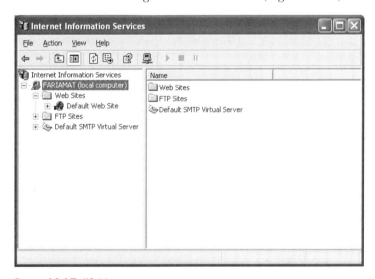

Figure 12-17: IIS Manager

1. To create a virtual directory, you first create the physical directory on your hard drive.

2. Then, use the virtual directory wizard in IIS manager. Right-click the Default Web Site item (under your computer in the tree), and choose New ▶ Virtual Directory from the context menu.

3. Click Next to get started. The first piece of information required is the Alias (Figure 12-18), which is the name that your virtual directory will have for web requests. Click Next to continue.

4. The second piece of information is the physical directory that will be exposed through the virtual directory. This can have the same name as the virtual directory, but it doesn't need to. Click Next to continue.

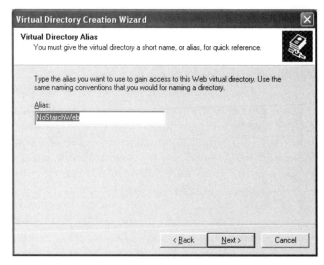

Figure 12-18: The Virtual Directory Creation Wizard

5. The final wizard window gives you the chance to configure the permissions for the directory (Figure 12-19). The default settings allow clients to read the directory and run ASP.NET pages, but not to make any modifications. This is the recommended configuration.

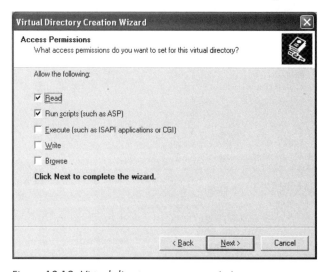

Figure 12-19: Virtual directory access permissions

6. Click Next and then Finish to end the wizard. You will see the virtual directory in the IIS Manager tree display with a package icon next to it. Once you have created a virtual directory, you can create a web project in it using Visual Studio.

TIP   *When you create a virtual directory with the IIS Manager wizard, it's also marked as a web application. That means that the ASP.NET files in this directory will run in their own isolated memory space, use their own set of local session data, and have their own independent configuration settings. If you create a subdirectory in your virtual directory, this directory will also be accessible over the Internet, but it will be a part of the same application. For example, if you create the virtual directory Sales for the physical directory c:\WebApps\01, the subdirectory c:\WebApps\01\Special will be available as http://localhost/Sales/Special. Any ASP.NET files in this subdirectory will be considered a part of the Sales application, and will have the same settings and run in the same memory space.*

What Comes Next?

ASP.NET almost qualifies as a programming framework of its own. If you work through the concepts in this chapter, you're well on your way to creating substantial web applications. However, if you want to become an ASP.NET guru, there are a few further topics you might want to start exploring:

- Performance can be critical when you're working on the Internet. Seemingly small changes can affect efficiency quite a bit. To improve performance, you might want to use the caching features. You can read up on the `System.Web.Caching.Cache` class in the Visual Studio Help.

- Get to know all the built-in web controls that you have to choose from, and try them out. As you become more experienced, you might even create your own. Controls like the `Calendar`, `GridView`, and `AdRotator` completely hide the underlying HTML.

- As indicated earlier in the chapter, once you create a form in the Web Form Designer, it's translated into an ASP.NET-enriched flavor of HTML. To glimpse what's going on underneath the hood and get a subtler understanding of ASP.NET, click the Source button in the Web Form Designer.

- Consult the Visual Studio Help to learn about higher-level features. For example, ASP.NET has premade solutions for data binding (which you saw briefly in this chapter), website navigation, web page standardization, validation, and security. And if the Visual Studio Help is too dry for your tastes, try the quick get-up-and-go tutorials at www.asp.net/Tutorials/quickstart.aspx, which are dense but informative.

- And lastly, if you're interested in reading an entire book that delves into web programming, you could do worse than my own *Beginning ASP.NET 2.0* (Apress, 2001).

13

WEB SERVICES

Web services are code routines that you can call from another application over the Internet. They're built on an impressive foundation of open standards and backed by a range of technology vendors from Microsoft to IBM to Sun Microsystems (the creators of Java). Since their creation, web services have spread through almost every current programming platform. Today, they power an ever-increasing number of web-enabled Windows applications, unite the business processes of different companies, and allow just about anyone to share functionality over the Internet.

.NET makes web services incredibly easy to program, while retaining their cross-platform credentials. The web services you create in Visual Basic 2005 can be used seamlessly by applications written in different programming languages and running on different operating systems. But the best part is that you don't have to worry about the plumbing, because ASP.NET handles these details automatically.

This chapter starts by asking, "What is a web service?" and takes you through the process of creating, deploying, and interacting with one. Luckily, .NET makes web services so quick and convenient that you can be creating simple examples in no time at all. However, it may take many more months of experimentation before you start to realize all of the possible ways web services can be used. The end of this chapter includes some helpful web links to live examples of web services.

New in .NET

Web services appeared in the VB toolkit for the first time in .NET 1.0. However, they are still usable (with a little more work) in classic VB 6. The difference is that in previous version of VB you needed to use a separate component, named the Microsoft SOAP Toolkit, to get web service features. For most VB developers, .NET is the first time they'll encounter web services.

In fact, web services are so well integrated into .NET that they are sometimes identified synonymously with the entire .NET platform. Of course, now that you have read Chapter 1 of this book, you know what .NET is really about—a compatible set of retooled languages, a runtime that provides high-level services, and a rich toolkit of features. How large a part web services will play in Microsoft's strategy of integrating languages, embracing open standards, and programming the Internet remains to be seen.

The Vision of the Interactive Web

What is a web service, anyway? Clearly, many sites on the Internet provide useful "services." A common example is a shipping company, which allows you to look up the location and delivery date of packages using a tracking number. Is this a web service?

The delivery date lookup meets one of the criteria of a web service—it's a discrete unit of functionality that serves a single purpose: returning information about your package. But in order to get this information, you have to navigate to the correct HTML page, select an option from a menu, and then enter your tracking number. In other words, you have to use an Internet application—represented by the shipping company's website—in order to get the information you need. A web service doesn't force you to use a web page, and it doesn't have any user interface associated with it. Instead, a web service is a piece of functionality that can only be used by another *application*.

Web Services: COM for the Internet?

One of the great developments in Windows programming was COM (some parts of which are also called ActiveX), a technology that allows code components to be easily shared among applications. When COM was introduced, it added flexibility. Instead of using monolithic applications, custom utilities could be created that reused a subset of all the capabilities provided in COM components.

In this respect, web services are like COM for the Internet. With a web service, you can take a unit of logic in a web application and allow it to be seamlessly accessed and used by other Windows or Internet applications. A web service is like a business object: It accepts information and returns information. Your program uses web services without involving the user, and takes care of providing the appropriate user interface to present the results. This is particularly important in the world of the Internet, where a user might be accessing information from a full-featured Internet Explorer browser or from a stripped-down interface on a cell phone or other wireless device. In each case, the web service used would be the same, but a different application would take care of the display. Like a COM object, a web service doesn't need to be tied to any specific interface.

In one important way, however, web services are *not* like COM technology. COM relies on a proprietary Windows standard, which means that it's useless for Macintosh computers, Unix systems, or any other non-Microsoft platform. Web services, on the other hand, are built on open standards such as SOAP and WSDL, which are based on XML and are described in this chapter. This means that any application can interact with web services (though few so easily as a .NET application) and can transmit data painlessly over HTTP. Because data is exchanged as text in XML format, there's also no problem sending a web service request or receiving its response, even when the web service is behind a corporate firewall.

Web Services Today

You are probably already making use of "first-generation" web services. These are examples of Internet procedures that are integrated into desktop programs, but require company-specific and site-specific standards. For example, you may use a personal finance desktop application that can automatically retrieve stock portfolio information from the Internet. This type of application retrieves information from the Internet, and it doesn't bother you with the details of the process. However, it relies on having information provided in a specific way, which was been planned and set up in advance, according to the particular application. It does not use an independent, widely accepted standard, as web services do with .NET. As a consequence, other applications can't easily extend or work with its functions and features. They must be recreated for every application that requires them.

Now imagine a world with thousands of web service components, where a desktop application has access to all kind of features that require up-to-the-minute information from the Web. Everyone has some type of "always-on" broadband Internet access, and users often are not even aware that an application is interacting with the Web. Programmers no longer have to constantly redesign off-the-cuff solutions that schedule Internet downloads or parse HTML files manually looking for specially formatted information.

Of course, that's still in the future. But today, web services already allow you to modularize Internet applications and provide components that can be consumed and reused by any other application. Web services can also use authentication and login procedures, allowing you to support various subscription models. In other words, you can sell units of application functionality to other developers, just like programmers have sold ActiveX components in the past.

Are Web Services Objects?

Web services are *not* objects, at least not in the traditional sense of the word. The main distinction is that web services don't maintain state, unless you specifically take extra steps to store information in a database or ASP.NET's session state. In fact, a web service that maintains state is rarely a good idea because it means the web server must allocate a portion of its precious memory for each client, which can quickly impose a noticeable performance penalty as the number of clients increases.

Web services also don't support object-oriented basics like overloaded methods and property procedures. Constructors work, but the web service class is constructed for each request and then automatically destroyed, even if the client maintains a reference. This ensures that web services perform well, but it also means that they can't be used like a local business object. It's best to think of a web service as a utility class made up of shared members. You can call a remote function to get a piece of information, but you shouldn't expect to keep a web service around and store information in it.

Creating Your First Web Service

Creating a web service is easier than you might think. All you have to do is create a class that incorporates some useful functions. This class should inherit from the System.Web.Services.WebService class (for maximum convenience), and all the methods that are going to be made available over the Web must be marked with <WebMethod> attributes. The following sections walk you through the process.

Setting Up a Web Service

In order to provide a web service, you first need to create a virtual directory using the IIS web hosting software described in the previous chapter. There's a simple reason for this requirement—namely, the clients of your web service need to be able to contact the service, so it needs to be at a well-known, fixed location. If you use the web server that's built into Visual Studio, the web service will only be available while you're debugging it, and it won't be accessible to other computers. (And even if it were publicly available, the URL used to contact the web service would constantly change, because each time the integrated web server starts it chooses a new, random port number.) Trying to keep clients up to date with this ever changing location would be almost impossible.

What's a web service developer to do? Here are the steps to follow:

1. First, follow the instructions in the section "IIS Setup" on page 419. This ensures that IIS is installed on your computer and ready to host a web service.

2. Next, create a virtual directory for your web service using IIS Manager, as described in the section "Virtual Directories" on page 420. Use any directory you like, but make sure you make a note of the virtual directory name.

3. Fire up Visual Studio, and choose File ▶ New Web Site. This opens the New Web Site dialog box (Figure 13-1).

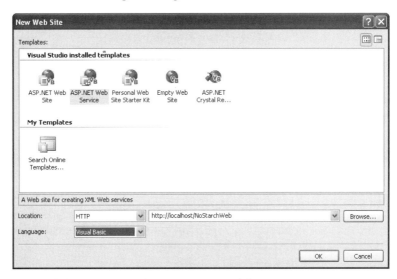

Figure 13-1: Creating a web project in a virtual directory

4. Choose the ASP.NET Web Service template.

5. In the Location box, choose HTTP instead of file. Then enter the exact URL that points to the virtual directory. For example, if you created a virtual directory named NoStarchWeb on the current computer, you would enter the URL http://localhost/NoStarchWeb, as in Figure 13-1.

6. Click OK to create the web application in the virtual directory. When you run any web pages or web services in this web application, the IIS web server will handle your requests instead of the built-in Visual Studio web server. The end result is exactly the same, except that you won't see the random port numbers in the URL.

It is possible to create a virtual directory through Visual Studio, without using IIS at all. Just skip steps 1 and 2 in the list. However, the virtual directory you create will be mapped to a new directory in the C:\Inetpub\wwwroot, which might not be what you want.

When you create a new virtual directory it may not be configured to support Integrated Windows authentication, depending on your IIS settings. This is a problem, because Visual Studio needs this support in order to allow web service debugging. If you receive an error informing you of the problem when you try to launch your web service, follow these steps:

1. Launch IIS Manager.
2. Browse to your virtual directory, right-click it, and select Properties.
3. Go to the Directory Security tab.
4. Click the first Edit button at the top of this tab. A dialog box titled Authentication Methods will appear.
5. Make sure the Integrated Windows Security check box is checked.
6. Click OK to commit the change.

The Web Service Project

When you create a web service project, you're actually creating the same sort of web application you used in Chapter 12. The only difference is that a web service project starts off with one web service instead of one web page.

TIP *The web service and web application projects are both ASP.NET applications. In fact, any web application can host a combination of web pages and web services.*

As with ASP.NET web forms, each ASP.NET web service actually consists of two files. An .asmx file for web services plays a similar role to the .aspx page for web forms. It is the file the client requests in a URL to access the web service. However, there isn't any content in the .asmx file. Instead, it simply links itself to another source code file with the extension .vb.

When you create a new web service, you'll start out with two files—a web service named Service.asmx, and a corresponding code file for that web service, named Service.vb (see Figure 13-2). The code file is stored in the App_Code directory, because ASP.NET uses a slightly different compilation model for web services than it uses for web forms.

Figure 13-2: A web service project with one web service

As you continue on with the following sections, you can use and modify this sample web service (by editing the code in the Service.vb file), or you can create a new web service that's all your own. To create a web service, select Website ▶ Add New Item, choose Web Service, and supply a filename, as shown in Figure 13-3.

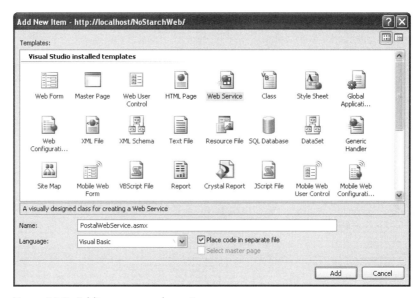

Figure 13-3: Adding a new web service

NOTE   *Web services consist of two files (the .asmx file, which is how other applications access your service, and the .vb file, which contains the code). You're free to rename either of these files, but you should use the same names (with different extensions) to prevent confusion. However, if you change the class name in your .vb file, you must also edit the Class attribute in the .asmx file so that it matches. Otherwise, ASP.NET won't realize the two pieces are linked.*

The Web Service Class

Now consider a very rudimentary example of a web service class for providing information about a package tracked with a shipping company. To enter this class on your own, select Website ▶ Add New Item, choose Web Service, and supply the filename PostalWebService.

Here's the complete code:

```
Imports System.Web.Services

Public Class PostalWebService
  Inherits System.Web.Services.WebService
```

```
<WebMethod> _
Public Function GetDeliveryDate(ByVal TrackID As String) As Date
    Dim PackageInfo As Package
    PackageInfo = GetPackageRecordFromDB(TrackID)
    Return PackageInfo.DeliveryDate
End Function

Private Function GetPackageRecordFromDB(ByVal TrackID As String) _
  As Package
    ' Some database access code here.
End Function

End Class

Public Class Package
    Public PackageID As String
    Public DeliveryDate As Date
End Class
```

The Package class encapsulates information about a package. Notice that it doesn't inherit from the WebService class or use the <WebMethod> attribute because it isn't a web service. Instead, it is used internally in the PostalWebService class, to pass information.

The PostalWebService class has two methods. The GetDeliveryDate() method is marked with a special attribute, <WebMethod>, which indicates that it will be provided in the public interface of the web service. No other methods are available. The GetPackageRecordFromDB() method is used internally by your code to get information, but it is not made available to any clients.

Now, believe it or not, any application using this web service will have access to the features and operations of the GetDeliveryDate() function. All you need is a method that uses the <WebMethod> attribute. Could it be any easier?

Touching Up Your Web Service

To improve your web service, you might want to add a description to the <WebMethod> attribute. This description may be displayed for the client developing the application that will use your web service, depending on the type of development tool they are using.

```
<WebMethod(Description:="Use this function to...")>
```

You should also specify a namespace for your web service. Ideally, your namespace should be uniquely identified with you—your company name, for example, or best of all, your web address. If you do not specify a namespace, the default (http://tempuri.org) will be used. Be aware that this is an XML namespace, and it has nothing to do with .NET namespaces.

NOTE *An XML namespace is used to identify different types of XML markup. Most XML namespaces look like an URLs, because the organizations that create the namespace use names of domains that they own. This prevents the possibility of more than one company using the same namespace name for completely different XML-based formats.*

To specify an XML namespace, change the first line of your class declaration to use the `WebService` attribute:

```
<WebService(Namespace:="http://mycompany.com/post")> _
Public Class PostalWebService
```

Enhancing the PostalWebService Class

You can also make a more useful web service that returns a custom object with several pieces of information at once, as shown in the following example. Notice that the Package information has been separated into two classes; we'll assume here that you will not want to provide the entire database record to the client, in case it includes sensitive information (such as a credit card number).

```
<WebService(Namespace:="http://mycompany.com/post")> _
Public Class PostalWebService
  Inherits System.Web.Services.WebService

    <WebMethod(Description:="Gets tracking information about a package.")> _
    Public Function GetPackageInfo(ByVal TrackID As String) _
      As ClientPackageInfo
        Dim PackageInfo As Package
        PackageInfo = GetPackageRecordFromDB(TrackID)
        Return PackageInfo.BasicInfo
    End Function

    Private Function GetPackageRecordFromDB(ByVal TrackID As String) _
      As Package
        ' Some database access code here.
        Dim PackageInfo As New Package()

        ' To perform a crude test, uncomment the following two lines.
        ' PackageInfo.BasicInfo.PackageID = TrackID
        ' PackageInfo.BasicInfo.DeliveryDate = Now

        Return PackageInfo
    End Function
End Class

Public Class Package
    Public BasicInfo As New ClientPackageInfo
    Public CreditCardNumber As String
End Class
```

```
Public Class ClientPackageInfo
    Public PackageID As String
    Public DeliveryDate As Date
End Class
```

Database and OOP mavens will realize that there are many different ways to implement this type of scenario. (You may also wonder why the credit card is stored with each package.) In a real-world example, security concerns will shape the whole construction of the database (and the applications that access it).

In any case, this example demonstrates that a .NET web service can pass many types of information to the client, including a DataSet, custom objects, arrays, and simple variables. Keep in mind, however, that if you were to pass an object with a built-in method, the method would be lost. Only the data is preserved.

Testing Your Web Service

Maybe you're still wondering exactly what is provided with the web service we've created. So now that you have created it, how can you use it? Fortunately, ASP.NET includes a handy feature that allows you to preview and perform a limited test on any web service.

Your Web Service in Action

To try out this useful feature, run your web service. Remember, web services are designed to be used from inside other applications, not executed directly. However, when you choose to run a web service in Visual Studio, your browser will display the test page shown in Figure 13-4.

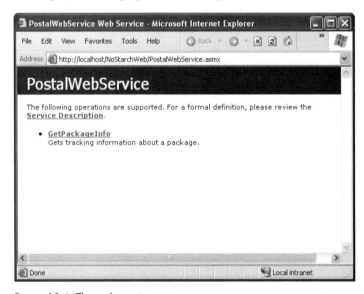

Figure 13-4: The web service test page

This window lists all the available web service methods. (In this case, only one, GetPackageInfo(), is available.) The Service Descriptions link will display the WSDL description of your web service. (WSDL is described in the next section of this chapter.) Click the GetPackageInfo link, and the test page shown in Figure 13-5 will appear.

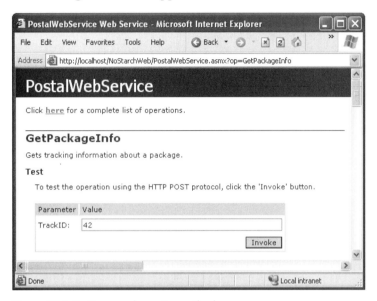

Figure 13-5: Testing a web service method

Ignore the puzzling XML code further down the page for now, and concentrate on the first portion of the page, which provides a prefabricated way for you to test your application. Try it by entering a package ID and clicking Invoke.

When you click the Invoke button, the browser posts a web service request to the .asmx page (the web service URL). IIS handles this request. Because .asmx files are registered to ASP.NET, IIS passes the request along to the ASP.NET worker process, which then creates an instance of your web service class. The web service runs the appropriate method and returns the result, which ASP.NET converts into XML. The web service object is then destroyed. The end result appears as a page in your Internet browser.

If you've entered the preceding example, and uncommented the hard-coded package values, you will receive a result like the one shown in Figure 13-6.

At this point you'll probably start to wonder if your web service has worked at all. However, on close examination, it turns out that the appropriate information is present; it's just been marked up in a special XML format. What you have received is a translated version of the ClientPackageInfo class. The class is marked with a beginning and an ending tag, and inside are the tags for the members, including the PackageID and a DeliveryDate field.

You don't need to understand the format of this information if you are programming in Visual Basic 2005. As you'll discover later in this chapter, .NET provides special utilities that abstract away this layer of XML. These features allow you to call a web service and retrieve its data as though it were a local function inside your application. However, understanding this format can give you some additional insight into what's really going on with web services.

Figure 13-6: A web service response

The Open Standards Plumbing

Much of the excitement over web services results from the fact that they are built on open standards. It's this foundation that makes them more flexible and extensible than previous attempts at allowing distributed component-based programming, including such existing standards as DCOM (Microsoft's own Distributed COM), and RMI (Java's Remote Method Invocation).

XML and WSDL

Web services are based on the XML standard (which was introduced in Chapter 8). XML, however, is only the starting point. XML is just a tool for describing data, much as SQL is a tool for accessing databases. Both are generic, and both can be used in countless different ways. What is needed is an agreed-upon standard for encoding information in XML before it's packaged in a web service message, guaranteeing that other clients will be able to decode the information by following a uniform set of rules. You also need an agreed-upon standard for describing the functionality that's available for a web service, so your programming framework can interact with it without you needing to worry about all the low-level details. There are two web service standards that fill these gaps: WSDL and SOAP. Both are XML-based languages.

The standard way of describing web services is the Web Services Description Language (WSDL), an XML-based language that has been accepted by Microsoft, IBM, and a host of other vendors. WSDL tells clients what methods a web service contains, what data types it uses (for example, it will define the ClientPackageInfo class used in the previous example), and how to contact it.

If you want to find out all the low-level details of WSDL, you can read up on it at http://msdn.microsoft.com/xml/general/wsdl.asp. However, for most developers, these details won't hold any more interest than do the details of the technologies that underlie many of the other aspects of the .NET platform. What is more interesting is examining the WSDL information that ASP.NET generates automatically for your particular web service. To display this information, click the Service Description link on the web service test page. You'll see a lengthy—and perhaps intimidating—document that describes the types and the functions used in your web service. A portion of the WSDL document for the PostalWebService is shown in Figure 13-7. Among other details, this section of the WSDL document defines the ClientPackageInfo class.

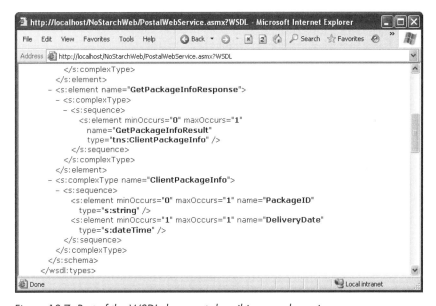

Figure 13-7: Part of the WSDL document describing a web service

If you pay careful attention to the URL that's used when you click the Service Description link, you'll realize that you don't really need to go through the web service test page (although it is very convenient). Instead, to see the WSDL contract for a web service, just add ?WSDL after the web service file name. This works for any .NET web service, including those that have been created by other developers. For example, the web service WSDL contract for the PostalWebService can be retrieved with this line (assuming it's in a virtual directory called NoStarchWeb on the local computer):

```
http://localhost/NoStarchWeb/PostalWebService.asmx?WSDL
```

SOAP

WSDL describes your web service, but another standard is needed to communicate with it. In fact, there are three different ways to communicate with a web service. The first is HTTP POST, which Internet Explorer uses automatically when you click on Invoke on the web service test page. The second is HTTP GET, which is very similar to HTTP POST. Internet veterans will realize that a POST request sends information in the body of an HTTP request instead of in the query string. ASP.NET ignores HTTP GET requests for security reasons. The final method is SOAP, which is what .NET uses transparently when you create a client (as shown later in this chapter).

SOAP is another XML-based standard, and it predates the .NET platform. Essentially, when you send information to and retrieve information from a web service in a .NET application, your requests and responses are packaged in the SOAP format. The SOAP format looks similar to the XML response you saw in Figure 13-6, but it's a little more detailed. To take a closer look at the SOAP message format (for curiosity's sake), launch your web service in Visual Studio to head back to the test page. Then, select a method (in this case, use the GetPackageInfo() method). When the method page appears, scroll down to see the format for a SOAP request message (the message a client sends to a web service to request information) and a SOAP response message (the answer the web service sends back). Figure 13-8 shows these details for the PostalWebService.

Figure 13-8: The SOAP message format

The next section looks at how .NET applications consume web services by using SOAP calls, which allows you to retrieve the results of a web service in a .NET program instead of in a browser.

Consuming a Web Service

At this point, you've seen your web service in action, but you haven't usefully incorporated it into another program. Clearly, if users had to rely on the web service test page, they would be better off with a full-featured Internet application!

In this section you'll learn how to create a web service client that uses your web service (or *consumes* it, to use programmer-speak). Best of all, you'll learn how to get Visual Studio to create all the infrastructure code you need.

The Proxy Class

Web service clients communicate with web services through a proxy class that you can create automatically with the .NET Framework. The proxy class translates your actions into the appropriate SOAP calls and then interacts with the web service. The whole process is seamless, so you might not have even realized it was happening if you hadn't seen Figure 13-9.

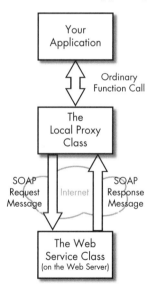

Figure 13-9: Web service interaction

Creating a Client Application

Once you've created your web service, it's always available. Even if you shut down Visual Studio, IIS keeps running. Whenever it receives a web service request it fires up ASP.NET and passes along the SOAP message for processing.

As a result, you have a good deal of flexibility when it comes to creating a client for your web service. For example, you can start a completely new Visual Studio solution with a client application in it. Your client application can be any type of .NET application, including a console (command-line) application, a Windows application, a web application, and so on. However, if you're still testing your web service, the best approach is to put both your client and your web service project in the same solution. That way you can easily debug both, and even step from your client code into your web service code.

To set up this relationship, open your web service project (if it's not already open), and choose File ▶ Add ▶ New Project. Put this project in a completely different directory. Unless your client is also a web application, it doesn't need to be in a virtual directory. This project should not be created in the virtual directory where the web service is located because it will not be hosted on the web server.

Once you create this new project, you'll see both applications in the Solution Explorer, as shown in Figure 13-10.

Figure 13-10: Two projects in Solution Explorer

At this point, there are still a couple of configuration steps to take care of. First, right-click your client project, and select Set As StartUp Project. That way, when you start this solution, the client project is launched (not the web service test page). Also, you may want to save the solution you've created so you can open this combination (the web service and the client) later for more testing. To save the solution, select the solution name in the Solution Explorer (which is the very first node) and then select File ▶ Save *[SolutionName]*.sln As.

Adding a Web Reference

Although you now have a client project, the client currently has no way to know about the web service. To configure a client to use a web service, you need to use a Visual Studio feature called *web references*. Web references are special types of links, stored in your project, that identify the web services your code uses. The neat bit is that when you add a web reference, Visual Studio also generates the code you need to communicate with the web service, saving you a lot of work.

To add a web reference, right-click your client project in the Solution Explorer and choose Add Web Reference. The Add Web Reference window will appear (Figure 13-11). In the address box, type in the full URL of your web service (like http://localhost/NoStarchWeb/PostalWebService.asmx), and click the Go button. Assuming you've typed the reference in correctly, you'll see the test page for your web service.

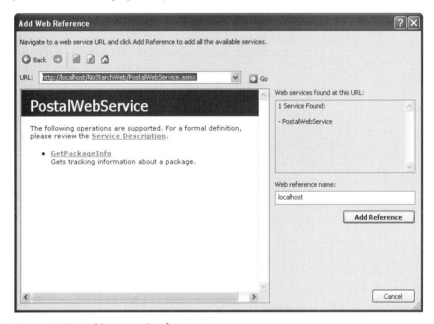

Figure 13-11: Adding a web reference

TIP *To save some keystrokes, you can use the browser functionality that's built into Visual Studio to find web services on the local computer. To do this, click the Web Services On The Local Machine link that's initially shown in Add Web Reference browser box.*

Optionally, you can change the web reference name at this point. The web reference name determines the namespace where the proxy class will be created. By default, Visual Studio uses the server name (in this case, localhost). To add the web reference, click the Add Reference button. At this point, Visual Studio copies some information it needs (like the WSDL document) and generates the proxy class. It also adds a configuration file to your project to store the web service URL. This file appears as app.config in the Solution Explorer, but every time you build your application, a copy is placed in the output directory, with the name of the application plus the extension .config. For example, the application MyClient.exe will have a configuration file MyClient.exe.config.

Sometimes, a web service might move to a new URL after you create a client for it. In Visual Studio you can easily change the URL you use by selecting the web reference (under the Web References node in the Solution Explorer) and changing the Web Reference URL in the Properties window. But what do you if you've already deployed your client, and you don't want to recompile it? Fortunately, .NET has the answer. Just look for the configuration file, which has the same name as your client (such as MyClient.exe.config).

You can edit the configuration file with any text editor. Inside you'll find the current setting, looking something like this:

```
<setting name="PostalClient_localhost_PostalWebService"
  serializeAs="String">
    <value>http://localhost/NoStarchWeb/PostalWebService.asmx</value>
</setting>
```

You can change this setting to update the web reference URL, without recompiling a lick of code. When you launch your client, it always uses the URL in the configuration file. Of course, if the web service changes more drastically—for example, the name of the web methods changes—you'll need to modify your client application and recompile.

Inspecting the Proxy Class

Visual Basic 2005 hides the proxy class that it creates from you, because you don't really need to see it or modify it directly. However, it's always a good idea to peek under the hood of an application and get a better understanding of what's really happening along the way.

To see the proxy class, select Project ▶ Show All Files from the menu. Then, expand the Web References node, which contains all your web references. Expand the node with the web reference you just added (which is named localhost by default). Finally, look for a file named Reference.map. Once you expand this node, you'll see the Visual Basic proxy file, which is named Reference.vb, as shown in Figure 13-12.

This Reference.vb file includes a proxy class with all the code needed to call the methods of your web service. It also includes the ClientPackageInfo class that you need to use to retrieve the information from the GetPackageInfo() method. It's important to understand that the Reference.vb file is constructed out of the *public* information about your web service. This information, which includes the method names, their parameters, and the data types they use, is drawn from the WSDL file. It's impossible for a client to snoop out the internal details of a web service. For example, you won't see the private GetPackageRecordFromDB() method in the proxy class, and you won't find the Package class in the Reference.vb file, because they are only used internally. Similarly, you won't be able to see (or learn anything about) the code inside your web service. If you could, that would constitute a significant security risk.

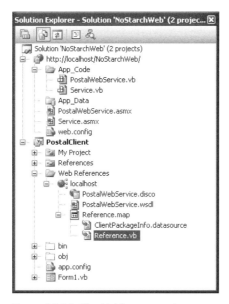

Figure 13-12: The hidden proxy class

Take a quick look at the modified version of the GetPackageInfo() function contained in the proxy class. (To simplify the display, the information in the SoapDocumentMethodAttribute is not included here.)

```
<SoapDocumentMethodAttribute(...)> _
Public Function GetPackageInfo(ByVal TrackID As String) As ClientPackageInfo
    Dim results() As Object = Me.Invoke("GetPackageInfo", _
      New Object() {TrackID})
    Return CType(results(0), ClientPackageInfo)
End Function
```

This function converts the TrackID input string into a generic object, retrieves the result as a generic object, and then converts it into the appropriate ClientPackageInfo object. In between, it accesses the web service through the appropriate SOAP request and waits for the response, although all this is taken care of automatically in the Me.Invoke() method, with the help of the .NET attributes that provide additional information to the Common Language Runtime.

Using the Proxy Class

The proxy class is the key to using a web service. Essentially, you create an instance of this class, and call the appropriate methods on it. You treat the proxy class as though it were a local class that contained the same functions and methods as the web service.

To try out the `PostalWebService`, add the following code to the `Click` event handler of a button:

```
Private Sub cmdCallService_Click(ByVal sender As System.Object, _
  ByVal e As System.EventArgs) Handles cmdCallService.Click
    Dim ServiceInstance As New localhost.PostalWebService()
    Dim PackageInfo As New localhost.ClientPackageInfo()
    PackageInfo = ServiceInstance.GetPackageInfo("221")
    MessageBox.Show("Received the delivery date: " & _
      PackageInfo.DeliveryDate)
End Sub
```

Now run the application and click the button. If Visual Studio loads up the web service test page, you have a configuration problem. Stop the project, right-click the Windows application in the Solution Explorer, and select Set As Startup Project. If you have configured everything correctly, you'll see the window in Figure 13-13.

Figure 13-13: Calling a web service

Once again, the technical details are pretty sophisticated, but the actual implementation is hidden by the .NET framework. Calling a web service is as easy as creating one, once you have set up the web reference.

TIP *There's a handy shortcut for using the proxy class without needing to explicitly create it yourself. You can use VB's built-in* `My.WebServices` *object. For example, to call the* `GetPackageInfo()` *method from the* `PostalWebService`*, you could use* `My.WebServices` `.PostalWebService.GetPackageInfo()`*. The proxy class is used in exactly the same way; the only difference is that you don't need to instantiate it.*

Debugging a Web Service Project

When debugging a solution that includes a web service project and client, you will find that any breakpoints or watches you set for the web service code are ignored. That's because, by default, Visual Studio only loads the debug symbols for the startup project, which is the client.

To solve this problem, you need to configure Visual Studio to load both projects at once. Right-click the solution name in the Solution Explorer (the first node), and select Properties. Then, browse to the Common Properties ▶ Startup Project tab and specify Multiple Startup Projects, so that both your client and the web service will be built when you click the Start button (Figure 13-14). Also, make sure that the `Action` column is set to Start for both projects. Then click OK.

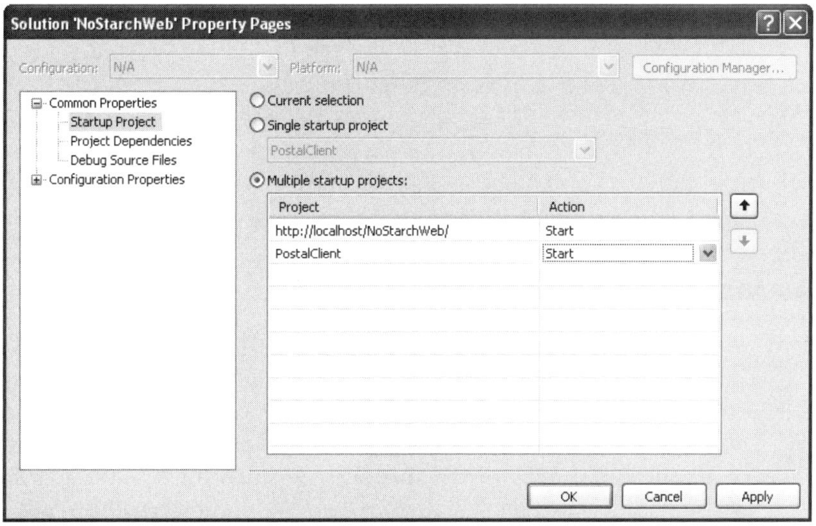

Figure 13-14: Starting the web service and client at the same time

You still need to make one more change. By default, Visual Studio starts the web service project by displaying the web service test page. In this case, however, you don't want any action to be taken other than loading the debug symbols so that the web service code is available for debugging. You don't want to see the test page.

To set this up, right-click the web service project, and select Property Pages. In the Start Options section, select "Don't open a page. Wait for a request . . ." as your start action (Figure 13-15).

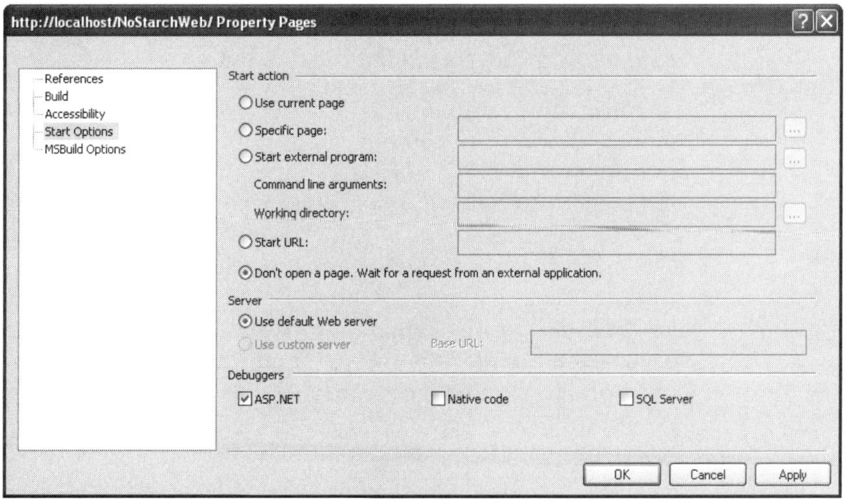

Figure 13-15: Loading the web service debug symbols

Click OK. You can now use the full complement of debugging tools, including breakpoints, with your web service and client code.

TIP   *You're free to change your web service without breaking your client. As long as you only change the code inside an existing method, there's no problem. However, if you add a new method, or change the signature of an existing method (for example, by renaming it or adding new parameters), the client won't see your changes automatically. Instead, you need to rebuild your web service and then rebuild the proxy class. To rebuild the proxy class at any time, right-click the web reference in the Solution Explorer, and choose Update Web Reference.*

Asynchronous Web Service Calls

You may have noticed that the proxy class actually contains more than just the GetPackageInfo() method. It also includes a GetPackageInfoAsync() method that allows you to retrieve a web service result asynchronously. For example, your code can submit a request with GetPackageInfoAsync(). That request will start processing on another thread. Meanwhile, your application can perform some other time-consuming tasks. When the result is ready, the proxy class will fire an event to notify you. This allows your program to remain responsive, even when waiting for a response over a slow Internet connection.

Before going any further, you should modify the GetPackageInfo() web method so it runs more slowly. This makes the asynchronous behavior much easier to test. The easiest way to make this change is to add the following line of code to the GetPackageInfo() web method, which artificially delays execution for 20 seconds:

```
System.Threading.Thread.Sleep(TimeSpan.FromSeconds(20))
```

Now you're ready to forge on and see how it all works.

Asynchronous Support in the Proxy Class

As you learned in Chapter 11, you can perform any task in .NET on a separate thread. However, the built-in support for asynchronous web services is a lot more convenient. When your web service finishes its work, you're notified on the main application thread, which makes it safe to update controls and change variables. In other words, the asynchronous support in the proxy class allows you to dodge many of the threading headaches discussed in Chapter 11.

In order for this system to work, the proxy class also adds an event for each web method. This event is fired when the asynchronous method is finished. Here's what the event looks like for the GetPackageInfoAsync() method:

```
Public Event GetPackageInfoCompleted As GetPackageInfoCompletedEventHandler
```

And here's the delegate that defines the event signature, which the proxy class also creates:

```
Public Delegate Sub GetPackageInfoCompletedEventHandler( _
  ByVal sender As Object, ByVal e As GetPackageInfoCompletedEventArgs)
```

But wait, there's more. The proxy class simplifies your life by creating a custom `EventArgs` object for every web method. This `EventArgs` object exposes the result from the method as a `Result` property. That way, when the asynchronous processing is finished and the completion event fires, you can use the `GetPackageInfoCompletedEventArgs` object and check its `Result` property to get the `ClientPackageInfo` object you're interested in. If an error occurred contacting the web service (or in the web service code), you'll receive an exception as soon as you try to retrieve this result, so be ready with some exception handling code.

An Asynchronous Client Example

The easiest way to understand this pattern is to see it in action in an application. You can use your existing Windows client, and modify it to have asynchronous support.

The first step is to attach the event handler so that you can receive the completion event. You should attach this event handler when the form first loads:

```
Private Sub ClientForm_Load(ByVal sender As System.Object, _
  ByVal e As System.EventArgs) Handles MyBase.Load
    ' Attach the event handler.
    AddHandler My.WebServices.PostalWebService.GetPackageInfoCompleted, _
      AddressOf GetPackageInfoCompleted
End Sub
```

This example uses the default instance of the proxy class that's exposed through the `My.WebServices` object. This is useful, because you need to make sure you use the same proxy object in all your event handlers. Another option is to create your own default instance as a form-level variable.

NOTE *It's easy to make the mistake of attaching the event handler just before you make the call (for example, in the Click event handler for a button). Don't do this. If you do, you'll wind up attaching the same event handler multiple times, which means your event-handling code will be repeated several times in a row.*

You still need two more methods to complete this example. First, you need the event handler that triggers the asynchronous task when the user clicks a button. This is fairly straightforward. You simply need to tweak your code so it uses the asynchronous `GetPackageInfoAsync()` instead of `GetPackageInfo()`. Here's what your code should look like:

```
Private Sub cmdCallService_Click(ByVal sender As System.Object, _
  ByVal e As System.EventArgs) Handles cmdCallService.Click
    ' Disable the button so that only one asynchronous
    ' call will be allowed at a time (this is optional).
    cmdCallService.Enabled = False

    ' Start the asynchronous call.
    ' This method does not block your code.
```

```
' The second parameter can be any object you want. You must use the
' same parameter if you choose to cancel the request.
ServiceInstance.GetPackageInfoAsync("Call001", "Call001")

MessageBox.Show("Call001 has been started")
End Sub
```

Notice that when you call GetPackageInfoAsync() you need to supply a tracking ID as a string. This allows you to uniquely identify the call, if multiple calls are taking place at once. You can generate a unique ID in your program using a random number or a GUID, but in this example there's only one call, so the ID is hard-coded. The ID isn't too useful at this point, but it becomes very handy when we consider cancellation in the next section.

The last detail is the event handler that responds to the completion event, which is named GetPackageInfoCompleted() in this example. To complete this example, you'll need to add that event handler to your form. Here's the code you need:

```
Private Sub GetPackageInfoCompleted(ByVal sender As Object, _
   ByVal e As localhost.GetPackageInfoCompletedEventArgs)
   MessageBox.Show("Received the delivery date: " & e.Result.DeliveryDate)

   ' Re-enable the button for another call.
   cmdCallService.Enabled = True
End Sub
```

TIP   *Have no fear—web service completion events are always fired on the same form as the rest of your application. That means you don't need to worry about interacting with other controls or synchronizing your code. Behind the scenes, the proxy class uses the* BackgroundWorker *component that you considered in Chapter 11.*

Now you're ready to try out this example. When you click the button, the code will use the GetEmployeesAsync() method to start the asynchronous process. In the meantime, the form will remain responsive. You can try moving the form, minimizing and resizing it, or clicking other buttons to verify that your code is still running while the web service request is taking place. Finally, when the results are in, the proxy class fires the completion event, and a message box will appear alerting the user. (A more common action might be to use the information to update a portion of the user interface.)

Canceling an Asynchronous Request

The web service proxy class has one more feature in store—cancellation. It's possible for you to halt a request in progress at any time using the CancelAsync() method. The trick is that you need to have the proxy object handy in order to call the method, and you need to use the tracking ID that you supplied when you first called the method.

To change the current example to support cancellation, add a new button for cancellation. When this button is clicked, call the `CancelAsync()` method, using the same tracking ID:

```
ServiceInstance.CancelAsync("Call001")
```

There's one catch. As soon as you call `CancelAsync()`, the proxy class fires its completion event. To prevent an error, you need to explicitly test for cancellation in your event handler, as shown here:

```
Private Sub GetPackageInfoCompleted(ByVal sender As Object, _
  ByVal e As localhost.GetPackageInfoCompletedEventArgs)
    If Not e.Cancelled Then
        MessageBox.Show("Received the delivery date: " & _
          e.Result.DeliveryDate)
    End If

    ' Either way, re-enable the button for another call.
    cmdCallService.Enabled = True
End Sub
```

What Comes Next?

This chapter has provided an overview of how web services work and how to use them. Leading-edge companies and developers have invented all kinds of imaginative web services. One example includes Microsoft's Passport, which allows other companies to provide authentication using the engine that powers the Hotmail email system.

If you want to continue learning about and working with web services, here are some interesting places to start:

- Microsoft provides a web services portal that provides such information as low-level technical information about the SOAP and WSDL standards, code samples of professional web services, and white papers discussing the best ways to design web services. Be warned—it's highly technical. Check it out at http://msdn.microsoft.com/webservices.

- Eager to create a client for some sample web services? Try playing with the examples on www.xmethods.com, which provide currency exchange rates, stock quotes, and prime numbers. Most aren't written in .NET, but you can still add a web reference to them and use them just as easily.

- Have some classic VB 6 applications kicking around? Remarkably, they don't have to be left out of the party. Microsoft includes the SOAP Toolkit—a COM component that allows other applications (like VB 6) to contact web services (like those you create in .NET) and get the same information a .NET client would. Check it out by surfing to www.microsoft.com/downloads and searching for SOAP Toolkit.

- Web services isn't the only distributed object technology on the block. .NET also introduces a feature called *remoting*, which allows two .NET applications to interact over a network. Remoting is a strictly .NET solution—cross-platform applications need not apply. It also doesn't use IIS—instead, you need to launch an application that hosts the remotable object, and make sure it keeps running. However, remoting also adds a few features that web services doesn't have, such as the ability for any application to act like a web server and receive requests from others. Also unlike web services, configuring remoting can be fiendishly difficult (and forget about peer-to-peer applications on the Internet, because there's no built-in way to get around firewalls and proxy servers). To learn more, check out a dedicated book or head to the Visual Studio Help.

14

SETUP AND DEPLOYMENT

If you've read through the last few chapters, you've gained the knowledge you need to make a professional, useful application in Visual Basic 2005. In fact, you may already have created one or more programs that you want to share with others, deploy internally, or even market to the world. But how does a .NET application make the transition from your workstation to a client's computer?

To answer that question, you need to have an understanding of assemblies, the .NET way of packaging files. You also need to understand file dependencies, or, "What does my program need to be able to run?" Both of these subjects were tackled in Chapter 7.

Once you've learned which files you need, you can copy and set up your program on another computer. If the program is only being used internally (for example, from a company server), or if your only goal is to transfer the program from one development computer to another, you won't need to do much more. In some cases, you can even use a rudimentary batch file or script to copy all the required files. However, if you're deploying a program to multiple users or selling it as a package, you probably need a more convenient, automated solution. Using Visual Studio, you can create a full-featured setup program that selectively copies files, allows the user to configure options, and creates appropriate shortcuts and registry settings. You can also use ClickOnce, a new technology for rolling out automatically updated applications using a website. This chapter describes these features and shows how you can use them to create professional, off-the-shelf products.

New in .NET

Visual Basic 6 provided a utility called the Package and Deployment Wizard to help you create setup programs for your applications. Unfortunately, there was little support for customized deployment or advanced configuration options. In this chapter you'll see the changes in Microsoft's new deployment philosophy, which provides two new setup options.

ClickOnce

Developers who are searching for a streamlined setup option may appreciate ClickOnce, a new .NET 2.0 feature that's tailored for creating setup applications that users can install from a website. Without a doubt, the greatest feature of ClickOnce is its support for automatic update checking, while its most significant limitation is that it provides very few options and stubbornly resists all customization.

Visual Studio setup projects

Visual Studio includes a much more powerful feature for building setup projects that can be added directly to your solution files and configured extensively. With a Visual Studio setup project you can copy whatever files you want, create shortcuts, configure the registry, and more. You may never need to resort to a third-party installation tool again.

Setup Programs

In Chapter 7, you learned how .NET assemblies work, and you learned how you can deploy an application just by copying it to another computer, so long as the target computer has the .NET 2.0 runtime and you copy all the .dll files that your application uses. However, the simple copy-and-run approach doesn't suit a professional application. Most users expect a more user-friendly interface, including a wizard that walks them through the process and puts a nice shortcut in the Start menu (or on the Desktop). A setup program can put these details in place.

If you develop products that will be distributed to other users on CD media or over the Internet, you will almost certainly want to create a full-fledged setup program that takes care of creating shortcuts, making any important registry settings, and copying the actual files. While .NET is intelligent enough that a simple copy operation can transfer an application, it still makes sense to provide a customized, wizard-based approach for your product's end users.

To make life more interesting, .NET actually includes two deployment technologies:

- ClickOnce is a new setup approach that made its debut in .NET 2.0. It's designed to be simple, and sports two interesting features: installations from a website, and automatic download of updates. However, ClickOnce's emphasis on security and simplicity means it lacks most of the snazzy installation features users of a professional application typically expect.

- Visual Studio setup projects are a more powerful option that lets you hand-craft your setup application through a set of designers. Although you won't get the automatic updating features of ClickOnce, you will get much more power to customize the target computer, including features that allow you to create registry values, create custom shortcut icons, and launch utilities to perform custom actions.

You may want to evaluate both technologies before settling on an approach for your application. However, a few basic rules of thumb can help steer you right. ClickOnce is best for line-of-business applications in huge companies, where deployment needs to be simplified and standardized as much as possible. In that environment, the ClickOnce approach of removing features in order to guarantee simple deployment makes sense. ClickOnce may also be a good choice if you want application updates to be automatically downloaded to the user's computer. In any other case, the Visual Studio setup project is a far more powerful option that allows you to build a traditional setup application.

Requirements for .NET Applications

One aspect of application setup that's all too easy to ignore is the fact that so-called copy-and-run deployment isn't quite as easy now as it should be in a few years. The problem is that while your assemblies have all the metadata they need to identify themselves and their dependencies, they will still only work on another computer with the .NET Framework. If you copy your application to a computer that does not have the .NET runtime, it won't work. And because you're creating your application with .NET 2.0, you need the .NET 2.0 runtime—earlier versions are no help.

The easiest way to ensure that a computer is .NET-ready is to install the .NET Framework through the Windows Update feature (select Windows Update from the Start menu). The .NET Framework runtime is fairly small (much smaller than Visual Studio itself), but it's an optional install, so many computers won't have it. You can also use the .NET Redistributable to install .NET, and even include it with your own setup projects. The easiest way to find the .NET Redistributable is to surf to Microsoft's MSDN site (http://msdn.microsoft.com) and search for ".NET redistributable 2.0."

ClickOnce

ClickOnce provides a streamlined solution for application rollout that may appeal to programmers who want minimum fuss, including automatic updating and web-based deployment. However, it's short on the features that traditional consumer-level setups need, and provides almost no customizability. (And that's the point. With ClickOnce, standardization is king.)

The very long list of ClickOnce limitations includes the following:

- ClickOnce applications are installed for a single user. You cannot install an application for all users on a workstation.

- ClickOnce applications are always installed in a system-managed user-specific folder. You cannot choose the folder where the application is installed. You cannot install additional files in another folder. And you won't know what folder ClickOnce uses, because it's all managed behind the scenes.

- If ClickOnce applications are installed in the Start menu, they show up as a single shortcut in the form *[Publisher Name]* ▶ *[Product Name]*. You can't change this, and you can't add additional shortcuts (for a help file, related website, or an uninstall feature, for example). Similarly, you can't add a shortcut for a ClickOnce application to other locations like the Startup group, the Favorites menu, and so on.

- You can't change the user interface of the setup wizard. That means you can't add new dialogs (for example, to include a user registration step), change the wording of existing ones, and so on.

- You can't install shared components in the Global Assembly Cache (GAC).

- You can't perform custom actions (like creating a database, registering file types, or configuring registry settings).

In the following sections, you'll take a quick walk through ClickOnce. You'll learn how to create an automatically-updating setup that users can install from the Web, and you'll see how to create a more modest install package for a setup CD.

Publishing to the Web or a Network

ClickOnce install packages are called *publications*. Because of the way ClickOnce works, you need to choose a single, specific location where your publication will be stored. This is where users will go to run the setup and install your application. This location can be a UNC path to another networked computer (like *\ComputerName\ShareName*). Or, you may prefer to use a web server, in which case you use a URL of the form http://*ServerName*/*VirtualDirectoryName*.

NOTE   *For more information about web servers, refer to Chapter 12. Before continuing in this section, you should make sure that IIS is installed and correctly configured. You may remember that you can use a web server for computers in a local network, or you can use a web server that publicly accessible over the Internet. For the first option, you simply need to install IIS on your web server computer. For the second option, you'll probably need to buy space at another web hosting company, and upload your files via FTP or some other mechanism.*

Here's the important bit. Before you can create your ClickOnce setup, you need to pick this location. If you decide to change the location later, you'll need to republish your setup. That may sound like an irritating limitation (and sometimes it is), but it makes sense because the ClickOnce setup location is also the update location. ClickOnce's premier feature is automatic updates and in order for this feature to work, ClickOnce needs to know where it should head to check for newer versions.

That means if you decide to publish your application to http:// *IntranetComputer/SuperApp*, the client will automatically check the http://*IntranetComputer/SuperApp* location to look for new versions.

You don't need to have your publication site ready before you create your publication. It's perfectly acceptable to store the publication files in a local directory, and then transfer them to the right site (network share or website) for deployment. However, you do need to know what the ultimate destination will be, because you'll supply that information when you create your publication.

To get a better understanding of how this works, you can load up a completed project and create a new publication. (Any of the sample applications from previous chapters will work for this purpose; if you haven't created them for yourself, you can use the downloadable samples as described in the introduction.)

The easiest way to publish an application through ClickOnce is to choose Build ▶ Publish *[ProjectName]* from the Visual Studio menu, which walks you through a short wizard. This wizard doesn't give you access to all the ClickOnce features you can use, but it's the best way to get started.

Here's what you need to do:

1. Select Build ▶ Publish *[ProjectName]* to start the wizard.

2. First choose the location where you'll save your publication. You have a few choices. First, you can copy your files to a local directory and *then* transfer them to their final location (manually). Alternatively, if you're installing your ClickOnce application to a website on the local computer for a quick test (as in this example) and you've installed IIS (as described in Chapter 12), you can use a URL that points to the local computer (as shown in Figure 14-1). Visual Studio will create the virtual directory and transfer your files automatically.

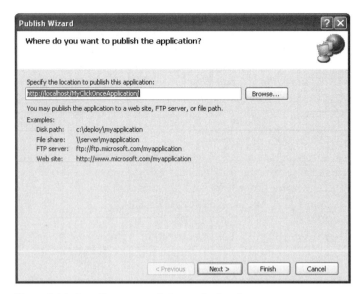

Figure 14-1: Installing to a website on the local computer

3. If you've chosen a local directory, you'll see an extra step (Figure 14-2). This is the point where you supply the final destination for your setup files. The assumption is that you'll transfer your files here before anyone runs the setup. If you don't need to use the automatic updating feature of ClickOnce, and just want to create a setup program that can be run from anywhere, with minimum fuss, you can use the From A CD-ROM Or DVD-ROM option, which is described later in this chapter. If you supplied a URL in Step 2, Visual Studio assumes that's the final destination for your files.

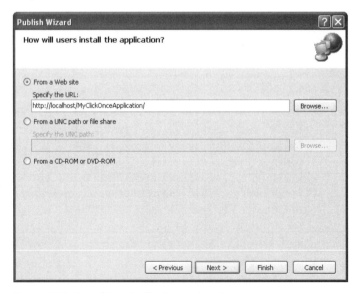

Figure 14-2: Specifying the final setup location

4. The next window (Figure 14-3) asks whether you want an online or an online/offline application. An online/offline application runs whether or not the user can connect to the published location after the initial setup. With this option, a user heads to the automatically generated install page (named publish.htm) and runs the setup. A shortcut for the application is then added to the Start menu, and the user can subsequently run the application from there. However, if you choose to create an online-only application, no shortcut is created. Instead, the user needs to launch the application from the automatically generated web page every time. The only advantage of this approach is that it ensures there's no way to run an old version of the application. As with a web application, only a user who can get online and connect to your site can run your application. (The difference is that the application will still be downloaded the first time it's launched and then cached for optimum performance.)

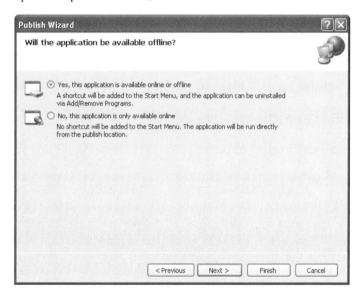

Figure 14-3: Choosing whether to allow offline use

5. Finally, you'll see a summary (Figure 14-4) that explains all your choices. Click Finish to generate the deployment files and copy them to the location you chose in Step 2.

NOTE *Keen eyes will notice that the URL specified in Step 2 (see Figure 14-1) has been modified in the final summary. The first URL used the computer name localhost, which always refers to the current computer. However, the problem is that if you try to use this URL on another computer, localhost points to that computer (not to yours). To correct this problem, the ClickOnce wizard substitutes your computer name in the last step. Now all clients on your network can use the same URL, and that's the URL that's stored in the publication.*

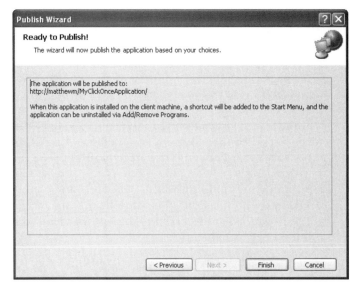

Figure 14-4: The final summary

Installing a ClickOnce Application

The ClickOnce publication includes several files. Here's what you'll see for a typical application:

```
c:\MyClickOnceApplication\setup.exe
c:\MyClickOnceApplication\publish.htm
c:\MyClickOnceApplication\MyClickOnceApplication.application
c:\MyClickOnceApplication\MyClickOnceApplication_1_0_0_0.application
c:\MyClickOnceApplication\MyClickOnceApplication_1_0_0_0\MyClickOnceApplication.exe.deploy
c:\MyClickOnceApplication\MyClickOnceApplication_1_0_0_0\MyClickOnceApplication.exe.manifest
```

As you publish newer versions of your application, ClickOnce adds new subdirectories for each new version.

The most important file is setup.exe, which installs the application. The setup program uses a bootstrapper to check for system requirements. For example, if the target computer doesn't have the .NET Framework 2.0 runtime, it launches that setup first. Provided the requirements are installed, the setup.exe file installs the application.

If you're installing from a website, ClickOnce includes a publish.htm file. Users can browse to this page and click Install to install your application (see Figure 14-5). When you finish generating a new ClickOnce publication, Visual Studio opens this page for you automatically.

To install your application, click Install in the web page or run the setup.exe file directly. The application will download, install, and run in one quick step. If you're installing from the web, the only pause you'll see is a security message asking if you want to trust the application (similar to when you download an ActiveX control in a Web browser). Clearly, ClickOnce does everything it can to make a setup painless and (almost) invisible.

You'll also see a new shortcut in your Programs menu that you can use to run the application. You can uninstall it using the Add/Remove Programs section of the Control Panel.

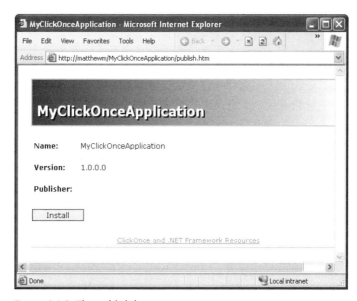

Figure 14-5: The publish.htm page

Updating a ClickOnce Application

The most exciting ClickOnce feature is its support for automatic updates. But before you try this out, it's worth reviewing the update settings, which are mostly left out of the ClickOnce wizard.

To see the update settings, double-click the My Projects node in the Solution Explorer, and select the Publish tab. This tab provides quick access to all the ClickOnce settings. To control the update settings, click the Updates button. (The Updates button isn't available if you're creating an online-only application, because an online-only application always runs from its published location on a website or network share.)

You'll see the Application Updates dialog box (Figure 14-6).

To use automatic updating, you must check the The Application Should Check For Updates check box. You then have two choices about how updates are made:

- Before the application starts. In this case, every time the user runs the application, ClickOnce checks for a newer version in the publish location. If an update is found, the user is prompted to install it, and *then* the application is launched.

- After the application starts. In this case, ClickOnce checks for new versions periodically. You can choose whether this checking is performed every time the application is launched, or only after a certain interval of days. If an updated version is detected, this version is installed the next time the user starts the application.

Figure 14-6: Configuring update settings

The first option ensures that the user gets an update as soon as it's available. The second option improves load times, and is recommended if you don't require immediate updating. Of course, an update won't be made if the user can't connect to the site where the application is installed. If you're really concerned about missed updates, you can use the online-only model to ensure that the user it always forced to use the latest version.

You can also specify a minimum required version if you want to make updates mandatory. For example, if you set the publish version to 1.5.0.1 and the minimum version to 1.5.0.0 and then publish your application, any user who has a version older than 1.5.0.0 will be forced to update before being allowed to run the application. Ordinarily, there is no minimum version, and all updates are optional.

To see automatic updates in action, follow these steps using the same application you chose in the section "Publishing to the Web or a Network" on page 454:

1. Select the Before The Application Starts update mode.
2. Make a change in your application. For example, add a new button.
3. Republish your application to the same location.
4. Run the application from the Start menu.
5. The application will detect the new version, and ask you if you'd like to install it (see Figure 14-7). If you accept the update, the new version will be installed and then launched.

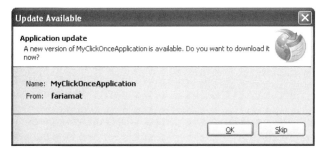

Figure 14-7: Automatic updates in action

Publishing to a CD

If you're not interested in automatic updates and web-based deployment, you can use a simpler strategy. ClickOnce allows you to create a publication that can be installed from any location (including a setup CD). Here's how to create it:

1. Select Build ▶ Publish *[ProjectName]* to start the wizard.
2. Enter a file path for your installation location (like C:\MySetupFiles). You can burn them to a CD or copy them to some other location later. Click Next.
3. Choose the From A CD-ROM Or DVD-ROM option, which turns off the online-only features. Click Next.
4. In the last step, choose The Application Will Not Check For Updates to turn off the automatic updating feature. (If, on the other hand, you want to make an application that is deployed by CD but can be updated via the web, you would specify the website where you also plan to copy the publication files.) Click Next.
5. Finally, you'll see the summary. Click Finish to generate the deployment files.

Of course, if all you want to create is a CD setup that copies your project, you'll find a much more customizable, flexible model with Visual Studio setup projects, as described in the next section.

Creating a Visual Studio Setup Project

Although ClickOnce is an exciting technology targeted for a specific set of users, it pales in comparison to full-fledged setup projects. Most users will prefer to use Visual Studio setup projects.

Unlike the other project types discussed in this book, Visual Studio setup projects are not language-specific. Instead of writing scripts, you configure setup options through special designers and property windows. You don't ever write any code.

You can create a stand-alone setup project, and then import the output from another .NET project, or you can add a setup project to an existing solution that contains the project you want to deploy. This second option is often the most convenient.

First, open an existing project. You can use any existing project, although Windows and Console applications are obviously the most likely choices.

NOTE *You can create a full-blown setup and a ClickOnce setup for the same application. However, you won't be able to benefit from the automatic updating of ClickOnce unless you install the application from the ClickOnce publication.*

Then, right-click the solution item in the Solution Explorer window, and choose Add ▶ New Project. Choose Setup Project from the Setup and Deployment Projects group, as shown in Figure 14-8.

Figure 14-8: Creating a setup project

Then enter a name for the setup program, and click OK to add the project. You will now have two projects in your solution, as shown in Figure 14-9.

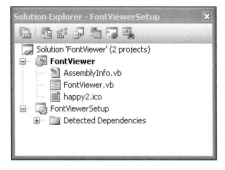

Figure 14-9: A solution with a Windows application and its setup project

Make sure you set the application (not the setup project) to be the startup project. To do this, right-click your application in the Solution Explorer and choose Set As StartUp Project.

Compiling a setup file can take some time, and it's only required when you want to deploy the finished application, not during testing. To create the .msi setup file at any time, just right-click the setup project and choose Build. An .msi file for your setup will be created in the bin directory, with the name of your project.

Basic Setup Project Options

The setup project is unlike any other type of .NET application. Instead of writing code, you configure options in a variety of different designers. Finding the designer you need and setting the appropriate options are the keys to creating your setup project.

To start, use the Properties window to set some of the basic setup options, such as Author, Manufacturer, ManufacturerURL, Title, ProductName, and Version. Most of these settings are descriptive strings that will show up in the Setup Wizard or in other Windows dialog windows, such as the Support Info window (which can be launched from the Add/Remove Programs window).

You can also set the AddRemoveProgramsIcon (the icon that represents your program in the list of currently installed applications for the Add/Remove Programs window) and the DetectNewerInstalledVersion setting (which will abort the setup if a newer setup program has already been used to install software). Each setting is described individually in the Visual Studio Help.

To configure more sophisticated options, you will have to use one of the setup designers. To navigate to the main designers, right-click on your setup project in the Solution Explorer, and select View. There are six different designer options, depending on the settings you want to configure (Figure 14-10).

Figure 14-10: The setup designers

You can also jump from one designer to another quickly by clicking one of the buttons in the Solution Explorer. As long as you've selected your setup project, you'll see one button for each designer.

In the next few sections, we'll quickly explore each of these setup options. The first and most important is File System.

File System

Initially, your setup project is a blank template that does not install anything. You can change this by using the File System options window, which allows you to specify the files that should be installed during the setup procedure. Once you've configured this window by adding your application, along with any dependent files and shortcuts, you can create a fully functional .msi file simply by building the project. All the other windows provide additional options that you may or may not need.

By default, a short list provides access to commonly needed folders on the destination computer. You can add links to additional folders by right-clicking in the directory pane and choosing Add Special Folder (Figure 14-11). There are options that map to the computer's Fonts folder, Favorites folder, Startup folder, and many more, allowing you to install files and shortcuts in a variety of places. Folders that have already been added to the list are grayed out so that you can't choose them again.

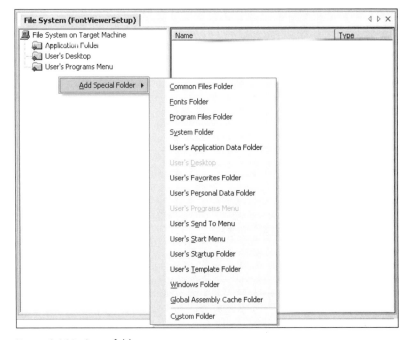

Figure 14-11: Setup folders

Adding a Project File

On their own, these links don't actually do anything. However, you can add files and shortcuts into the folders they represent. For example, to add an application file, click the Application Folder item. Then, on the right side of the window, right-click and choose Add ▶ Project Output.

The other project in your solution—that is, your application itself—is automatically selected in this window (Figure 14-12). Choose Primary Output and click OK. (Primary output is the .exe or .dll file a project creates when you click on the start button.) Figure 14-13 shows a setup project with a project output added and ready to be installed to the user-selected application folder.

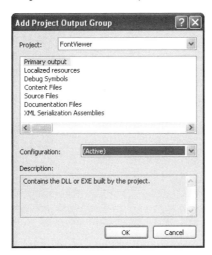

Figure 14-12: Adding a project output

You should also note that you can right-click in the file list and select Add to insert any other dependent files, such as pictures or XML documents. You can also create as many layers of subdirectories as you need. Lastly, you can click any folder to display additional information about it in the Properties window. You can see, for example, that the standard format for naming directories (*ProgramFiles\[Manufacturer]\[ProductName]*) is used by default for the application directory.

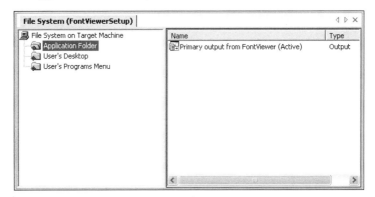

Figure 14-13: The FontViewer project output

Adding a Shortcut

You can also use the File System designer to add shortcuts for your application. Add a shortcut directly to the desktop by including it in the User's Desktop folder, or add one to the Programs group in the Start menu by using the User's Programs Menu folder.

Once again, just right-click in the file list space on the right. Choose Create New Shortcut. A special window will appear that allows you to choose the linked file from one of the other folders. For example, you can browse to the application folder and choose the application's .exe file for the shortcut target. Figure 14-14 shows a setup project with a shortcut added to the Program menu for the main application executable (project output).

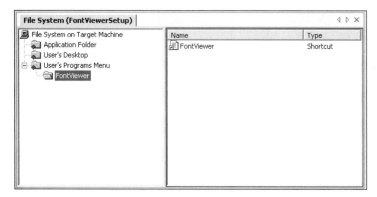

Figure 14-14: The FontViewer shortcut

You can then use the Properties window to fine-tune your shortcut, changing its name, icon, default window state (the ShowCmd property), and startup or working folder. Note that in order to assign a special icon for the shortcut, you must have added it to the setup project.

NOTE *At this point, you've created a fully functioning setup that can install your application, complete with a basic wizard, a shortcut, and an uninstall feature. All you need to do is build the setup project and double-click on the .msi file. All the other options we'll consider in this chapter are for adding enhanced features to your setup program.*

Registry

The Registry designer (shown in Figure 14-15) allows you to create registry entries in the destination computer as easily as you create shortcuts and copy files. The display is similar to the familiar Windows regedit program which you can use to edit the registry. To add a new registry key in the Registry designer, browse to the proper location on the left, right-click the list at the right, and choose New ▶ String Value. Any values you specify in this way will be created automatically during the setup.

If you want to use one of the setup variables in a registry setting, enclose it in square brackets. For example, if you use [Manufacturer], the setup program will use the corresponding Manufacturer value defined in the project properties. This is a good way to design a generic setup that can keep up with frequent product updates, or even with company name changes.

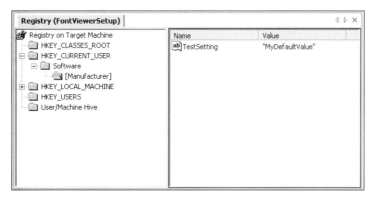

Figure 14-15: The Registry designer

It's a good idea to reduce your reliance on these registry settings. Even if your application is designed exclusively to be deployed through your custom setup, there may be situations where you want the ease and convenience of a simple file-copying deployment. In this case, your application should be intelligent enough to use default registry settings if none are specified, or raise a nonfatal error and query the user for more information. You should not rely on the success of this setup program. The best use of the registry features in a Windows Installer project is to preconfigure directory settings, based on the location where the application is installed. The application should *not* fail without this information.

File Types

The File Types designer allows you to associate your program with specific extensions, a trick that was awkward with the Package and Deployment Wizard in earlier versions of Visual Basic. A file association allows Windows to automatically launch the correct program when you double-click on a file (for example, .pdf files are opened in Adobe Acrobat, and .txt files are usually opened in Notepad).

If you are deploying a document-based application, you may want to use your own registered file types. Make sure, however, that your file types have reasonably unique names, to prevent them from conflicting with other programs. File types do not need to be restricted to three characters. Also, never try to take over such basic file types as .bmp, .html, or .mp3. It is almost certain that the user will have a preferred program for accessing these types of files, and trying to override such preferences is certain to annoy your clients.

Figure 14-16 shows a complete File Type entry. To add a file type association like this, begin by right-clicking anywhere in the File Types designer and choosing Add File Type. Before the file extension is considered complete, you must specify the following details:

- The name of the type of document (Name)

- The associated extension (Extension)

- The program to launch for the extension (Command)

- Ideally, a nice icon (Icon) and a two- or three-word description of the format (Description)

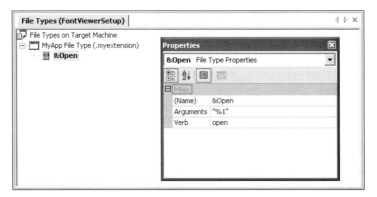

Figure 14-16: A custom file type

You can then add actions to each of your file types. The most common action is Open. When you double-click a file or right-click it and choose Open, the owning program will launch, and should open the file automatically. By convention, the filename is passed to your program, and it is your program's responsibility to check its command-line arguments and take the appropriate action (in this case, opening the file). The "%1" string in the Arguments property indicates that the action passes the filename to your program as a command-line parameter.

In some cases, you might want to add other actions, such as a Print command that would automatically open your application with the selected document and print out the corresponding file. To do this, alter the Arguments property to some other format that your program can recognize. For example, you could set it to /p "%1" and specifically check in your program for the /p parameter.

Before you use this setting, you should test it out with your program, and fine-tune it as needed. You should also look at how the icon and description appear in Windows Explorer. To test a custom file type, add it manually using Windows Explorer. (Choose Tools ▶ Folder Options from the menu, and select the File Types tab.) If you're trying this out for the first time, it will also be helpful to see how other file types are registered.

User Interface

For a simple setup, you can let the Windows Installer generate the entire user interface for you using its default options. For a more sophisticated setup, you may want to configure some of the Setup Wizard options using the User Interface designer.

The Windows Installer user interface is *not* created using .NET, or even using Visual Basic code. Instead, it is configured through a series of options that you can specify within your setup project. These limitations are designed to make setup creation easy and to restrict setup variations so that Setup Wizards follow a highly consistent pattern.

With the User Interface designer, you can see the windows that will be displayed to the user. Windows are listed in the order in which they will appear, are grouped by setup type, and are further subgrouped by setup stage, as shown in Figure 14-17.

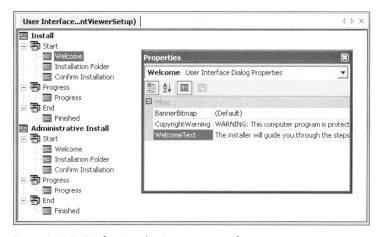

Figure 14-17: Configuring the Setup User Interface

NOTE   *You will see two versions of your setup listed: a normal user install and an administrative install. To access the administrative install, you run the .msi setup file with the /a command-line parameter. Usually the administrative install is used if you need to provide a network setup.*

To customize your setup, there are four tasks you can perform:

- Modifying options for a window, using the Properties window.
- Rearranging the order of windows by right-clicking one of them and choosing Move Up or Move Down.
- Removing a window from the setup by right-clicking it and selecting Delete.
- Adding a new window to the setup by right-clicking a setup state and selecting Add Dialog. All windows are chosen from one of the predefined window types available to you.

Predefined Window Types

You can add one of several predefined windows to the Setup Wizard (Figure 14-18).

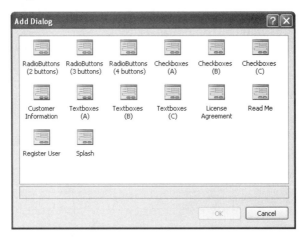

Figure 14-18: Adding setup windows

Each window is designed for a single purpose and provides an extremely limited set of functions. Some options include:

- A Splash window, which displays an image file for the product, and is sometimes used as the first window in a setup project.
- A License Agreement or Read Me window, which shows information from a linked .rtf file. If you add a license agreement, users must accept it, or they will not be allowed to continue.
- A Register User window, which launches a custom program if the user clicks the Register Now button. You can also add a Customer Information window which requires a name, an organization, and a serial number that can be validated by comparing it with the format specified in the SerialNumberTemplate property.
- A choice window, which uses radio buttons, check boxes, or text boxes to allow the user to enter additional information.

These windows are described in more detail in the Visual Studio Help. Generally, though, each of these windows provides only a small set of properties, which are self-explanatory.

Some aren't even configurable at all! Also, you will notice that a combination of four check boxes or three radio buttons is the most sophisticated interface that you can use. The Setup Wizard does not provide more complex options, the idea being to force you to create a straightforward setup that is consistent with other Windows products.

Choice Windows

Choice window is the catchall term I use to describe the setup windows that request additional selections from the user, through such basic interface controls as check boxes. Because a setup project does not allow you to write any actual code, you might be wondering how you can use the results of a user selection. The answer is quite straightforward.

First of all, you must choose a choice window to add to your project. Each choice window is based on a single type of control. The different versions of each window (A, B, and C) are identical, but each window can only be used once. Clearly the language used to create Windows Installer files is not built using .NET class-based technology! However, Microsoft is unlikely to change this system in the future. Presenting more than three configuration windows using similar controls is a nightmarish scenario that would frustrate many average users. If possible, a setup should always default to the most common value—or not provide an option at all. Remember, whenever presenting users with a choice, you are demanding that they make a decision.

To create a simple choice window, add a check-box window. You can set values for up to four check boxes by modifying the corresponding properties: CheckBox1Visible, CheckBox1Label (the descriptive text), and CheckBox1Value (the default setting, either checked or unchecked). You match this check box to a global setup variable by setting the property named CheckBox1Property.

If the user checks CheckBox1 from the example in Figure 14-19, the variable MYCHECKBOX1 will be set to True. (This introduces another ugly feature of setup project design—variable names are almost always typed in uppercase.)

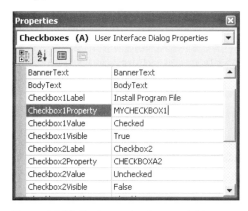

Figure 14-19: Setting a CheckBox variable

Conditions

To use the MYCHECKBOX1 variable, you need to assign it to a Condition. Conditions are provided as properties of all sorts of elements in the setup project. For example, you can find a file or a shortcut using the File System designer, or a registry setting using the Registry designer, and set its condition property to MYCHECKBOX1. If this value evaluates to True (meaning the check box was selected from the original window), the file will be copied or the entry will be added. Otherwise, the operation will be skipped. For example, Figure 14-20 shows a conditional file operation that will only be carried out if MYCHECKBOX1 was selected.

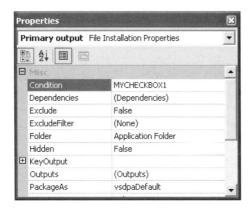

Figure 14-20: Making a file operation conditional

If you are working with a text data type or with a radio button window that assigns different numeric values to a property, you can still create a condition. For example, you might create a condition such as SELECTEDBUTTON = 1, assuming you've added a radio button choice window with the ButtonProperty of SELECTEDBUTTON, and assigned the value 1 to one of the buttons (for example, Button1Value). This condition will only evaluate to true if the user chose the SELECTEDBUTTON with the value of 1.

Conditions and choice windows provide a fairly crude way to manage user selections, but they are ideal for the simplified Setup Wizard application. Always make sure that the choice window is displayed *before* the setup action that evaluates the condition. For example, if you place a choice window at the end of your setup project, after the files have been copied, you won't be able to make the file copy operation conditional.

Built-in Conditions

The choice window isn't the only source of conditions. There are also about a dozen conditions with some basic information that are always available. These are special environment variables that provide information about the destination computer.

All of these built-in properties are described in the Visual Studio Help. Some of the most useful are COMPANY and USERNAME (which correspond to the information entered in the CustomerInformation window, if you are using it), LogonUser (the username of the currently logged-on user), ComputerName, PhysicalMemory (the number of megabytes of installed RAM), VersionNT (the version number of Windows NT/2000/XP/2003 operating system), and Version9X (the version number of a Windows 95/98/ME operating system).

Custom Actions

Custom actions allow you to run code at the end of the installation process to perform additional configuration. As you've seen so far, the features built into the Windows Installer are extremely easy to use, but they provide a set of defined options with little extensibility. If you need to perform other tasks, such as configuring a database, adding a user account, or setting up some other type of application-specific configuration file, you can create a separate .exe file for this purpose, and run it when the setup is complete by using a custom action. You can even make custom actions dependent upon other options, such as a choice window or the version of Windows installed on the current computer. Keep in mind, however, that if a custom action generates an unhandled error or fails, your entire setup will be rolled back, and the program will be uninstalled.

You can add a custom action to one of several different installation phases (Figure 14-21). Right-click the appropriate phase, and choose Add Custom Action. You must choose the program from the files included in your setup project (as there is no guarantee that any other files will be available).

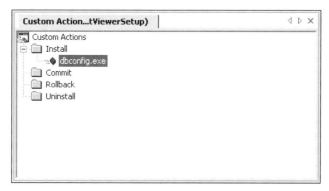

Figure 14-21: A custom action

Of course, most users like to set up a program with a minimum of fuss. Also remember that in many environments, the person installing the program is not the person who will be using it. For these reasons, it is sometimes better to add a special configuration window to your application (perhaps one that launches the first time the program is executed), rather than adding a custom action to your setup program.

Launch Conditions

Launch conditions allow you to specify the ingredients that a setup must have in order to run. If these conditions are not met, the setup will be automatically cancelled and an error message you specify will be displayed.

A launch condition has two parts. First, there is a search operation, which hunts for the registry, file, or component that you identify. You have to set a variety of properties in order to set the scope of the search and the type of match. A Boolean True or False is set using the corresponding property. For example, if you add a Search For File operation and set its property to FILEFOUND, that will be the global variable you can use in other conditions.

You can use the search result at any point in your application, but it is typically used with a corresponding item in the Launch Condition group. Just set the Condition property to the appropriate variable name (in this case FILEFOUND), and specify a Message property that specifies the error message that the setup will display if the condition is not met. Figure 14-22 shows a launch condition that searches for a particular file in the Windows folder and prevents the setup from continuing if the file cannot be found.

Launch conditions are really just an extension of the Windows Installer way of dealing with conditions. You can create a search and use the global variable for another conditional operation (a file copy, for instance), or you can create a launch condition that uses one of the built-in variables (such as Version9X or VersionNT). By default, every setup has a launch condition that verifies that the .NET Framework 2.0 is installed. You can (foolishly) remove this requirement, or customize it to give a more detailed error message if .NET 2.0 isn't found, or even point the user to another URL where they can find it. (The default is http://go.microsoft.com/fwlink/?LinkId=9832.)

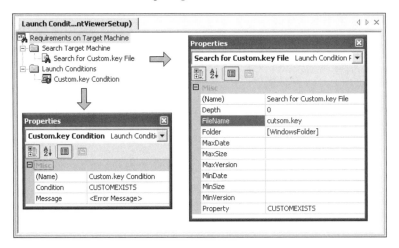

Figure 14-22: Anatomy of a launch condition that searches for a file

What Comes Next?

This chapter introduced the new ClickOnce setup infrastructure, which gives you a quick way to deploy lightweight applications over the Web and ensure that they're updated automatically. Then we considered the more powerful technique of creating a full setup project. Rather than reviewing a full setup example, we took a comprehensive look at the available designers. Setup projects are simple to create, and there aren't any hidden dangers. However, you need to know exactly what is possible and what isn't. Remember, setup projects aren't written in VB code and really have little in common with true .NET projects, other than the fact that they are easy to create in Visual Studio.

To see an actual setup project, refer to the online samples for this chapter, which include a simple setup program for a FontViewer utility. The FontViewer utility is relatively modest—it simply provides a list of all the fonts installed on the computer and allows the user to preview each one— but it provides a good example of a fully configured setup project. (As a side note, the FontViewer utility also shows you how to enumerate the fonts on your computer and how to draw directly on a Windows form using the .NET class library.)

INDEX

C

C#, language similarities, 12–13
caching, web, 423
call stack, effect on exception handling, 256
CancelAsync(), BackgroundWorker method, 368
CancelButton, Form property, 103
Catch statement
    described, 256
    filtering with, 260
choice windows, setup, 470–472
circular reference, 154
class blocks, 63
class library
    contents of, 49
    described, 11–12, 49
    projects, 223–224
    reference, 49
    useful namespaces, 57–59
Class View window, 170
classes. *See also* cloning; collections; inheritance
    accessing in a namespace, 53
    brief definition, 52
    business objects, 209–210
    casting, 185
    constructors, 148–152
    destructors, 152
    disposable, 201–202
    events, 155–159
    forms, 104
    garbage collection, 152–154
    instance vs. shared members, 53
    instantiating, 141–142
    interfaces, 194–198
    null reference error, 144
    partial, 144–145
    properties, 145–148
    reference vs. value types, 142–143
    releasing, 142
    representation, 177
    serialization, 290–293
    shared members, 165–168
    simple Person class, 140–141
    support for cloning, 198–201
    three-tier design, 209
ClickOnce
    compared with setup projects, 451
    files used, 458
    install from CD, 461
    install from network or web, 455–457
    limitations, 454
    publications, 454–455
    updating with, 459–460
Clone() method. *See* cloning
cloning
    arrays, 74
    compound objects, 199–201
    objects, 198–201
    possible errors with, 201
    through serialization, 292–293
Close(), Connection method, 319
CLR (Common Language Runtime), 11
code samples, 3
code snippets, 35–37
cohesion, 176
collapsible code display, 31–32
collections
    custom, 208
    described, 203–204
    generic, 207–209
    keys in, 203
Columns, DataTable property, 347
COM. *See* Component Object Model (COM)
Command class
    command types, 322–323
    creating, 322
CommandBuilder, 342–343
comment tokens, for task list, 34
comments, XML, 305
Common Language Runtime (CLR), 11
comparable objects, 202–203
compilation, 44, 212
Component Object Model (COM)
    vs. assemblies, 213–215
    vs. GAC, 227–228
    interface-based programming, 196–197
    vs. web services, 426–427
component tray, 89–90
components. *See also* assemblies; Global Assembly Cache (GAC)
    class library project, 223–224
    clients, 224–226
compound objects, cloning, 199–201
compressing files, 281–283
concurrency
    database concurrency problems, 344–345
    thread concurrency problems, 381

conditions, setup, 471–472
.config file
    described, 230–231
    storing connection strings in, 320–321
    web.config, 392
configuration tool, for .NET, 231
configuring assemblies, 230–232
Connection class, 318–319
connection strings
    described, 318–319
    storing in config file, 320–321
console applications, 41–43
Console class, 41–43
constructors
    default, 152
    described, 148–149
    inherited, 180–182
    with parameters, 149
    using multiple, 150–152
container controls, 99–100
containment, 189
ContextMenuStrip, 126
context-sensitive help. *See* help
Continue statement, 78–79
control designers, 90–91
controls
    creating dynamically, 117–119
    DataGridView, 350–351
    events. *See* events
    grouping, 99
    invisible, 90–91
    locking, 91
    providers, 132–133
    subclassing, 192–193
    web, 405. *See also* web forms
conversions, data type, 67, 75
conversions, objects, 185
cookies, 414
current date, retrieving, 71
custom actions, in setup, 472–473
custom collections, 208
custom event arguments, 157–158
custom exception objects, 262–264
custom file types, registering in setup, 467–468
customizing the toolbox
    to add/remove .NET controls, 29–30
    to import ActiveX controls, 30

CType() function
    using to handle multiple events, 102
    using for object casting, 186–188
    using with session state, 412
    using for variable conversions, 75–76

D

DAO (Data Access Objects), 311
data binding
    in an ASP.NET application, 415–418
    in a Windows application, 350–352
data source controls, 417–418
data tier, in three-tier design, 209
data types
    arrays, 71–74
    with binary files, 278
    conversion, 75–76
    dates and times, 71
    integers, 65–66
    as objects, 67
    strings, 67–70
DataAdapter class
    filling a DataSet with, 334
    using FillSchema, 337
database stored procedures. *See* stored procedures
database transactions, 331–332
databases. *See* ADO.NET
DataGridView control, 350–351
DataReader class
    vs. disconnected access, 317
    ListView example, 324–325
    reading records, 322–324
DataRelation object, 338–339
DataRow class, 335
DataRowState enumeration, 341, 343–344
DataSet class. *See also* ADO.NET
    creating by hand, 347
    data binding, 350–352
    deleting records, 336
    disconnected use, 333
    filling with a DataAdapter, 334
    GetChanges method, 347
    inserting records, 336–337
    with multiple tables, 338
    object model, 335
    ReadXml method, 348
    with relations, 338–339

Math class, 76
MaximumSize, Form property, 96
MaxValue, Integer property, 245
MDI forms, 123–125
MdiChildren, Form property, 124
MdiParent, Form property, 124, 300
Me keyword, 116, 205, 252
MemberwiseClone() method, 198
menu, 126
MenuStrip, 126
metadata, 15, 213, 216–220
MethodInvoker delegate, 373
methods
   ByVal and ByRef parameters, 80
   calling, 79–80
   default parameter values, 82
   delegates, 84–86
   described, 52, 79
   optional parameters, 81
   overloading, 82–84
   overriding in derived classes, 183–185
   Return keyword, 81
   shared, 165–167
Microsoft Intermediate Language, 13
Microsoft .NET Framework
      Configuration tool, 231
Microsoft.VisualBasic namespace, 59
Microsoft.Win32 namespace, 59, 302
MinimumSize, Form property, 96
modal forms, 107
modeless forms, 107
modules
   block structure, 63
   vs. shared members, 168
monitoring file system events, 288–290
mouse events, 102
MSIL (Microsoft Intermediate
      Language), 13
Multi Document Interface, 123–125
multiple inheritance, 188
multithreading. *See also* threads
   with the BackgroundWorker, 360–368
   debugging, 280
   design scalability, 311
   interacting with user interface, 373
   vs. single-threading, 357–359
   synchronization, 381–385
   thread management, 375–376
   thread priorities, 377
   thread starvation, 377–378
MustInherit keyword, 186

MustOverride keyword, 187
My object
   core objects, 60–61
   described, 60
My.Application, 61, 265
My.Computer, 61
My.Computer.FileSystem, 61, 273–274
My.Forms, 61, 106–107
My.Resources, 61, 235–236
My.Settings, 61, 321
My.User, 61
My.WebServices, 61, 447
MyBase keyword, 181

N

name collision, prevention in GAC, 228
Namespace keyword, 64
namespaces
   aliases, 57
   described, 49–51
   importing, 55–57
   project-wide imports, 56–57
   setting the root namespace for your
      projects, 64
   useful ones in .NET, 57–59
   XML namespaces in web services, 432
.NET class library. *See* class library
.NET Framework
   Configuration tool, 231
   overview, 10–15
NetworkAvailabilityChanged, Application
      event, 109
New keyword, 67, 141
NewRow(), DataTable method, 336
nodes
   TreeView. *See* TreeView
   XML. *See* XML
nondeterministic finalization, 152
NonSerialized attribute, 292
Northwind database, 314
Nothing keyword, releasing an object
      with, 142
NotifyIcon control, 129–130
Now, DateTime property, 71
null reference
   with conversions, 186
   dealing with using AndAlso and
      OrElse, 78
   error, 144
NullReferenceException, 144

W

Watch window, 252–253
weak typing. *See* Option Strict
web applications. *See also* ASP.NET;
 web forms
 application state, 413
 ASP.NET file types, 392
 controls, 394–395, 405
 creating a website, 390–391
 page life cycle, 403–404
 query string, 409–411
 session state, 411–412
 view state, 403, 407–408
 virtual directories, 420–422
web development outline, 390
web forms
 AutoPostback, 400
 controls, 394–395, 405
  adding, 395
 data binding, 415–418
 event handlers, 398–399
 flow layout, 395
 HTML output, 402
 Page.Load event advisory, 404
 processing cycle, 403–404
 transferring information between,
  408–411
 view state, 403, 407–408
web pages, reading, 280–281
web references, 440–442
web services
 adding a reference, 440–442
 calling, 443–444
 calling asynchronously, 446–449
 creating, 430–432
 debugging, 444–445
 described, 426–428
 vs. objects, 428
 SOAP, 438
 test page, 434–436
 using with My object, 447
 virtual directories for, 428–430
 WSDL, 436–437
Web Services Description Language
  (WSDL), 436–437
web.config file
 automatically adding, 397
 compilation settings, 397
 described, 392
 session state settings, 411

view state encryption settings, 408
WebMethod attribute
 described, 432
 using to configure method
  descriptions, 432
 using to configure the namespace,
  432–433
WebResponse class, 281
WebService class, 428
windows
 debugging. *See* debugging windows
 IDE. *See* Visual Studio windows
 splitting windows
  in a form, 97–99
  in the IDE, 32–33
Windows Form Designer generated
  code, 113–116
Windows forms. *See* forms
Windows registry, 301–303
WithEvents keyword, 118,155
WorkerReportsProgress, BackgroundWorker
  property, 366
WorkerSupportsCancellation,
  BackgroundWorker property, 368
WrapContents, FlowLayoutPanel
  property, 99
wrapped printing, 296–297
Write(), BinaryWriter method, 276
WriteAllBytes(), My.Computer.FileSystem
  method, 274
WriteAllText(), My.Computer.FileSystem
  method, 274
WriteLine(), StreamWriter method, 268
WSDL (Web Services Description
  Language), 436–437
wwwroot directory, 420

X

XML
 attributes, 305
 collapsed whitespace in, 304
 comments, 305–306
 described, 304–305
 DOM, 309
 elements, 304
 vs. HTML, 304
 reading from a file, 307–209
 storing DataSets, 348
 in web services, 436
 writing as a file, 306–307

Electronic Frontier Foundation
Defending Freedom in the Digital World

Free Speech. Privacy. Innovation. Fair Use. Reverse Engineering. If you care about these rights in the digital world, then you should join the Electronic Frontier Foundation (EFF). EFF was founded in 1990 to protect the rights of users and developers of technology. EFF is the first to identify threats to basic rights online and to advocate on behalf of free expression in the digital age.

The Electronic Frontier Foundation Defends Your Rights!
Become a Member Today!
http://www.eff.org/support/

Current EFF projects include:

Protecting your fundamental right to vote. Widely publicized security flaws in computerized voting machines show that, though filled with potential, this technology is far from perfect. EFF is defending the open discussion of e-voting problems and is coordinating a national litigation strategy addressing issues arising from use of poorly developed and tested computerized voting machines.

Ensuring that you are not traceable through your things. Libraries, schools, the government and private sector businesses are adopting radio frequency identification tags, or RFIDs – a technology capable of pinpointing the physical location of whatever item the tags are embedded in. While this may seem like a convenient way to track items, it's also a convenient way to do something less benign: track people and their activities through their belongings. EFF is working to ensure that embrace of this technology does not erode your right to privacy.

Stopping the FBI from creating surveillance backdoors on the Internet. EFF is part of a coalition opposing the FBI's expansion of the Communications Assistance for Law Enforcement Act (CALEA), which would require that the wiretap capabilities built into the phone system be extended to the Internet, forcing ISPs to build backdoors for law enforcement.

Providing you with a means by which you can contact key decision-makers on cyber-liberties issues. EFF maintains an action center that provides alerts on technology, civil liberties issues and pending legislation to more than 50,000 subscribers. EFF also generates a weekly online newsletter, EFFector, and a blog that provides up-to-the minute information and commentary.

Defending your right to listen to and copy digital music and movies. The entertainment industry has been overzealous in trying to protect its copyrights, often decimating fair use rights in the process. EFF is standing up to the movie and music industries on several fronts.

Check out all of the things we're working on at http://www.eff.org and join today or make a donation to support the fight to defend freedom online.

ELECTRONIC FRONTIER FOUNDATION · 454 SHOTWELL STREET · SAN FRANCISCO, CA 94110 · 415.436.9333

SILENCE ON THE WIRE
A Field Guide to Passive Reconnaissance and Indirect Attacks

by MICHAL ZALEWSKI

Author Michal Zalewski has long been known and respected in the hacking and security communities for his intelligence, curiosity, and creativity, and this book is truly unlike anything else out there. In *Silence on the Wire*, Zalewski shares his expertise and experience to explain how computers and networks work, how information is processed and delivered, and what security threats lurk in the shadows. No humdrum technical white paper or how-to manual for protecting one's network, this book is a fascinating narrative that explores a variety of unique, uncommon and often quite elegant security challenges that defy classification and eschew the traditional attacker-victim model.

APRIL 2005, 312 PP., $39.95 ($53.95 CDN)
ISBN 1-59327-046-1

WICKED COOL JAVA
Code Bits, Open-Source Libraries, and Project Ideas

by BRIAN D. EUBANKS

Wicked Cool Java contains 101 fun, interesting, and useful ways to get more out of Java. It is not intended as a Java tutorial—it's targeted at developers and system architects who have some basic Java knowledge but may not be familiar with the wide range of libraries available. Full of example code and ideas for combining it into useful projects, this book is perfect for hobbyists and professionals looking for tips and open-source projects to enhance their code and make their jobs easier.

NOVEMBER 2005, 248 PP., $29.95 ($40.95 CDN)
ISBN 1-59327-061-5

VISUAL BASIC 2005 EXPRESS: NOW PLAYING

by WALLACE WANG

A beginner's guide to Visual Basic 2005 Express with a twist—short movies on CD-ROM that show exactly how to write programs. Best-selling author Wallace Wang explains not just *how* to do things but also *why*, making this book perfect for novice programmers. *Visual Basic 2005 Express: Now Playing* starts with a short primer on the general principles of computer programming, so readers will master the fundamentals and then apply them to Visual Basic Express. The first CD includes numerous short source code examples that readers can run and modify, along with movies demonstrating how to accomplish specific tasks; the second CD contains a full working version of Visual Basic Express.

MARCH 2006, 480 PP. W/ 2 CDS, $29.95 ($38.95 CDN)
ISBN 1-59327-059-3

WRITE GREAT CODE, VOLUME 1
Understanding the Machine

by RANDALL HYDE

Many of today's programmers lack a formal education in computer science. The Write Great Code series is here to fill those gaps in education. Volume 1 of this series teaches machine organization, including numeric representation, binary arithmetic and bit operations, floating point representation, system and memory organization, character representation, constants and types, digital design, CPU instruction set and memory architecture, input and output, and how compilers work.

NOVEMBER 2004, 464 PP., $39.95 ($55.95 CDN)
ISBN 1-59327-003-8

WRITE GREAT CODE, VOLUME 2
Thinking Low-Level, Writing High-Level

by RANDALL HYDE

Today's computer science students aren't always taught how to choose high-level language statements carefully to produce efficient code. *Write Great Code, Volume 2: Thinking Low-Level, Writing High-Level* shows software engineers what too many college and university courses don't: how compilers translate high-level language statements and data structures into machine code. Armed with this knowledge, readers will be better informed about choosing the high-level structures that will help the compiler produce superior machine code, all without having to give up the productivity and portability benefits of using a high-level language.

MARCH 2006, 640 PP., $44.95 ($58.95 CDN)
ISBN 1-59327-065-8

PHONE:
800.420.7240 OR
415.863.9900
MONDAY THROUGH FRIDAY,
9 A.M. TO 5 P.M. (PST)

FAX:
415.863.9950
24 HOURS A DAY,
7 DAYS A WEEK

EMAIL:
SALES@NOSTARCH.COM

WEB:
WWW.NOSTARCH.COM

MAIL:
NO STARCH PRESS
555 DE HARO ST, SUITE 250
SAN FRANCISCO, CA 94107
USA

UPDATES

Visit **www.nostarch.com/vb2005.htm** for updates, errata, and other information.

COLOPHON

The Book of Visual Basic 2005 was laid out in Adobe FrameMaker. The font families used are New Baskerville for body text, Futura for headings and tables, and Dogma for titles.

The book was printed and bound at Malloy Incorporated in Ann Arbor, Michigan. The paper is Glatfelter Thor 60# Smooth, which is made from 50 percent recycled materials, including 30 percent postconsumer content. The book uses a RepKover binding, which allows it to lay flat when open.